All the Shah's Horses

To Mary

All the best

Gail Thompson

All the Shah's Horses

by

Gail Rose Thompson

WWW.OAKLEAPRESS.COM

Sulu, Helen, Denis

For my three children:

Helen Parrot, Denis Rose and Sulu Rose-Reed

I wish you life and long prosperity,

May God protect you from adversity!

May heaven prosper all you say and do,

May evil glances never injure you,

Whatever purposes you hope to gain

May all your efforts never bring you pain,

May wisdom be your guide, may fortune bless

Iran with prosperous days and happiness.

ABOLQASEM FERDOWSI

From Shahnameh (The Persian Book of Kings)

CONTENTS:

Author with Ezat, Manuchehr, Kambis, Ali Rezai

FOREWORD

I lived in Iran during the "Golden Years" from 1972 to 1976 during which time I worked for the Imperial Court Secretary-General; I was the trainer for the horses and riders of the Imperial Stables and the Iranian show jumping team. In this capacity I met many high officials and International visitors and was privy to a great deal of information about the regime, and His Imperial Majesty Mohamad Reza Pahlavi, Shahanshah of Iran. As well I was able to learn about the Persian way of life and to become a part of this magical country.

I wrote this book, which is as collection of stories and anecdotes from my days working for the Imperial Stables, the Royal Horse Society and the Iranian Show Jumping Association, forty years ago. As I reflect on that past I have so many memories that flash through my mind. There were joyous times that made me feel happy, amusing times that made me laugh, stressful times that made me shudder in my boots, times of accomplishment that made me proud and sad times that made me cry. It was a time of all emotions.

I feel sorrowful when I reflect on the Revolution that overtook the country that I loved so much. It was a beautiful place full of interesting and wonderful people of all walks of life, so many of whom were lost through that Revolution

To-day seventy percent of the population of Iran is under the age of thirty five. These young people have grown up through changing times and the revolution was not their fight. Life in the country now has become more and more as it was in the time I was there and show jumping is still a popular sport and going strong.

I hope you will read this book and enjoy it for what it is: one woman's peek at another world.

FACT FINDING TRIP

I answered the telephone one morning after we had been living in Iran for about a year and was surprised to hear a voice say, 'Would you please hold the line Mrs. Rose, Mr. Kambis Atabai wants to speak to you.'

I held the line for a few moments wondering what this powerful man of whom I had heard so much and met a few times could want from me.

'Haalo, Mrs. Rose? What did you want to speak to me about? Oh, no I am sorry, actually I want to speak to you, don't I?'

'I presume that you do, as it seems you have telephoned to me!' I replied.

'Yes, yes, I am very busy as you know. I was hoping you could come down to my office to speak with me. I have something very important that I would like to talk over with you. Could you come tomorrow morning at say, ten thirty?'

'Yes, of course I'd be delighted to come down to meet with you.'

Now what could this important Iranian who held a list of many titles want from me? Most puzzling. Kambis Atabai, Master of His Majesty's Horse, Secretary General of the Royal Horse Society, President of the Iranian Equestrian Federation, President of the Iranian Football Association, Director General of the Imperial Court, were the ones known by most. He was personal assistant of the Shah and was said to be a man that was capable of getting things done due to his powerful political and social influences.

The first time I had met him was in February of 1972. My husband Don and I were in Iran on a fact finding trip; finding out, in fact whether or not we would like to live in Iran where Don's company, Reynolds Metals wanted to post him. After two weeks of sightseeing, I was desperate to find out if there were any horse activities. All our contacts had been quizzed by me and I had drawn a complete blank, so I made a telephone call to the Imperial Country Club, as I had read in a tourist guide book that the Country Club had a riding section. It took at least four calls for me to get through to the stable section and then after a garbled conversation with a non-English speaking groom, I found myself speaking to someone who spoke perfect English.

'I am calling to inquire about the riding activities of the Club,' I said.

'Well, yes, what would you like to know?'

'What are the possibilities of renting horses to ride for a nonmember visitor to Tehran?'

'Well, we only have horses for beginner riders.' the voice said.

'Oh,' I said haughtily. 'What do you do about experts who come into town?'

'Are you an expert?'

'I consider myself one.'

'What do you know about Pony Clubs?' I was questioned.

'Quite a lot. I was the District Commissioner for the Hamilton Hunt Pony Club in Canada for quite a few years. Why?'

'Oh, this is just the most wonderful luck! You know we are just starting a Pony Club in Tehran and we really do need some help. Could you possibly come tomorrow with me to see the woman who is starting it?'

'Why yes, I would be very pleased to do so. Where should I meet you and who are you?'

'My name is Igor Filipides and my father is the manager of the Hilton Hotel. Could you meet me in the lobby of the hotel at say ten o'clock tomorrow morning?'

'I'll be there, Igor, and I'll look forward to meeting you.'

The next morning at nine-thirty I went to the lobby of the hotel in which we were staying to be informed that it was *Ashura*, the deepest mourning day in the Shiite Muslim religion, and there were no taxis to take me to the Hilton Hotel. I was stricken! The desk clerk seeing my obvious distress and being a typical Persian, said he would do what he could. About ten minutes later I was escorted to a rather battered looking pick-up truck and we chugged up the long hill to the Hilton.

In my mind's eye I pictured this Igor Filipides to be a tall dark and handsome twenty year old. Perhaps a university student.

When I saw him in his riding togs waiting in the lobby I was slightly taken aback. He was tall and handsome but fair and about sixteen years old. How mature he had seemed on the telephone. We got into his awaiting car and started off for a place he called Nowruzabad. It seemed that this Nowruzabad was a stud farm for the miniature Caspian Horse and the mistress of the stud, Louise Firouz was a guiding light in the horse world of Iran. She was married to an Iranian prince from the Khadjar dynasty although she herself was from the horse country of Virginia. She sounded like a really interesting person. She alone had rediscovered the Caspian Horse which had become part of the heritage of Iran. She had helped to found the Royal Horse Society of Iran which was in its inception. This organization had been set up to protect and improve the Iranian breeds of horses as well as to encourage the improvement of horsemanship in the country. And now she was helping to start a Pony Club in Iran.

We drove over the most desolate country I had ever seen. There was not a tree nor a blade of grass in sight, just rolling hills and mountains of sand and rock. All brown, many shades of brown, but BROWN. The freeway that was very modern, just having been completed for the 2500th anniversary of the Persian Dynasty in 1971, passed a big industrial development. This is where we left the highway and drove along a dirt road.

'There it is!' said Igor. 'That is it; where you see all those trees!'

I strained my eyes to see far in the distance an oasis of trees. We continued on over the dirt track in the desert, through a garbage dump inhabited by hundreds of the wild *jube* dogs that were found in Iran and came to the gates of Nowruzabad. Actually, there were no gates and there was no great wall! Suddenly the dirt track went through a forest of tall pine trees and then on either side of the drive were beautiful orchards and finally we came to a cluster of one story brick and mud buildings.

As I alighted from the car music came to my ears; flutes, guitar, piano. Most eerie! We walked into a courtyard, not large. On one side three horses' heads appeared over the bottom half of the Dutch stall doors. Opposite the horses was the main entrance to the house. The door opened into a large room with high beamed ceilings; straight ahead was a group of about eight or ten young people most of whom were playing a musical instrument. Upon our entrance the music stopped and a tall attractive blond woman of about thirty-five came to meet us.

'Guess who I have brought to you?' panted Igor.

'Well Igor, I just couldn't,' replied Louise Firouz with a distinct Virginia accent.

'This is Mrs. Rose who knows all about Pony Clubs and maybe she will be moving to Iran with her husband. She is an expert rider and a great show jumper from Canada and she is really very nice as well.' This was my garbled introduction to the horse world of Iran!

We chatted and went to see the horses in the stable. I was most impressed with the little Caspians that looked just like a miniature thoroughbreds.

Narcy, Louise's charming husband came home and again we discussed my experiences with Pony Clubs. After lunch Narcy decided that he wanted to see if I really was a rider or not, so I was asked to give my opinion of a couple of horses.

I had been used to large Thoroughbred type horses and when an Arab stallion of about 15 hands was brought for me to ride, I felt quite lost. I rode the horse around for a few minutes only to discover that he was not terribly well schooled on the flat, in fact he was a real "kick and pull" horse but he did have a very comfortable gait. He was a beautiful Darashuri type Arab that had become almost extinct in Iran at the time.

Once again on the ground I was presented with a three year old gelding that was in the midst of his early training. This was a Turkoman horse. I had never seen this breed before but had read that some of the foundation horses of the Thoroughbred are actually Turkoman not Arab. For instance, the Brierley Turk, Lister Turk, and Brownlow Turk to mention just a few that are said to be the origination of the race horse of to-day. The conformation is very similar to the paintings one sees of the Thoroughbreds in the 18th and 19th century. I found this young horse quite a pleasure to ride, a good mover and ready to respond. The third horse I rode was a Kurd which was also a small horse but very muscular and short coupled. These horses were used, mostly, as mountain and pack horses. They were said to be extremely strong and have amazing stamina. I was to learn that they didn't make very good jumpers but they were used in Iran for polo quite successfully. Having been requested to show my prowess on a jumping horse, I put this little grey beast over a few obstacles of about a meter or so. Only after I had dismounted was I told that this horse was a bad stopper and the Firouz family was quite impressed that I had been able to prevent the horse from refusing. I guess that was my trump card! I had made a sale, even though I had not been trying to do so.

Having proved that I was not a fake, we went back to the house where I was given a detailed account of this Pony Club that was being started. I was verbally introduced to Colonel Neshati who did most of the advanced instruction; Mr. Afshar, who rode himself and taught the beginner class; and Mr. Kambis Atabai, whom I was told was a very important man but

very DANGEROUS. Over cocktails it was decided that two days hence
Narcy would pick me up at the hotel early in the morning and take me to
the Imperial Stables, where every Friday Princess Farahnaz and Crown
Prince Reza Pahlavi would have a riding lesson along with some of the
children of high ranking Iranians at Farahabad, as the Imperial Stables was
called.

Friday morning at eight o'clock my husband and I were driven down
by Narcy, to the Imperial Stables. Driving through the gates we were impressed by the fact that there were hundreds of trees, actually a forest on
either side of the road and when we reached the stable area, the neatly laid
out gardens, the green grass and the beautiful big deciduous trees around
the stable yard, were almost unbelievable in a country that is naturally so
brown and barren of any vegetation.

Having arrived at the ring side where the children were beginning to
gather, I was given a horse and told to jump it over a course. I was rather
surprised as I hadn't been introduced to any of the people who were hanging around the railings and as I had had no intention of riding was wearing
a pair of slacks not riding britches. However, I looked the horse over and
checked the jumps, none of which was more than a meter ten, and mounted.

It was a large chestnut half bred gelding; the Iranians called the breed
Varamin due to the fact that at the Imperial Army Varamin Stud they bred
a type of horse especially for parades and gave the name of the stud to these
horses. There was some Thoroughbred blood in these horses from two or
three stallions that had been imported from England in the late 1950's.
Some of these horses were reputed to become quite super jumpers although
after having worked this one on the flat for about ten minutes, I felt that he
was not one of them. I popped him over a few small warm up fences and
then jumped the course that included a great hoop to jump through. Amazingly enough the horse was quite responsive and jumped a good clean
round. I gave him a good pat on the neck and handed him back to the groom

who led him away. The one funny thing about that horse is that I never ever saw him again during the following five years and once I had started to seriously work in the horse world, I wondered why. I inquired several times about the animal but never got more than a shrug as an answer.

Now I was presented to all and sundry as "the Great Mrs. Gail Rose from Canada!" and they all complimented me on my beautiful riding! Personally I had felt it was a rather mediocre ride on a mediocre horse and my legs were rubbed and sore due to the fact that my slacks had ridden up, but I went along with the game!

Shortly after I had dismounted there was the whirr of helicopters that became louder and louder and then two huge blue and white choppers came into sight. Both landed about 50 meters from the ménage sending some of the horses that were milling around waiting for the class to commence, into fits of bucking and playing. To my amazement out stepped the Shahanshah himself and the two eldest of his children. He mounted a beautiful chestnut horse that was brought up for him and galloped off with an entourage of about ten other horses and riders. His children meanwhile came into the ring and got on the horses that had been awaiting their arrival.

I stood by watching as Colonel Neshati gave the lesson and did have a few chuckles. Having spent a lot of time teaching young children myself, I was slightly appalled at his military method, but all the twelve children that were riding seemed to be in ecstasy just being there. They went round and round and round and round. At one point one of the Firouz children had a bit of trouble with her horse so Narcy asked me to get on it, which I did, and after ten minutes it seemed to settle down so I put her back up and took her to one side to help her with her difficulty. The next thing I knew, Colonel Neshati asked me to go over and take his class for him. For some reason he wanted to see me as an instructress. I had the young riders work over trotting poles, small cavaletti and doing a lot of change of pace. I tried to explain a bit of theory of which it was obvious they knew nothing by some of the answers they had given as I questioned them during the ride. The prince and princess seemed to be really enjoying themselves. All too soon, the time was up, the Shah was back, the Royal children were whisked off, the helicopters left and class was dismissed.

As we were about to leave, Kambis Atabai rode into the ménage mounted on a large Arab type horse. I later learned that this was a Moroccan Barb that had been given to His Imperial Majesty by King Hassan of Morocco. He asked me to watch him ride and give my opinion of the horse. After watching for only a few minutes, I realized that the rider had not much idea about balance or the correct aids. When he had a great deal of difficulty getting the horse to depart onto the correct leg at the canter I, in my ignorance, stepped into the ring.

'Mr. Atabai, I think if you would bend the horse in the direction of the circle, use your inside leg at the girth, holding his shoulder out and the outside leg just behind the girth holding the haunches in, you might find that the horse would depart onto the correct lead.'

'I beg your pardon, Mrs. Rose?' was the response.

'You do understand, Mr. Atabai that the horse must lead at the canter with the inside hind and inside fore legs in order for it to move in a balanced cadence, don't you?'

'Oh yes! Was the horse on the wrong lead?'

'I am afraid so. Now do as I said. Use your inside leg at the girth, the outside leg behind the girth and turn the horse's head into the circle just so that you can just see the corner of its eye, and squeeze. Always ask a green horse to canter on the turn. That's right, now SQUEEZE. Good! Do you feel the difference? The horse is now on the correct lead.'

'Yes, yes. Now let me try it the other way. Inside leg at the girth, outside leg just behind, head in and squeeze.' He repeated what I had told to him. He squeezed and the horse broke into the canter from a trot onto the correct lead. 'That is it, isn't it?'

18

'Very good! You make a good student, Mr. Atabai.'

'And you make a good teacher, Mrs. Rose. Thank you'

He dismounted and came over to chat with the Firouzes, James Underwood, the journalist, my husband and me. There was general discussion that eventually turned to the chances of Don and me returning to Iran to live. All present felt it would be a great thing if the Roses were transferred to Iran; what a help it would be to the horse world! I of course, took most of this empty flattery with a grain of salt but the amusing thing is that much of it turned out to be not far from the truth.

As Mr. Atabai took his leave he turned to me, 'Mrs. Rose I do truthfully hope that you and your husband will return to Iran because you will be most helpful to us I am sure. If you do, I would very much like you to help me with this horse I was just riding. I really love this horse and would like to make a good jumper of him.'

'I would be most pleased to help you in any way I can.'

'In the meantime Mrs. Rose, we are having a meeting of the Board of Directors of the Pony Club on Sunday at three o' clock; I would be obliged if you could come to give us some of your ideas.'

'Thank you for your invitation, I'll be there.'

'Good bye then.'

'Good bye, Mr. Atabai, it has been a pleasure to meet you.'

Slowly people began to disperse. We had been invited to have lunch at Nowruzabad with the Firouzes and so departed for the other side of the city with Narcy.

The lunch was very informal but absolutely delicious. I have never tasted such corn on the cob. Grown at Nowruzabad and frozen in their freezer, it tasted like fresh picked. The new snow peas cooked in their shells were a true delicacy and a leg of lamb raised at the farm was quite savory. There had to be at least forty people there that day, ranging from ambassadors to sergeants in the American Army, all of whom seemed to be great friends in this melting pot of Nowruzabad.

During the lunch Louise came to sit by me.

'You must be very careful of Kambis Atabai' she said. I really was a bit taken aback. I had found him quite charming, rather attractive in the Persian sense, he had a most winning smile and a "little boy like" personality. I did not understand the warning.

'Listen, Gail! I've lived in this country for thirteen years and I know a lot more than you do. Kambis Atabai is a very dangerous man and I know from the way he reacted today that he wants you. Actually, he needs you in order to accomplish many of the things he is trying to do in the horse world. Please listen to me and don't let him trap you the way he did me!'

'But in what way has he trapped you? You have your own set up. Why do you have to answer to him?'

'Never mind just now. You will learn if you do move here. I just beg of you to heed my warning. I will say no more.'

I was, to say the least, most puzzled with this conversation but I did not really pay too much attention to it. I had no aspirations and to me Louise, Narcy, their children and their friends were becoming my friends. I was only too happy to heed the warning, but had no comprehension of how it could ever affect me.

I attended the Pony Club meeting, at which I did stick my neck out a bit in telling them they did not really have a Pony Club in Iran but a Junior Riding Club. I was informed that the Queen had promised to give the money to build a model stable that would be for the Pony Club which would be run on a commercial basis. I still reiterated that it could be a Riding Club geared to help the Junior Riders but it was not a Pony Club. In a Pony Club the children all learned to take care of their own horses, they groomed, saddled, cooled out, and mucked the stalls. This sort of work was not done by the Persian children; it was beneath them and they had grooms to do those things. Thus, I argued it was not a Pony Club. In the end it became the Farahabad Riding Club!

FIRST DAYS

Don and I left Iran unsure of whether or not we would be returning to become residents. Return we did! With the family of our two children and one Basenji, named Sam. About a week before we arrived in Iran, while we were in England, I learned that I was pregnant and due to a past history of miscarriages, I was warned not to ride until I had produced.

Upon our arrival in Iran we contacted the Firouzes, who in their characteristic manner, welcomed us with open arms. I was commandeered by Louise to help her children and their friends with their riding as an instructress; a job that I did most willingly.

During the course of the subsequent months I helped Louise turn her Nowruzabad into a commercial riding establishment. She hired two girls from the U.S. and I took on the training of the advanced riders. We got together with Ali Reza Soudovar who was the first Iranian to import foreign horses for show jumping in Iran, and had a series of horse shows through the summer and fall months. I acted as program chairman, steward and judge with the capable help of my husband. Being out spoken, I was both popular and hated by the horse world, but we did have fun. No one took these Jumper classes too seriously and all who competed each Friday were friends. We alternated holding shows at Nowruzabad, and Dashete Behesht, Ali Reza Soudovars' place. By the end of the season we had all the local clubs competing with the exception of the Imperial Stables. We had sent an invitation each week to them but Mr. Atabai refused to let his team compete in these unofficial competitions.

In Iran the horse world was organized into clubs. Anyone who wished to compete in any competition must be a member of a club and could only enter competitions as a club member. The Imperial Stables, which was the personal stable of His Majesty the Shahanshah, had a riding team that was supposed to enter the local horse shows as a representative group of His Majesty's Stable. Mr. Atabai was the Master of the Horse and so all the decisions lay with him. He declined all the invitations. It seems that at the time the Imperial Stables had a dearth of good horses and refused to enter competitions where they felt there was not much chance of their winning.

During the fall of the year, 1972, I was sent an official invitation, written in Farsi, to be a member of the Jury of the Aryamehr Cup which was the only Show Jumping Competition that His Majesty actually attended and subsidized. It was quite an experience. There were at least 15 people in the jury box and I spoke little Farsi at the time. Somehow I muddled through and pointed out a few infractions. Once the competition was over the Jury and other officials lined the pathway upon which the Shah would take to leave on his awaiting helicopter. As he passed me he nodded his head and smiled at me.

Towards the end of October I was asked to judge at the Iran-Russian Competition. The Iranians had invited a Russian team to compete in Tehran and the latter had accepted. They surprisingly enough sent a good team including the horse "Equidor" which had done passably well in Europe and had competed at the Olympics completing the course at Munich. During this competition I unfortunately had to eliminate Mr. Atabai for jumping a fence that had not been replaced after he had refused it and knocked it down. The decision lost me some popularity. The Russians, carried the Friendship Cup back with them but one Iranian won the final class. It was Hushang Temouri from the Imperial Guard, riding his Varmin stallion, who made a fantastic effort over a Table A with time to count and beat the Russians by two seconds.

The newspapers were full of show jumping news the next day. James Underwood wrote:

"A ROSE IS A ROSE

When we said Gail Rose had been instructed to hold on to her unborn baby until the recent spate of show jumping competitions was over, we may have been mistaken. The decision could only have been hers, it seems.

For when the wife of Iralco's popular Don Rose was judging the final day of the Irano-Soviet jumping at Farahabad on Friday her firmness on the interpretation of International regulations led the ring judge to refer a querying rider in a loud voice to 'the decision-making lady.'

This in turn led to a wag commenting that 'a rose, is a rose, is a rose - except when it's Gail Rose!'

The delightful Gail, who hopes to be back in the jumping ring as a competitor next season, was among the guests at the latest horsey set party the previous night when a few non-horsey people managed to get in, too. It was hosted by the set's Majlis representative."

My next big event was producing Susan Louise, named after our good friends Susan Khaki and Louise Firouz. The Jam Hospital was very modern and clean and the medical staff excellent. After I was visited by two of the Shah's top generals and a couple of ministers I was treated like a celebrity. Due to some minor complications I was kept in the hospital for about ten days and when I was finally released I thought I would never sit on a horse again. About two months after this, the phone call came from Kambis Atabia.

I took a great deal of care with my appearance as I was sure that something big was about to happen. I wore a navy blue pant suit, black patent leather boots, and white silk blouse with a puffy bow at the neck and a simple gold chain and antique pocket watch around my neck. It was soon to be replaced by a ball and chain! I seldom made up but I did put eyeliner on and a dab of powder.

I very nervously drove downtown to the office on Pasteur Avenue. The traffic in Tehran was something one needed to see to believe; it made Paris or Rome look very tame indeed. I had only been driving for a little more than a month as I refused to do so during my pregnancy. By the time I arrived at the Imperial Court offices my hands were dripping with perspiration and I was five minutes late. I scurried up the one flight of stairs and down the long hall to enter the ante room of Kambis's office panting slightly. There were at least five people waiting in this small reception room. I walked up to the desk of Parvin, Mr. Atabai's secretary, to announce my arrival and she just looked at me bewildered.

'You don't know how busy Mr. Atabai is today, Mrs. Rose. He has four people to see before you, and he must leave in a half an hour for a meeting at the palace. I don't know how he will ever find the time. But please sit down and wait.'

I picked up the English newspaper to see what was going on in the world. The usual bold headlines about the Shahanshah on the front page with smaller print informing the readers about other members of the Imperial Family. One little blurb read, *"The Shahanshah cables congratulations to the Sheik of Oman on the occasion of their national day."* I turned to the back of the paper to find the international news. The U.S. was preparing for their election year; there were the results of the presidential primaries. England was having trouble with their labor government, and so forth. Next to the comics I found James Underwood's column on *"Leper farmers of Behkadeh."* Empress Farah was doing great works as the chairman of the Lepers' Aid Association.

I was brought to the present by a bustle about me.

'He is coming out now, Mrs. Rose, but he will not have time to see you as he is on his way up town to a meeting.'

The door opened and out came Kambis Atabai. He was a tall man for a Persian, with a thick head of black hair, slightly wavy. He had a chiseled face with quite a prominent brow line making his heavy eyebrows seem more so. The deep set eyes were of course brown, a velvety dark brown. His nose was a typically projecting Iranian nose almost hooked and close to a full mouth with a slightly pouting lower lip that was somehow overlooked due to the strength of his chin. His slight figure was beautifully turned out in a deep, but not navy, blue silk hand tailored suit, from Paris most likely, immaculately polished shoes and Yves Saint Laurent tie. A very dapper figure.

'Oh, Mrs. Rose! I had forgotten about you. I must go up to the palace now. Do you have your car?'

'Yes. I do,' I replied, slightly confused.

'Good, Good. I'll get my driver to drive your car behind us and you will drive up with me and we can discuss this thing as we go.'

Five or six people were following us out the door of his waiting room, all trying to have a word with him before he left his office. I was whisked through the corridor and down the stairs by my escort while these people followed behind asking all kinds of questions and giving messages ranging from a reminder about a dinner appointment to a request for permission to order more hay for the Imperial Stables.

Once at the street entrance to the office, the driver was given my car keys and I was ushered into a small beige Mercedes Benz. I was quite curious by now as to what the conversation would entail but as we started up towards the north of the city we only passed pleasantries of the day and asked after each other's health and family. He had a most attractive wife of whom it was said, was at one time picked among a number of other young Iranian girls to be the wife of the Shah; His Majesty had ultimately married his own choice Farah Diba. Kambis had two young boys of about the same age as my two eldest children, so we chatted about the mutual interest we had. I was beginning to feel that I had come downtown for no reason at all when he finally broached the topic to be discussed.

'As you know, Her Imperial Majesty has given some land at Farahabad and is about to build a stable for a riding club geared towards the development of junior riders in Iran. I, as the Master of His Majesty's Horse and Secretary General of the Royal Horse Society, am asking you if you would consider taking this stable on and running it along the North American lines. We want something very professional that will really begin to develop some good young riders here, because we feel that the future of show jumping in Iran lies in the hands of the young. We of course, would not expect you to do this job all on your own and would want you to hire an assistant from the United States, Europe or wherever.'

'Well, I do thank you for the compliment of offering me such a job but really I don't think that I could accept such a responsibility. You probably know that Mr. Bozoghmeyer offered me the job of running the stables at the Imperial Country Club but I refused him firstly, because I don't want a full time job, and secondly, because the Club has not officially fired Colonel Khalvati and while he is away on vacation they are trying to find a person to fill his position. I think that it's quite an unethical thing for the Club to do and I don't want to be a part of it.'

'Yes I had heard the story about the Club and I do think you did the right thing; however, why don't you want a full time job?'

'With three small children and a husband it is an impossibility. I am sure that you can understand. My riding activities throughout my life have been mostly amateur and I have followed this field because I love it and I can't see any reason why I should turn my pleasure into my profession.'

'Of course, Mrs. Rose I do understand. I am unhappy that you won't take the position but perhaps you could help us to compose an advertisement to put in some American magazines and also help us chose the person that would be capable to take this on.'

'Of course, I'll help you in any way I can,' I replied effusively.

We discussed the acquisition of the Imperial Stables' new German Show Jumpers. It seemed that Kambis's father Abolfath Atabai who was one of the Shah's closest advisors and treasurer of the Imperial Court had gone to Germany to buy some carriage horses, as the eight white horses that had been pulling the Imperial coaches were getting older and ready for retirement. When he was in Germany he had bought five show jumpers as well. A few European horses had been imported for show jumping the previous year and these horses proved quite successful in the competitions and so Abolfath decided that His Majesty should have some European horses as well; also his own son who had been educated at Sandhurst in England, was very keen on Show Jumping wanting it to become a noteworthy sport in Iran.

The horses had arrived in Tehran along with a very nice young German chap by the name of Fischer, who had come with them to help the Iranians get started on them. He had spent a week in Tehran doing all he could and left with a great feeling of failure.

In Germany people had laughed at the Iranian group that came to buy horses. Their requests were as follows: eight matched greys for the carriage, two grey mares from which to breed more carriage horses; one grey stallion; one black show jumper; one show jumper with a white face; one chestnut show jumper; one very good show jumper for the son of one of the members of the delegation (that was for Kambis); one large, very large, good looking chestnut horse for his majesty to ride in parades. When one looks critically at the stock that was eventually bought for two hundred and fifty thousand dollars one must admit that they did not do too badly. Eight matched, more or less, grey geldings arrived with a German coachman to help the horses settle in. Two grey mares arrived; one was a flea bitten grey but a nice sort of big heavy Holstein mare that produced three quite nice foals, the other didn't get in foal and was so crazy that she landed three riders in the hospital at different times. The stallion was just rising three years when he arrived, also a Holstein; he sired a number of attractive foals and competed quite successfully in the show jumping events as time went on. Of the five show jumpers they were all, most useful for the Imperial Stables; I will mention that the mount for his majesty turned into a show jumper because he was afraid of the music and they were certain that the Shah could not tolerate a runaway horse when he inspected the troops.

'You see Mrs. Rose my father spent quite a bit of His Majesty's money on those horses so I am embarrassed to admit that we cannot ride them properly; we need help. Actually, I need help because His Majesty is going to want to see what we are doing with these new horses very soon and I don't want to make a mess of the whole thing.'

'I'm sure that you don't want to do that.'

'Would you be so kind as to go down to the stable and ride the one that is supposed to be for me and tell me what you think.'

'I would enjoy doing that. It'll be fun to ride a good horse again but I really can't promise you anything. I am certainly not fit and haven't done any serious riding for quite some time.'

'Oh, I'm sure that you can help. Could you go down say, ... how about tomorrow morning? I will tell them at the stable that you will be there.... at what time?'

As I had nothing in particular to do that day I agreed to go to the Imperial stables at Farahabad the following morning about ten o'clock. The conversation was ending as we drove into the gates of The Marble Palace which was the working palace of the Imperial Court of Iran. The guards acknowledged Mr. Atabai with a cursory glance and opened the gate for the car to pass through. It was a huge rectangular building, quite modern, constructed of a soft rose colored marble. It looked more like a small hotel than a palace. Kambis said his farewells as his door was opened by a man in the uniform of the Palace Guard. Then he rushed off to his meeting while I alighted to find my own car parked not ten feet from the front door of the palace. I got in, drove to the gate and relished in the bow I received from the guard as he opened the gate for me to leave.

Louise Firouz far right

My mother with James Underwood

THE IMPERIAL STABLES

At nine-thirty in the morning the traffic in the south of Tehran could be impossible, and that it was, as I drove down to the Imperial Stables that Sunday morning in April. In Iran Friday is the Holy Day, thus Saturday is comparable to our Monday, and Sunday is just another day in the working week. I had been driven down to the *Shikar Ghar Sultaniti*, as it is called in Farsi, on a number of occasions when we had first visited Iran and later when I was sitting on the jury for the Horse Shows, but that first drive on my own was quite an experience; not only were there cars to dodge but camel trains carrying their cud or dung, donkey carts, sheep, goats and of course, the pedestrian who in Iran feels that the road is made for walking. When I finally drove into the gates of the Imperial Stables, I was a nervous wreck but I was on time. It was exactly 10 a.m. I had no problem at the gate; they had been expecting me.

There was a small attractive man in the livery of the Imperial Riders waiting at the parking lot for me. He opened my car door and with a grin tried his English on me.

'Meeses Rose. You know me. Ali Rezai. I am good rider. You see me ride the last year? We wait for you. You come, see here is one horse for you ride.'

When I look back I realize that it was quite a speech for the man to make as his English was limited. He only had education to fifth grade but was a very clever horseman and could have gone far most places in the world.

I was led down the tree lined gravel path toward the main ring. The ring itself was enclosed by a buff colored brick wall with seating above it on all four sides. The middle of one side had the circular royal box; a separate glassed building that was used only when his majesty or another member of the Royal Family was visiting the stables, was by one corner of the ring. The footing of the ring was sand mixed with sawdust and wood shavings. It really was a springy good surface and as I discovered not too hard when one fell off.

In the ring was a large chestnut horse with a white face, all tacked up, being led around by a groom in uniform.

'This is Rokhsar.' said Ali. 'You know what *sar* is and *rokh* is very nice.' I did not know that *sar* in Farsi is face and *rokh* is a pretty one, but I learned. At this time in my career, I did speak some Farsi but my vocabulary was quite limited. I was given a leg up on to the horse and adjusted my stirrups. I rode the horse on the flat for about half an hour getting to know him. He certainly had been well schooled in dressage, as most of the German horses are. He took the bit very well and responded to the legs. His departures to the canter were excellent and his extension and collection at all paces was very good. He did a very nice half pass, renvers, travers, shoulder in and so forth. It really was quite fun to ride such a horse.

Ali who along with about four other men had been watching steadfastly asked, 'You want jump this horse?' I really did not want to, with all those eyes on me, but I thought what the heck; I might as well have some fun.

I had seen that there were some jumps set up in the adjoining ring which was about the same size as the main ring and was usually used for a warm up area at the horse shows. I rode through the gate and popped the horse over a few fences at the trot and then a few more at the canter. After this little bit of work Rokhsar began to show that he was not in shape to do much more. He had been in the country for about three weeks and was feeling the effects of acclimatization. I got off and handed him to the groom who was waiting.

'Meeses Rose, zat was gud. Zat horse gud jump.'

I thanked him for the compliment and asked if I could have a tour of the stables. We first entered the main stable that was close to the ring. It was a long building with twenty four stalls. Each stall opened to the outside with a Dutch door but there was also a center aisle which was used for feeding and observing the horses. The horses stood about six inches higher than the aisle so those five German horses looked huge standing in their stalls. The other horses were Persian breeds and all looked well cared for. Of course the first two horses, in the stalls of honor, were the favorites of His Majesty; Azar, his Anglo Arab parade horse that was born in 1957and raised at Farahabad looked much younger than his years. The other horse was also an Anglo Arab, but not raised at Farahabad; Alvand, was the mountain horse of the Shah. The stalls were all large and bedded with what looked like peat moss but I was to learn that it was *paeen* or dried manure which actually made a soft bedding. The mosaic tile on the stall walls was colorful and a true Persian touch. The horses were fed in big tiled mangers that were on the center aisle side of the stall. We moved on to the second stable, a duplicate of the main stable, but for only twenty horses; in that barn were found the carriage horses. There were a couple other buildings with stalls but I was not shown them as they were not "show places". There was a show tack room, a working tack room and a grooms' tack room. I was to learn how confusing that whole system could be.

I was really impressed to see the veterinary facility which had a half-finished operating room and pharmacy. The only disappointing thing was that four years later it was still not finished. Like many of the various projects at the Imperial Stables they were started—-that looked impressive. I think one of Kambis Atabai's follies was that many of the projects he started were never finished. He either lost interest or budget funds dried up and things weren't finished, and that was the end of it. I hate to think of the waste that I saw at the Imperial Stables alone, during the time I lived in Iran. If one contemplates that this was just a minute part of his Majesty's domain, it is frightening to guess at the amount of waste that went unnoticed in the country as a whole.

My tour over, I walked towards my car, escorted by the ever present Ali Rezai and a few other of the "boys" from the stable. As I was about to enter my vehicle I bade my farewell and thanked them as best I could for an interesting morning.

'But Meeses Rose, you come here *farda*?' Would I come the next day?

'I think Ali, that Mr. Atabai just wanted me to ride his horse today. I do not come back tomorrow.'

'No, no! He tell you come all days for two o'clock.'

'I cannot come all days and especially at two o'clock; I cannot come in the afternoon!' I answered.

'I don't say you come afternoon, I say you come all days for two o'clock. You know *do sauat* you ride here.'

'Oh, I see! You want me to come each day for two hours, is that it?'

"Yes, yes, Mr. Atabai, he say you come all the days.' He was quite insistent. I reflected that I really didn't have much else to do each morning aside from being a mother. Denis and Helen were in school until twelve and Sulu slept most of the forenoon.

'All right Ali, I will come back tomorrow if you like, but I will come earlier. I will be here at nine o'clock, *sauate noh*.'

'Good, good Meeses Rose. We wait for nine o'clock. We are very happy you come. Maybe you see my horse tomorrow.'

'Okay Ali, till tomorrow. Bye, Bye.'

'*Khodafez, Khonume* Rose,' they all chorused.

The next day when I arrived I noticed, as I drove past the ménage that there were two horses being walked around. I proceeded directly to the ring and mounted my "Pretty Face". I spent about 45 minutes working with him giving five minute walks on a long rein after about every ten minutes of work. As I had discovered the previous day, he was not in very good shape and I usually like to intersperse my horses' work with periods of relaxation. When I had finished I handed him to the waiting groom to be cooled out and put away. 'You not jump now?' Ali asked perplexed.

'Of course not Ali, he worked well today. He had a few jumps yesterday, he really does not need to jump today.'

'We jump every day you know, Meeses Rose.'

'Not when I am here you don't!' was my haughty reply.

While I had been working Rokhsar, I had noted the lad on the other chestnut horse. He had been fighting the poor animal the whole time. The horse was leaning on the bit, uncollected and bent the wrong way. When questioned as to what I thought of this horse I hardly knew how to answer. I felt that the poor thing was being tormented by his rider but dared not say so. He appeared to be a man in his mid-thirties and one whom the others seemed to respect. Reza Tarash. Reza became one of my favorites and remained faithful to me to the end. He was one of the few Iranians who was true to face, always said his piece, and was always honest. He offered me his mount which I reluctantly took. I was not in shape and didn't relish a fight with a 17 hand German beast. I suppose in hind sight it was a challenge from the Imperial riders for they knew the horse was difficult and I was later to learn that Shahab, as they called him, had not been out of the stable for over a week. I was able to collect him at the walk and did some flexing with him and leg yielding in order to try to soften his mouth and relax him. All went well during the ride at the trot. It was not until I attempted to put him into the canter that the stampede commenced! I felt he was a little tense and that he was humping his back but I was there to show that I could ride the horse and so, as this was Iran, one did not finish the work with a trot, one must canter. Perhaps my aid was a little strong, more than likely it was much too strong. The reaction was like an explosion! He bucked, I would say three good ones and then took off like a bat out of hell, with me like a flea hanging on for dear life. Try as I would there was no response to my leg-hand command to slow down. It was like riding a mechanical horse over which the actual rider had no control. I decided that most likely this horse was in about the same shape as Rokhsar and would soon tire and slow down so I sat for a nice gallop around and around in ever diminishing circles to await for the inevitable. I didn't reckon on what was to happen though. As I was just getting some control and had him in a small circle in the center of the ring one of the old grooms came up to us at a quick run and with a swing of his cane hissed at the horse. That was all he needed. We were off again. Again I was about to gain control and the same man came running over. Off we went! I couldn't believe what was happening and by this time I was a might tired to say the least! After several more attempts I was finally successful. All eyes were upon me.

'Oh, Meeses Rose that was good.' Who else but Ali would make such a comment?

I was exhausted, embarrassed and a little shaken but I could not help myself as I burst into gales of laughter. When I was finally able to speak again I asked, 'What was that fool trying to do to me? Every time I collected the horse he scared the poor bloody animal and it took off again.' Ali obviously did not understand just what I had said but he tried to answer.

'Khodavadi, is old man. He makes horses quiet. You know if you say "Sssssst, sssssst" it makes horse stop. He try to make horse stop. He had bad leg so he need stick to walk maybe stick scare horse.'

'Well where I come from and I will bet where these horses come from "sssst,sssst" does not mean stop. It means go or it means jump. Don't say 'sssst' to these horses anymore.'

I handed the poor panting, sweating horse to his groom who had had a ringside view of the exhibition, and told him to walk the horse until he was dry as it was too cool to bathe him.

I figured that was about the end of my days of riding at the Imperial Stable but as I said my *"Khodafez"* Ali was there again.

'What time you come tomorrow?'

'Maybe I don't come tomorrow, Ali.'

'You must come! We need you to help us Meeses Rose.' He actually seemed desperate in his plea. They had to be nuts to want me to come back after the performance of the morning, but why not? I did enjoy riding and I would certainly get into shape quite fast if I continued with the rodeo riding.

'Nine o'clock then.'

At the appointed hour the following morning there were three horses and two riders awaiting me. All went uneventfully. I tried to help the two riders with their horses. We worked over cavetti and I agreed to arrive the same time next day. Wednesday there were three riders. Thursday there were four riders, and Friday was a day of rest! Did I need it!

When I arrived on Saturday at the agreed upon hour I was given a piece of paper with a brief profile on each of the horses I was obviously expected to work with.

Shabrang. Black Hanoverian gelding. 7 years. 1.65M. Jumped in Germany under the name of Lutsig in S level competitions.

Rokhsar. Chestnut Hanoverian gelding. 7 years 1.67M. Competed in Germany under name of Ambos. Won 3 M competitions and competed in S.

Shahab. Chestnut Holstein gelding. 1.70M. 7 years. Competed under name of Snob in Germany. Competed at M level.

Shabahang. Chestnut Holstein gelding. 1.68M. 7 years. Competed in M and S level in Germany.

Rostam. Chestnut Anglo-Holstein gelding. 1.75M. 6 years. No record of competitions.

Gotaard. Grey Holstein gelding. 4 years. Has not competed.

I was given Mr. Fischer's instructions as to how to work the horses during any given week.

'Now,' said Ali, 'We work with you every day, Meeses Rose. You know me, Ali Rezai. Rostam is my horse but he is not good. He cannot jump. I have better horse. It goes in carriage but can jump too. You will see. This is Reza. He ride on Shahab. That horse that take you for good race. Ezat Vodjdani he must ride on Shabrang because Shabrang almost kill Mr. Atabai when Shahanshah came to see horses. Ezat very good rider. Davoud has Shabahang but maybe Shabahang is horse for Shahanshah to ride in parade. Reza Hadavand can ride what horse you say. You see Mr. Atabai, he fix everything for you when he came here yesterday.'

He certainly did fix everything. I now had five men and six horses to work with each day.

As I began to work with these five young men I learned that they did not know even the most basic of the principles of horsemanship. They did not have any understanding of balance. They did not have any conception of trotting on the correct diagonal. There was no knowledge of cantering a horse on the correct lead. So I began my work with them as though they were beginners who knew nothing. I did have a language problem but Ali was adequate and I began to learn the important words quickly.

I tried to follow Mr. Fischer's schedule, as it had been given to me for a purpose and it was something to start with. When it came to lunging the horses over fences without a rider which my predecessor had emphasized was necessary, I was in a bit of a predicament. I personally didn't really feel that type of work was very beneficial. I liked a free school in either an oval or just a straight chute; however, I decided to try lunging. Each of the riders was to bring his horse out to watch me as I demonstrated with Rokhsar, the horse that I had more or less taken over, and then have them follow the example. Luckily my horse had been superbly schooled and he was no problem. I was able to lunge him over a good vertical fence of about 1.10M and an oxer 1.20M. He was put away and I then started with Ezat and Shabrang.

He didn't know how to lunge the horse and got the line all tangled up and tripped, the horse ran away and it was a real mess!! What was I going to do? I obviously had to take the horse and try it myself. But first we had to catch it and it was having a great time gallivanting around the ring. By the time he was finally captured there were at least twenty men in the ménage all screaming, yelling and hissing. I was helpless. They would not listen when I tried to get them all out of the ring and, of course, they didnn't understand me anyway.

The horse caught, I had to lunge him for quite a while to calm him down before attempting to put him over anything. When I did attempt, I was amazed. This horse had real ability and he seemed to love to jump. He played over the small obstacles and with a beautiful bascule and popped over an ascending oxer of a 1.20M with no trouble at all. I had luck on my side for the remainder of the morning, for I lunged the rest of the horses myself and they all behaved well. My Iranian students stood by speechless.

None of the boys ever became proficient at lunging but they did try. Towards the end of my time at the Imperial Stables I could trust most any of the boys to take a horse out and give it some good exercise on the lunge. I think that it was because work on the lunge can become tedious that the Iranians didn't have the perseverance which one needs to do a good job.

They really did not understand what real work on the lunge could do. They liked action and action meant gallop and jump.

The beginning of the following week I had a call from Kambis Atabai asking if I could please go to the stable one afternoon because he wanted me to give him a lesson. I was a little startled that he wanted to ride in the "class" as he referred to it, with the boys, but I said I would arrange to go to the stables in the afternoon the following day.

When I arrived at the stables at the appointed hour it was obvious that Kambis had not arrived so I went ahead supervising the tacking up of the horses. It was the first time I had actually watched this process. I had wondered why I had had to adjust bridles and untangle reins and martingales every time I got on a horse but now I learned why. No horse had its own bridle. The good bridles were saved for Mr. Atabai, His Majesty, the Royal children and special guests, and no one else was allowed to touch those "good" bridles. Each Imperial Rider had a bridle of his own but seeing as each rider had four or five horses in his care some of which were small and some of which were large this was not too successful a system. I found six bridles that fit the six horses in my care and insisted that no other horses use these bridles and it did not matter who rode the horses, the bridle belonged to the horse. This was impossible the head tack keeper said. I was in the middle of this argument when Kambis arrived. He got right into the argument which lasted for another ten minutes but I finally won my point. I was quite surprised when I heard him say in Farsi to all the men and grooms that were standing around observing this scene, 'I said that whatever Mrs. Rose wants goes. You must do what she says.'

Why had I been given such an honor? He repeated to me in English what he had said, not realizing how much Farsi I was beginning to understand.

'And if you have any problems at all, you just call me at my office and I will straighten it out for you.

I have told the men that you have a free hand. We need your help and don't want to hinder you in any way. Now shall we get on the horses? I have been hearing from the boys what wonderful things you have been teaching them and I want to catch up.'

He rode Rokhsar and I was on the big cumbersome Rostam. As we walked our horses out to the ménage he said, "You know Mrs. Rose this is a really unique situation in Iran that you see here at the Imperial Stables. His Majesty has bought all these expensive horses for the stablemen to ride in competition. You know these boys, or men as you may call them, are Imperial servants. Most of them are second or third generation Imperial servants, some of them more. This Imperial Stables has not changed in its organization for generations. It was the Imperial Stables of the Kadjars and the Pahlavis just kept it on. My father was a groom during the reign of the last Kadjar king. He then served His Majesty Reza Shah the Great and was appointed Master of His Majesty's Horse and now I have been appointed to the position. This is a place where we like to think that everyone is equal. You see these young men that you have been working with; they are just servants and yet His Majesty knows each one of them. They may go up to their king with a problem. I want to ride in your classes but I want you to realize that I'm not to be treated any differently than any of the other boys. Just because I am, you may call it, the boss, does not mean anything when we are learning something. We are very democratic here at the stables; however, there are rules and everyone knows the rules. You will learn after you have been here for a while longer.'

He continued, 'Now your job will be to train these men and me, as well as General Khosrodad, to be members of the showjumping team of His Majesty's Stable. He wants nothing more than a representative team to compete in the National Competitions. All of us are to be equals in your eyes; and if you think that a certain rider is not good with a particular horse, you may change them at any time. You'll find that I am a fairly easy person to get along with no matter what you might have heard to the contrary. I know how the gossip goes. Now, shall we get to work?'

It was quite a speech but it became the basis of what I practiced during the time I worked at the Imperial Stables. All, in my eyes were equal. That was the way the Shah wanted it and that is the way it would be for me. Unfortunately, Kambis was not always able to practice what he preached to me so emphatically.

Kambis commenced his riding lessons. He was an attentive student and had a good mind. It really was a pleasure in those beginnings to have him in the class. He could laugh at himself, as he did especially when he was learning to do the rising trot without stirrups. I think I laughed harder than he did over that one, though. We decided to change the riding time to six thirty in the morning so that Kambis would be able to come to ride before he left for the office at nine o'clock. That was the only concession we made for him in those early days of our relationship.

L to R Author, Col. Neshati, Ali Monazami, Abulfath Atabai

Riders at Farahabad Club

Danny Elganian

Farahabad stable yard

Mashed Mahmad and Rajab with mares and foals

Lessons at Nowruzabad

James Underwood and Sulu

NEW AQUAINTENANCES

One afternoon when I had first visited Iran in February 1972, I was at the Imperial Country Club helping Igor Filipides with his horse when a small balding man about thirty-five years old came up to me.

'You must be Mrs. Rose. I have heard all sorts of weird and wonderful things about you. I am Fred Elghanian. I have a few horses and love to ride. I'm not very good but what I lack in talent I make up in enthusiasm.'

'I am pleased to meet you. I don't know about the weird and wonderful things of which you speak but I am Gail Rose. Igor introduced me to Louise Firouz who has more or less thrown me into the horse world here.'

'We heard about how you rode that horrible horse they gave you at Farahabad the other Friday. We could not be there last week but we plan to go this week. Will you be there?'

'I'm afraid not, my husband and I fly out on Thursday.'

'I want to invite you and your husband for dinner before you leave. Could you make it on say, Tuesday? I have a friend who has just returned to Iran from Europe and he is planning to import some European horses here. He is a really good rider and wants to get show jumping really going here. I know he will want to meet you before you leave.'

'Thanks Fred, as far as I know Tuesday is fine. Let me check with Don and let you know,' I replied.

'Well, why don't we leave it like this; if Tuesday is alright, we will pick you up at your hotel at eight-thirty? If it is not, you call me before, at my office. You may have realized how difficult it is to make a telephone call here, so no sense in calling if you don't have to.

'That sounds like a good idea. So it's Tuesday, eight-thirty at the Commadore Hotel.'

'Now tell me what you are trying to do with Igor and that piggy horse he has. It really is no good you know. I have been trying to persuade his father to buy him a new one for quite a while now. These Persian horses are really hopeless you know.' It was obvious that Fred did not feel about the Iranian horse the way Louise and Narcy Firouz felt.

'I have always believed that one must work with the tools that one has at hand and that was what I've been doing with Igor this afternoon. It really depends upon what he wants to do with the horse. It knows nothing. It will take a very long time to make a jumper out of it which he seems to want to do but otherwise it's not such a bad animal. It looks to me to be the typical Turkoman type and that's not so bad.'

'Oh, come on. You know that no Turkoman could ever make an international jumper. They are too small for one thing. Anyway, it is too long an argument to get into now. We can discuss it at dinner on Tuesday.'

Freddie's friend turned out to be Ali Reza Soudovar, a young Iranian man in his late twenties who had been educated in Europe. He had just returned from Switzerland where he had been at university. He had a place in the country near Karaj, about a one hour drive from Tehran where he planned to set up a stable for show jumpers. He was about to import a truckload from Switzerland within the month. His horses were meant to be a hobby but from our conversation at dinner that evening it seemed to me that they were more important to him than his job at Mercedes Benz, the family company. He was a most congenial chap who seemed to know a great deal about horses. He felt that with all the money available in Iran and with all the people seeking leisure time activities, show jumping had a real future. We tentatively agreed that if Don and I did make Iran our home, Ali and I would work together to improve things in the show jumping world.

During the summer of 1972, while I was helping out with Louise Firouz, Ali and I saw a lot of each other. We pooled our ideas and the two of us organized the weekly shows that became so popular that year. There were no rules or regulations for show jumping in Iran, so we used basically the FEI rules with some modifications to suit the Iranian situation. The group of people who had been competing in our local shows became quite knowledgeable and all adhered to the rules without complaint. It was felt to be a great step forward.

Until that year there had only been four yearly horse shows. The Imperial Country Club had one spring and one fall competition and the Imperial Stables at Farahabad had a summer competition and the Aryamehr Cup in the autumn.

It was now time for the Aryamehr Cup which was always attended by the Shah and his family. It was a very formal and social affair; anyone who was anybody must be there. The preparation went on for weeks. The gardens around the stadium were totally replanted, the royal box was redecorated, the stands were repainted, garlands were hung over the railings and not least of all the Imperial Horse Museum which contained hundreds of horse related items, some Royal Collections and some gifts from International visitors, was totally cleaned and reorganized.

Three weeks before the event I received a very formal looking letter written in Farsi that I could not possibly read at the time. When I had it translated, I learned that it was an Imperial order to be a member of the jury at the Aryamehr Cup. I really was quite thrilled to have the honor of serving at this competition and as it turned out, I was the first ever foreigner to be on the jury for that important show held in the presence of the Shah.

About a week before the competition I received a telephone call from the Royal Horse Society asking that I attend a meeting to discuss and help design the parcours for the Cup. When I arrived at the appointed time I discovered that Colonel Neshati and I were the only ones at the meeting. Kambis Atabai did poke his head in at one point to see how we were getting along. The Colonel's English was about as good as my Farsi! It is quite amazing how the language of the horse is really international and we did make out very well. Four days before the competition we went down to the Farahabad main ménage to put the course we had jointly designed. I was aghast at the method of setting the course. The Colonel was in charge. He was a truly good looking Iranian man standing about six feet tall, very erect, dark wavy hair, chiseled features, high cheek bones and the almost Mongol type eyes of the Turkoman. I knew that he truly resented me in every way but he had been told that I was to help so what could he do. There were about twenty uniformed Imperial *djelodars* (grooms) in the ring ready to help. As we had the course already designed, I felt we could lay poles on the ground in the places where the obstacles would be set and then get a crew of men to work on each jump. No! Not in Iran. All twenty men put up each jump one by one. There were so many people around the fences that were being constructed that it was impossible to see them. The old adage "too many cooks" certainly did hold true. After four hours work we had most of the jumps in place but they were in no way ready to be jumped so it was decided that we would return the next morning.

The following morning I arrived at the dot of nine to find that the whole course had been changed. It bore no resemblance to the course that we had put up the previous day. The explanation was simple. Mr. Atabai had not liked the other course so he had taken the design of the 1964 Queen Elizabeth Cup in England which he had seen drawn in a book and had the men build that. We had to change the distances in the combinations and lines which with twenty helpers took quite some time. By noon things were looking quite good, or so I thought.

Then Mr. Atabai arrived. The *djelodars* were prostrate as he passed. He ascended the steps of the Royal Box and beckoned the Colonel and me to come up.

'I think that the wall in the center hides the triple bar on the other side of the ménage, don't you? You know the triple bar is such a spectacular jump that we must have it in a place where His Majesty can see it well. Let's change that with the planks just over here.' were his first suggestions.

Sharp orders were given to the uniformed men who scurried hither and tither dropping poles and tripping over each other.

After another two hours things were just the way he wanted them. At least for that day. I was to return the following day to help the landscape gardener "decorate the ring."

The rumor was that the members of the Imperial Stables team jumped the entire course that afternoon with the horses they planned to enter on the Friday. I would not guarantee that there were not hoof prints in the sand the next day; I did understand there was quite a bit of cheating in those days. I do know that when I took charge of the Stables I never allowed jumping any of the obstacles that were set up in the ring for a competition.

It really was quite a spectacle to see the Shahanshah, the Shahbanu and the Royal children arrive. There was much helicopter activity on the pad for an hour before the competition was due to commence. The Savak, or secret service men were seated in every third seat of the grandstand when I had arrived two hours early and I was told they had been there since sunrise. I had seen the Imperial Guards going over the royal box and the immediate area the day before with electronic detectors and machine gunned guards were everywhere.

At ten minutes to ten the twin Imperial helicopters appeared in the sky.

They looked like huge blue and white dragon flies as they hoovered and then landed. Into the ring came a beautiful landau pulled by four white horses. In this sat the Shah and Shahbanu. I really did not believe when people had told me he had an aurora about him but I did feel it that day. A second carriage followed drawn by a team of four black horses. In it were the four royal children and their nanny.

We members of the jury were lined up on either side of the red carpet laid out for the Royal party to walk on before they ascended the steps of the Royal Box. As the Shahanshah passed me I had the distinct feeling that he was looking directly at me, and what he would have seen? A seven months pregnant short lady! I felt like a little round barrel, but I will admit it was quite an exciting experience.

The competition went on. I am certain that Empress Farah was bored to death as she had no interest in horses at all, but His Majesty appeared quite interested as did the children when they were not running amuck in the garden behind the Royal Box. There were two classes. The first was a speed class, Table C over twelve fences of one meter ten. There had to have been at least 30 riders in that part of the competition. The second class was a Table A with one jump off. There were ten fences and fewer horses but everyone was in the jump off!

We had thirteen people in the jury box. I was stuck in the far right corner; far enough from the automatic time clock that I couldn't see it and also far enough that I had a hard time hearing the times as they were being given. Most of the conversation was in Farsi but I could tell that it was mostly gossip and nothing to do with the competition. I had a sweet little man who was to become a fast friend, Colonel Arab Shehbani, sitting on my left; I was told that he was a chief of one of the Bakhtiar tribes in Khusustan. He was attentive and watched the competition judiciously carefully scoring his card. The Table C class was a farce and I really had no idea who had won as I could neither see nor hear the times, but in the Table A I did note a few knock downs that were disregarded and drew attention to them. A few embarrassed looks told me that those were not to be noticed but I made a point through this little colonel of making sure they were counted. When one three star general came in the ring and had three refusals, the members of the jury would not ring the bell to eliminate him, so I reached over, took the hammer and gonged! The shock on all twelve faces was astounding. 'But that was General Khosrodad! You cannot eliminate him!'

'I am sorry but I was asked to come here to be a member of the jury and that rider had three refusals which means that he was eliminated. I don't care who he is.'

I really stuck my neck in a noose but all sheepishly pretended that they had not seen the first refusal.

Many people were surprised at the outcome of the two competitions. The Shaki Riding Club won both classes and thus the overall championship for the year 1353. A prize of seven hundred Tomans was given that year. That would amount to about five thousand dollars U.S. The Shaki Club could certainly use that money as they worked on a shoe string. The Colonel was of Russian decent and some say that he was one of the army colonels who supported Mossadegh when he tried to take over the government of Iran; thus he had been given an early retirement with a very small retainer. His wife was a "go getting" German woman who had lived most of her life in Iran. She actually ran the Shaki Riding Club while the Colonel enjoyed his drink and picked fights with all and sundry in the horse world. Unfortunately, the Shaki's never got the money. When their club won the competition The Royal Horse Society decided to put a condition on the money, that being, that the winner use the money to improve the facilities of their club. It was decided that the Shaki Club was in such bad shape that it did not deserve any improvement and should be torn down! The club continued to stand but never got any improvements!

During the winter months after I had had Susan Louise, Ali Reza Soudovar and I spent quite a lot of time together compiling an Iranian Show Jumping Rule Book. When we had completed this it was early May and I had already commenced my work at the Imperial Stables. We felt that these rules along with a translation of the FEI rules should be the foundation of the Iranian Equestrian Federation and Royal Horse Society competitions. I mentioned our work to Kambis one morning while we were riding and he was surprised and impressed that we had done this. He asked to see the results of our work with the intention of sanctioning it if he felt the regulations were applicable. We set up a day for a meeting the following week. Ali, of course, arrived about an hour late but it didn't really matter because most of the time I had been waiting in Kambis' office he had had two telephones to his head and at least four other people in the office all talking at once. When we got to our proposal he agreed whole heartedly to have the new rules translated into Farsi and printed in a booklet form in both English and Farsi. Ali who had not had much of a formal education in his native language suggested that we have a translator assigned to us. To this he readily agreed.

When Ali had left, Kambis asked me to stay on for a few minutes. He had something to show me. What he showed me was a rather large office with one desk, a chair and three file cabinets.

'This,' he said, 'is your office. I would like very much for you to plan the horse show season for us this year and I feel that you should have proper place to do this. We will supply you with secretarial help and anything you need. I thought that perhaps a couple of days a week after you have finished your work at the stable you could come in here and do this. I would like to make you Chairman of Show Jumping for Iran. That means we are totally in your hands. I want to have one competition a week for the next two months and then I would like to have a season of twelve weeks in the autumn. I have made Ali Reza Show Jumping Technical Advisor to the Riding

Federation but I expect most of the work to come from this office. I know what good friends you two are and so I feel with the cooperation of the Federation and Society I can really make Show Jumping into something here in Iran.'

'I hardly know what to say, Kambis. As you know, I don't want a full time job. I will do as much as I can but please don't expect too much. Ali and I have already discussed the possibility of more shows this year and we will get together and make up a schedule for your approval. Please don't expect miracles.' I felt that I was beginning to be buried in a snow drift.

Ali Reza and I spent two or three days a week together working out schedules. We split it up so that the Federation and the Horse Society would take alternating weeks. We made provision for an Iranian National Championship to be held at the end of the show season each year—-the winner to be declared the Champion of Iran.

One noon I arrived at my office to see a bearded young man lolling in a chair at a desk that had not been in my office the day before. I was a bit taken aback. Who was this strange looking fellow with his right arm in a cast?

'Mrs. Rose, I am Hossein. I am the translator for the rule books.'

'Hey! That is wonderful!' was my reply and it was, so I thought. 'I've been waiting for about three weeks for you to turn up. How did you happen to come to work here?' I asked.

'Well you see I am actually a dramatist. You see, I translate plays and poetry into Farsi or from Farsi into English. I really didn't want to do this but I have been in some trouble and my father got me this job with Mr. Atabai and told me I had to do it. I hope I can do the translation to your satisfaction.'

'Well all we can do is try. I'll give you this rule book of National Regulations. We have already made a rough translation but feel that we need someone to read it and correct the grammatical errors. This book is quite short so I hope you can have it ready in say, three days.'

'Oh, no problem, man! I'll have it for you on Wednesday.'

Wednesday the translation arrived. I was thrilled. It looked great to me but all I could read in Farsi were the numbers! I sent it over to Kambis' office and he ratified it in a matter of a few days so we were all ready to go to press.

Meanwhile the following Saturday when I walked into my office I noted a third desk and behind it a rather plump but handsome man. He was busily cleaning his pipe. A real worker I could tell!

'Hi,' he greeted me. 'I am Amir Pahldad. I have been appointed your assistant.'

'Well, that's something! Here I am not, really having a job, and I have someone appointed to be my assistant. Not that I don't need you. I'm sure that I can get you to do all sorts of things that I don't have the time to do.'

'I might as well tell you that I am sort of a spy,' he said.

'A what?'

'Spy. You know... I really work for security and Mr. Atabai's father. He wanted me to work here at the Royal Horse Society to see what is going on. I am supposed to spy on Kambis and you and all these other people. I have to make a report at the beginning of every week.'

'Well thanks for letting me know. I can't imagine that you will find much of interest to report, but be my guest and spy away.

'Now why don't you take this rule book and the translation and call up some printers. I want the English in the front and the Farsi in the back which, of course is actually the front for Farsi. I want it about ten by fifteen cm with a hard cardboard cover in bright orange. Get me some estimates. Then you decide which one is the best and submit it to Mr. Atabai. I want to see the rough proof before the thing is printed. That should take care of you for a while.'

HIM riding Azar

Farhahabad Helipad

THE CONTRACT

My telephone rang. It was Kambis' secretary, Parvin. Could I please come across the road Mr. Atabai wanted to see me about an important matter?

My friend Colonel Arab Shehbani had said to me when I saw him at the previous week's horse show, 'I think you will be very pleased about your salary.'

'I beg your pardon, sir. I don't quite understand?' I was confused.

'Oh dear, didn't you know? Don't tell anyone that I told you, but the Royal Horse Society Board has agreed to hire you with quite a nice salary. I hope this pleases you.'

I was taken aback by this but I had been working as a volunteer in a full time capacity; I guessed it wouldn't be bad to get paid for what I had been doing. Don and I discussed it at the dinner table the night I had heard the news, trying to decide how much I should be paid; we decided on a figure that would be excellent pay in the States and certainly be a lot of money in Iran. I didn't think I would be offered that much but it was a place to start in any bargaining there might be. In Iran there was always bargaining! So I did have some warning when I walked into Kambis' office.

'Good morning, again, Gail. Would you please read this while I sign these few letters,' was his comment as he handed me three white sheets of paper covered with printing top to bottom.

It was headed: *Contract between Mrs. Gail Rose and The Imperial Court of Iran.*

The contract stated that I would be an employee of the Imperial Court of Iran and that I would be the Trainer of the Imperial Stables of the Shah, the Director of Show Jumping for the Royal Horse Society and the Iranian Equestrian Federation as well, I was to be the trainer of the Iranian National Show Jumping Team. I was to work whatever hours would be necessary to discharge my duties in accordance with the operational requirements of these positions. I would abide by all applicable rules, regulations and other practices. . . .

The interesting thing about the contract was that the salary I was being offered was exactly the amount Don and I had decided would be fair.

When I had finished reading it he called to his secretary to have her hold all calls. It was obviously important to him because Iranians very seldom hold calls.

'Well, what do you think?'

'First of all I am overwhelmed. I really don't want a real job and you know it. I feel that you have tricked me into this. I am happy as a volunteer and actually when you consider the amount of money you are offering me I think I would rather work for one Rial a year. The other thing is that I have committed myself to spending two months in the USA this summer and I can't take on a job one month and leave for two months vacation the next.'

'I will give you more money if that's what you want and as for your summer off, that's no problem; we can lay off the jumpers during the hot months anyway. Please Mrs. Rose we really need you to help us and I cannot allow volunteers at His Majesty's stable. It is just not allowed. I have spoken to His Majesty himself and he is in favor of you doing this work. You know this is quite an honor. I should not tell you this but you are a very unique person. We have had other people here to try to teach us about show jumping but none of them stayed. Either they didn't like us or we didn't like them. We had a French man about three years ago. He went away in disgust. Last year we had a German man come to do a clinic. He was to stay for six weeks and he left after just two weeks. Mr. Fischer was shocked when he came with the German horses and he couldn't teach the boys anything. But you understand us. You seem to have a certain key that makes us like you and respect you as well. You have been helping out at the stables for just about six weeks and I know that the boys who work with you would do anything for you. We all think you are a good teacher and a good person. Maybe it is because you are a woman. You know how the Iranian women have been suppressed. They are supposedly liberated now, but no Iranian woman would be as strong and demanding as you are. This is what we need.'

'Listen, Kambis, I really have to think about this. You are giving me a great compliment in offering me this contract but I don't know that I can fulfill it.'

'You can't turn down an offer from His Majesty's Court; it is not allowed. You are a guest in this country and he and I want you to do this job. Just think of it as a formality in an informal relationship. I know you can do it. As a matter of fact I have stuck my neck out to get this contract. Won't you please sign it?'

Sign it I did! Who could refuse? As I drove home to my little family that afternoon I couldn't believe what I had done. The ways in which my life would be complicated were nowhere in my thoughts. In retrospect my ignorance makes me truly laugh. How could I believe that the fun and amusement I had been having would remain in a static position. We all know when a financial commitment has been made it alters everything beyond recognition. If I had realized, I certainly would have had second thoughts; however, I would not have attained the sense of fulfillment and the excitement that were to become a part of my life during the next three years.

Two weeks later Kambis came to me in my new office at the stables after we had finished riding for the morning, with an envelope in his hand

'I have something for you, Gaeel.' He always pronounced my name with the log 'e'. I was handed the envelope. I took it and placed it on my desk.

'Well aren't you going to open it? It's your first pay check.'

'Oh, thanks Kambis," I answered him but left the envelope on my desk.

'You need to open it so you can see how much it is.' he told me smirking slightly.

'I know how much it is. I signed the contract against my better judgement so I know what it will be'

'Still, please open it while I am here. I want to make sure they spelled your name correctly.'

I slit the envelope with the silver letter opener that was on my desk and took out the check as well as an accounting of the check. I couldn't believe it! I was in total shock! My salary was double the amount we had agreed upon and I had been given two months retroactive pay for the time I had been working.

Smiling, I gave Kambis a big hug, saying, 'Thank you so much. I can't believe it! I am in complete shock. Now I'm really going to have to work hard.'

'We are confident that you will be worth every Rial that we pay you. Oh, and by the way, we will pay you during the months you are on vacation.'

EARLY DAYS OF TRAINING

Towards the end of the first month I had been working at the Imperial Stables Ali Reza Soudovar and I had arranged the show jumping schedule for the spring season. The initial show was to be held at the Imperial Stables the first Friday of the Iranian month. We had decided to have four classes to start off the season. A junior competition open to all junior riders under eighteen years of age with horses that were to be considered C Jumpers which could negotiate a course of obstacles up to 1.10M. We had three competitions for riders in the senior division. A, C class for novice horses, a B class for horses that could jump up to 1.20M and an A class for horses that would jump up to 1.45M.

Ali Reza and I had set up the parcours jointly and purposely made it a very jumpable course with no tricks; we kept the height and width of the obstacles well under the maximum allowed. We felt this first competition to be held under the new regulations should be fair to all and we especially did not want to discourage any of the smaller clubs from entering subsequent shows. As everyone knows without the competitors there is no show.

That first show we did not expect many entries but there would be an extraordinary number of curious spectators from all those organizations that did not actually send competitors to represent them. We had had excellent publicity from the newspapers and expected a really good crowd. On the morning of that first show which was to be my debut as the trainer of the Imperial Stables and as a competitor in Iran, I was more nervous than I had ever been. As I reflected upon the past six weeks of my work, I was hoping that everything would go well.

My job as trainer had now expanded. After the third week Kambis had suggested that I take on the training of the six top riders with all their horses as well as himself and General Manucher Khosrodad. Each rider would ride two horses with my tutelage each day. This meant I had to spend at least three hours each day training. As the weather was getting warm during the middle of the day I really didn't mind arising early when it was cool. In Tehran the sun rises about five o'clock starting the middle of May and it gets earlier as we approach the vernal equinox. I began starting the training period at six each morning.

The first set of horses was usually the older Iranian horses that had been spoiled and were not much hope as future jumpers or anything for that matter. I used this session to do three quarters of an hour of limbering exercises and drill work for the riders. The riders had never done any of this and as I mentioned previously, they hardly knew about diagonals or riding of the canter on the correct lead, so we worked on all of these basics that had been missed out. None of them could use their hands independently from the body and thus I did a lot of arm exercise and bending and stretching. As well we worked up to the point where they would ride the whole period without stirrups. I remember one day after I had finished all three sets of horses one of the riders came up to me and said: 'I am blood, Mrs. Rose.' I didn't understand what he meant until he pointed to the knee of his too baggy cotton britches and I saw a patch of dark brown. I realized that this was blood. They didn't really enjoy this exercise period or think it was necessary but by giving them this form of torture I made them realize that they weren't as fit as they thought they were. I never had them do an exercise that I didn't demonstrate and do myself. During this part of our training I usually rode a young horse that needed slow quiet work and walked and trotted in an inner circle while the seven or eight riders performed their work in the outer circle. At this time I was able to learn a great deal of Farsi for when I demonstrated something they would call out the command for such exercise. I had Kambis there to help out and he really did insist that I repeat the command in Farsi with the correct accent. I found that eventually I was able to take the whole forty-five minute period and not utter a word of English. I got to know a lot about the riders during this this lesson time, too. I learned who had perseverance, who tried to be a perfectionist, who was enthusiastic, who cared for his horses and who really wanted to learn. After I had been at the stables for about six months this class became almost too cumbersome because all the *djelodards* not just my show jumpers were ordered by Kambis to participate. Through this exercise period they were able to develop a good seat and more independent hands. I sat mounted in the ring tormenting these poor Iranian men, silently laughing to myself at the discomfort they were going through. I was like a little Hitler. Upon occasion I had been referred to, as such!

The second riding period consisted of the the new German horses. Here we worked each day on the basics of command by the rider and response from the horse. It was a slow, slow process especially teaching about collection. This was very complicated especially as there is no word in Farsi that truly means collection. *Jamcon* means to collect up and is used for collecting up things that are on the floor or in different places. But to teach about getting the horse to move actively on the hind quarters and lightening the forehand was quite difficult.

These German horses had all had a very good training in collection, extension and many basic dressage movements. Somehow I had to show these men how to ride to the ability of the horse.

I usually rode Rokhsar, my "Pretty Face," or Rostam, the huge cumbersome animal with such a super disposition. They both were able to demonstrate all I wanted to teach. I hate to think how I repeated myself during the first months and how discouraging it sometimes was, but eventually we did get there.

We worked the horses over trotting poles a fair bit and I used a gymnastic grid once or twice a week. The first few weeks I didn't allow the men to jump a complete course. We worked on the approach to individual fences and lines; also great stress was put on slowing down after the fences. During my year in the country I had been ever shocked at the way all the riders streaked around the courses at a dead run and I felt that if I did not allow anyone to jump a course they might forget about speed. Apparently the idea was that the faster the horses moved the more impulsion they would gain and impulsion is what is needed to jump well. Through trotting fences of 1M and 1.10M they began to learn that speed was not necessary. It was how well the hind end was working. Without activation of the hind quarters, the horse could not do its job.

The third riding period was spent with the young Iranian horses. I really had had no intention of doing any work with these horses, but one morning Mr. Atabai asked me to watch him jump his young horse. He came into the ring mounted on a very pretty white faced Turkoman stallion which stood about 15.2. He trotted and cantered the horse for a few minutes and proceeded to gallop it towards a small oxer of about one meter. The horse hesitated but then jumped the fence with lovely form. Such a lovely little horse! He put him over one or two other jumps before he attempted to jump the combination. The horse would not attempt it. He stopped, ran out and then started to balk in the corner of the ring. I didn't blame him because Kambis had been left behind on almost every fence.

After I had watched the spectacle for what seemed like an eternity, I walked over and said, 'Would you please let me try the horse?'

'Of course you can, get on the bastard! He is no damn good! If you can get him over that combination, I will give him to you… Just to train that is!'

I mounted, adjusted my stirrups and walked the horse around for a few minutes. I trotted him a bit to get a feel of him and then cantered around the ring once each way. The first thing I noticed was that the animal had no idea about leg aids and its mouth was as dead as lead. I feared that I would have the same problem as Kambis. I trotted back and forth over a small vertical of about ninety centimeters a few times. Just as I was about to try a couple of the bigger fences in the ring, I noticed that Colonel Neshati was lurking about on the side lines. Spying as usual! He was the official trainer of the Imperial Stables at present and needless to say had become very nervous with my advent. I decided that I had better do a good job of this.

I jumped three or four individual fences and then in a flowing rhythmic canter I turned towards the combination. The horse did not hesitate but jumped the two fences perfectly. I pulled up and patted the horse on the neck then walked him over to where Kambis was standing.

'He really has a super feel to him even though he is a small horse,' I opened the conversation.

'That was very surprising to watch. He does jump with a good style. I really didn't think you could do that with him. Why he never even hesitated did he? I guess I will have to keep my word. Roshan is yours for as long as you are here with us.'

'Really Kambis I don't expect you to do that. He is your horse and I know you are fond of him. I have heard you say that so often. I wouldn't dream of taking him from you.'

'No, it is actually because I do love him that I will give him to you. I know you will make a really good horse of him. I have been training him myself under the tutelage of Colonel Neshati, who by the way is over there watching you. '*Salam Jamsarhang! Khale shoma*!' he called to Neshati.

'*Gorbonetun! Salam. Salam Khonumne Rose*. Very Goot.' Colonel Neshati shouted back.

'*Salam Jamsarhang. Merci.*' I replied in as friendly a tone as I could muster up.

'To get back to the case of Roshan,' Kambis began, 'I bought him myself in the Turkoman Sarah last year. My father doesn't think that I made a good buy. First of all he is not a good horse in the mountains. You know he stumbles a lot and he tries to attack other horses. He almost killed me this winter attacking another horse when we were up on a ledge. I fell off and he fought the other horse while I lay under them. No, I want you to make him a good jumper because then I will be able to show my father! You know he is always around watching me to make sure I am doing things the way he thinks they should be done. He held this position for many years before I came home from England and he just won't let go. You can't imagine how it makes me feel. It's as if I had never grown up and am still under his control.'

'I do understand about that Kambis. I will take Roshan and do my best. I don't particularly want him fighting over top of me though!' So I had committed myself to the training of an Iranian horse.

When I took the horse back to the stable the five riders I was working with were standing around gossiping in their usual fashion.

'Well, Meeses Rose, you like Iranian horse?' asked my friend Ali Reza.

'I like this one Ali, and now that I'm going to be training him I am sure I will get to like him better.'

'We all have Iranian horse to train, you know. Why you not help us with these horses?'

'Actually because it's not my job, I think you work the Iranian horses with Colonel Neshati in the afternoon, isn't that right?'

'Yes, but he does not teach goot. He let us do what we want. We not working like when you is my teacher. You very hard teacher and you make us hurt but we know what you teach we keep up here.' He pointed to his head.

I was quite flattered but explained that until Kambis asked me to help with the Iranian horses I could not do it.

The next morning Kambis said that the boys had asked if I would help with the Iranian horses and would I be interested. It was actually a rhetorical question.

'I don't want to quicken the ire of our fine Colonel. I think it might hurt his feelings if you let me have the Iranian horses to train too.'

'You leave that to me. I can take care of the Colonel. I want you to have a look at the Iranian horses that these five boys have and see what you think. You can start today after we finish with the German horses.'

So I commenced having a third instruction period. I had the five Iranian horses brought into the ring after the second set was finished. Three of them were quite nice horses but the other two were small and poorly put together however, I would have to work with what I had. I allowed the boys each to give me their own demonstration of what the horse could do and then I gave them a constructive criticism individually. I stopped three of them from jumping until further notice; one of the three was the horse assigned to Ali Rezai and he was furious. The other two were older horses that I gathered had been used for competition. They would have to do some changing but they were not impossible.

From then on I took this third period and worked individually with the men and the horses rather than taking them as a group, mostly because the horses were at very different stages in their training.

Usually by about nine-thirty or ten I was finished and I could spend the time I wanted with Roshan and Towsan, another horse I was working on.

For the first show I had entered all the German horses in the B and the A classes and I had entered two of the boys on their Iranian horses in the smaller divisions. Ali Reza was to ride big Rostam; he was not too happy about that. Ezat Vodjdani, who was to become Iran's champion, rode

Shabrang, the big black; Hosein Karimi Majzoob was to ride Shabahang, the chestnut with the Roman nose; Reza Tarash was on Shahab, the chestnut white faced horse which had such a super jump and had carted me around, my second day at Farahabad. Golam Reza Hadavand was riding Kobalt, one of the carriage horses which had caught my eye and having read its file I discovered that it had had some work over small fences in Germany. This horse was entered in the C class. Kambis would be riding Rokhsar and Gen. Khosrodad, who trained quite sporadically, would ride Goothard. Kambis had told me that I must compete myself and so I had entered Roshan in the C class and Towsan in the B.

Colonel Neshati had entered a group of riders in the C and B classes. I had followed his spying technique one morning and watched his training session from the bushes as I was walking my horse to the lower ménage. In turn the riders galloped full tilt over the course while he, in the center of the ring, yelled '*Burro! Burro! Sud! Sud!*' which means, Go! Go! Fast! Fast! The timbers cracked, the riders flailed, he screamed and I laughed uncontrollably. I was sure my group of riders would beat his.

The day of the show was fine. A typical sunny Iranian day. Tehran gets an average of three hundred sunny days a year. As expected there was a large crowd and actually more horses than we had counted on. In the C class there were about thirty entries, which pleased all of us who were involved in the organization of the show.

The junior class went first. I had young Davoud Bahrami entered on Mojgan, his little Anglo Arab-Turkoman cross mare that had been bred by the Imperial Stables. I had worked with Davoud every morning. He came in time for the exercise part of the lessons which he really enjoyed and rode one of his two horses in that and the other, I worked with while the *djelo-dards* were changing their horses. Akbar Bahrami, Davoud's father, was Kambis' favorite *djelodard* and had actually acted as Kambis' guardian while he was growing up at Farahabad. So Akbar was allowed to tack up

69

his son's horse and bring it for the boy so that he could have his lesson with me before he was off to school. Davoud was about 14 at the time I started working with him. He was a small boy for his age and had very short legs which were quite a detriment. He had lovely hands and a talent that is hard to find. He was a bright young lad, who had a true feel for the horse and loved riding. He always listened well and in the few weeks that I had been working with him he had developed his style, that I knew had potential when I had seen him the previous year, into something that no other rider in the country had at the time.

When Davoud entered the ring on that lovely little grey mare, which always went around the ring with her tail flying, it was a real picture. Both he and the horse went beautifully. In the jump off he was the only junior to go clear. I had my first winner at the Imperial Stables. I was elated.

In the C class Ezat Vodjdani was third in the prizes on his Turkoman horse, a pretty little grey stallion that during the next few months was to do very well with Ezat. We were all upset when Kambis told us that he had sold the horse to one of the engineers who worked on a number of stable projects at Farahabad. He bought it for his son Farzin Keymadar, who rode the horse very successfully in the junior division for the following two years.

The other horses in that division did not do very well, but I hadn't expected very much. The horses that Colonel Neshati had entered all went disastrously. Only one completed the course, that being Ali Karadjbani, who went around on the Turkoman mare Shirin, like a bat out of hell, with Shirin cat jumping and lunging between fences like nothing I had ever seen.

When I entered the ring on Roshan I was very nervous. It was my first time in the show ring in Iran and, of course, all eyes were upon me. The horse naturally felt my tenseness and I could feel his muscles tightening up. I went to the jury to make my salute and then proceeded to make another circle before I crossed the starting line. As I passed through the start

70

line which was rather close to the in gate, Roshan started to resist my aids and began to balk the way I had seen him do with Kambis. I had to teach him a lesson and the hell with making a pretty picture for all these people, or winning a prize. I made another circle with him resulting in three faults and gave him a good sound crack with the whip. I think he was quite startled but it did put him in the frame of mind I wanted and we completed the course without another fault. It had been his debut and mine and I felt it was not so very disgraceful.

The B class was a very interesting beginning for the boys with their German horses. It was a Table C competition where knockdowns are counted by adding seconds to the total time of the round. I had told all the men that I did not want to see one person ride for the clock, which was the Iranian way. I wanted them clean and slow because this class was to be a prep for the A Jumper to follow. Kambis followed orders to the point that he was too slow and accumulated time faults, but he did have a very nice clear round. Reza Tarash on Shahab was a disaster. The horse ran away from him losing all impulsion. Reza, who could barely seem to steer him and rode him through five fences; poor Reza. He was terribly upset about it but he felt the fault was definitely not his. These German horses were just not what was needed in Iran! Reza Hadavand, I had entered as a post entry after I had seen that he and Kobalt went well under good control in the C class even though they were not in the prize. In this B competition he had two fences down but rode better than I had expected. Our glamour boy, Ali Rezai, on Rostam went very well until the last four obstacles when Ali decided it was time to speed up and galloped full tilt hitting all four. General Khosrodad on Goothard had three fences down but it was not a disastrous round. Then came Ezat Vodjdani on Shabrang. The horse knew exactly what was happening as he entered the ring. He became quite excited as the bell rang, but Ezat was able to keep control and he had a good clear round. It was a little fast to my mind but it was a very good start for that combination of horse and rider. The outcome was that Ezat won the class and Hossein Karimi Majzoob was second with a clear round on Shabahang who handled the course very well. The third prize went to someone from another club and I was fourth on Towsan. He was a beautiful little gray Moroccan Barb that was given to the Shah by King Hassan of Morocco. The horse had a reputation for stopping and I had been working on him for the past few weeks trying to give him confidence, for it seemed to me that he was a bit frightened. On course he went very well but coming into the combination, he started to stop. I pushed him, but he went through the first element of the obstacle, somehow he regained his impulsion and jumped out clear and finished the course with only the four faults.

The final competition of the day was the main event, the A Jumper, Table A with one jump off. I had tried to give each rider a critique of his ride in the B competition in hopes that he would be able to rectify some of the more obvious mistakes and hopefully get a better performance. The first to go over the course was Reza Tarash on Shahab. Poor Reza was white with fear as he entered the ring. When the bell rang the horse took off like a bat out of hell. Reza gamely pointed him in the direction of the first three obstacles which were cleared in fine fashion with Reza holding on for dear life. He had very little strength in his legs and had absolutely no control at all. Without the use of a rider's legs pushing the hind quarter forward no amount of pulling of the reins will stop it. It is the interrelationship of the hand and the leg of the rider that is the steering gear, accelerator and brakes to his mount. I hate even to picture the next few moments of Reza's ride. Shahab galloped around the ring in the fashion that he had taken me so many weeks before. When finally his rider was able to slow him down he did not attempt another fence but just came right out. I approached the exit gate as Reza rode through it. '*Nemitunam, aslan nemitunam, asbe Almani, savarmisham!*' panted poor Reza. He just could not and did not want to ride these German horses. I as kindly as possible, told him not to worry about it that we would sort things out the next day. I could see that this kind man was near to tears.

Ali Rezai was next of our group and he went in with great confidence that he was going to improve on his mistake of the previous round. He did go much slower and under better control. Rostam needed a lot of leg though and Ali just did not have the idea of the collecting leg yet. I was able to see where I hoped to help him during the weeks to come and was quite pleased with his round, only two fences down. In the end he was just out of the prize but there was lots of promise there. He was a talented man, had a lot of guts and was probably the only horseman of the lot I was working with at Farahabad at the time.

As he jumped off his horse, letting the groom take over, he called to me, 'Messes Rose. You see that much better! I go slow that time.'

'Yes Ali, that was a lot better.'

'Messes Rose. I say something to you. You geeve me the horse of Reza. He is best horse and I am best rider. With that horse I know I can ween. What you say?' He really was an outspoken devil but I knew that he would be able to get along well with Shahab. 'I will have to talk to Mr. Atabai about that. We will discuss it on Saturday morning.'

'Oh, Messes Rose. Thank you very much.'

Shabahang and Majzoob went around the course with just four faults. At the time of their round it was the best so far. Davoud, as we called Hossein, for some inexplicable reason, rode with a great deal of calm and calculation; I was quite surprised. Ezat Vodjdani rode the big black Shabrang well and came out of it with one stop for three faults. That put him on top to that point. There was just Kambis left to go and when he and Rokhsar had a clear round, I was astounded. I think Kambis was as well. But he had won the competition. He was in seventh heaven. So we had Kambis on Rokhsar, Ezat on Shabrang, Hossein Karami Majzoob on Shabahang in the first three spots. Hushang Temouri from the Imperial Guards, who had done well in the Russian Competition was fourth and the other spots were riders from other clubs. In all there had only been twelve horses in the big class but it was a start. The first A competition had been quite a success, especially in my eyes. I had been very lucky.

Saturday, the day after the competition, I was at the stable later than usual for I only intended to check out the horses that had jumped the previous day and chat briefly with each rider before I left for my office in town. All the horses had come out very well, no swelling or undue heat. I instructed the boys to take each horse out and cold hose the legs for about twenty minutes, then walk them for thirty minutes and again bandage them and put them in their stalls.

The outcome of my discussions with the riders was that Reza Tarash did not want to ride German horses. He was happy with his little Barb stallion that had been given to the Shah by the King of Jordan. This horse Sheyhey, was an honest animal with a heart as good as gold. When I first saw him he had three seasons of jumping under his belt. Granted there had only been four shows a year; nevertheless, the Imperial horses jumped many times a week and so he had not been easily used. I had to agree with Reza, who was the eldest of the men I was training, if he did not like to ride these large horses, there was no point in his wasting his time or mine. I would speak to Kambis about it.

The second outcome was that Ali Rezai was determined to have Shahab assigned to him. I had to agree that it would be a good combination, however, I would have to be careful because perhaps Kambis would want the horse. When I mentioned that fact to Ali, he shrugged, 'Well, Meeses Rose you must say to him Shahab is not goot horse. Or you say to heem that Rostam is goot horse for heem. It is not problem.'

'Well actually Ali, you know that Mr. Atabai is the boss here and if he decides that he wants a horse I can't tell him otherwise. You are not running the place, he is.'

'But I must have goot horse. I am goot rider the horse. You see. You geeve me Shahab I make *Garamon* (champion) of Iran. You must have *Garamon* in Imperial Stables.'

'Ali, you are impossible. I will see what I can do. Actually, I like Rostam quite a bit and I think it proves that you are not such a good judge of horse flesh if you don't want to ride him. I ride him a lot and I don't have a problem. If you would learn to use your legs properly and listen a bit you might be the Great *Garamon*.'

'Yes, thank you Meeses Rose. You is goot teacher, you my teacher. I show you, I listen. You give me Shahab, I listen. You know I listen you. Mr. Fischer was here I not listen. I not ride. Mr. Fischer was not goot. You goot so you see I work with you.' He was incorrigible this man but I had to admit quite perceptive and I was sure he would become a Champion of Iran.

THE JUDGES

On Sunday I met Ali Reza Soudovar at my office to discuss the pros and cons of our first show. We were really very pleasantly surprised that things had gone as well as they had and we just had a few rough edges to iron out for the next week's show. One of our main problems was that there were not enough qualified people to act as members of the jury.

When we went into Kambis' office to critique The Royal Horse Society's first show of the season he was also worried about the lack of judges.

'Why don't we run a Clinic or a series of lectures on the subject? Or better yet a real course at the end of which the participants who pass the final test gain a certificate that qualifies them as an official judge for the Iranian Equestrian Federation,' I suggested.

'Now, that is a good idea, Mrs. Rose and I have just the two people to run it, sitting here in my office.' Ali and I looked around but found that for once we were the only people in the office. That meant us. 'You see, Ali can be there to interpret for the Iranians and you can be in charge of the English part of the lectures. Yes, that is an excellent idea, Gail. I think you and Ali should start on this thing right away, to-day, so that we can have the course as soon as possible. I think that next week would be a good time, so you will really have to get it all planned today and we will have the notices sent out tomorrow so that we can have the first lecture a week from now.' That was our sign that the meeting was over and off we went to my office to do some work.

In all actuality we composed the circular that would be sent out to all the clubs, me doing the English and Ali the Farsi. We had it typed up and sent to Kambis' office for approval and arranged to have it sent out the next morning.

We spent a couple of afternoons that week working out the format for the course. We arranged for the rules and regulations to be photocopied as the books had not yet been printed. We planned to make the opening session a general introduction to the new rules that were being put into effect this show jumping season and then spend two days going over the rules, section by section. The final two days we would ask the participants in the clinic to judge the rounds of a number of horses that we would arrange to have jump a course we set up in the main ring at Farahabad one day, and at the Farahabad Riding Club ring the second day. After each round we planned to discuss it with participants and answer any queries or explain any problems that might have arisen. The judging cards would then be collected and marked by us. We planned then to use these participants as members of the jury during the show season. We would both review their cards after each show and then at the end of show season dinner and presentations, we would present certificates to those we felt deserved them. The idea was that after this initial course we would have other people who were interested in judging be "learner judges" under the guidance of an official judge. After a season of learner judging we would grant a certificate if the official judges felt these "learner judges" were qualified. It all sounded very idealistic but the amazing thing is that it actually worked.

My husband, Don, became the chief jury member in the country and within the next four years he broke in a lot of people who did the judging for many years to come. I think that if it had not been for his hard work, it may not have worked as well, for the Iranians were more inclined to gossip than do the job; but he was always a hard task master in the jury box and so the competitions were judged fairly.

We used the new carriage house that was under construction, as a lecture hall. I had arranged to have blackboards brought in; hopefully we would have the opportunity to use them. Slowly people began to arrive. The time on the invitation had said 3 p.m. and by 4 o'clock we had about fifty people assembled. Ali Reza arrived a half hour late in his customary dress of blue jeans. The rules in both Farsi and English arrived as we began.

Of those in attendance about half were members of the foreign community in Tehran, ten were riders from the Imperial Stables, five were from Tehran University Riding Club and the other ten were members of the Iranian riding community. It was quite disappointing that there were not more of those people who were constantly complaining but it was I supposed, too early to expect them to show their faces.

I made the opening remarks in English and then Ali made a similar speech in Farsi in which we stated that without a competent jury we could not expect show jumping in Iran to progress and that we felt all in attendance were potential people to draw upon for our juries this season; as well, we were grateful that they were giving some of their valuable time to the horse world.

As we were about to hand out the copies of the rules we saw a hand waving from the back row of seats. When I noted from whose body the hand was waving I was determined not to notice and was just about to tell Ali to do the same when he courteously acknowledged the individual. Actually the hand was not so bad, it was that human being attached to it that made me feel our Clinic might become a farce. Too late Ali realized the problem.

Colonel Shaki had certainly had a few drinks before he arrived. Using his most formal Farsi he addressed all in attendance, 'I have come here not as an individual who expects to learn from this ridiculous lecture but as the greatest rider and instructor of all time in Iran. I want to inquire of all of you in attendance today why you would come to listen to a foreign interloper who has already infiltrated too far into our Iranian world of show jumping and a hippy freak who has spent most of his life outside our wonderful country? The Master of His Majesty's Horse is nothing but a *Farengi* lover! Why would he give this woman so much authority otherwise? Why, Soudovar cannot even speak his mother tongue any better than a common laborer. I ask all of you who are loyal Iranians, why you did not come to me or to my dear friends Colonel Sohrab Khalvati or Colonel Neshati. This is the disgrace, that you did not utilize the people in Iran who could do the job.'

Pulad Mansapur, who was to become the President of The Royal Horse Society and Kambis' right hand man, had come to observe this first meeting. To this point I knew him only as a wishy washy "yes" man. I was flabbergasted when he stood up to Colonel Shaki and said, 'If you think you and these other two colonels you mention are so great why were you not the ones to get this whole thing going? You certainly have had the chance. You say you have been the master of show jumping in Iran. Tell me then why are you so behind in this field today? It must be that you are not up to date. It takes two young people who are knowledgeable about what is happening in the horse world outside our country to help us catch up with the rest of the world. Now if you wish to make difficulties you may leave at once, if not you may now sit down and listen!' The Colonel sat.

On the whole the five days of lectures and practical work went very well. All save Colonel Shaki came back to complete the remaining four days. Of those who graduated, we were able to rely more on those members of the foreign community for the first two years but gradually more and more Iranians became interested in helping out especially as it became a prestigious thing to do. Colonel Tom Drake was one of the most faithful. He was an American Army Colonel who was one of the chief advisors to the Iranian Officers Staff College. It was a great loss to the horse show world when he left to go back to the U.S. and retire from the Military. Sargent Walter Link, Skip as we called him; and Ted, as our journalist friend, James, always referred to him in the paper, was also a faithful member of our jury in those early days. He withdrew from the activities when Colonel Khalvati insulted his family at the Esfahan Horse Show by calling them "those freckled faced little American people." Skip figured that was as bad as being called an "infidel". His wife, Margarite, did continue to help out and she and her children made all the rosettes for the shows.

The Jury, Don Rose right

THE GOOD COLONEL

During the period of the first two and a half months that I worked at the Imperial Stables, Colonel Eshmail Neshati was still the official trainer of horses and riders for the Imperial Stables. This did not really bother me especially as I was really employed to train only the foreign jumping horses. I think that I bothered Neshati, not that I blamed him. Here was an interloper that was slowly taking all his job functions from him. He began to assert his authority over the *djelodards* by making it mandatory for all to appear in the main stable yard at 5 a.m. every morning to do calisthenics. The men had to strip to their undershorts to do this.

I remember the first day that I arrived earlier than my usual 5:15 a.m. and I encountered twenty riders and grooms half nude doing exercises in the yard. I though taken aback, was not embarrassed but I could see that the men were. Neshati was enjoying every minute of it.

'What are you doing to my riders, Colonel?' I asked.

'It is a decree from His Imperial Majesty that all members of the Imperial staff be fit,' was his reply.

'That is fine with me, just don't wear them out, please.' That afternoon he had everyone out to run up the mountains for two hours. The morning after, my riders were to say the least, slightly despondent and not eager to do their usual exercise routine especially as they had, again that morning, had to do twenty minutes of calisthenics. I watched on without making comment for three more days. I finally pointed out to Kambis that these men were being asked to do the impossible —-early morning calisthenics, exercises on horseback, ride at least two more horses in the morning, perhaps ride one or two out in the early afternoon and then from 4 p.m. until 6 p.m. they were running across the desert and up the mountains. I wondered if there might be some way we could change this schedule.

'Well, you know Mrs. Rose that Colonel Neshati is the official stable manager which includes the men as well as the horses and if he sees fit to make the men fit what can I say?' was the answer of my illustrious boss.

'Frankly, I agree with you what business is it of mine? However, you have asked me to see what I can do with a few of the riders and their horses and if these few are exhausted what can I do with them? Is there any way that we can extricate these five men who ride with me from the schedule?'

'I am sorry to say that all the *djelodards* are considered equal here and to grant permission for a few to be exempt from Colonel Neshati's torture would not be fair.'

'Kambis, couldn't you use the excuse that they are going through the same torture on horseback with me every morning at 6:30 a.m. and why should they have to do it twice.'

'I am afraid not. Anyway, I feel it doesn't hurt them to work once in their lives. They have it so cushy here that they need to find out what it is to be exhausted once in a while. It won't go on forever. Colonel Neshati will be out of here by the time you come back from summer vacation. At that time you will take over all of his responsibilities.'

'I think that I might be glad to have him here at that time, if I'm expected to do all his jobs. You know I didn't sign on here as a stable manager. I came here originally to help you out with a few German jumping horses that you were having some trouble with. Please keep that in mind. I'm not a jack of all trades. Also, my first job is to Don and the children.' I tried to sound emphatic.

'Don't go getting so upset. I thought you would like to have the Colonel out of here so that he would not be meddling in your affairs. Isn't that so?'

'Actually it's not! I think he would like to have me out of here! It seems I'm meddling in his affairs more than he is in my affairs!'

I could see that Kambis was becoming exasperated. It was time to stop pushing. True, I didn't like to have that man tiring out the riders I was trying to teach however, I didn't want to have all the extra responsibility that went along with his job.

Meanwhile the stables that Her Majesty had built for the junior riders of Iran were near completion. These stables were about one half a mile through the woods from the Imperial Stables. They were at the main gate to the Imperial Game Preserve upon which the Imperial Stables were situated. Soon twenty-seven box stalls and twelve standing stalls would be ready for this junior riding club. To date there was no one to run this establishment.

Kambis called me into his office one afternoon to ask me if I would put some advertisements in the American publications so that I could do the interviewing and hiring of someone to run and do the training at the Farahabad Club, as it was to be called, while I was in the States that summer. I felt that it was quite a responsibility and did not particularly want to do it, but I felt I could not refuse. I composed an advertisement that looked attractive, using my father-in-law's address for the replies, and hoped that I would be lucky in finding someone.

It turned out that an old friend of mine Ed Lane, who was working in the saddlery business in New Jersey saw the ad and contacted me. He had been a rider and trainer in New York State and was all in for the adventure; he came with his wife and children and did a great job for the next two years.

Colonel Neshati began to spend more and more time at the Farahabad Riding Club below. He lost interest in the morning exercises and actually moved his office down to the new club. He begged, borrowed or stole a number of horses and commenced giving lessons at the new establishment even though it was not officially open. One morning he came to me and said, 'Mrs. Rose I will not be bothering you at the Stables anymore. I am moving below. I hope you can do the job that will be expected of you. It is much harder than you would think!'

'Colonel Neshati, I really have never had any designs on your job. Kambis asked me only to come here to help train the German jumping horses. I have never wanted or been asked to take over your job. Actually I will be going away for two months in the very near future. Please don't move out just like that. Does Mr. Atabai know what you are planning?'

'*Abe nadere*, (it does not matter) Mrs. Rose. It will all work out for the best. *Norahat nemisheed* (Don't worry).'

I was becoming more nervous by the day. Not only was I usurping this man's job at the Imperial Stables, but now I had put an ad in some American publications to hire someone to take the position that Neshati now seemed to want. What was I to do?

The next time I saw Kambis I mentioned the fact that Colonel Neshati was now thinking of taking over the Farahabad Junior Riding Club and should I perhaps dispense with thinking of hiring an American to work there.

'No, no! By the time you come back with your American teacher not only will Colonel Neshati have left the Imperial Stables but also he will no longer be at the Farahabad Club. There is no problem. Just continue on as we have discussed.'

I was *norahat*! It turned out that the Colonel did not leave the Farahabad Club but thank goodness things worked out between him and Ed; they actually became very good friends and worked well together.

The spring show season rolled along. Each week we had more and more horses entered in the competitions, especially the C class. We still had few A horses but there had been another three or four imported by Ali Reza Soudovar; among them Upa Negrino, a horse that had been on the Swiss International Team. Freddy Elghanian bought this horse but unfortunately never did ride it himself.

The day before I left with my family for the two month summer vacation we had planned, we organized a competition open only to the imported horses in the country. Ezat Vodjdani won the class on Shabrang and Ali Rezai was second on Shahab which he had been riding since the first competition in which Reza Tarash had had such trouble. I rode big Rostam. It was really a joke to see me upon that huge German monster. He was actually quite a good jumper but unfortunately, he had not had very much experience and we did rush him a bit but he won a fair number of competitions in his day and he held the record for puissance in Iran at 1.75 for some time. I had quite a time with him that day though.

Colonel Neshati had put up a really good course. The first round Rostam ran out at the second part of the triple combination and dropped me right on my ass! Slightly demeaning. In the second round of the class which was being run as a Grand Prix I was the only horse clean. Actually the only one for the day. That didn't help the ego much though!

Off I went for a great eight weeks of vacation having left detailed instructions for each *djelodar*. When I returned we would have twenty five days of intensive training before we flew off to Russia for an international competition. The competing nations were to be Poland, Czechoslovakia, Rumania, U.S.S.R., and Iran. What a terrifying thought!

TO RUSSIA

Everyone in the Horse World was excited about the prospect of sending a team of show jumpers to Russia. The invitation had come to the Iranian Equestrian Federation in reciprocation for the previous year's Iran-Russian Friendship competition that had been held in Tehran. I had been quite surprised when I had seen the specifications for the various competitions. Our riders and horses would be expected to jump courses of 1.30M and 1.45M consistently. The big division was a bit over our heads but just the same it should be a good experience.

I was asked my opinion about members for the team but it was really a foregone conclusion before the discussions started. Kambis Atabai would go with Rokhsar and Rostam; General Khosrodad would go with Goothard, whose name he had by this time changed to Gholitossi, which means big grey giant loosely translated. There was a chance that the General would not be able to make the trip, so if this happened his horse would be ridden by Hossein Karimi Majzoob who would also ride Shabahang. Ezat Vodjadani had Shabrang, Ali Rezai would ride Shahab. Reza Tarash would take little Sheyhey; General Nader Djanahbani would ride his new French horse Vercingetorix and Ali Reza Soudovar would ride Fred Elghanian's Upa Nengrino. The final member would be Husshang Tehmori from the Imperial Guards with his two Varamin horses. As most of the horses came from the Imperial Stables we would have the majority of the training sessions there.

Ali Reza had been out of training for a couple of years; he had been spending more of his time training the young children of Fred Elghanian as well as Fred himself and General Djahanbani. He had spent the two months that I had been away getting into shape. I was very impressed the first day I saw him compete about two weeks after I got back. He rode both Upa Negrino and Djahanbani's horse Vercingetorix very well and was in the prize on both of them. After the show he confessed that he didn't have the nerve he used to and that he hoped he would be OK for Russia. I figured he would be as good as or better than the others for at least he had experience riding outside Iran. None of the others had ridden anywhere else.

We got together as a team one day a week so that we could work on jumping the bigger fences and combinations. I tried to plan for any combination of fences in a multiple obstacle that we might encounter. During the four joint training sessions we had, I think we covered all the probabilities; we tried to prepare for what we could expect to find in Kiev.

The first of our joint training sessions was held in the Farahabad lower ring early one morning. I had set up a course of obstacles between 1.20M and 1.30M. There were ten fences in the ring plus a vertical and an oxer in the warm up ring. I didn't intend to have the horses jump a complete course but had set up the jumps so that there were series of three or four related fences that could be worked on as a unit before going on to the next problem.

The riders all warmed up their own horses and as they were ready they came to me to discuss what they were to jump. As always Rezai was ready first; he never did any more preliminary work than absolutely necessary. He felt that he could jump the horse whether it was warmed up and supple or not. This is one thing that I never could understand about him because he really was quite a good horseman and he did have a feel for the animal; he was always in a hurry no matter what he was about. I glanced around to see that he was the only one ready, so decided to take him alone and get it over with.

He popped over the practice jumps and then proceeded to attack each set of obstacles as I requested. Both he and the horse were doing very well, so after a brief rest in order for the horse to catch its breath I had the jumps raised for him. I set the double vertical fences with eight meters in between at 1.40m expecting this to cause a problem, but he flew over without any trouble at all. I had put the oxer at 1.45M followed in three strides by a triple bar at 1.50M. After successfully conquering that, I sent him and the horse to the stable to be cooled out. Ali in particular needed cooling out because he felt he had done a great job and was ready to observe and criticize the others when they had troubles as he knew they would. Unfortunately he was back within ten minutes, having obviously given his horse to the groom to bathe and walk out.

I had been watching the other riders out of the corner of my eye as I put Ali over the couple of big ones and I could tell who would be ready and who seemed to be warming up with trepidation. I loved to work with them when they were a little nervous because those were the times when they listened the best. Ali Reza came up to me on his first mount and asked that he be allowed to jump the fences just at the low height of 1.20M to 1.30M. He said that not only was he not fit but the horse was not ready for the big stuff this week. I certainly didn't mind because Ali really was his own trainer and it was just a formality to have him come to Farahabad once a week. He schooled Upa Negrino over the fences and when the horse had jumped everything once he called it a day for him and got on his next mount. He was schooling Vercingetorix for General Djahanbani while the latter was away on some sort of military mission; it was obviously a secret because no one knew where he had gone.

By this time I knew that some of the others were ready for their schooling but were unwilling to come forward. I called Reza Tarash who with the grin of a Cheshire cat trotted over in his usual style of rising much too high with his hands jerkily keeping time with his body movement. Poor Shehey, but he never seemed to mind; he always went as well as he could for Reza. After mentioning the hands and his style of posting I put horse and rider over the practice jumps four to five times. Reza explained that he felt the vertical combination was a bit too high for him for the first time. I always listened to the boys when they made such a request if it was reasonable because I was beginning to understand the Iranian temperament and if I did not listen I knew that out of spite they would muff something to prove how correct they had been. Often I would discuss the problem and hope to convince the rider that there was really not a problem. Only if the rider remained adamant would I change the jump. In this case I did lower the combination and I shortened the distance for Shehey because he was a lot smaller than the rest of the horses and would have trouble with the eight meter one stride combination. Reza did well on the course. He did knock the first of the double verticals so had to do that again and he had an oxer down as well. I like to build up the rider's confidence as much as I can towards the end of a training sessions so I put the triple bar up to one fifty for Reza. He jumped it without a problem and was able to leave the ring puffed up like a pouter pigeon.

As I was about to pounce on Kambis I noted his father coming into the ring. He was a very tall stately older gentleman with a full head of beautiful white hair; he supported his moderate paunch proudly; it went along with being a true Persian statesman. He was one of the Shah's closest personal advisors and thus carried a lot of influence.

'I thought I would come over on my way to my office to see what you are doing here, Mrs. Rose. You know I come by often to have a look but I don't think you notice. You seem to be too absorbed in your job. I like that; to see someone who is not too easily distracted. Well, don't let me interfere. Go on with what you are doing.'

Kambis rode his horse over to speak to his father and I decided to take Davoud first. He did very well having trouble with just one combination.

When he had cleared it I put each element up ten centimeters and he jumped it again without fault. I put the triple bar up for him too and he made the 1.50M jump seem easy. I really was not keen on schooling horses high but in Iran the riders seemed to need the odd high fence for psychological reasons more than anything else.

The old man seemed to be quite pleased with what he had seen and asked me if Kambis could do the same thing. He was riding Rokhsar at the time; the horse had started stopping with him and I was a little leery; however, I replied that I was just about to school Kambis.

As he approached me for his warm-up jumps I said to Kambis, 'This had better be *par excellence*, you know. You have to show your father how well you are riding; he was one of the ones who was against your hiring me, you told me. Just keep as sharp as you can and don't choke up!'

'Please don't put the jumps up too high I don't want to make a mess of things.'

'OK, away we go; I will keep things cool.'

Kambis never could learn to trot into a fence so his warm-up jumps were not exemplary. He got left behind a couple of times.

'Kambis just sharpen up a bit. Go with the horse. When you feel he is ready for take-off just hold your body position; let him jump up to you. Now canter in. That's better. Just wait until I put this fence up a hole . . . OK, keep an even pace ... DON'T PUSH SO HARD ... it's only a small fence; keep a rhythm and let the horse do the work.' I could not help shouting at this man and as it turned out, I was to learn, he was much happier when someone was screaming at him than when he was being praised. He went over the rest of the fences with just one stop at an oxer. I figured that was about it when *Agha Bazorg*, (Grandfather), a term that most everyone called Abolfath Atabai, called to me asking why his son did not jump the big jump that Majzoob had just cleared.

'I think the horse has had enough for today; he seems to be a bit bothered by the heat.' I lied. I actually didn't want Kambis to make a mistake in front of his father and if he was nervous of the higher fence surely it could be disastrous.

'Well Mrs. Rose, I paid a lot of money for that horse and I want to see if he can jump the high one.'

'OK, I will fix the fence. I went over and put it up to 1.40M. Kambis jumped that without any trouble and I could see that the old man wanted it up again. Kambis looked pleading me with his eyes not to put the jump up again but I was angry that his father was interfering and I decided I would put the fence up again. Up it went another five centimeters and over they flew. I now put the jump cups in the top hole and motioned Kambis to approach the fence. Over went Rokhsar in fine style; to say his rider's style was fine, I would like to, but I cannot. It was a picture from Sartorius; toes down, legs straight, hands up and the true old English position well behind the center of balance. Well, at least he was over it and the old man seemed pleased as he didn't really know the difference.

'Measure the jump!' he commanded. We did and discovered it was 1.50M. Kambis almost fainted when he heard the height but secretly he was elated that he had been able to get over it.

'Well, my style was not very good over the last one but at least I made it. My father went away happy and that's important. You know he holds all the purse strings to this place.'

The rest of the session went well enough. When we were finished Kambis went off to his office and I got down to my regular every day work.

Hushang Tehmouri had been given a berth on the team for Russia; he was a member of the Imperial Guard that had a stable about two miles from the Imperial Stables of the Shah, but on the same Farahabad property where I was working.

It was decided that for the pre-Russia training Hushang would bring his horses up to Farahabad every morning and then when he had finished working with them he would ride two of our horses with me so that I could reinforce some of the basics such as diagonals , leads , collection, etc . He, like the others, had little idea about these basics. He was a very congenial fellow, about thirty six years old, short and stocky; he had close knit eye-brows and rather smooth features for an Iranian but there was real kindness in his face. I think in all the time I knew the man I never saw him scowl. He was a happy-go-lucky fellow who felt that every day was new, and for having fun. He really did add something to the group. When he came to train with me I began to realize that the men at the Imperial Stables didn't smile or laugh much; they were too serious. With the advent of Tehmouri the fun and jokes began and they didn't leave until I did.

I assigned him two horses that were the least favorite of the *djelodars*. One was Ghesar, a grey gelding that had been imported with the rest of the Holstein carriage horses. It was said that he tripped and he shied from the cars when in harness. According to Robin Cutler, our Irish resident veteri-nary, he had some type of arthritis in his back and was no good for anything except perhaps carrying Hushang Tehmouri. Robin was not terribly fond of Hushang. They had had a couple of run-ins about the treatment of the forelegs of Ramsar, one of Tehmouri's horses. The other horse I was to give Tehmouri was an English Thoroughbred stallion Partheon Shaft. He had been imported some years before for breeding purposes but like every horse at the stables he had to be in a work program. I actually liked the old horse and had a go at jumping over little things with him but he showed no real talent so I had put him in a slot as a useful exercise horse for my lessons and a guest horse.

Now, up to the time Hushang came to work with me, his total daily work consisted of riding two horses a day and standing guard duty as an Imperial Guard at Niavaran Palace, the home of the Royal Family, twice a week. On the first day he came to train with me I saw him sending his horses back to their stables below with the groom. I stopped him; I took him and the groom to our wash stalls and showed them how we bathed the horses with warm water and hosed their legs after they had worked. I could see that the groom was not too thrilled with this extra work but my beady eyes prevented any complaint. This finished, I explained that he might now walk the horses down to the guard's stables but if they were not dry by the time he got there he was to walk them until they were.

Tehmouri started towards his souped up Ria; that was the Persian Version of an American Motors Rambler; this one was bright red; it had mag wheels, fender skirts and the rear end was lowered. A huge aerial arose from the front of the car and looped over the roof until it was tied down to the back bumper. There were many stencils of horse's heads and shoes plastered all over the vehicle.

'And just where do you think you are going, Hushang Tehmouri, Sir?' I queried.

'I'm going home; my work is finished.'

'Oh, no you are not! You have two horses to ride for me. Do you always go home this early?'

'I am allowed to go home when my work is finished at the Guard's stables; of course, I don't start as early there. Why do I have to ride more horses? I am only riding my own two in Russia.'

'Because, Hushang, you need to improve you're riding skills. You look like a sack of potatoes on the back of a horse and I don't intend to let anyone represent Iran who looks like you do. We are going to do all sorts of fun and exciting things for the next four weeks and at the end you will not only be fit but you will be a better rider.'

'That's fine with me, Khonume; what do you want me to do now?'

'I would like you to go over to the tack room, get your bridle and saddle and tack up a horse called Ghesar; he is in the fourth stall on the right in the twelve horse stable, then come to the ring with the rest of the boys.'

I stood by watching him go to the saddle room. The other boys were getting ready to tack up their mounts for the exercise class. I could see them chiding Tehmouri about the fact that he was in for a really rough time. They had been through the first shock of exercise on horseback and I could see that they were thoroughly enjoying being able to observe a newcomer. As he came out of the stable I asked him to come over and let me examine his saddle. I noticed that it had a sprung tree and could not be doing the back of any horse much good.

'Hassan, would you please get me one of those new saddles?' I asked our *djelodar* in charge of tack.

'You mean the ones that came from America, Mrs. Rose?' I had bought about twenty thousand dollars' worth of tack from Millers wholesale outlet in New York when I was on vacation.

'Oh, I put them away in the other saddle room. Why do you want one?'

'I am going to give it to Tehmouri while he is riding with us. His is broken and is not good for the backs of the horses.'

'I couldn't do that, Khonume. I don't think Mr. Atabai would like you're giving a saddle to Tehmouri.'

'I don't care, I don't want him using his own saddle on our horses.'

'I can't take the responsibility of letting you give a saddle to Tehmouri.'

'Hassan,' I laughed, 'don't hassle me. Just get me one of the new saddles. I will take the responsibility.'

Grumbling, Hassan got the key from the hook and limped over to the other tack room. When he came back with the saddle I gave it to Tehmouri telling him that he was to come to me after the classes were over to learn how to take care of this brand new saddle. I could tell he was very pleased and I felt a psychological victory was won.

I will have to admit that Ghesar was not the most comfortable ride being rather broad in the back. A rider's legs tended to be uncomfortable, if used to being astride narrower horses as was Hushang. It could be agony. I certainly didn't overwork him with the exercises that first day; however, he still managed to end up in the sand twice before he was finished with the clumsy grey. He was unhurt and quickly stood up to shake off the sand; the rest of the riders were in hysterics; my, how the Persian sense of humor loves to ridicule another. He gamely remounted each time and continued the exercise period. One time I saw Ghesar stumble, however he regained his balance and walked ploddingly on. Temouri being the joker jumped down pretending to fall off! Again all were in gales of laughter and so was Tehmouri . He worked very hard and learned quickly. He did have a good talent and like Rezai a real feel for the horse; I think he actually liked the animals more than Ali; he became quite fond of lumbering Ghesar and Partheon Shaft towards the end of his four weeks.

The Persians love a race; one morning after we had worked rather hard on the first three horses we were all kibitzing about on the fourth horse; actually, I was waiting for one or two stragglers before sending the men out on a hack. Tehmouri began to expound on the virtue of the English Thoroughbred as a race horse; he was on Partheon Shaft. One of the older *djelodars* was in the ring with a broken down old Turkoman horse that had been quite a good race horse in his day. He took up the handkerchief and with a wink to me challenged Tehmouri to race him once around the ring. Tehmouri questioned me as to whether it would be permissible. 'Why not?' I knew Rajab would start his horse off but would not gallop more than half way around the huge ménage. One of the boys started the great race off; as I had predicted Rajab pulled up half way down the far side but Tehmouri who was in front didn't realize this. He came galloping around the far end and as he started down the other long side of the ménage he realized the joke was on him so he began to pull up. I should say, he attempted to pull up; as he took hold of the old stallion's bridle he seemed to take off. Suddenly he realized that he was being asked to pull up, and began to slow down but by this time he was getting close to the end of the ring. He suddenly slammed to a stop throwing Hushang over his head, landing him on his butt facing the horse in the corner of the ring. The ever cheerful Imperial Guard stood up with a grin and mounted ready to go out for a walk in the country.

About two weeks before we were due to leave on our fabled trip the press requested permission to watch us schooling. Due to the fact that General Khosrodad could only ride in the afternoon that week we had the schooling in the late afternoon down below in the ménage belonging to the Farahabad Riding Club. As well as the press there were a number of curious onlookers who had heard that this press conference was to be held. I had waited in the ring fixing the fences with the help of some of the non-competing *djelodars*. It was a lovely sight when I looked up to see twelve horses and riders coming out of the pine forest with the barren mountain lit golden in the background.

I had put up two rather easy combinations and about six other fences. The wall was about 1.45M, for the press only, and I had put a triple bar about 1.45M as well. You may wonder why I used so many triple bars; they are so easy to jump and they look so hard to the unschooled eye! All went extremely well until it was Kambis's turn. He had insisted that he jump last; I guess he thought it would be like saving the icing of the cake until the end. It was quite an icing for he fell headfirst into the wall dismantling the whole thing.

In the interview following his comment to the obvious question of why did he crash was 'All riders fall; today just happened to be my day. Actually I think the sun got in my horse's eyes as we approached and he misjudged the takeoff.' I had not expected him to give such a cool answer.

When the TV people found out we had given a schooling for the newspapers they wanted their turn. This time General Khosrodad was able to make the morning session. The big blue mobile truck of the National Iranian Television pulled up about seven o'clock. It took them an hour to untangle all the wires and set up the one camera.

All went well; I didn't really pay much attention to what these people were filming because it was getting close to the departure of our illustrious team and I was trying to train, not be a TV star. It seemed I came across on film as a stomping screaming wench. To add further to my annoyance the only rider they showed in any detail on the sportscast was Hossein Karimi Majzoob who had a disastrous morning hitting too many fences and nearly coming to grief twice. Then came the interview part. General Khosrodad talked non-stop for about ten minutes and then asked me to make a few comments in Farsi because it was so cute! I made my cute comments and gratefully watched them "retangle" the wire and stuff the equipment back in the blue truck.

Then there was the morning Mr. Alam wanted to see the horses jump. Mr. Alam was the Court Minister, the second most powerful person in the country next to the Shah, more powerful than the Prime Minister. He came to look and make a report to His Majesty. At seven o'clock we heard the accustomed whirr of the Imperial helicopter and shortly after, it landed on the pad not twenty meters from the horses. He was a very tall distinguished man, on the thin side with aquiline features. His hair was slightly thinning but you could not call him bald. Each time I had met Mr. Alam I had liked him more. He was very friendly and yet so quick to get all the facts without seeming to ask any questions. It always gave me confidence in the Shah's regime to think that he had men like this around him; intelligent, kind and very easy going. During our brief chat I filled him in on our training schedule and our hopes for Russia; they were certainly blind hopes, for we had no idea what to expect.

Without exception the boys were extremely nervous. I think Kambis was the worst; it seems that the court minister was constantly teasing him about making a fool of himself in the show ring. The master of His Majesty's Horse rode his two mounts rather well though and just had one refusal at the final oxer with Rokhsar. The others gave good neat rides with the exception of Reza Tarash who was a mess. For some reason Shehey knocked down several fences. With relief, I sighed as I saw the helicopter depart and head toward Niavaran Palace where undoubtedly the Shah would hear all.

We had only one disaster during the whole training period and that occurred two days before we were due to leave for Russia. We had been schooling over the new water jump and the Liverpool because these jumps were new to the riders. Ali Reza Soudovar didn't have such jumps at his home stable so the only time he had the opportunity to practice was when he was at Farahabad. Our last school was to be on that day and he decided to bring the two horses that were going to Russia from his stable and leave them at Farahabad until departure.

We had actually finished the schooling for the day when Ali said, 'I would like to try the Liverpool one more time; I just wasn't happy with the way Upi jumped it the first time. Would you come and watch me?' I did and was shattered! In midair Upi peddled, caught the poles and did a complete summersault landing in the water. Ali was thrown clear and unhurt but poor Upi, after we had extricated him from all the poles, came up sore. We called for Dr. Cutler who came running into the ring to give a quick look but he diagnosed that it was most likely nothing too serious, a couple of abrasions, hopefully no pulled muscles. He would poultice the horse and keep an eye on him the next two days. Breathing a sigh of relief, that I could expect to take our best hope with us, I walked back to the stable where I began the task of packing.

The day before leaving I sent all the horses out for an hours walk while I supervised the final loading of tack boxes and feed on the trucks that were to take everything to the airport.

At that time the Imperial Stables did not have a proper horse lorry; when we moved the horses they went by open truck, something that never ceased to terrify me, even though I did get used to it. As this was the case we decided to lead the horses the two miles to the Doshan Tappe Airport. This was actually a military airport in the southeast of the city. It would be of strategic importance I am sure with the exception that the runways were too short to take off with a full load of fuel, so the planes had to fly the few miles to the west side of the city to Mehrabad Airport to fuel up before flying to any place of a real distance .

The horses were to leave the stable at five-thirty in order that they would be all ready to be put in the crates by six- fifteen. We were to begin loading the planes at six-thirty sharp! I was at the airport at the appointed hour but the horses had not arrived. Panic!

'Mrs. Rose! Where are the horses?' inquired the load master. I drove with screeching tires out of the airport only to find the horses coming in as I went out!

Robin Cutler leisurely arrived, 'What's the panic? We'll still be here by noon. I have flown horses around this country in Imperial Iranian Air Force planes enough to know that nothing happens on time. We'll be lucky if we go at all,' he commented.

There had been a mix-up a few days previously. We were due to fly out September 14th but all of a sudden it was changed to the 15th. Some say it was that Kambis could not get away until the 15th other say it was because the papers for the horses and riders were not ready but I never did learn the real reason.

By seven o'clock everyone who was coming on the trip was shuffling, standing or sitting on crates wondering what the delay happened to be. Ali Reza Soudovar was becoming more and more nervous. He didn't like to fly at any time on a regular commercial airline but to fly on theses military C-130s was too much. We had the horses in their crates which were securely strapped two to a pallet. There was only one problem. There was not a C-130 in sight!

The sun was up and the day began to get warm. Soon we heard the drone of a plane. All held their breath. Sure enough, a few minutes after we saw a big C-130 buzzing its way slowly onto the runway. It came so close to the horses that a few of them began to kick and spook; the wing actually passed over the heads of two of them. Great! Now we could get loaded and be on our way.

Suddenly a large black Mercedes-Benz pulled up next to the plane which was just dropping its back door. Out jumped a nameless general with members of the family and friends. The chauffeur of the Benz opened the trunk and handed up picnic baskets and beach bags along with some water skis. The General was off for a day's skiing on the waters contained by the Darius dam in the Shiraz area.

Time dragged on and as seven-thirty came and went I began to despair that we would never leave Iran. Finally we heard the drone of another two C-130s and soon the huge monsters were taxiing in. At the same time General Khosrodad who in the end had not been able to take the time off for the trip flew in with his helicopter. He came to bid us all farewell and good luck. I complained to him that we were behind schedule but he replied, 'Don't worry, you will get there eventually.' He went over to talk to the pilots; he seemed to be in deep, serious conversation.

When he came back he said, 'The brakes have locked on one of the planes so it can't leave. We have radioed for another but it will take an hour to check it out so you'll be later than you expected. But I always say better late than never!' he chuckled to himself. By this time everyone was becoming impatient to be off and the horses were restless.

Robin and I decided that if we started loading the horses in the one plane that was operable we could send it to Mehrabad for refueling and the baggage and the rest of the people travelling with us could be quickly loaded into the second plane when it arrived. The loading was a long, tedious process and terrifying to watch. Each pallet was moved by the tiny forklift vehicle, and shifted slowly over to the plane entrance where it was carefully lifted up into the doorway, then moved forward enough to get the pallet onto the rollers. Meanwhile we had a groom at the head of each horse because the front bar of the crates was a little low and we were afraid that they would jump out. For the next trip we did raise the front of the crates by about two feet. Once the horses were all on, there was much discussion as to who would go with that plane. Ali Reza flatly refused to go with the horses in the first plane. I myself was a bit nervous but Cutler pressed me to go with him; I hesitated; it would be fun if I could keep calm; I finally decided to wait for the second plane. Cutler left us with cries of 'chicken' on his lips.

The second plane arrived just a few minutes after the first had departed and we loaded as quickly as possible and took off in pursuit for Mehrahabad, refueling and immigration. I had never been in one of these huge cargo planes before so it was an exciting experience. The noise was deafening as there is no insulation such as is found in the commercial planes. We were seated in nylon rope seats that were not terribly comfortable for a four hour flight though there was enough room that we could stretch out if we wanted.

At Mehrabad there was some commotion about our Russian visas not being ready, but after a call to Kambis's office we were able to get it fixed up. Kambis was not with us on this flight; he was to follow two days later as he had pressing business for the court.

Having waited around the Immigration Room for about forty-five minutes we were finally able to get everyone cleared out. Those carrying Iranian Passports had handed them in to the Government Tourist Office twenty-four hours before leaving the country and they picked them up upon departure. As this was a military flight there was some complication and it took some time to find all the passports but eventually they were found. The reason for this handing into the government of passports was so that each person leaving the country could be cleared by Savak, the secret police. If it happened that Savak found some reason to detain a person, the passport would just not be at the airport. It must have been unsettling not knowing if you would be allowed out or perhaps if your passport would get lost in the shuffle. It did work though, for thousands of Iranians traveled abroad each year.

Shortly after eleven o'clock we took off for Kiev. We were finally on our way! The first thing that the grooms and servants from the stables did was to open their box lunches. Taking this as a cue Ali and I opened our bottles that had been purchased at the duty free shop. I felt like a kid smoking a cigarette behind the school because we poured the champagne behind our coats and drank out of the paper cups. Iranians, being Muslims, do not generally drink but also it was not quite the thing to be expected from the lady trainer of the National Show Jumping Team of Iran.

We flew and flew and flew and flew until I realized that we had been flying for five hours. I had understood that the flight time would be four hours, thirty minutes. What was the matter?

I looked over at Colonel Alai, our military escort, and noted that he was also observing his watch, so I got up and went over to where he was seated across the suitcase littered aisle.

'It seems that the flight is taking longer than expected,' I said.

'Yes, I think I will go to speak with the captain,' he answered in his halting English. He always spoke perfectly with a little trace of an accent but each word was carefully mouthed in a way that made me very nervous.

I watched as the colonel went forward to the opening on the left, climbed the ladder and disappeared into the cockpit. He was gone about ten minutes during which time Ali and I decided that there was definitely something wrong.

'I will be that those f——ing Iranians f——ed up on the clearance papers or something and that we will f——ing well have to return to Iran!'

was Ali's opinion in which he was able to use his favorite Olde English three times in a row.

'Oh, no! It just couldn't happen! Listen, Ali, after all the work that we've done for this thing and all the strings that were pulled by Iranian Big Deals, the Russians would not dare prevent us from landing in Kiev!'

'We are circling,' said the colonel when he returned.

'What do you mean, we are circling?' Ali asked him in Farsi.

'We don't have clearance to land; it seems we are awaiting clearance. Somehow our flight plan has not reached the Russians yet.'

It took me a moment to translate and digest what he had said.

'I told you, Gail, we will never get to Kiev. I promise you. These stupid Iranians are so f——ed up that they couldn't get a trip like this together! I should know, I am one of them!'

'I don't believe it! We will get it straightened out somehow.'

We flew some more. I could see that the others on the plane were getting a little restless. Tension is an easily transmitted emotion. They wanted to know what was happening. I didn't have the heart to say anything except, 'We are just awaiting order to land.' We waited in suspense until the Air Force Steward poked his head out of the door to the cockpit and beckoned for the colonel to come forward.

'I'll bet that we turn back,' commented Ali.

'I couldn't bet. They would not dare do that to us!'

'Well, here comes our news,' said Ali as the colonel appeared.

One of the pilots was on the ladder and came toward us.

'We are going back,' he said.

'But why?' I protested.

'We do not have clearance to land in Kiev. It seems that we had clearance for yesterday but not for today. You see we have come on the wrong day and they will not let us land. I spoke on the radio with Tehran and they notified Kambis Atabai and the Imperial Court protested but the Russians will not let us land so we must turn back. It is four more hours back and we have fuel for only five more hours and the Captain says that we must turn back now. Maybe it will be fixed and we can go tomorrow but for today it is finished.'

'Shit! What did I tell you, Gail? It was all that f——ing Kambis! If we had left yesterday the way we had originally planned we would be there by now. F—— Kambis! F—— the Iranians! F—— this plane! Now we have four more hours of vibration and noise to go through. Where is that bottle of stuff you brought? Let's get drunk!'

I reached into my tote bag and pulled out a bottle of Martini Dry and a bottle of Cinzano Sweet Vermouth. I always drank a Diplomat as the half and half was called in New York. I mixed up two in the plastic cups from our box lunches and without a hint of disguising our act we toasted the failure of the Russian adventure.

We had sent the colonel over to break the news to the boys who were on the plane, and the look of disappointment on their faces was just too much for us! We drank again!

When the colonel arrived back to our side of the plane we offered him a drink out of politeness though we knew he was a practicing Muslim; we were astonished when he accepted! He had only one while Ali and I finished off the bottles during the next four hours.

The landing was perfect! Not a bump. Here we were back on Iranian soil at Mehrahabad Airport. It was nine-thirty. What a day it had been and we were not nearly finished yet.

I couldn't wait to hear Cutler's remarks. Our vet was well known for his tactless remarks about the Iranians.

Ali and I jumped out of the plane to find Dr. Cutler huddling beside the other plane that had carried the horses. They had landed before us. He was obviously four sheets to the wind; a normal state for our leprechaun. Robin Cutler had been hired by the Imperial Court two years previously to take care of the Shah's stable. He had been out of Trinity Veterinary School in Dublin just long enough to get married, have a son and start up a small practice in Sussex which was not an easy row to hoc as far as financial gain was concerned, so when he saw the ad in the Veterinary Journal for a veterinary to attend the Shah's horses at an excellent salary he immediately applied. He was interviewed by Louise Firouz and hired almost on the spot. A great sense of humor and winning smile were two of his first impression attributes that influenced all who met him to like him, and have confidence in him. He was now considered a fixture at the Imperial Stable and the fact that he imbibed rather too frequently was cast aside as an Irish characteristic.

'What the f—— is going on!' he greeted us.

'Who knows?'

'Another Iranian f—— up!' replied Ali.

'Here have a drink.' He offered us a bottle of Pinch barely touched. 'It's my second bottle!'

We both took a good long swig as the evening was chilly; a little antifreeze never hurt anyone.

'I didn't know this stuff was so good. It gives a real glow, doesn't it?' said Ali, surprised. He usually liked the leafy things that most of the young people in his group smoked.

'Well, I'd say this is a great predicament to be in,' it was the good doctor who took a real look at the situation. As Ali and I, not being used to the condition in which we found ourselves, were less able to be realistic.

'Here we are with twelve horses in a big C-130 at Mehrabad Airport. The pilots will not fly us back to Doshan Tappe nearer the stables due to the fact that that strategic Iranian Military Airport had no facilities for take-off and landings after dark. We have no transport to get the horses from this Airport to the stables; there seem to be no lift trucks to even unload the horses. I think we are in for a very interesting evening. What do you say, trainer Gail, should we try to jump the horses off the plane?'

We hung around the plane for about forty-five minutes quietly nipping at the bottle of Pinch and as we got to the end of it Robin cautioned us, 'Now take it easy, you two, you are not used to this stuff and unless you have a secret stash hidden away this may have to last us until the morning. Now it may be that the two of you will have passed out by then but your good veterinary surgeon will still be about needing his nip every now and again.'

About that time that cheeky devil, Ali Rezai, came up to us with a plastic duty free bag in his hand in which was a bottle of Scotch.

'Doctor ,' he said, 'I see that your bottle is almost finished and now that I am back in Iran I will not be able to use this; I give it to you as a present.'

Robin was ever grateful to Ali; he could last the night and ethically he could not offer Ali a drop, what luck!

Eventually three army troop trucks arrived on the field. These were the type with seats on either side of the back of the truck and canopy tops supported by metal tubing; it was impossible for a human being to stand upright in these vehicles let alone put a horse in them! However, the Sergeant who was in charge of these three trucks, insisted that they had been sent for the horses. Cutler and I refused to even consider these for transport of horses even though the man ordered the lift trucks to come out to the planes to unload the pallets and place them aboard his vehicles. It would have been an impossible feat and yet we could not make him understand.

Some minutes later a large army tractor trailer with a huge flatbed behind it arrived. The driver of this contraption insisted that he had been sent to take the horses back to the Imperial Stables. He and the sergeant in charge of the other three trucks argued vehemently for quite some time.

Next to arrive was our usual Imperial Stables Army truck and its driver Djahanguir. We were happy to see him! We knew that we could put six of the horses in his truck and if necessary we could have him make two trips. His jovial laugh gave us confidence.

In due course we had three pallets of horses lifted off the plane and the horses put in the truck. This was a very delicate operation for the truck did not have a ramp so the pallets were lifted over to the truck and the horses had to back off the pallet onto the truck. It was pitch dark! The only light being that of the various trucks in the vicinity and the internal airplane lights.

Two of the horses put up a great fuss at having to back onto the truck and one got his foot caught in the crack between the pallet and the floor of the truck, but eventually six horses were safely in Djahanguir's hands and they and their grooms left for the Imperial Stables.

Now, what to do with the rest? The flat bed was very close to the ground, probably used for transporting tanks normally, and it seemed impossible that the pallets would be able to be properly secured. Robin, Ali and I were absolutely against loading the horses in their pallets onto that contraption.

About this time three big Mercedes-Benz's drove up to us and out hopped Kambis and some of his cohorts. How sorry he was about the mix-up but of course it was a true bureaucratic error on the part of the Russians. Actually, he had not been informed of the problem until just a few minutes ago at which time he came directly from a dinner with His Majesty to see what he could do to help. After much discussion we decided we would try to put the pallets on the flat bed. We were able to get the three remaining with their six horses loaded and with bands and chains they were tied and secured to the vehicle; off they went. Amazingly enough the horses all arrived intact at the stables about an hour later.

Another vehicle had appeared on the scene while we had been fussing about the horses and into this huge, very modern bus we few who were remaining at the plane were ushered. Kambis himself came with us leaving his chauffer driven limousine to find its own way home. We were whisked through immigration so quickly that it was not realized until the next day that the passport of one young boy who was going along as a helper-observer was lost. This was that of my friend Igor Filipides. The loss turned out to be quite a problem in the end because he was travelling on a Greek passport and due to the Military government restrictions he was to have a very difficult time obtaining another. It was managed eventually, but it took quite a few months.

After we left the airport Kambis informed us that he had arranged for a celebration dinner for us at the Hilton Hotel. So off we were driven to meet our husbands, wives, friends and relatives to celebrate the return of the Russian Show Jumping Non- Event!

It was the next morning that John Bierman, the BBC news reporter, called his daughter Katy who was the nanny of our three children to see if all was well. She replied that of course all was well and that actually Mrs. Rose had returned from her trip earlier than expected.

John being the thorough news man that he was came directly to the house. I, in no uncertain terms told him that I felt the Iranian Equestrian Federation should be given an apology from the Russians for this mistake no matter who was at fault. As far as the information I had was concerned we, the Iranians, had fulfilled all our obligations as far as veterinary papers for the horses and visas for personnel as well as having gained permission for the Imperial Iranian Air Force Plane to land in Kiev; it was therefore up to the Russians to make an apology. To think of all the money and effort of so many it took to take that abortive trip, would make the head spin. We had stressed the twelve best jumping horses in Iran for no reason. If there had been something to show for it at the end, it would have been a different matter but to do it for nothing. That was just too much! All these comments I made at the dining room table in my house over a few cups of coffee.

The next morning Kambis called and asked that I go to see him in his office.

'I have heard that you are expounding your opinion about the Russian affair. It is not for you to do. You may not have an opinion. You are not to expect any apology from Russia or from anyone. Don't forget your place. You are employed by the Imperial Court and the Royal Horse Society to train horses and riders, not to give opinions. I know what you have said and I do not like it. Please, let this be a warning first and last, that while in my employ you will not make any comments whatsoever to do with anything that happens in this Iranian Horse World.'

'I don't know what you think I have said? What I said was just, and Iran should be given an apology by those lousy people who wouldn't let us land our horses in their country.'

'I have heard everything you said to that BBC man, what's his name, Bierman or something. The one whose daughter works for you. I have heard the conversation word for word. As a friend I am warning you please be careful what you say, Gail. You are not in Canada or the US now; you are living in Iran and you have a job that entails that you are checked by security constantly. It is for your own safety.'

I said nothing of this conversation to anyone at the time. Unfortunately for John Bierman he broadcast a BBC report on the subject and the following day he was given forty-eight hours to get himself and his personal belongings out of the country. The excuse given by the Iranian Government was that the Shah had not liked the 90 minute close-up on Iran that the BBC had shown two weeks previously but I knew, and Kambis knew, the real reason.

Ready for Russia: Ezat, Temouri, Ali Reza,Davoud, Kambis, Reza Hadivand, Reza Tarash

Ezat and Shabrang

Ali Reza Soudovar and Vercingetorix

General Khosrodad and Upa Negrino

THE RIDERS

Now that the Team had returned from its Russian sojourn what else was there to do but go on with the show. For the next six weeks until the Aryamehr Cup and the three Championship shows, we were so busy with training, shows, and the aftermath there was little time for the disappointment of not having competed in our first away International Show to take too much hold.

Ezat Vodjdani, the most handsome and talented of the riders at the Imperial Stables won more competitions than any other rider that year. With this boy I had to be very careful that I didn't criticize him in the presence of anyone; in particular, the many attractive young Iranian girls who followed him like puppies. Ezat was a real prima donna and felt that any menial work in the stable was far beneath him. Each rider had an assigned groom who looked after his four horses; luck was with Ezat when he was assigned Hossein Peykani, for this young man was not only the most intelligent of the grooms at the stable, he also really loved the horses. Shabrang was Hossein's favorite, partly due to the fact that the horse did have a true personality and of course partly because the horse was winning a lot of prize money and a portion of this would be given to Hossein at the end of the Show Jumping season.

After each show I would make the rounds of the stable to see that the horses had been properly done up and to find if there were any problems that had been noticed by either the grooms or riders. Shabrang lived in a prominent box and would stand with his huge white starred Hanoverian head out over his half stall door with his ears pricked forward toying with the rosettes that Ezat always hung outside his stall the day of the shows. About the fourth Friday into the season while I was making my rounds I missed that ever present head. Shabrang had not been in the prizes that day due to refusals in both his classes. As I approached his stall where there were no rosettes hanging, I heard him kick at the side wall.

Hossein came running from nowhere. *'Khonume Rose, Shabrang naurahat hast; kheli naurahat!'*

This word *naurahat* means upset, unhappy, ill, bad tempered, argumentative, unkind, misguided, colic stricken or lame depending upon the intonation. My Farsi at that point was fair but I really didn't know what Hossein meant.

'You see, Khonume, he did not take a prize today so he is very angry.'

'You're sure he is not colicky? I just heard him kicking.' I went over to the stall door. As I approached Shabrang laid his ears back and kicked at the air a couple of times. I had never seen him behave in this manner. Being a generally placid and well behaved horse, he disturbed me with this strange behavior.

'I think you had better keep an eye on him tonight, Hossein.'

'Of course I will, Khonum, but I know that Shabrang is only *naurahat* that he did not win today. You will see, next week he will take everything so he will be happy.'

I was worried when the horse seemed to be off sorts all week. He worked well, and after a veterinary examination in which Robin passed him as 100% sound and healthy, I could not actually say he was "off" however, his strange behavior in the stall puzzled me. Hossein kept insisting that it was only a case of bad temper accounted for by his poor performance the previous week.

Friday came and Shabrang won the A class as well as taking second place in the B speed competition. When I was making my post show rounds I noted that our star for the day had that big head of his over his stall door and his ears pricked forward; he was playing with the two colored rosettes that hung on his door. As I approached he came up to me for a customary pat and gave me a real nuzzle. Ezat and Hossein came up laughing.

'You see, Khonum, Shabrang is happy today; he won the prize so he will talk to us. I told you there was nothing wrong with him. He is my friend and I know him well.' Hossein did know his horse.

Over the next three years we learned that Shabrang in fact was very sensitive about his poor performances. Each time he didn't win a placing he would hang his head in the corner of the stall until the next competition. We tried hanging a ribbon out even though he had not won; this was a disastrous idea for he not only ate the thing but sulked much more that week than he had before. I have never believed horses were intelligent but this one animal certainly did have a real sensitivity to his own success and failure.

And then there was Reza Hadavand! A true Turk was my boy Reza. Iran and Iranians are as much a mixture of races and peoples as any place in the world; it was professed by the dynasty that the real Iranians were "The Aryans", thus the title Shahanshah Aryamehr. Be that as it may, there are many distinct groups of peoples. The Turkomans, as I have mentioned, come from the Turkoman Sarah and are a race of tribal people, with the peoples in the Russian Sarah and the Afghani Turkomans. The Baluchis inhabit the southern parts of the country while the people in the west and southwest are the Arabs; until the early 1930s this part of Iran was Arabia. In the north and the northwest are the Armenians who are the true workmen and businessmen. The Kurds of central Iran are the warriors of the country; it was these warlike tribesmen that caused Reza Shah the Great such troubles; it took him many years to conquer them; during the Pahlavi reign they became Kurds first but loyal Iranian citizens second. In the far north we find the Turks who are kin to the people of Southern Turkey; there is a saying that "If he is a Turk he must be crazy and if he is not crazy he must be a liar!"

Reza was tall, strong and bore a definite mark of being Turk. He was not totally crazy and he didn't lie to excess, but these characteristics were evident in his personality. A gifted rider, he could not be called, although he did listen hard and tried to the best of his ability to follow instructions. Reza rode the inexperienced Cobalt to many prizes that first season and was later to ride Shabahang when Davoud left for his course in England. When I first started to train him he had the misfortune of being totally overcome by his nerves each time he entered a competition. He had never been given the opportunity to compete until I arrived at Farahabad and eventually, he did come into his own and actually won a few competitions. In these early days I had to baby him through each ride. As we walked the course he seemed to take all the advice I was giving to the whole group from the stable very seriously; he would repeat a certain problem to me as I waited with him at the gate but the moment he entered the ring and heard the bell ring pandemonium broke. His arms would start to flail, his legs would furiously pump and he would go steeplechase fashion.

'Bekhbakshid, Khonume! (I am sorry).' He would say as I awaited him at the exit gate. I tried being kind and understanding towards him; when this got no results I worked on the anger technique; the cold treatment was of no use; no matter how I tried to solve his problem I couldn't calm him down in the ring.

My final attempt rather frightened me. I was discussing my dilemma at a party one night before a show when an acquaintance overheard and came over to say that he had an idea that he thought would help. He was a person whom might have been written about in 'The Valley of the Dolls'. Out of his pocket he pulled a silver pill box. He gave me one dark shiny yellow tablet and two lighter yellow ones.

'You give Reza this shiny tablet one hour before his first class tomorrow and I am sure that he will do well. But be sure to give him these other two to take when he goes to bed at night. They are just valium!'

'I really don't think I could do that. You know I don't hold with all this pill business.'

'I promise you that you'll find a real difference in your man. I have seen him ride myself and can see just what he is going through.'

So I thought what the heck, if Reza will try it couldn't do much harm. After we had walked the course for the first class in which Reza didn't have a horse I took him aside and explained the idea to him. He was quite pleased at the thought of trying something new for his nerves and readily took the shiny little tablet. By the time he had warmed up and was awaiting his turn I was a nervous wreck. He entered. The bell rang. And I watched with baited breath.

First the hands started to flail, then the legs began to bang the sides of Cobalt, next something new, Reza began pumping back and forth with all his effort with every stride of the horse and of course he went hell bent for election! He had to be worse than before! And this time what could I say when he came out of the ring? It was too sickening. I was sorry and he was sorry but what was done was done. I gave him the valium to take upon retiring in the evening and didn't give the episode another thought until the next day. Reza did not show up for work. I inquired about his absence and after lunch learned that he was sleeping. What had I given him? I was panic-stricken. The following morning he arrived looking quite well. 'Khonume Rose, what pills you gave me! First of all I could not sleep at all the then when I finally did get to sleep I could not wake up. Yesterday my wife couldn't awaken me and I was so tired when I did finally open my eyes I just went back to sleep and waited for today. You know I don't like to miss a day with my horses, especially Dalear. I hope you had someone ride them.

'Oh, Reza, I am sorry! I guess we won't try that one again will we?

But don't worry. I rode Dalear myself and the other horses were all taken care of by one or other of the boys.'

Reza was at the time working on five horses, two of them German and three Iranian horses. Dalear was a Holstein Stallion that had been bought at the same time as the jumpers; it was hoped that he would be used as sire as well as being a potential jumper. He was just three when he was brought to Iran. I had started his basic training in the spring and then turned him over to Reza. I had enjoyed working with the horse even though he was moody and quite difficult, but I couldn't find the time that I needed for him, as well as working Kambis's two horses, Roshan, and getting on one or two others each day. Reza had done a fine job on Dalear; I was well pleased.

It was just a few weeks after the "valium" episode that I arrived at the stable at six to find Reza awaiting my arrival.

'Mrs. Rose, you must help me!' was his opening plea.

'Why, Reza, what's the matter?'

'Khonume, you know how I like my horses. You know that I work as hard as I can. You know that I am not cruel to my horses.'

"Why, yes, Reza. I know all that.' I was puzzled.

'Khonume, Colonel Arab Shahbani has reported me to Mr. Atabai. He says I was beating Dalear and being cruel. Mr. Atabai wants to take the horses away from me and send me as a game warden to the mountain preserve. Please Khonume, don't let him do that. You know I have a wife and she is just about to have a baby. I can't be so punished now.'

'You are sure that you have been unjustly charged, Reza?'

'I did hit Dalear three or four times when he became studdish in the ring yesterday. You know the way he gets; you yourself told me not to let him get away with it. You know Colonel Arab Shahbani does not like me; he thinks I am not sensitive. He is a Gashgai (one of the old Arab tribes) and I am just a dumb lying Turk. Please plead my case. '

'I'll do the best I can Reza, you can count on that. I trust you and I'm

117

pleased with the work you do. I know when I ask you to do something that it will be done. We'll see if our boss brings this up this morning.'

Sure enough, when Kambis arrived one of his first topics of conversation pertained to Reza.

'I am most disturbed, Mrs. Rose.' Oh, oh! The formality warned me he was about to bring up something that would not be pleasant.

'You are always telling me what confidence you have in Reza Hadavand and I have never doubted your judgment about the boy. I have elevated him to a higher pay scale on your recommendation, and then I receive a report from another trusted friend that Reza is cruel to his horses and beats them mercilessly. Do you know what Mr. Arab Shahbani saw yesterday? Reza beat that poor little Dalear about a hundred times just for making a little buck. Now that is cruelty! What have you got to say on the matter before I order Reza grounded and send him up into the hunting grounds?'

'I think that most probably you are slightly exaggerating about what Mr. Arab Shahbani told you; I think he may have exaggerated what he saw and I think that Reza may have played down his version to me. He has already told me about the episode.' I commented.

'Are you saying that you would rather believe a lying Turk than me or Mr. Arab Shahbani, Mrs. Rose?' he was annoyed.

'I'm saying nothing of the sort. What I'm saying is that I was not there, you were not there. It's very difficult to judge. You know that I'm very fond of Arab Shahbani; I think he is a wonderful, kind man who loves horses, but he is an old man and he does not like Turks. I don't doubt that Reza lost his temper but I'm sure he was not any crueler than I am sometimes or than you have been on a few occasions that I have observed. I will give Reza a severe reprimanding in front of all the boys; I will warn them all; I will also prohibit Reza from riding Dalear unless it is with me in attendance. But please, don't go sending him up into the mountains. He is a good hard worker and we need him here!'

'You have made your point but you will be responsible for Reza and his actions personally, from now on!'

Thus things were solved. I had won some ground; Kambis had given in some. It was the first of a lot of ground he was to give and the beginning of my many harassing responsibilities that were to eventually inundate me!

Ali Rezai was like an enthusiastic child. His two best horses were Shahab, the German horse, and Zahak, a young Turkoman that was beginning to come into his own in the C classes. When he walked the course with me Ali listened attentively but I could tell by the look on his face that he was not always digesting what he heard. He strutted around the ring with the attitude that he would definitely win the competition and that the other entrants had no chance whatsoever. With Zahak in particular, he would enter the ring and ride a fast steeplechase round; the frustrating thing for me was that he could often win that way. Zahak was a careful horse and over a course of 1.10M he could speed without any trouble at all.

'Ali that was a dreadful round! What do you think you are doing in the ring? This is not a speed class! You have a jump off; there was no need to go so fast!' I said over and over again as he came out of the ring after one of his lightening like clear rounds.

'But Meeses Rose, it was clear. I ween this time. You see.' And he would win but he was not learning the finer points of show jumping that way. Ali was born in 1940 by the Christian calendar and the year 1319 by the Muslim calendar. They say it is hard to teach an old dog new tricks; the same Ali had been riding all his life. His father was in charge of the carriages and carriage horses of the Imperial Stables, a position he had held during four reigning monarchs. He made the transition from the Kadjar dynasty to the Pahlavi's without blinking an eye. As a young boy Ali hung around the stables and when he was big enough he was allowed to ride out on exercise of the mountain horses. As he gradually showed that he was adept on a horse and because he was a good size he was used to break in young horses each spring.

Kambis who lived on the grounds while he was a boy, became Ali's friend; the two had many happy times together the way boys do. It was these two who decided that jumping would be fun, in the days when show jumping as such did not exist in the country. A few of the army officers had been sent to Sameur in France for part of their training and came back with pictures of horses and riders jumping over obstacles; these in due course came into the hands of Kambis's father Abulfath who had shown them to his son. And so Kambis and Ali would go out into the pine woods to jump their ponies over the fallen logs. The interest in jumping of the son of The Master of His Majesty's Horse, was discovered by some of these Saumeur trained officers. They in turn offered their services to help at the Imperial Stables in training a few of the horses to jump. Until Kambis was sent away to school in England he and Ali were playmates enjoying the fun only two children with a love of horses can have together.

When Kambis had returned to Iran at the age of 26 he became the master and Ali the servant; gradually Kambis took over the duties of his father at the Imperial Stables and eventually he was given the title of Master of His Majesty's Horse. He and Ali were still friends but the relationship was very different; Ali, of course, knew that he was a servant boy and had to accept it but of all the young men at the stables he was the one who was unable to accept the fact that he and his boyhood friend were not equals any longer.

It was Ali who had the nerve to try the bigger jumps that Kambis put up in the ring and together they began the jumping team of the Imperial Stables. Kambis with his experiences from England and his books and Ali with his nerves of steel and his talent. Ali became the best in Iran and at the time I started to give him instruction he believed that this was the truth and most probably, it was.

I had more success in teaching him to ride Shahab because the muscular German horse could not jump at the top speed that his new rider wanted.

He had to be well collected and jump off his hocks; when asked to move faster by Ali's ever nagging legs the horse would only flatten out and hit the fences.

Many times I would give Ali my final instructions, 'There is no time; take it slow and collected. *Jamcon, jamcon!*'

When he came out of the ring having his two or three fences down he would sheepishly smile and question, 'Was it too fast, Meeses Rose?' I would have to go over the course fence by fence with him telling him where and why the impulsion was lost; it took some time but he did learn to get the horse together like an India rubber ball and towards the end of the season he became a real threat to Ezat and Shabrang.

But Ali was a cocky devil and just when he was a sure winner, his over confidence would take a hold and he would muff the whole thing! Ali came up to that first Iranian National Championship with a really good chance of winning. There was great speculation as to which of my riders would take the honors, Ali or Ezat. Even though there were fifteen entrants that year the two were so far superior to the others that there was not going to be much contest. Kambis who was the only one with two horses, was not getting the results I wanted and was extremely inconsistent. He won a few classes that fall but he had little confidence in himself which was the real problem; the rider must transmit confidence; a lack of this confuses the horse and many start to refuse. This was happening with Rokhsar. I began riding him every other competition and that way we were able to keep him from stopping for a time.

One day early in the fall of 1973 while I was at my office in town I was called in to Kambis's office. 'Mrs. Rose, I have something very special for you to do this afternoon.'

'You know I like to spend my afternoons with the children, Kambis, but if it's that special I'll try to help you out. What is it?'

'I just talked on the telephone to His Majesty and he would like to see his jumping horses do some training. I thought you and the boys could get some fences put up in the main ménage and we could give him a little show. I won't be riding myself because I will have to be with him to explain what you're doing. I would like to have you ride a horse to demonstrate your style and then we could get Ali, Ezat, Davoud Majzoob, and Hadavand to ride the German horses. I want some jumps that look big and difficult. His Majesty likes things to be big! But for God's sake, don't make a mess of things.'

'I am sure I won't make a mess of things, but I will say, that I think you should ride at least one of your horses.'

'Oh, I suppose you are right but you know I do get so nervous in front of him. Why don't we just play it by ear? You get the horse ready and if I see fit I will signal to you and you can bring the horse out. Now you had better get going because this is to take place at three-thirty and it's now almost one. And please don't make a mess, I beg of you. If you knew the trouble I went to get you hired on at the Imperial Stables! I will be ruined if you make a boob. I almost put my job on the line for you so remember that.'

'Look, Kambis, I'am not going to make a mess as you say. You wouldn't have hired me if you thought I couldn't handle such a situation. Let's pray that the boys will not choke up and if you ride, don't you! Now let me get out of here. I have to drive all the way home to get my clothes changed and then get back to the stable to arrange the jumps. Could you please call the stable and ask Maleki to get out the big white wall, three large brush jumps, two smaller brushes, about ten sets of standards and about twenty poles?'

'Let me write that down and I'll get my secretary to call. White wall, three large brushes, two smaller ones, ten pair of standards and twenty poles. OK away you go; I'll see you there at three thirty.'

The northbound traffic usually thinned out about noon so I was able to speed up the Vanak Expressway, cross Mirdamad Avenue and get to the house which was just off of Old Shemran Road behind the Hosseini Ershad Mosque in record time, just 20 minutes.

Every time I passed the mosque I recalled that Friday in 1972 when as I lay having an unaccustomed nap I heard shouting and cheering nearby. We had not been very long in our house so I thought there was perhaps a soccer stadium in the vicinity.

Later in the day, Don had walked over to the main road on his way to visit an Iranian friend and discovered that the mosque had been cordoned off and the corner was surrounded by armed riot police. When he came home to tell me what he had seen, I really didn't think much about the episode. It was later in the day when Parvin, our maid, failed to return from her time off that I began to worry. She was often at the mosque praying, I had assumed. Days later, when she still had not returned, I was discussing the fact with an Iranian friend who told me that there had been some trouble at the mosque. The Mullah (religious leader), had been preaching anti-régime doctrine; this fact had been reported through a Savak informer and the riot police took the Mullah and his followers by surprise that Friday afternoon. It had taken tear gas and Billy clubs, but eventually all the congregation and the leader were taken away to a political prison in police wagons. I presumed that Parvin was with the group and hired another maid.

Once at home I grabbed a quick sandwich, had a few minutes with my baby daughter and rushed upstairs to change my clothes. I put on my best brown field boots, rust britches, a cream shirt with a choker collar and my newest tweed jacket. Observing myself in the full length mirror I decided I did not look too bad for a thirty-three year old shrimp. I pulled my long dark brown hair back over my rather too big ears and plopped my favorite *Esfahani* hat on my head. I would put on my hard hat when I got to the stables.

By the time I left the house it was just after two, so I would have had lots of time to get to the stables, set the jumps up and make sure the horses were ready. I didn't reckon on the traffic, however. As I drove across the back roads I had no trouble at all but when I got to *Chelo Pang Metri* (forty-five meter) Road I was stopped! The three lanes going each way had developed into five and the road was a sea of autos all blaring their horns. Things stayed at a standstill for about five minutes which to me in my nervous state of mind seemed like an hour. We finally moved forward slowly, very slowly, so that when I came to the first turning I made a right and headed south. Tehran is an extremely easy city in which to become lost because there are many huge *nars* and *jubes* over which there are not many bridges. I thought I knew where I was heading but by the time I had been driving around for ten minutes I was headed in the wrong direction not knowing how I would get back to a familiar street. I finally wended my way back to *Chelo Pang Metri* where the traffic seemed to be moving, but very slowly. As I waited to get into the stream of traffic I recognized the car and driver that had been directly behind me before I decided to make my clever little detour. Amazingly enough he let me in my original place. I gradually made it to my other shortcut which took me through the Imperial Guards quarters and in the back gate of the stables. When I switched off the engine it was five minutes to three. The ride that usually took me fifteen minutes had taken almost an hour. Things would have to move fast.

I knew things were in a state of confusion when I had ten different people come up to me and say 'Khonume Rose!' before I had my whole body out of the car.

Maleki got the floor first, 'Khonume, what jumps do you want in the ring and what ring are we going to use?'

'You mean you didn't get the message from Mr. Atabai's secretary about the jumps?'

'No, Khonume. I have done nothing.'

Thinking as quickly as I could I had Maleki follow me into the main ring, meanwhile I had five men each bring in one pole from the jump storeroom. I placed the five poles in the positions I wanted for the five obstacles.

I then took Maleki from pole to pole and in detail explained what type of jump I wanted in each place.

'Now all you have to do Maleki, is to use these five men to bring the jumps and put them up. I'll be in the ring in twenty minutes at which time we will set them at the heights I want.'

Rushing over to the tack room which was congested, with about twelve people all trying to do something different I blew my stack. What were all these people doing in this small room? I first singled out the riders who would ride the jumpers in front of the Shah. They were to immediately get the horses tacked up and get out to the practice ring and work on the flat. Oh! Problem! They could not get out there quickly because their grooms were being used to tack up the horses for the Shah and the others who would be riding with HIM. The others were Kambis who always rode out when the Shah did, Kambis's father and a few security men who would also be accompanied by about ten Imperial Guards mounted on their own horses. I made it quite clear that the Imperial Riders could tack their own horses, especially as it turned out that Abraheem, the groom for Roshan, was saddling up the horse the Shah himself was to ride; that meant I had to tack up my horse. Off they went. In the nick of time young Davoud Bahrami appeared, having just come back from school. Seeing him gave me a brilliant idea.

'Davoud, you know the Shah is coming today. I'm going to ride Roshan and there is no groom to tack him up. Would you please take care of that and then get Mojgan ready and you can jump her around for His Majesty to see.'

'But Khonume, I'm not in good riding clothes."

'That doesn't matter. You look presentable. Now come on, let's get a move on.' My idea of having Davoud ride for the Shah was that he was popular with the Royal Family because he won most of the junior competitions and he had a very pleasing, quiet style to watch. Also the mare

Davoud would be riding was bred and raised at the Imperial Stables.

When I went into the still boiling tack room to get my spurs I found that Akbar, Davoud Bahrami's father, and the most senior of the riding *djelodars*, was fussing about not having a horse to ride out with the Shah. He always rode with His Majesty but three of his horses were already taken, for they would be ridden by His Majesty himself, Kambis and one of the security men. His clear blue eyes always startled me for their color was so unusual in this country of brunettes, but today they were misty and I could see that he was almost in tears. Akbar had two other horses but they were both lame; he did tend to be rather hard on his horses. He was quite a heavy man and why he was given young small animals I could not figure out because they became sore easily with his weight and heavy handed riding. I hate to see a man cry so I wracked my brain and finally thought of a fairly well behaved young Turkoman horse that we were trying to train to jump. It was one of Ezat's horses and as he would be jumping in front of His Majesty I told Akbar to take the horse even though I knew Ezat would be annoyed. None of the *djelodars* liked to see another man on his horse and especially Akbar. I would have to do some fast talking later and meantime hope that Ezat would not find out and get in one of his petulant moods. I wanted him to put on a good show.

By now it was three-thirty and I had not yet fixed the jumps so I rushed out to the ring. Maleki and I ran around setting them all at 1.10M and 1.20M for the first two horses would be Roshan and Mojgan, and they would not be jumping high. I then picked a man to stand by each jump and to adjust the heights when I signaled. I had five grooms in the ring and had organized the whole thing when Mashmahmad, the head stud *djelodar*, came running into the ring. He was Ezat's father and one of my favorite people at the stable. Later on as I began to be responsible for the breeding stable as well, we became very good friends.

'Khonume Rose, I would like to watch my son jump before the Shahanshah so would you please put me by one of the jumps; I will take the place of one of the other men.'

'Why, of course. You take the triple bar. Let's go over so that I can show you where to put the poles each time I give you the signal to raise it.' I showed him very carefully how each pole of the spread would have to be raised one or two holes depending on the signal. I then had a great idea.

'Mashmahmad, for sure His Majesty will ask what the height of the jump is, so you had better take this measuring stick. The only thing I want you to do, is when the Shah asks the height you measure it. Now you and I know that these standards only have holes up to 1.55M so the pole will not be higher than that but His Majesty will be a long way off and will not see the numbers on the stick so you could very easily say that it is 1.60M. That way it will look as though Ezat and Ali who will jump the highest fence are doing very well with His Majesty's expensive show jumpers. What do you think?'

'Baracala! Khonume, I think that is a good idea. I will say the jump is one eighty.'

'No, I think if you say 1.60M that is enough, 1.80M is too high; he will know that.'

I had Maleki send the extra man to the practice ring to help with the warm up jumps and ran to the stable to get my horse. Davoud had Roshan all ready to go and gave me a leg up.

'Davoud, hurry and get on the mare. I'll jump Roshan first and you'll go second so come out and warm up now. We want to be all ready when His Majesty arrives.'

As I began trotting Roshan in the practice ring that was right next to the helipad I thought it was a good thing that His Majesty was being Iranian; we could never have been ready on time. As I warmed up I realized that all the bustle had kept me from getting nervous. Here I was about to make my debut in front of the owner of the stable where I was working, and he was the Shahanshah of Iran. What would I say to him? How would I address him? Where was Kambis? I had to ask him all these questions. What if I made a mess or fell off or something?

I remembered that in one of the spring shows The Prince's Cup, I had ridden a horse belonging to Ali Reza Soudovar; Bristol was an Irish mare that had little talent and no manners. I had ridden her because there was not a horse for me in the Imperial Stables that I felt was ready for the competition and Ali Reza had asked me to show the mare. I had not expected to even get in the final, but when she went clear in the qualifying round I had to jump in the final. When she came into heat the day before the show Ali was a bit upset but not as upset as I when she put on the brakes at the Liverpool and nearly dumped me in the water. With one knockdown she had a total of seven faults but it was not a very good showing. Especially when the Crown Prince, who was watching, said, 'So that's the new trainer that there's been so much talk about. I don't think she is so great!'

I was startled out of my dreamy recollections by the whirr of helicopters. I looked up to see the two blue and white Imperial Hughies gliding across the sky towards Farahabad. In another five minutes my act would begin.

When I glanced about to see that all the riders were ready to go, they all appeared to be panic stricken from the looks that I saw on their faces. I trotted over to them where they walked side by side with a frozen look of fear in their eyes.

'Cheer up everyone. You are not going to the *zendon* (prison). You are fortunate enough to be giving a demonstration to your Shah. It's an honor! You should all have smiles on your faces!'

'But Meeses Rose, what if we fall or the horses do not jump good?'

'Forget the "what ifs", Ali. The horses have been training well lately so why should they go badly today? *Naurahat na bashid!* (Don't be nervous). If you make a mistake so what, this is supposed to be a training session and we all make our mistakes during training. I'll be out there yelling at you all just as if it were a training period in the morning. Think of me! It's not my King and I am just working for him. What if I make a mess?' I laughed outwardly but deep down my thoughts of doubt were going to work. I needed to relax a little myself.

'Oh, Meeses Rose.' they were all chuckling, 'you won't make a mistake! Except the way you speak Farsi!'

'Well neither will you, boys. Let's just concentrate on having a good time in there and pretend it is fun. I am sure His Majesty wants you to be happy riding his horses, so smile.' I grinned from ear to ear to demonstrate what I meant.

The choppers were now hovering over the pad. We all stood our horses so that they were facing the landing noises, both to settle them and to show respect to His Majesty. When they had settled I speculated upon which one was carrying the Shah and of course was incorrect, for he emerged from the one closest to the ménage followed by Kambis and a number of security guards. As His Majesty walked out the gates to the road where his riding horses were waiting, Kambis signaled me from the other side of the fence. I cantered over to be informed that His Majesty had decided to go for his ride now and would return in about three quarters of an hour to watch the schooling.

It was a let-down for all of us but it did give me some time to go into the ring to prepare the jumps a little better. When I had finished I went back to the practice ring where I was able to warm each of the boys up individually. After their warm-up I had them get off the horses and walk them around until His Majesty returned.

I had just finished giving a few practice jumps to Roshan when I heard the clatter of hooves on the tarmac which signaled me that the riding party had returned. His Majesty usually liked to start off and finish his ride at the canter leaving the cooling of the horse to one of the grooms.

I entered the main ring to see His Majesty seating himself in one of the chairs that had been placed on the east side of the ménage. Because this was an informal occasion he would not use either his Royal Box or the covered stand that we reserved for when we had dignitaries visiting. I approached him observing that he was ever the King in attitude. His brown booted legs were crossed and both his hands held his riding crop which lay across his lap.

I began to get real butterflies in my stomach. I had forgotten to ask Kambis what to say; I knew that '*Valasrat*' was the Persian for Your Majesty but I didn't know whether I should speak in English or Farsi. I can't remember having such a case of nerves before or since. The aura that I noted the first time I had seen the Shahanshah Aryamehr was once again with him.

I stopped before him. Placed my whip, held in my right hand, to my forehead perpendicular to the ground and bowed my head in the way that it was customary for women to salute the jury in a competition. I then looked him in the eye and said in Farsi, 'I am honored, *Valasrat*, to give you a demonstration of jumping. I am riding Roshan, which is a Turkoman stallion, just in his first year of jumping.'

His Majesty said something I didn't hear properly but later Kambis told me that he said, 'Your husband is with the Aluminum project?' It was a rhetorical question but he must have thought me quite stupid not to have made some reply. I did hear him say 'You may commence.' and this I did.

I did love that little stallion with his feisty personality but that day I loved him most, for despite my terrible nerves he jumped each fence in perfect style allowing me to show my best form; I can say without boasting that it was a very beautiful performance. I again saluted to His Majesty, patted my horse, then dismounted and gave him to one of the grooms who was to take him to the stable.

I signaled for Davoud Bahrami to come in with Mojgan. He saluted the Shah and then jumped the same course that I had jumped. Davoud and the mare performed very well. Kambis was next to the Shah as was his father; they would no doubt, be explaining about each horse and rider.

We had raised the fences for the German horses so they would jump the oxer that was now 1.30M, the wall was 1.40M and the triple bar was at 1.45M.

As Ali Rezai came into the ring I could tell there was going to be trouble; he had that look on his face that meant he would blow the deal. He jumped the oxer well but brought his horse far too short on the turn leading into the wall and of course the horse stopped. I could see it three strides out and Ali did nothing but throw the reins away and I guess, say a prayer to Allah!

I was furious! *'Ali Rezai! Hamishe vakhte que kare bokonid eshtebah mikonid! Chera? Makhsh naderid! Fekremikonid! Asb vasate daste paetun bayad bashe!'* (What are you doing? Every time you do that the horse stops. The horse can't jump from there! THINK!)

Ali made his approach and jumped the fence well although for me again a little too far away. The triple bar he cleared in fine form. Both Ezat and Davoud jumped around without any mistakes.

I had the triple bar put up to 1.50M and the wall to 1.45M and this time all three jumped well. I then put the triple up to the top 1.55M and had them each jump the oxer and the triple bar. I was very pleased that all three cleared the high triple bar with room to spare. As I knew he would, His Majesty called down to Mashmahmad, 'How high is that jump?'

Mashedmahmad took out the stick and measured; there was a hesitation and finally he called back, 'It is just a fraction over one meter...... fifty five, *Valasrat.*' He could not lie to his King!

His Majesty seemed impressed enough, called a thank you and rushed off to his awaiting helicopter.

When Kambis came back to the stable having seen the Shah off, he was effervescent. 'Gail, that was wonderful! His Majesty was very impressed. And you know he especially liked the way you gave the instruction in Farsi. He said he thought it was so cute! You know it does impress him when a foreigner tries to learn our language and the fact that you were not afraid of making mistakes in front of him pleased him very much! You job is very secure now.'

Kambis invited me across to his house which was only a couple of hundred yards from the stables. It was a beautiful large country house styled after the English country homes of the mid-1800s. Avid, Kambis's wife, had just completed the redecoration of the house the previous spring. The servant was there to take off our boots as we entered the huge wine colored entrance hall. The beautiful marble floors were partially covered with exquisite antique Persian runners and carpets. Avid had had a tray of drinks and tea set up in front of the large regency sofa in this hall. Here we sat to have our refreshment and relate to Avid the events of the afternoon. It was such a relaxed atmosphere I was able to express my feelings of nervousness and laugh about it with these two friends. All too soon, I felt I should leave to go home to my family who would also be waiting to hear how I had fared in my first official meeting with the Shah.

Khosrodd, Kambis, Author, Majzoob winning Prince's Team Cup

THE FALL SEASON

The season of autumn horse shows was one without a moments rest. I had the early morning training sessions, my midday work at the office and many times, special command performances at the stable in the afternoon. An ambassador from Italy had his granddaughter visiting and she wanted to see the stables of His Imperial Majesty. Could Mrs. Rose possibly be there to take the guided tour? A minister or guest of a minister would be riding at the stable in the afternoon. Could Mrs. Rose please be there to see that all went well? No, she did not have to give any tour, just be in the background supervising. General Khosrodad could not attend the morning training session this week (as usual) could Mrs. Rose please meet him at the stable at four instead? (I was lucky if he arrived by 6 and often he did not make it at all.) And so forth went the supposedly infrequent days that I would be expected to spend time at the stable in the afternoon. Of course my contract did say: 'You will work whatever hours may be necessary to discharge your duties in accordance with the operational requirements of the directions given by the Royal Horse Society, The Iranian Equestrian Federation and the Imperial Stables and will abide by all applicable rules, regulations and other practices . . . . '

The show days, even though most fulfilling in the fact that the results of my training sessions would be evident, were the most trying. The previous day I would have the list of horses and riders typed up and placed on the bulletin board; alongside of the name of each horse was the groom's name who would be in charge of actually getting the animal to the practice ring. The *djelodar* responsible for each horse did have to double check that the horse actually left the stable with its *metard* (groom) at the correct time, but even so, we had more slip-ups than I would like to remember and the majority of them were with General Khosrodad's mounts.

I think that actually everyone in the stable was terrified of this handsome man. Whether it was his reputation of being a strong general, the knowledge that he was a close friend of the Shah, or the fact that he so closely resembled the Shah in appearance, I couldn't decide, but all were truly petrified of the man. And of course, true to the Persian way, when it is really important and the heat is on, the goof-up happens. I think that I had more tongue lashings from the General during my time at the Imperial Stables than I ever had from my boss, Kambis. How many times did I hear, 'Messes Rose? Where is Upa Negrino?' (which he had bought from Feridoun Elghanian), 'There are just ten more horses to go before me and I cannot find my horse. No one in the stable takes care of me. You make certain that Kambis's horse is always ready but you don't care about me! Those dumb boys in that stable, they don't know who I am! I should have them reported!'

'*Timsah*, just hold on for a minute. I will take care of things. I'm sure the horse is here.'

I would rush to the nearest *djelodar* ranting and raving about the General's horse and nine times out of ten I would see some poor harried looking *metard* dragging Upi or whichever horse he would be riding up the road from the stable. I would approach and admonish but what could I say when I always got the same reply, 'But Khonum, no one told me I was to take Upi today. Just now, Reza said he saw my name on the list so I brought the horse as fast as I could.'

'But! But! But! Hashem you know your name was on the list. You need to read the list. Before each show! Read it the day before!'

'Khonume, *sabot naderam*. (I cannot read.)'

The worst mix up was the day we were at Nowruzabad for a horse show; the horses had all arrived safely, or so it was reported to me after the trucks got there. Robin was at the loading end at the stables and I was at the show on the receiving end. The General came running up to me screaming, 'Khonume Rose! Where is my horse? I can't find him; all the horses have been unloaded and Golitussi is not there'.

'I'm sure he is here Timsah, Sefola reported to me that all had arrived safely.'

'Well not my horse!'

I walked over to the stabling area and found Sefola. 'Where is Golitussi?' I inquired.

'Let me see Khonume.' After a moment he came back, 'He is not here; maybe he jumped out of the truck. His groom is sure he was loaded but he was not here when we off loaded.'

'This is impossible, Sefola! We have never had a horse jump out.'

'Well actually we did have it happen one time when we were taking the horses to Kish Island; it wasn't injured, though.'

About that time Narcy Firouz came over to us from his house, 'Gail, I just had a call from Dr. Cutler, apparently they left one of the horses at Farahabad so he wants you to send a truck back to get it. He said it was an important horse.'

'Only General Khosrodad's!..... Sefola you go back with the truck to get him and be as prompt as you can.'

And then, I had to school each rider with each horse in the practice ring. If I was not there to school them they would not school. Oh, no! They would not take the responsibility of warming up the horse themselves. I always tried to give them some jumps, a few horses before their turn and then I would give them last minute instructions as they waited at the gate before going into the ring. I was running back and forth between the rounds of the various riders, all of whom I wanted to see in the ring.

I usually had one horse in each class myself. Not that I really had the time or the energy; I was expected to ride, and show that I could not only train horses and teach riders but, I could compete too.

I remember that in one show I did not compete; I had been exhausted the week before and I decided that I would try train only and not worry about getting myself psychologically up for competition as well. The horse world was up in arms. Why was Mrs. Rose not riding? Had she turned chicken? What was the matter? The next day at the stable all the boys came up to me and told me in strict confidence that they felt that I should ride in each show because it was very bad for my image to stand on the sidelines. Kambis also told me that he felt it was a good idea for me to ride so from then onward I would see that I had a competitive horse to show.

Soon the end of the season was upon us and ahead were the Aryamehr Cup or King's Cup and the Championship. I really wanted to win both of these events with horses from His Majesty's stable.

The first event was the Aryamehr Cup. This event was the one that meant the most to the Iranian riders because it was the one competition to which His Majesty actually came. The Shahanshah, was truly a horse lover, and supported the sport of show jumping by having his stable of horses compete in all the National competitions; he also had given permission to have his Imperial Stables facilities available for all or any show jumping competition. Since this facility was the best in the country the majority of the competitions were held there.

Slowly other venues were being developed, such as the Royal Horse Society Nowruzabad Riding Club which had a beautiful big sand ring with stands on all sides; also General Nader Djahanbani, one of the country's great enthusiasts who had bought Chatfield Hills, that great horse of Iris Kellet's that was ridden by Eddie Macken for Ireland, had a beautiful spot near Karaj. He was the great grandson of Faith Ali Shah, thus a prince of the last dynasty, as well his brother was married to Princess Shahnaz the Shah's eldest daughter so he was well connected! He had the one and only grass show jumping ménage in the country and usually hosted two shows a year. His shows were always spectacular. The place was decorated with flowers and greenery making it look like a European venue. He had his own Royal Box where he seated any royals he could persuade to accept his invitation to the fancy show and delicious luncheon he always served; there was champagne and caviar served as a mid-show snack. Most of the Iranian competitors fussed about the slipperiness of the grass and what they were going to do about the shoeing of the horses for the competition. But everyone who was invited to show always accepted one of the biggest social events of the season.

The Aryamehr Cup was to be a Team event for B class horses to be run under modified Nations Cup rules. Each year the regulations changed but that was it for the year 1352. I wanted to have a winning team, no matter what! I did have a great team that I felt could not fail to win with Kambis Atabai on Rokhsar, Ezat Vodjdani on Shabrang, Ali Rezai on Shahab and Hossein Karimi Majzoob on Shabahang. The only problem with that was the fact that it left General Khosrodad out and he must ride in the event.

He was a favorite of the Shah.

The story goes that in 1963 when there was so much religious trouble in Iran the then Major Manuchehr Khosrodad made his name. Three young Iranian girls without chadors had been walking down one of the main streets of Tehran in miniskirts. The Mullahs and religious fanatics were at the time trying to enforce the chador and repress the women who had been liberated by the Shah and given equal rights the previous year. These three girls were attacked and finally stoned to death by a group of fanatics. This precipitated a state of anarchism in the city of Tehran. Described by friends who lived through it, the period was when no one was safe on the streets; most people huddled in their houses afraid to stand up for fear of stray bullets. A group of Mullahs including Ayatollah Khomeni staged a demonstration against the government and the Shahanshah at Sepah Square, the main city square. During this demonstration they preached the anti-regime doctrines. This was too much for the dictator, no matter how benevolent, to stand so he sent the military in. The handsome Major Khosrodad, whose looks so resembled His Majesty, led the armored attack upon the demonstrators at Sepah Square. When the tanks and artillery left there were many dead! However it was the end of the anti-régime doctrine for the time. The Ayatollah was arrested along with twenty eight other ayatollahs and sent into exile, eventually settling in the Shiite community of Najaf in Southern Iraq. The Major was promoted and had remained a favorite. He was always fair and a great sportsman. They say he was one of the few Iranian generals who would not accept Bakhshish. (Bribery)

I had to find another team on which to put the General. He and his horse Golitossi were certainly not the class that would make a winning team. I did have Reza Hadavand on Cobalt who would do creditably well and Reza Tarash could ride his little Moroccan Barb Shehey that would make three members for the second team. About two mornings before I was to present my team lists to Kambis I had a telephone call from Freddy Elghanian.

'Gaily, how are you? What are you doing?'

'Well, actually, Freddy, I am trying to get my team entries together for the Aryamehr Cup. I have some political problems that I am not sure how to settle. You of course know, that the General will want to be on the number one team but I have to win the Cup so I want to put him on a second team. I think it's going to cause some problems.'

'I was calling you about that. I was wondering if you would want to ride Upa Negrino in the competition. I know you don't have a horse for the B and A divisions and Upi doesn't have a rider. Do you think Kambis would let you ride an outside horse on the Imperial Stables team?'

'I am sure, Fred, that if it is Upi there will be no problem. How can the *Timsah* (General) complain about riding on the team with me? Thank you so much. I will tentatively accept your offer and check later with Kambis. I'm sure there will be no problem but I'll call you back later.'

Kambis agreed it was a great idea and wasn't it kind of Freddy to let us have his horse. But I had to handle the General.

'He is my friend, you know Gail, but if I tell him that he's not on the same team with me he will get very angry. You'll have to think of a way to make him happy. If he is angry and starts complaining to the right people there will be trouble in this place and I don't want to, how do you say, roll the boat.'

I sent in my official entries and when the general came down for his training the following afternoon I informed him of the Imperial Stables teams.

'You see, General, Kambis has to captain one of the teams and I feel that you should be the captain of the other. If you were on the same team as Kambis you wouldn't be the captain and I would have to captain the other team; now I feel that it would look badly to have me a foreigner, the captain of His Majesty's jumping team so I put you in as captain of the team upon which I will ride Upa Negrino and we will have the two Rezas with us. I think that it's a good team and we have as good a chance as the other team if we have a little luck.'

'Yes, Mrs. Rose. That ees a very good idea. I would not have thought of that but you are right. We should have a good chance. How did you get Elghanian to lend you that good horse? You know I always loved that Upa Negrino; I would love to ride him sometime.'

'To tell you the truth *Timsah*, Freddy just called up and offered me the horse for the competition. You know that he can't seem to get along with him and I think he would like to sell him. I don't know about the price but you might check into it. I think he is a super horse.'

139

So the day of the competition arrived. The pomp and glory was as it had been the first year. This year, though, I was more a part of it. We had two carriages; one pulled by the team of greys in which His Majesty and the Shabanu rode and the other had a team of black Hungarian mares in which rode the royal children and their nanny. At the head of the procession rode Abulfath Atabai. He rode a really beautiful grey Turkoman stallion which was at the time one of the favorite mounts of the Shah. I had ridden the horse and really didn't like him; he had a mouth of steel and was totally insensitive to any aids. Well, that day was his undoing, for as the crowd began to cheer for the Royal entourage Shetab took off at a gallop. I was amazed to see that the old man was able to stay on! He somehow slowed his mount down when he came level with the Royal Box and there he jumped off and let the horse go! As the Royal carriage carrying His Majesty and the Queen drew up, Shetab decided to mount one of the carriage horses. Their Majesties either did not notice or were very cool because neither flinched as they descended to the red carpet. One of the outriders was able to catch the horse without too much trouble, but poor old Shetab mysteriously disappeared from the stable about two weeks later.

Their Majesties were seated and the show commenced. At the end of the first round General Khosrodad's team did not have much of a chance. Reza Tarash had been eliminated at the combination which meant that he went into the second round with 20 faults added to the faults of the worst rider of the first round, for his score. Reza Hadavand had twelve faults, I had seven and the General himself had twelve.

Kambis' team however, had a total of eight faults for the round. All the horses had done very well on the demanding course but the Dashte Behesht team also had only eight faults. This surprised me and meant that the second round was vital to our winning. Kambis went in to have a refusal at the last fence after knocking one other fence for a total of 7. Ezat went clean. Then Hossein Karimi Majzoob astounded me by being eliminated at the last fence which was an oxer over the bridge. The Dashte Behesht team had only one knockdown so far in the round which meant that they were three faults better off. Their last horse had four faults which meant that we were one fault ahead. Ali Rezai had to go clean or we would not be the winners. As only three of the four scores counted we could drop Majzoob's. Ali's going clean would mean a win for the Imperial Stables. He was in the position he loved so much. Anchor man in front of his ruler.

It amazed me that he came through with a superb clear round on Shahab. The Imperial Stables A team won the Aryamehr Cup. The Dashte Behest team was second which they well deserved and General Khosrodad's team was nowhere!

Immediately following the presentation the Imperial Family exited from the back door of the Royal Box to drive in their limousines the short couple of hundred yards to the helipad. The Aryamehr Cup of the year 1352 was successfully completed.

His Majesty was so impressed with his horses and riders that he decided that the members of the Imperial Stables Team should have special team riding jackets. In due course the jackets were designed and made by one of Tehran's most fashionable couturier. They were beige with bright colored Baluchi embroidery trim on the collar and sleeves. Very handsome in the Iranian way.

The first year of the Iranian National Championship was held on a Friday, Tuesday and Friday. The Tuesday it happened to be Aid de Gorbon which was a 'Happy Day' and thus a holiday available for a horse show. There are many holidays in the Persian calendar but the majority of them are mourning days and not able to be used for having competitions. The Iranians took their Muslim religion very seriously and expected that all people would have the decency to keep a quiet front on the mourning days.

The first competition was a Speed Class to be scored under Table C.

In my mind it was a foregone conclusion that Ali Rezai would win the class with Shahab, so when we drew for positions in The Royal Horse Society office and he drew last in the order I was even more confident.

Ezat went about midway down and had a spectacular round with Shabrang. It was a round that would be very hard to beat.

Finally it was time for the last horse. Ali had watched about half the class go before he had warmed up his horse. I could see in his eyes that he was totally confident that he would win the class hands down. Just before his turn I went up to him to check that he knew the course; one of his failings was going off course. He knew it. I warned him of a few of the more difficult questions again. As he was called up to the gate I warned him, *'Mobazeh bashid, eshtabah nemikonid, Fekr mikonid!* (Be careful, don't make a mistake and Think) *Bon chance*, Ali.' The French word is used for good luck for there is no such word in the Persian language.

I stood tensely watching Ali enter the ring. I was sure he was going to blow it. I could always tell with Ali. He was such a talented man on a horse and yet he had that temperament that was so unpredictable. His round was superb; he cut the corners in each place I had suggested; he seemed to be thinking clearly about every move. Shahab had a spectacular style. He seemed to explode over every fence. I watched carefully as Ali made the last turn to take the vertical poles and then a long straight gallop to the last fence which was a large square oxer. Incredulously, I saw him ride right past the second last fence and jump the oxer. As he crossed the finish line he threw his hands in the air confident that he had won the class.

I think I have never seen such a crestfallen face as that one when the bell to eliminate him rang. He still did not realize that he had missed the fence!

As he came out of the ring I could not hold my anger but then I saw the tears in his eyes. I could only walk away, for to me this was a terrible thing to see a man cry. I was not the only one stunned. All who had seen the mistake were shocked and of course during the next few days before the second competition Ali was confronted many times about his drastic mistake. The outcome of the class was that General Djanahbani won putting Ezat in second place. Kambis was 5th and General Khosrodad and Majzoob nowhere.

In the second round Ezat again went clear, Kambis had one fence down on Rostam and Majzoob had a couple of fences down. It was up to Ali whether or not he would at least win this one event even though there was no way he would be able to win the Championship. He went in and rode a spectacular round to the last fence. There he asked Shahab to leave the ground way too long so he rolled the far pole on the oxer with his hind feet.

It was Ezat on top. Unless General Djahanbani won the final event and Ezat was last there was no way anyone could beat my boy. I had no intention of telling this to Ezat though. He would probably not realize that he really could not beaten easily. Djahanbani did have the one win and even though he was placed about 9th in the second event I would let Ezat think he could be a threat. Keep the boy sharp!

Thursday, the day Ali Reza Soudovar and I had set aside to put up our joint course for the final event was rainy and miserable, which was in Tehran at that time of year was unusual. It would be a difficult course.

We had a hard time getting the eighteen fences in our main ménage even though it was large. When we had finished it looked good even if crowded. The drizzle started again so Ali left as soon as we were finished. We had been plied with those miniature cups of tea they served in Iran all during our course building, but even the effect of that was wearing off. I gave Ezat and Davoud Majzoob a final pep talk and was about to leave when Kambis arrived. We had to walk the course so that he would have it in his head for the next day.

'Now tell me, Gail, what chance do I have if I win tomorrow? I know not much of a one. Actually, what is the point of going in tomorrow if I don't have a chance to win?'

143

'First of all, you couldn't win even if you did win the competition to-morrow. But you have a chance of taking second place and that's not bad however, you must enter because I feel it shows very poor sportsmanship if you decide not to enter just because you don't think you can win. If everyone did that there wouldn't be many entrants.'

'Well, Gail, the one thing I will say is that at least we are having a Championship. It is the first time in Iran. We have had the best season, per-haps the first true season of show jumping in Iran, and you were a part of it; perhaps I could say that you made it. If you hadn't come along when you did we might still be having our four shows a year. I am not one to give praise often as you know but I do want to congratulate you on a job well done so far.'

'You embarrass me, Kambis. What can I say but thanks? You know I only do it because I love horses and enjoy working with you and all the others. I hope we can continue to do as much as we have this year. And again thanks.'

I took my leave and rushed home to a hot bath. The only problem was that we were out of butane gas for our instant water heater and there was no hot water. Azizeh in her usual defensive way said that she had ordered the gas the previous day and that it should have arrived. I did my usual rant and rave during which the gas men did arrive. Saved, I could warm up!

Mr. Alam, the Court Minister, was the official guest at the Champi-onship Final. Due to the extreme cold he sat in the heated royal box. This was very unusual, for the pavilion is kept only for the Royal Family.

'Ezat, make it a clear one to win.' It would look much nicer for him to win it that way.

'*Sahee mikonam, Khonum.*(I'll try)'

Ezat rode a beautiful round clear that was very professional looking. I am sure that it impressed Mr. Alam who was a great horse enthusiast and

144

patron of our sport. The whole Vodjdani family came rushing up to me and engulfed me with kisses and thanks for Ezat's win. When I finally extracted myself I said, 'But it wasn't me, it was Ezat. He did it. I just gave him his lessons. When it came to winning I had nothing to do with it. He did it all by himself!'

Mashmahmad, Ezat's father, spoke. 'No, Khonume, if you had not been here this would not have happened. It is our luck that you came and made our son famous.'

I stood with the family watching the presentation. It was an emotional moment being with these good people and sharing their utter joy and pride. It was all I could do to keep away the tears that were welling up in my eyes. Ezat would be on the front page of all the newspapers. He would be a hero for a day in Iran.

In the final standing Kambis was second which really pleased me.

The front page of the Kayhan International Newspaper had the following headline:

VODJDANI HORSEMAN OF THE YEAR

By JAMES UNDERWOOD·:

It was only a time fault which beat them. Nader Djahanbani really had the hard jumping Vercingetorix under firm control in the second round to wind up with only three faults and hold on to eighth place in the national standings. Arsia Ardalan took seventh place on Darmis.

A Twenty-two year old Ezat Vojdani: won the last stage of the national show jumping championship on his little black partner Shabrang at Farahabad yesterday and clinched the title of Iran's Horseman of the Year. The pair had clear second round to clinch the title. Babak Shaki got the unseating he deserved when he quite unexpectedly gave Eyvollah, who was going beautifully, a sharp cut with the whip but they fully meritted their fifth place finish in the second round and for the day. Kambiz Atabai held on to his second stage place to clinch the runner-up title on Rostam. Unluckiest rider of the afternoon was Hushang. Teymouri on Ramsar, who was eliminated after a good first round for failing to pass the finish line and then followed up with a clear round in the second part of the competition. Hosein Karimi-Majzoob and Shabahang just pipped Javad Varzidekar on Pasha for third, which gave The Imperial Stables the first three leading places. This was hard luck for Varzidekar and the little Turkoman who had put up a fine show.

A second article in the paper read:

FROM STABLE BOY TO TOP OF THE TREE:

It was the story of the stable boy who beat the best in the land when Ezat Vojdani won the title of champion rider of Iran at Farahabad yesterday.

The son of a stableman at The Imperial Stables he has followed his father in the same job. And the horse he rode to gain the honors belongs to the Shahanshah himself.

Ironically it was the man who gave him his big chance who he beat to land the title, Imperial Stables boss, Kambis Atabai, who was a clear second at the end of the competition yesterday—and at its opening looked the only one with a chance to beat Vojdani—picked out the stable lad with the riding talent a few years ago and since has given him every opportunity to improve himself.

Fate nearly robbed Vojdani of his big chance. Shortly before the start of the contest, ten days ago he chipped a bone in his knee when he had a fall. Only at the last minute was the doctor persuaded to postpone the operation until next week so that he could ride.

As he received his trophy from Court Minister Assodollah Alam at the end of the afternoon, with Atabai standing next in line it wasn't' difficult to imagine how for this young Iranian, who gets married to a girl from another of the Farahabad families very soon, this was a dream come true

After Kambis had seen Mr. Alam off in his limousine he came back to the group of people that were left standing around having tea. He made a

146

formal little speech thanking me for all I had done and the event was over. The post show party would be down at Dr. Cutlers. That was where we always seemed to congregate after the shows. It would surely be a gay party that would last until the wee small hours or until we all decided to move on elsewhere to have dinner. Don was already down there acting as bar tender while the doctor and I checked out the horses after the jumping.

For me it had really been a great day. My riders had made me proud; Ezat had won and Kambis and Davoud had been second and third. In four days I was off to Brussels, Belgium, with Kambis to represent Iran at the FEI meeting. I had something good to look forward to. A perfect day.

The Shah and his children at the stable

Col. Khalvati presenting Davoud Bahrami with Poulad Mansarpour

Presentation of Prince's Cup L to R Khanlahani, Abulfath Atabai, Crown Prince (head and back), Gen Khosrodad and others

New coats: Manuchehr and Kambis

Ezat and Shabrang

MY TRIP

We were due to leave on Wednesday morning early so I tidied up all the loose ends at the stable on Sunday and Monday making certain that all and sundry had plenty to do while I was gone. At the end of the show season it was bit of a letdown for the riders who had been participating for ten weeks; they needed something to take the place of the constant psychological up and down they had before and after each show. It was the time of year that I liked them to get to work again on the three year olds they had broken during the spring and we had let off work to rest and grow during the summer and fall. As well, each rider was allotted a two year old, rising three that would be broken come March, so work was begun with these babies, teaching them to lead properly and commencing the elementary work. The jumping horses would all be laid off until the middle of February but there were plenty of young horses that needed attention.

Tuesday was the day I set aside for my office and making sure my passport and visa were ready for me to take. I first collected my FEI Agenda that I would read over on the flight to Brussels. I then picked up the fifty copies of the CSIA Prize List that I would take to distribute to member nations that might be interested coming to Iran. As it was Asian Games year the Equestrian Federation had proposed to the Joint Sports Federation that Iran hold a Friendly Jumping Competition at the same time as the Games. This was approved and Ali Reza Soudovar and I had worked for weeks

150

preparing the program for the event. I was shocked to find that it had been printed up, beautifully on Sports Federation official paper, and signed by General Hojat, the head of the Iranian Sports Federation. Everything seemed to be in order. Certainly a first. I had expected to have to rush around for hours getting everything finished.

When I went into Mr. Mehran, the man who takes care of all exit visas of Imperial Court employees, I found my passport ready and waiting; exit visa all entered and stamped. Mr. Mehran all smiles, 'You see, Meeses Rose, I your friend, everything is ready so you go to big meeting with Mr. Atabai.'

There were many times that things were not ready to go when it came to this little man's department. I had seen him admonished many times by Kambis. No wonder he was smiling. No tongue lashing today!

I had no plane ticket, no idea of when we were to leave or on what airline, so I had to stop in at Kambis's office. As usual it was swarming with people. His secretary was telling them all that he could not see anyone else because he had to go to the palace but would see them the following week. She was making appointments in her book that I knew would never be kept by him. These poor people would come back on the appointed day at the appointed hour and find that Kambis was at the palace or he had not come in or he was out of the country, but that was the way of the Iranian business world.

'You may go in, Mrs. Rose, Kambis is waiting for you.' As I opened the door I saw that as usual he had one telephone up to his ear and was holding the other. He was giving someone a hard time, 'Do you know to whom you are speaking? . . . Yes that is my name but I am the Secretary General of His Majesty's Imperial Court do you realize to whom you are refusing to give two first class seats? ... I have had these reservations for one month and now the day before I am due to leave you say that you do not have room in first class because of the foreign stars who have been here visiting for the International Film Festival. I will have your job! I am immediately going to call the General. He is a very close friend of mine.' He slammed the phone down.

'Good morning, Gail. You don't know what a mess things are in this country. Just by chance I had my secretary call Iran Air to check our reservations and they informed her that we were on the plane but we would have to sit in Tourist section because they had filled up first class with all these stupid film stars who are returning to Europe after the Festival. We've had these reservations for a month. I told Mrs. Nazami to call another airline to get us first class to Brussels. I wanted that Iran Air flight direct to Paris; it's the only non-stop out of Tehran but I am not going to sit in Tourist even if they say they will give us first class treatment. I like the wider seats and the quiet of first class . . . Just a minute.' The phone was ringing again. He had a short conversation at the end of which his secretary came in.

'I got you on Lufthansa to Frankfort with an hour layover until you catch the Sabena flight to Brussels where you will arrive about three in the afternoon. It is the best I can do.'

'That sounds fine. I refuse to fly Iran Air! That airline is such a mess!' The phone was ringing again. Mrs. Nazami reached over to pick it up.

After a few moments she covered the mouthpiece and said, 'It is Iran Air. They have your first class seats and they are very embarrassed about the trouble. What shall I tell them?'

'Tell them I refuse to fly with them. They have probably just put someone else out of the seats because they found out I was so important. I am going to smarten them up!'

She did so.

'Now get me the general on the phone. I want to tell him about this airline that he is supposed to be running.'

In a few seconds the general was on the phone and Kambis was blasting him like I have never heard him blast anyone before. Obviously there was no love lost between the two of them.

152

'This will not be the end of this affair, *Timsah*, you can be sure of that. I will not let this rest. It is people like you who are so incompetent, running our government businesses, that give this country such a bad name. If you are the Chief Executive of the airline, the running of it is your direct responsibility; if you cannot run it you should not be there!' He slammed down the telephone.

'You know Gail, there are so many people like that stupid general who have very important jobs in this country and they can't think of anything but their own importance. They run a very poor show and then the whole country gets the reputation of being disorganized and running a bad show. It just makes me sick. I'm not going to let this thing rest. If those people had given us back our first class seats they would have put some foreigner back into tourist. How would that look to a celebrity who has been here to promote films? It makes me sick. Anyway let's not talk about it. Have we any unfinished business to take care of?'

I gave him his copy of the FEI agenda and told him he should read it over before we get to Brussels.

'Why don't you read it tonight and then you can brief me on the plane tomorrow?' Great idea! Just what I wanted to do. Spend my last night at home reading that tomb!

'OK, I'll see what I can do. Now what time do we leave? Where should I meet you? Seeing as our reservations have just been changed I presume there is no ticket yet.'

He got the information on the intercom from his secretary. 'The plane leaves at seven-thirty so I will meet you at the Lufthansa check-in counter about a quarter to seven. Pulad will be there too because he has to bring some papers down for me.' So it was 'til tomorrow.

I arrived at the airport at exactly six forty-five. I had Don's driver take me down. When I looked at the check-in area I could not believe my eyes. It was wall to wall people. There were only three or four counters in that old airport, the one that eventually caved in in December of 1974 killing many people. Each counter had an unbelievable line. I searched for the Lufthansa line and had the porter put my bags down at the end of it. I could find neither Kambis nor Pulad. I stood at the end of the line not moving an inch for fifteen minutes before I began to get panicky. Pulad finally turned up at five after seven.

'Good morning, Gail. Have you seen Kambis?'

'No I haven't and I'm getting a little worried.'

'Oh, don't worry. He's always late coming to the airport. The plane won't leave without you. We have the Court VIP people tuned in.'

We waited and waited. I could see when it got to be twenty after seven that Pulad too was beginning to fidget. At seven twenty-five I saw Jafar, Kambis's driver, running up the steps of the airport with two bags in his hands. Following leisurely, unconcerned was Kambis. Jafar pushed his way up to the counter, said something, left the bags and then came over to us.

'Good morning, Mrs. Rose. Sorry to be late. I hope you weren't worried.' It was Kambis.

'Oh . . . uh . . . no, not at all. I was sure you would turn up at some point. It was just when Pulad began to get antsy that I thought we might miss our flight.'

'I always arrive as late as I can. I hate crowds and I don't like to wait in line. I am sorry, I'll have to leave you now. I guess you call it segregation; I go through a special door you know, diplomatic passport and all. Jafar will take you through the other way. Just leave your bags here and they will be taken care of. I'll see you in a minute.'

I saw Jafar signal to someone about my bags and then he lead me up to the front of the line where hundreds of people were waiting to get through immigration. We went straight through without ado and on the other side of the door was Kambis waiting. We were ushered with VIP treatment out to the plane. No sooner than our seat belts were fastened, the door was closed and we were off.

'I really hate this airport. They have so many flights leaving in the morning between seven and nine that the place is a madhouse. That's why I come late and use my pull.'

'I'll have to admit to you, Kambis, I really thought that we wouldn't make it.' I said hesitantly.

'You should have more faith in me by now, Gail.'

The flight to Frankfurt was broken up by a stop at Ankara for about half an hour. We were not allowed off the plane but we did go out the door and stand at the top of the stairway to observe the desolate field where our plane was parked. It was cloudy and drizzling which made it more depressing. We were able to discuss the upcoming meeting, in which Kambis was not terribly interested but he listened and asked questions while I was briefing him. I was the one who would need to pay attention and know the answers if need be.

As well, we discussed my trip to Ireland. It had been suggested by Ali Reza Soudovar that I go on to Ireland after the meeting and try to buy some Irish horses for the Imperial Stables. Kambis was all for the idea but he said he was in a bad way budget wise, so it would have to be young, inexpensive animals that I would have to train. It would be a long process but it would be fun to pick my own and see what I could do. Kambis had a few names of contacts to add to the list I had already compiled with the help of Ali Reza. We agreed that I would have twenty thousand pounds to spend and should try to get four or five young animals for that price. It was going to be a difficult task. The money had already been wired to the Bank of Ireland in my name and all I had to do was pick it up in Dublin. It all sounded so easy.

When we arrived in Brussels, collected our bags that had miraculously arrived safely and found our way to the taxi stand, Kambis expected me to arrange for a taxi to take us to the Palace Hotel. After I had muddled through in my very rusty French and we were safely seated in the back of the speeding car he said, 'Your French is not much better than mine. I thought for a Canadian you would be able to speak fluently. '

'I didn't give that as one of my qualifications, did I?'

'Somewhere in my memory I recall that you won some French prize.'

'That was in high school and I know I didn't tell you that.'

'I think it was on one of the reports about you that I read when they were doing your security check.'

'They certainly are thorough! I have never mentioned it that to anyone in Iran that I know. I'm the first to admit that my French is atrocious. I haven't kept it up and I was never bilingual. We'll just have to muddle along together as best we can.'

We arrived at the hotel, checked in and were ushered to our rooms. We agreed to tidy up, get settled and meet each other in the hall in half an hour. I got the dresses I expected to wear in Brussels out of my bag and hung them, tidied myself and was all set to have a look at Brussels. When I opened my door in that ancient old hotel I saw that Kambis's too was open. I knocked tentatively and he called for me to come in. He was meticulously hanging up his beautiful French suits and laying out ties, Yves St. Laurent, Gucci, and Dior.

It would make a great story if I said that the beginning of our affair started then! It would make for juicy reading and I'm sure I would sell many more books if I could put a little sex in it but unfortunately I must be honest, there was no affair; Kambis and I had a good business association and we were friends. He was the boss and I respected him as such but we were good friends and I hope always will be even though we have had our ups and downs.

'Come on, Kambis, let's go and have a look at Brussels. I've never been here and I know you haven't been either. I'm sure you are not the sightseeing type but you have a Canadian lady with you who likes to have a look around when she goes anywhere.'

'I'm all ready. I would like to get out and have some fresh air anyway. I always get restless when I have spent the day in an airplane. Do you see my key? Where did I put it? Oh, here it is! Let's go.'

In the lobby we turned our keys into reception and were walking away when who should come walking towards us but my father. I was shocked. I knew that Dad had come to the FEI meeting a few times but I didn't think he would be here this year; he had been at the meeting the previous year.

'Hey, Dad! How are you?' I threw my arms around him. I hadn't seen him since the previous summer and we didn't correspond on a regular basis since he and my mother had divorced a year and a half previously. Next to him was a good looking blond woman in a beautiful mink coat. I wished I had brought mine along!

'Do you know Sheila?' was his introduction. I actually had met her in Canada years before.

'Yes, hello, Sheila. May I present my boss Kambis Atabai. This is my father Denny Whitaker and Sheila.' I could not say his wife. Poor Sheila, it was not much of an introduction.

'What are you two doing now?' my father asked.

'We thought we would go out for a walk to see what there is to see around here. Won't you join us, sir?' It was Kambis being his most charming.

'Well sure, if you don't mind. Do you want to go for a walk, Sheila?' She did so we all went out.

In the evening was the cocktail party given by Prince Philip, Duke of Edenborough, and President of the FEI. I could hardly wait! Since I had been a young girl I had had a great crush on Prince Philip; I found him and still do one of the most exciting men in the world. To me he is handsome, witty, and intelligent, and above all, a man that seems to accomplish things well, and he is a wonderful husband to the queen. When he had come to the Royal Winter Fair in Toronto, I had been standing with a group of my

young friends in the Tanbark Club having a drink after the evening performance when my father had brought him up to meet the entourage of
pretty young maidens with whom I was chatting. I was so overwhelmed
that I could not speak! Actually I thought that I was going to faint when I
was presented. I had read everything printed about this man to date and
held him in the highest esteem. I felt as though I was being presented to
God. I could not get enough control of myself to do more than smile va-
pidly and gurgle a bit in the back of my throat. I am sure that he felt I was
perhaps a poor young retard!

My father had met the Prince on numerous occasions so that they were
on more or less first name basis; I would naturally meet the Prince as a
member of the Iranian delegation and as the only female representative of
any nation. The only other woman at the conference was the female interpreter for the Russians but she was not an official delegate. I guess it was
quite an honor to have the distinction of being the only member of my sex
to be an official part of this International meeting.

As Sheila was not a part of the official delegation she was not invited
to the cocktail party so my father, Mr. George Jacobson, the other Canadian
delegate, Kambis and I all arrived together. We went directly up to the
Prince and my father made the introductions.

'Has the cat got your tongue tonight?' He laughed.

'No Your Majesty, he gave it back to me a few years ago!' was my
reply.

He was charming. He made mention of the fact that it was strange that
a father and daughter combination would represent two different nations.
When he had been in Iran with Princess Anne for the 2500th Anniversary
of Iran he had been presented with a pair of Caspian Horses and Princess
Anne had been given an Anglo Arab Pahlavan that had been raised in the
Imperial Stables, so Kambis was interested to hear news of how these an-

imals had made out. It seemed that the Pahlavan was a good hack and the Caspians had been sent to the only Caspian horse stud in England where a breeding herd was being built up.

I was able to open my mouth and utter a few intelligent comments; I did not gurgle and I hoped that my idol did not think me that unsophisticated young girl he had met many years before.

We all met many of the other delegates during the course of the party. Kambis was very taken by Prince Philip's gorgeous blond secretary and I think she was fascinated by his charm and handsome Iranian looks. When it came time for the party to fold my father and I had agreed to go out to dinner with the Canadian and Mexican delegations; Kambis declined to come as he said that he was very tired and wanted an early night.

The next day there were business meetings, both before and after noon. I found it all very interesting and not at all dry. I had the Irishmen sitting next to me who would crack jokes if none were forthcoming in the presentation at hand.

I was in a bit of a quandary at noon, for the Official Dinner was to be held that evening and my father had told me that it had always been a stag affair. As a delegate I had received an invitation addressed to Mr. Gail Rose. My father was not sure what I should do. The problem was settled when Chevalier H. de Menten de Horne, who was at the time Secretary General and Treasurer came to me while I was having lunch to say that it was drawn to his attention that I was a Madame, not a Monsieur, and he wanted to make it clear that I was definitely to attend the dinner. It was not intentionally a stag dinner party, it was just that there had never before been a woman delegate at the meeting.

The dinner was a very formal affair. The men were all in their black ties or formal military dress. I found myself surrounded by attractive men. I spent a lot of my time trying to promote the CSIA that we planning were to have in Iran in August but found few who were really interested. I did get Colonel Harry Llewellyn to agree to be our official delegate and I must say was very embarrassed when the whole thing fell through. I was pleased to see him in Iran though at our first true International Show in 1976. I felt that it made amends for the cancelled event.

After the dinner, Prince Philip made a very typical witty speech. We all laughed a lot but the only part I remember well was when he said, 'This year we have for the first time a father and daughter combination even if they do come from different countries. I hope that someday I will be able to top that combination by having my daughter up here where I am.' That did come to fruition when Princess Anne was elected to his position a few years later

Liqueurs were served, conversation flowed and soon it was midnight. As the party started to disperse I looked for my boss who was nowhere to be found. I presumed he could find his own way home so departed with Dad and some of his friends.

Saturday morning was the day to leave Brussels and I as yet, did not have a plane ticket in my hand. Kambis had been very elusive so when I awoke to find an envelope had been pushed under my door I was rather startled. Inside I found an airline ticket taking me to London, Dublin and eventually back to Iran.   First Class I was relieved to see! I called my father and Sheila to tell them that I did have a ticket so we made arrangements to travel together to London where Dad had business the following week.

I spent the weekend with them enjoying London, one of my favorite cities, and departed for Dublin on Monday morning agreeing to meet them in Adair, County Limerick, the following week.

From London I had called my great friend David Broome, the Canadian, not the rider from England, who said he would love to have me visit in Cork for the following weekend; he knew some people in the horse business and would enjoy taking me around. Unfortunately David's wife and my good friend, Willow, had not been able to take life in Ireland so after trying it out for a year had gone back to Canada again with the children. I could tell David was very lonely and quite unhappy about the situation. David and Willow had been my closest friends for a number of years. It was these two who had taken such great care of me and nursed me through my untimely widowhood, been enthusiastic about my second marriage and became great friends with Don, too. I looked forward to seeing David and hearing the sad tale; we had all been corresponding regularly until the previous summer but then there was a silence that neither Don nor I could understand.

The Royal Hybernium, in Dublin, did not have the red carpet out for me but I was expected. I was shown to a very comfortable room in this lovely old world hotel. I sat down on the bed long enough to sort out my schedule and decided that the first thing I had better do was to go to the main branch of the Bank of Ireland .

Upon asking at the front desk of the hotel I discovered that the bank was just five blocks away so I stepped out into the cloudy day. It was about noon and the streets of Dublin were full of people on their lunch hour who were leisurely window shopping or strolling to the nearest pub. No one in Ireland ever seems to hurry and I found that I too was able to take my time observing the lovely old stone buildings of Trinity College that I passed on my way to the stately old limestone building that housed the Bank of Ireland.

I passed through the huge stone pillars of the main entrance and was barely able to budge the large oak door into the main lobby of the bank. When I questioned the guard as to where I would go to receive currency that had been sent from abroad he said, 'Ya go straight on down the corridor t'other side of the hall. Ya'll have a haird time missing it.'

I did have a "haird" time finding it, for once I went through the corridor I discovered that it did not go straight! I had the choice of four different directions and could not decide which way was "straight on down". I finally chose the wrong corridor and after another few minutes and many inquiries I found a small office with "Foreign Exchange" written on the door.

I explained who I was and that I was expecting a draft for twenty thousand pounds in my name that would have been sent through The Bank Melli of Iran in London. The young lady was very obliging, checked all the incoming foreign currency and then informed me that nothing had arrived.

'That is impossible,' I said. 'Perhaps you missed it for I know the money was sent about two weeks ago.'

'Just wait a moment, please; I will see the department manager.'

When she returned she apologetically said that nothing had come but if I would call back in a day or two she was sure it would have arrived. 'You know these international transfers do take some time, Madam.'

There was nothing that I could do but go about my business of looking for horses and hope that the money arrived in time for me to pay for what I finally decided to purchase.

Frank O'Neil who had been the Irish delegate at the FEI meeting, had given me the name of a Jack White who was a veterinary and usually had the odd nice horse for sale. When I got back to the hotel I called him. He was most congenial on the phone. Yes he did have a couple of horses that might fit the ticket for me. Unfortunately, he himself was in bed with the grippe but one of his men would show me the horses if I could be there by about three-thirty in the afternoon. I should call at the house after I had seen the horses; he was looking forward to meeting me.

I then called about renting a car the following day, for I intended to wend my way slowly across to Cork for the weekend. It took about four tries but finally Murray's Pal said that they had a Hillman Hunter for me; I would be picked up at the hotel at ten the next morning. When I suggested that it was a bit late I was informed, 'But Madam, we don't open until 9: 30.'

Slightly surprised I said that I would be waiting at ten. I felt I had had a rather unproductive morning so decided to go to the main dining room for my lunch. It is a beautiful room, red plush wall paper and huge crystal chandeliers. I decided to splurge and ordered oysters, which I love, and were unavailable in Iran. I had a half bottle of Riesling as well. I was relishing my second oyster when I crunched something with my left molars. I hoped I had not cracked a tooth or maybe lost another filling! The latter had happened about six months before and had caused me quite some pain and anxiety. I cautiously mouthed the hard substance to the front of my mouth and then as delicately as possible spit it out into my hand. I could not believe it! It was a pearl! Whoever finds a pearl in an oyster these days? I wanted to yell out, 'Look everybody, I have just found a pearl in my oyster!' but how could I do that? Everyone in the restaurant was about 80 years old and would certainly think it most uncouth of the obviously "American" young lady sitting by herself. I just stared at the lovely little pearl then carefully put it in my wallet, drank a toast silently to my new found treasure and carefully ate the four other oysters, none of which contained a pearl. I felt that the find was good luck and perhaps an omen that the trip would be successful.

At three o'clock I ordered a cab and set off for Clonsilla and Jack White's place. My directions said that I should go through Phoenix Park, by Castlenock heading for Annfield. I would go through Porterstown and opposite the church would be the gates to Clonsilla. My driver either did not understand what I said or did not know where we were headed or perhaps both. It took a full half hour to get to our destination when Jack had said it would be a fifteen minute ride. Granted we had stopped to ask directions four or five times. My taxi driver was not terribly keen at the prospect of waiting for me but I knew that I would never find a way back to Dublin if I were to let him go.

The head lad was expecting me and showed me four or five young horses only one of which would suit me; this was a pretty filly of four years old but she had the most dreadful feet I have ever seen and I knew there was no sense in taking anything back to Iran with a foot problem. We had enough farrier troubles as it was.

When I went into the house, Jack's charming wife ushered me upstairs. I was brought tea and cakes and Jack and I sat, or rather, I sat while he lolled, drinking our tea and discussing horses in general and finally his in particular. I explained that I was looking for four or five young prospects to take back to Iran where I was living. I planned to train them and then sell them there. Kambis had told me not to mention that I was purchasing these horses for His Majesty's stable so I had to make up the little white lie that I stuck to during the trip. Jack was most understanding when I said that I really didn't find any of his stock suitable and gave me the names of two or three other people on the way to Cork who would maybe have a few animals to show me. Jack, was a big healthy looking man and it seemed incongruous to see him as he was, propped up by pillows in the huge antique bed. His wife had obviously very good taste for the bedroom was attractively decorated with a bright cheery chintz at the windows and on the bed ruffle.

Our business done we discussed horses and show jumping. My host and his wife were real horse people, extremely knowledgeable, and most entertaining. I was able to learn little bits of information about the people I would be seeing in the next few weeks; it made no matter from what part of Ireland they came, Jack White knew them and some anecdote that made these people much more real to me when I did meet them.

Darkness sets in about four-thirty in Ireland in early December so when I emerged from the house it was pitch black outside. The head lad had taken care of my taxi driver while I was inside but even though he had had a cup of tea or perhaps something stronger he was in no mood to tangle with. It was foggy and chilly, the type of weather that warmed my soul for some reason, so in high spirits I gaily mentioned the fact that I had an old school chum that lived at No. 10 Zion Road.

'Well, Lass, it is a bad night, ya knoow. I ken Zion Road but i' ya ha'n't
the lass's telephone she might na be in. I would hate t' go all t'hat way and
find her nat in. T'would cast ya a penny or two ya knaw.' I decided to forget
about seeing my old school chum.

Having returned to the hotel and finding no messages —funny thing -
I decided to try for the pearls again. I had a long hot bath, dressed in my
understated blue wool, put on my single strand of pearls and went down to
the lobby where I had a drink and quietly read my book. My vermouth finished, I went to the dining room where I was seated at a secluded table for
one. I once again ordered the oysters, hoping; I don't recall what else, for
I was so disappointed in not finding a pearl, it spoiled my evening.

A very pretty young Irish girl from Murrays Pal picked me up promptly
at ten the next morning. It was actually too prompt for me because I had
not paid my bill and when I presented my husband's American Express
card they refused to accept it! What was I going to do? Until my money
arrived from Iran I would be a little short on cash and I had relied on this
card to carry me through. It had worked well in London. The very proper
little man behind the desk called American Express in Dublin explaining
the situation and they did agree to wire Tehran to make certain the little
signed card I had was Don's and that I had permission to use the card; but
that would take a day or two to get a reply. I did not have time so decided
to pay with some of my cash. It would cut me short but what could I do? I
just hoped Murray and his pals would not put me in the same situation.

Murray was only too happy to accept my card and send me on my way
with many maps and instructions as to how I would get out of Dublin and
on my way to Kilmackthomas in County Waterford.

I felt quite at home in this little Hillman Hunter for it was the exact car
I had in Iran. Mine was called a Peykan and the steering wheel was on the
left hand side but otherwise, including the color and the loud humming the
clutch sometimes made it was the identical car. Little did poor old Murray

know that I had never sat behind a right hand drive and little did I know what a terrifying time I would have the first day of driving on the wrong side of the road. I drove away cautiously from Murray's shop hoping the girl waving me off would not notice my fixed grin and the strange way I was shifting the gears. Had they had any sense I am sure they would have refused to let me have a car. A few blocks away from Murray I stopped by the side of the road to get my bearings and try to figure out how I would get to the Nais Road that would be signposted Kilcullen. I finally found myself on the map and started off carefully resisting the urge to move over to the right hand side of the road. I came to a big intersection with a policeman directing the traffic and I became confused so I stopped in the middle of that intersection, looked completely lost, and asked the policeman the way to Kilcullen. He really was very kind and seemed to understand my predicament. He directed me well and I was soon bombing down the road towards Nais. What beautiful countryside it was! So green, the sun was shining brightly, lovely cottages flashed by as I sped on. This main road was indeed very quiet. There were very few cars going either way which was a relief to me when I made the invariable mistake of driving on the right side, I was quite safe with such little traffic. Only the pedestrians stared at me with unbelieving eyes and many waved frantically which woke me up to my mistakes.

Michael Hickie had nothing of interest to show me so I quickly headed for John O'Byrne and Kilmackthomas. I truly did enjoy my drive through the Irish countryside. Folksmills, Wexford and many little villages with quaint names. I was surprised when I didn't have any trouble finding Kilmackthomas.

I stepped out of my vehicle to be greeted by a very handsome young Irishman with a ruddy complexion. He was tall, sandy haired and had well-formed features even if his nose was a little too sharp. John introduced himself and we were off to have a look at what he had. I had talked to him myself the evening before telling him that I was looking for something between three and five thousand pounds; it should have some size, no apparent blemishes and have been backed. He showed me two or three that were far too big and clumsy for me. The final horse he had for me to see was a 17 hand bay gelding 5 years old by that great jumping sire Nordlays. We took the horse out on the lunge and jumped him over a few fences in the pasture and I could tell that even though the horse was a bit long in the back he really had a fantastic jump in him. I did like him very much but remained noncommittal. I explained that as this was my first day of actual serious looking I would not commit myself, but would be back in touch with him in a week or so. I bade my farewell, hopped in my little yellow car and off I went.

My next stop would be at Captain Morgan's in Lismore which was in Co. Waterford also. It should not be too far to my destination. I had no trouble finding the signposted road to Lismore and when I got to the wee town I stopped my car and asked the first person I saw, the way to Captain Thomas Morgan's place. That's what the good captain had told me to do.

'Ah, well, Captain Morgan's ya say?'

'Yes, Captain Thomas Morgan. He has horses.'

'Ah yes. Well I dunna knaw the best way to tell ya. Ya might just go up the big hill past the church, then ya might go round by the pub but I would guess the quickest way would be to go back the way you came and take the fairst right turning after you leave the town. When ya get to the top of the first hill stop and ask someone; they'll surely send ya right.'

I thanked the woman and turned around. When I got to the top of the hill sure enough there was a man outside his cottage hoeing. I stopped and asked him the way to Captain Morgan's.

'Well, lassie, and why would ya be going to see Captain Morgan?'

I explained, and the man then gave me some directions in a tongue that

I barely understood, but the main gist of it was that I should go back the way I had come! I thanked him, turned my chariot around again and drove back down into town. I passed the fat old lady who had first directed me and came upon a youth riding a bike. I flagged him down and again asked for Captain Morgan.

'Well, now, I would go on up the road a couple of miles. You will see a white cottage with a thatched roof, tha's no' it. Go on farther and you will come to three cottages on the left, tha's no' it. About a stone's throw from those cottages you will see a small road on the right; ya turn up there and go about three or four miles and you'll come to a field with a white fence. It's on the right. The next drive is the Captain's.'

When I passed the three cottages I saw an old man out front so to be on the safe side I asked him the way to Captain Morgan's.

'Well now, you are on the right track. It can't be much further on you take a right turn then you will run right into it. Ya couldn't miss it. They have lots of hosses you know.'

I miraculously found the road, turned right and drove on. It was now becoming dark and I felt sure that I would pass right on by the place but amazingly enough after three or four miles I spied a white board fence and turned in the gates even though there was no sign. I hoped it would be the place; I didn't see any horses, but then it was that dark!

I stopped the car and opened the door but quickly shut it again. I had never heard such barking or seen so many dogs in one place at once except perhaps in the hunt field. There were two huge guard dogs, German shepherds; two or three English fox hounds were baying and then there must have been six or seven terriers as well as a couple of dachshunds. I waited for the Captain, who had been expecting me, to call off the dogs before I stepped out. I daren't even open the window. It took a few minutes for him to take all the animals to the various pens I could see, and some he put in what looked like stall doors in the barn. It gave me time to collect my thoughts. I had told the captain nothing about myself on the phone, just that I was looking for young, inexpensive horses to take 'home'; he had not asked where home was but I could be sure that he would. I had to make my story good for this man.

The summer before, Kambis had gone to the Dublin Horse Show with Freddy Elghanian and during the show he had agreed to buy a horse from the Captain. It was a young three year old that had done well in the line classes and according to Fred, Kambis had taken a fancy to it. The price had been ten thousand pounds at which Kambis had not quibbled. The horse had been vetted and that had been the end. Kambis had never followed through. He had told me about almost buying the horse when he came back to Iran and when I embarked on my trip he had requested that I visit the captain to see if the horse had been sold or not. If not, I was to offer a lower price and buy it. The extra money would be forwarded upon receipt of a cable from me. Ha! I thought to myself as I waited for the dogs to be cleared. To date I had not received any money. Would I ever?

I decided to play it by ear. I was a Canadian woman living in Iran very involved in show jumping. I had a 'friend' in the military who was going to arrange for a plane to take the horses I bought in Ireland to Iran and the two of us were going to make a little 'business'. It sounded plausible. I was just another horse dealer. It would put me on a par with him.

'Mrs. Rose', the Captain extended his hand as I opened the door of the car. 'I am so pleased that you made it. We were becoming a little worried when it got dark and thought perhaps you had lost your way.'

'I am pleased to meet you Captain Morgan. I did have a bit of trouble, but not much.'

'Call me Tom. Do come in out of the damp'! It had begun to rain in that drizzly Irish way. We walked in through the kitchen door of a typical farm house and into a cozy library that had the ever present peat fire smoldering away. I was introduced to Mrs. Morgan who was at the time Master of her own pack of foxhounds. She was recovering from a bad fall she had sustained some weeks earlier. She had had a very severe concussion along with a few broken bones and was hobbling around in definite pain.

Tom got us all a wee drop of the Irish to warm our bones on a chilly night and we sat down to talk.

'Tell me again, Gail, if I may ask, what sort of horses are you looking for and what are your plans for them? I thought you said that you were taking them to some strange country but now I see that you are American; I am a might confused.'

'Actually, I am Canadian but I live in Iran, Persia, you know the Middle East, oil and so forth. I am planning to buy four or five horses and send them back there, where I hope to sell them for a wee profit once I have put a few months work on them.'

'Iran, you say. You had better be careful there. They are a difficult group to deal with. I actually had a most peculiar experience with one of them at the Dublin show this past year. You might know this fellow, I think he was something big in the government. Worked close to the Shah, he said. Quite a charming fellow he was. Interested in a nice young chestnut three year old that I had, won with it on the line in the Suitable to Become Hunters classes. He took a real fancy to this hoss of mine and I quoted him a substantial price at which he did not blink an eye. He said that he would take the horse if he were vetted sound. Asked if I would arrange for the vet. Not quite the way we would have done it here but I said I would take care of it for him and send him the certificate when it was in my hands. He said that would be fine and he would then forward the money to me and let me know how he would transport the horse. I thought the deal was done. Well, I got a sound certificate on the animal and forwarded it on to the fellow at the address he gave me in Iran. Do you know, that was the last I heard of it. I followed up twice more but nothing happened. I finally sold the horse elsewhere. But do you know that that sleazy little bastard never even paid the vet his ten pounds for vetting the horse. Yes, I would be careful of those people.'

'I know Mr. Atabai well.'

'That was the fellow's name! Atabai!'

'He really is a very charming man and means well. He is the guiding light in the horse world in Iran. I think what probably happened was that he got back to Iran to find that his budget at the Imperial Stables had been cut and he was too embarrassed to tell you. You know they are having an austerity program and I heard that all the sports budgets have been cut for the remainder of this year, which in Iran ends the 21st of March.

'Well, I would say that is no bloody excuse for him not replying to my letter. I could have sold the horse much better than I did but I thought I had sold him already. I will tell you I would like to see that fellow again someday.'

'I'm sorry to hear you had such a bad experience. The Iranians aren't really that way you know; it's too bad that you had to take a loss of some considerable sum and I'm sure that Kam . . . Mr. Atabai would be upset himself. But he is probably in a bind, or was. There are a lot of really marvelous people in Iran.'

'Well, I don't think I ever want to go there to find out about it or about the people.'

'To change the subject, what have you got in the 4 to 5 year old bracket, green, that has been backed but not had much work done to it?'

He did have three horses to show me that were not what I was looking for. I told him so on the spot and he did understand. He didn't know of any horses around in my price range that would be the type of class I was obviously after but he would let me know if he came across any. I left him David Broome's number. When we returned to the house from the stables we had another wee drop of the Irish to ward off the chill of the night air and to prepare me for my drive on to Cork.

It was only about an hour and a half away 'straight on' the road that passed by his place. Just five miles further on, the road in front joined directly to the main Cork Road. I would have no trouble finding Cork. Famous last words, I thought. I thanked both the Captain and his wife and went off to my chilly car.

I did not really find the chilly night air quite so chilly as everyone seemed to think it was. I had been to Ireland at most times of the year and I found the temperature to vary little. Maybe I had been lucky, but I found that if I wore slacks, a light wool turtleneck sweater and tweed hacking jacket I could be comfortable at any time of year. I always carried a mackintosh for the rain that invariably fell but I had never had a day when at some time the sun did not peek through the beautiful Irish clouds. Of course I love clouds, drizzle, fog and a light breeze so perhaps it was just that the climate agreed with me and I didn't find it cold.

As I drove on toward Cork, which miraculously was not a difficult drive, I wondered if I should have paid the ten pounds for the vetting of Kambis's horse. If I had had lots of ready cash I would have, but as I was short, I didn't offer. I was rather stricken that Kambis would have pulled such a trick. In Ireland if you have a horse vetted it is almost a guarantee that if the horse is declared sound you will buy it. I was glad that the Captain had sold the horse and wondered if he really had not made what he had expected to on the animal. I think Kambis was just a good sucker that he had hoped to pull one off on.

I had a little trouble finding David's house and found myself going around in circles for about a half an hour . I finally found a pub that was open and went in for directions.

'Mr. Broome's house you want? Why it is just on up the road. Ya take a right at the second road and then drive up to the top of the hill. His is the second gate on the right. It is about a mile from the top of the hill, mind you. You know his missus left to go back to Canada a few months ago. What a shame it was! She took them children along with her too. That boy was a problem cracking up his father's car the way he did but the little girl was as sweet as you'd ever find. I guess it gets lonely up there all bay himself, now.' He gave me such a look, that I wanted to crawl under the nearest table. I resisted the urge and thanked the man for his directions and then ran out to my car. I was in need of another wee drop of the Irish! And I was not a real drinker in the true sense of the word.

David, tall, be speckled and bald, but very attractive, opened the front door of the house when he heard the car drive in. It was marvelous to see him. He brought my bag in and put it up in my room which looked out over a beautiful valley I was to discover in the morning. The "impossible" house that Willow had written so much about was attractively decorated and did not look so "impossible" to me. When I mentioned this to David he agreed that he himself had always liked the house but being English this sort of turn of the century period house appealed to him. It was like the house he had grown up in. Willow's taste was impeccable and each piece of furniture seemed made for its place. The muted tones of color and thick mushroom broadloom made for a peaceful effect. We had a drink in the library telling each other our tales; David's was one of woe and loneliness but I was sure Willow had something on her side too.

I was glad that I didn't have to cope with both sides and that we were all living so far apart. No one was more pleased than me when about six months later I received a letter informing me of their reconciliation. We went out to dinner in the town of Cork. As I recall the white bate was especially fine. Later on there was a "business drinks" party at which David had to make an appearance. It was really quite a lot of fun and I met many charming Irish people. It also turned out to be profitable as I met a young woman who was into horses in a small way and said that she knew of a number of good young horses that I was to look at later on during my trip.

The next morning David was going to drive me to Cashel where a friend of his had a stable of horses. Tim Hyde was about thirty years old and had been a fairly successful steeplechase jockey until his father had died and he had to run the farm. He was in horses in a big way. Hunters, young horses to deal and even Thoroughbreds. The first horse he showed us was a very good looking seal brown gelding, a three year old. It was by the good sire Master Book and one of the nicest horses I had seen in a long time. This animal moved beautifully, so smooth and cat-like. When we had arrived at the farm I had seen the horse's head looking out over a stall door and had walked up with an enquiring look. Tim had said he was out of my price range but I decided to look anyway. It did spoil it for the other horses I looked at. The rest of them we saw that day, and there were about twenty of them, were all overshadowed by the nice Thoroughbred horse. Having finished our looking we went into the big old Georgian house to have a wee drop of sherry with Tim and his wife. Upon parting I said that I would probably have the Master Book horse vetted but would let him know in a week or so. I think he was quite surprised but I just had not seen anything else that took my fancy.

David and I stopped at the Palace in Cashel which had once been the Bishop's palace, to have a bite of lunch. The large brick Georgian edifice was surrounded by beautiful gardens. When we walked in the soft yellow front hall, flanked on either side by large fireplaces, we were informed that the dining room was closed but if we did not mind sitting by the fire we could order a cup of soup and a sandwich and eat it in the hall. We thought that was a good idea. There was a sofa on either side of each fireplace and the Doric pillars sectioned the room off into cozy corners. There were some beautiful paintings of the 18th and 19th Century that gave an aura of grandeur to the old palace; particularly interesting was a series of paintings of the winners of the Irish 1000 Guiness for a period in the 19th Century.

We left Cashel heading back on the Main Cork Road. We had both enjoyed the lunch and were having a quiet period.

David had given me the grand sightseeing tour on the way up. This old manor house had been one of the most prosperous farms in the south of Ireland until the famine of 1848. In that year the potato crop which was the staple diet of the Irish people failed. The consequences were far reaching. In a little over one year, half of the population of eight million people died or were forced to emigrate.

That place was the ancestral home of Lord so and so. As we passed by he had a story for most of the renowned old homes. David certainly did know the area.

I was not paying very much attention to the road but suddenly I noticed a lone car approaching us and it was heading straight for our small black jaguar. It took me a moment to pull myself out of my daydreams but suddenly I realized that we were driving on the right hand side of the road. I looked over at David and to my horror discovered that he was fast asleep!

'David!' I shouted as I jerked the wheel to the left narrowly avoiding what could have been a fatal accident. We swerved, the tires screeched, but we finally got the car under control. We were both shattered. It was only after the episode was over, that I recalled the fact that we had always joked about how long it would take David to fall asleep when he was driving the car. Willow had almost always taken the wheel about fifteen minutes after they set out on a drive.

It was time for Fox Hunting so a couple of days later I bade David a fond farewell and headed north to Limerick. According to the road map it was an uncomplicated drive to Adare, the turn-off being just before the town of Limerick. It was a beautiful misty morning as I started out, reminiscent of a Renoir painting. The main highway was more like a quiet country road; there was very little traffic as I wound my way towards my destination. I had heard so much of the IRA, bombs, feelings of dissension and general unrest in Ireland that to date I had been surprised to find none of these things. It was on the little road leading to the town of Adare that I saw the white crudely painted writing on a pretty old stone bridge. It read:

IRA

FREE IRELAND

DOWN WITH THE BRITISH

I had stopped to look at horses on my way so the journey that generally takes a couple of hours took almost all day. It was about four in the afternoon when I had turned off the main road towards Adare. It had started to drizzle about three and by four it was pouring and getting dark very quickly. Just after my IRA bridge I saw a figure standing at the side of the road waving. I was going slowly enough to see that it was an old man, obviously getting soaked. I stopped the car, something I would be afraid to do in North America or Iran, and asked if he wanted a ride.

'Why, Lassie, 'tis kind of ya t' stop fer an old man such as me. I wouldn't be unhappy to take a ride from ye.' In he got. On closer inspection he seemed to be in his seventies but I really could never tell with the Irish. There were some who had the complexion of twenty year olds and they were in their forties and some looked eighty while they were only in their fifties.

'And what would an American lass such as yerself be doing out on the road all by yerself on such a night as this?' was his opening remark to our conversation. I informed him that I was a Canadian and I was on my way to meet my father and spend a couple of days fox hunting.

'So ye like the harsses. That's my biggest love too. I grew up with the harsses,' he continued. 'Me father was head lad for Prendergast, a great trainer in those days. I worked about the harsses as soon as I was big enough. I did a bit of riding, how I liked the jumpers!' In Ireland "the jumpers" means the steeplechase horses.

'I even did a bit of training myself, tho I'd say I wasn't the best at it.

Wouldn't be a seller at the window now would I if I had been an O'Brien?'
he chuckled.

'Well, I am sure your job is interesting.' I tried to interject as I was expected to.

'Ye know, Lassie, I work with the racing commission. I go to all of the
meets in this part of the country. And i'tis an interesting job. And I know
most of the trainers and owners from way back. I sometimes get a good tip
and get one of me friends to buy me a pound ticket. Yes, I do make ends
meet. I love to be around the harsses.'

And so went the conversation for the next ten miles. At the edge of
Adare he asked me to let him off and directed me that half a mile further
on I would see the Dunraven Arms on the right. I could not miss it.

I did not miss it! A low, long building with a gambrel roof. I pulled up
in front of the main door and scooted through the teeming rain to the lobby.
I was immediately caught up with this old inn and knew that I would have
a wonderful time the next few days.

There was an attractive red haired woman behind the desk to whom I
introduced myself.

'Why yes, Mrs. Rose, we have been expecting you. Your father has
stayed with us many times before. We are so pleased to meet his daughter.
I do hope you will enjoy yourself while you are with us. Mr. and Mrs.
Whitaker have gone over to Hospital to see Mr. Fraizer about having some
clothes tailored. I will show you to your room and tell them you are here
when they return.'

My bags were brought up by an attractive blond Irish boy in his teens.
Miss 0'Sullivan herself came up to see that I was comfortable and that my
fire was burning.

My room was at the end of the hall off to itself. I had a big comfortable
double bed with lots of pillows. My two windows looked over the main
street which at this time was in complete darkness. I turned on the shilling

heater in the bathroom, and ran a hot tub. It felt so good to languish in the tub after having spent the day on the road that I took longer than usual. By the time I went back into my bedroom someone had unpacked for me and all my clothes were neatly hanging in my closet.

While I was dressing there came a knock at my door to inform me that my father was awaiting me in the lounge downstairs. I made the finishing touches quickly and went down.

We had a couple of drinks while enjoying the huge fire in the lounge. The atmosphere of the Dunraven Arms was one of informality and yet correctness. The inn was owned by Lord Dunraven who also owed Fork Union Stud and Dunraven Castle across the street. Adare is the ancestral home of the Dunravens. The current Lord was a young man who was unfortunately in a wheel chair, but he was very active both in running his stud, the inn and his castle.

We went across the hall to the dining room, where we had a delicious dinner of smoked salmon, grouse, fresh vegetables and a superb custard desert. The wine was French and most palatable. It would be an early night because we all were off to Tipperary to hunt the next morning.

The meet was at eleven which meant we would have to leave the Dunraven by nine. It was about an hour and a half drive and we would need a half an hour to find our mounts and get aboard. I had a dreadful time sleeping, even though I was so tired, due to the excitement at the prospect of hunting in Ireland for my first time. I had heard for years from my father how the fox hunting in this ancient country is the best in the world. I had also read accounts and heard tales of the frightful banks and ditches that often were the death of people and horses. I knew not what to expect but I couldn't wait to find out.

It was an overcast but warmish morning with little wind at all, the perfect conditions for scenting. Benny Supple, a cheery Irish fellow who had been driving my father and arranging for his hunting horses for years, was to drive us over to Tipperary. It was an uneventful drive save for the sheep, goats and cows that slowed our progress to a crawl at times. We were a little late in arriving so were put aboard our horses quickly upon reaching the meet. I had barely time to take in the appearance of my mount before I was given a leg up. Benny had told me I was very lucky in having a really good horse to ride that day. It was an event horse that the people didn't usually let out. At first glanced it seemed a very nice looking bay gelding.

Before I knew it we were off drawing a covert near a big old stone manor house. I heard the hounds speaking; I collected my reins and scanned the crowd for a gentleman, who looked like a true hunting type to follow. When one doesn't know the area it is always a good idea to tag along behind someone who is familiar with it and is a good strong forward rider in the field. We flew across the first field and I was up and over the first bank and ditch before I realized it. Not so bad after all. We had a good half hour's run before hounds marked the fox to ground. There had been only one huge drainage ditch that had frightened me. As I had approached from one side there was a small ditch and a moderate four foot bank, but the other side of the bank the ditch was about ten feet wide, very deep and with vertical sides. It had actually been machine made and was very difficult to negotiate. My heart was in my mouth each time we approached it and we did jump it three or four times in different places.

We were off and running again and again were approaching "my" ditch. I had taken to following a very good riding girl on a lovely chestnut mare. She really seemed to know the country and was very pleasant indeed. As we approached the ditch, I saw her horse go up the little bank, but as I waited my turn it did not appear on the other side. I turned and followed someone else behind me who was saying, 'That's a bad spot there; let's try a little further to the left.'

We negotiated the ditch without any trouble but when we got over to the other side we saw that my original lead was in trouble. Her horse had misjudged the landing on the other side of the ditch, had flipped over and broken its neck! I was stricken! Should the hunt stop and help this girl?

Not in Ireland! The chase continued. Too bad! Unfortunate. T'is sad to see a good horse go. Many comments but no one stopped to help, save the man riding a stable mate of the dead horse.

I was both exhilarated and exhausted after my first day's hunting in Ireland. As I lay, soaking my weary bones in the bath reflecting upon the day, I realized that it was the way I would love to spend the rest of my life.

The Dunraven Arms catered to fox hunting people during this time of year. Each morning after the day's hunting my boots and britches were placed in my room spotlessly clean ready for another day's wear. The white shirt and stock always crisp and starched, the laundress must have spent the whole night washing and ironing as the majority of the guests were hunting people.

I had many good days hunting, all the while keeping my eyes and ears open for horses that might be suitable for Iran. One day in particular sticks in my mind.

For years my father had raved about a hunter called "The Beatle". He had asked Benny to try to hire it for him but the three or four days my father was there the Beatle was not available. He was truly disappointed that he didn't get a chance to ride it because he had hunted this famous horse at least once every time he had been in Ireland. According to him, the horse was legendary; he was the most dependable hunter, like a cat; he knew where the fox was going before the hounds did.

My last day's hunting when Benny picked me up at the Arms he had an impish grin on his face.

'I've got quite a surprise for you this morning, Ma'am,' he said excitedly. 'All the time I've been trying to get "The Beatle" for your father to ride and now he is gone what happens —the man calls me last night to offer me the horse. I already had a mount lined up for you but I quickly cancelled it and took "The Beatle"' instead. You are going to have the ride of your life today.'

When we got to the meet there was one big chestnut horse, more a sorrel actually, that really stood out from all the others. It had to be "The Beatle". It was. Benny led me over, gave me a leg and bade me fair hunting.

It was amazing for no sooner was I on the horse when two or three people came up to me to say, 'You've got "The Beatle"!' or, 'How did you get "The Beatle?"' or, 'The Colonel has not been letting "The Beatle" out much this season. They say he is taking more care of him now that he is getting on in years.'

'You will certainly be up at the front today, riding that wonderful horse.'

Everyone in the field knew the horse and obviously admired him. He was owned by a retired Army Colonel who let him out once or twice a week for about thirty pounds to help pay for his keep. The Colonel himself hunted the horse one day a week.

I decided to keep my sights on the master that day. I stayed a discrete two or three horses back so as not to seem too pushy but "The Beatle" himself seemed to want to be right up there, and the two or three people between me and the master seemed to want me to go ahead of them, so there I was, right in the front. "The Beatle" was fantastic. He judged his every stride when we were approaching banks and ditches. We flew over a high steel cattle gate, I with my heart in my throat and my eyes shut, mind you.

The hounds were really running that day and at one point we got into some really overgrown country. We came to a huge ditch with a high bank the other side that was completely overgrown. The master tried to get through but his horse would not go. He turned to me. 'Would you take "The Beatle" and give me a lead?'

Now I am not long on nerve when it comes to doing something that I know someone else has been unable to do, but I was a guest, and the master, my host, had made a request . . . I gave "The Beatle" my boot, hung onto the neck strap , shut my eyes and headed for the bank. I prayed a little too! I heard and felt the branches breaking all around my body. My hat came off, my face was scratched, but suddenly I was on the other side of the obstacle and in one piece. The other horses followed without problems, for I had cleared a path in the bracken. What a wonderful horse! The whole day was full of really great hunting experiences; I was in ecstasy.

Lord Darsbury, Master of the Limerick Hounds, called Toby by all his close friends, had been a friend of my father's for many years so it was that he invited the three of us for dinner after hunting one night. Sheila and I were dressed to the nines and Dad was wearing a coat and tie.

'Don't be surprised when you see Toby tonight.' Dad said as we drove up the long lane to Alto Villa which was a very old Irish house that had been in ruins after most of it had been destroyed by fire at the turn of the century. The Lord who held an English title had bought it after the Second World War. He and his wife Boodlie had spent many painstaking hours and years in having it renovated. Unfortunately, she lived only a short time in this huge stone mansion, for she was killed while out hunting just a couple of years after they had moved in. Her horse had tripped in a ditch and went down pinning her beneath. She drowned!

The massive oak front door opened as we climbed the stairs to it and there stood the Lord in a maroon track suit. I was surprised and obviously my face showed it; I never was very good at the poker face.

After greeting us he turned to me and said, 'Hope you don't mind that I put on something relaxing.' He laughed and so did I.

We had drinks in the beautiful drawing room, the walls of which were covered with sporting paintings. On one wall was a very large Alken depicting the gathering of horses and riders before a hunt. Mary Atkinson, the Lord's right hand woman, acted as hostess and ushered us all downstairs to the huge paneled dining room. The table was set with the most complete set of silver I have ever seen. There were knives and forks for each of the many courses and in front of each person there was a variety of small silver boxes and trays. I never did figure out what they were all for but some were snuff boxes and there were cigarette boxes, pill boxes, small ash trays — to name a few. Each one was an individual piece hand tooled by some early silversmith. They were just a part of the Lord's famous collection.

After dinner we were taken on a tour of all three floors of the house. The purpose of the tour was to see the extensive collection of sporting paintings that were housed at Alto Villa. This was only a part of the collection of Lord Darsbury which was reputed to be second only to that of Paul Mellon, who has the largest private collection of sporting art in the world.

During the tour the Lord took me aside at one point when the others had moved on ahead.

'I must ask you something, my dear,' he said. 'I know I am getting old and sometimes forget things but I cannot figure out your mother. She has changed so that I didn't even recognize her and frankly I could swear that she is not the same person.'

Through my laughter I explained that indeed it was another person. My father had left my mother and married Sheila quite recently. The Lord had a good laugh about it and later chided my father for not telling him the difference. It seems that it was an intentional joke that did tickle the Lord's funny bone.

During the time I was staying in Adair and enjoying my hunting I had been in touch with the Bank of Ireland numerous times about the phantom money from Iran. When I had been two weeks in the country I decided to call Kambis. I put a call in and miraculously got through within a day.

'Mrs. Rose, it is so good to hear from you. How are things going?'

'It's good to talk to you, Kambis. I'm in a panic! I have found three definite horses, one a little more expensive than I had expected but really worth the money. However, the money has not arrived in Ireland. I'm sure the Bank of Ireland thinks that I'm nuts. I have called them so many times and they have nothing to tell me. Please get a tracer on it immediately.'

'That is a surprise. I will check it for you. When I got your cable last week I looked into it but they said that it had definitely been sent. Yes, I will certainly look into it again. But you are in no hurry to come home. You have set up a good schedule for the boys and they are all working along very well.'

'Kambis, do you realize that it will be Christmas in just one week? I do have a family and if I don't get home for Christmas dinner I'm going to have a very angry husband and three disappointed children.'

'Well, don't worry, I'm sure the money will be there in a few days. I will take care of it.'

We said our good byes and I was no further ahead than I had been be-fore the conversation. On top of that I knew that the Dunraven Arms did not accept American Express so I would be dipping into my dwindling cash again.

When I had gone back to David's I told him one evening, the woes of my money problems. He was a brilliant businessman and could not believe that I had left Iran to do a job without at first having been given an advance. Never having done such an errand, I had not thought about an advance. I knew the Imperial Court was good for it so why the hurry? By this time it was about the 19th of December and I was getting a little worried. I would either have to leave the country without paying for the horses and have no guarantee that the owners wouldn't sell them to other buyers before my money got there, or I would have to miss Christmas at home. I had to be home by the 24th. To me that was first priority.

David finally came up with the solution. He would arrange for a loan from the Bank of Cork which he would guarantee. I could then pay for the horses and other expenses and when the money came in he would see that the loan was paid off, get the release from his guarantee, and we would be home free. It was so simple and so trusting of David to make the offer. Naturally if the Iranians reneged I would have to pay him back from my own funds. That would have been a problem!

The next morning we fixed everything up with the bank and I went off to do some Christmas shopping. Also now that I had some money in my hot little hand I called the vet, a friend of our Dr. Cutler at the Imperial Stables, and asked him to examine the four horses I had picked out. In two days I had the soundness reports. All four had passed so it was time for me to get back to Iran.

By this time my father-in-law had joined me. He was visiting Europe and on his way to Iran for Christmas with his son and grandchildren. He and I gaily flew away from the Emerald Isle to London where we planned to spend one night and then fly back to the Middle East. When we tried to make reservations to Iran there were none to be had. I had a first class ticket but he was travelling tourist, the class I usually traveled, so I thought I could use that extra money I would be returned by cashing in my first class ticket. What a joke! The only way we could get to Tehran would be first class if we wanted to be there before Christmas. They did have two seats for the next morning and that was it, even for first class, until the following week. We bought the tickets.

We decided to surprise Don upon our arrival. When we landed at Mehrabad we took a taxi to the house and casually walked in the door. I noted that Don had all the Christmas decorations up and a beautiful big tree stood in the corner of the living room all decorated with decorations made by the children. Don was speechless for a moment.

'Why Mrs. Rose,' he said, 'I am surprised that you were able to come home for Christmas.'

Author riding : "The Beatle"

COLLECTING HORSES

HAPPY NEW YEAR STOP MONEY NOT YET ARRIVED FROM IRAN STOP WILL ADVISE UPON RECEIPT REGARDS DAVID

I took this telegram to Kambi's office the second of January. I was beginning to panic now for I had taken the loan, written the checks for all the horses and mailed them before I left Ireland. I now owned, or better, David Broome owned, four young Irish horses. In each deal I had stated that the owner of the horse would have to keep it on free board until I was able to arrange for the plane to pick it up in a month or so.

'Mrs. Rose, I really don't understand this. Let me call the man in the foreign currency department right now while you are here.'

He did. There was a long heated conversation on the end I was hearing. I could only imagine the obsequiousness of the banker on the other end. It would be straightened out within a few days I was informed when the receiver was in its cradle.

Two weeks later I received a letter from David with my Irish bank book, cancelled checks and record of payment of my loan by the Bank Melli, Kensington Branch in London.

It was arranged that Dr. Cutler, the stable veterinary, and I would go to Ireland to pick up the horses. I would be needed to make certain that those tricky Irish did not switch horses on us. I would never have thought of that but the Iranian mind is always ready for a chance to cheat or undermine and so is suspicious of others.

We were due to leave Mehrabad International Airport on a Monday morning early in February at six-thirty in the morning. We were taking two *djelodards* from the Imperial stables with us and would fly to Lynam Airforce base in England and spend the night. The following morning at seven we would take off for Dublin to pick up the horses and directly from Dublin we were to fly to Belgrade, Yugoslavia, where we would spend the night. The next morning we were to be delivered a Lipizzan mare that was a gift to His Imperial Majesty the Shah from President Tito. According to the Yugoslavs, the best and the true Lipizzans are in Yugoslavia. In Austria, there is the Spanish Riding School where the Lipizzaners perform, but Czechoslovakia, Italy and Yugoslavia all have Lipizzan stud farms.

We were to spend the night in Belgrade where the authorities would have stabling arranged for the four horses that we would already have on the plane and then we would load all five horses and return to our own country the next day. It all sounded so very organized.

Robin Cutler, Davoud Karimi Majzoob, Abdula Ghadimi and I all walked through the immigration and customs check at seven o'clock having waited in the main hall of that old antiquated airport for one hour. We had finally been informed that our plane had arrived on the runway and we could proceed through control. The captain of the plane would come to the lounge to get us when the plane was ready for take-off. Robin and the two *djelodards* went immediately to the duty free shop to stock up on cigarettes and booze. I bought myself a bottle of Madame Rochas, my favorite perfume and Cinzano Bianco, my favorite vermouth. When we checked each other's purchases it seemed that the good doctor had done better than the rest of us. He had three bottles of scotch and two bottles of champagne.

It was by now close to eight o'clock and still no sight of the captain of our Flight ELF 95.

'Join me at the bar for a quick one for the air,' Robin suggested. I joined him but had a cup of coffee. The boys sat guarding their purchases and ours.

188

I was beginning to get a little worried as I knew that we had a long flight ahead of us, and the C 130 is not as fast as a jet. If we were much later in taking off we would not be able to fly on to Ireland the following morning due to the regulations about the number of rest hours the pilot must have between flights. At nine thirty after having had two scotches Robin decided to try to call Khambi's office. He was not there and would not be back that day. He then called the office of Abulfath Atabai who when contacted said that he would check into the matter and let us know what the trouble was. We hung around the pay phone in the corner of the lounge until it rang. The information we received was that the pilots did not have the proper papers for a flight to England and Yugoslavia and these were now being processed; in another hour or so we would take off.

I sat down with my book, Robin with his bottle and the boys called their various families for another couple of hours. When by noon nothing had happened I assented to join Robin at the bar and had a couple of Bloody Marys. We sipped our drinks and filled up on pistachio nuts as we waited. I really expected to be informed at any minute that the plane was cancelled for the day, when miraculously we saw an Imperial Iranian Air Force pilot walk into the lounge. It turned out to be the navigator, actually. He walked up to the bar. 'I knew this was where I would find you, Dr. Cutler. Your reputation is well known in the Iranian Air Force. I am Ali Behegzadi, your navigator. And are you Mrs. Rose?'

'Yes. How do you do, Ali.' They always addressed the man first because even with all the women's liberation, to most Iranian men the female of the species was not at all equal.

We picked up our bags and walked out the door to the runway. There was no security check for us. The plane was only a few steps from the door, where we had seen it earlier in the morning. As we boarded we introduced ourselves to the rest of the crew and the captain.

'By the way, Mrs. Rose, we are not going to make it to England today.

We will be flying to Athens where we will spend the night. We will go to Lynam the next day and on to Ireland the following day.'

'Oh, no! '

'My orders were to inform you of the flight plan when you boarded. You are supposed to be head of the mission though I would think the doctor would be better, being a man! '

'Would you give me about ten minutes? I have to make a telephone call so that I can inform them in Ireland that we won't be there tomorrow. It was all arranged for the horses to be at Dublin airport at nine o'clock to-morrow morning. What time will we be arriving the next day?'

'Well, Mrs. Rose, I would suggest that you just tell them that we will advise the ETA when we are sure what it will be. You never know what might happen.' He was looking a little sheepish. I could tell, having dealt with Iranians so long that he had some plans that he was not letting on to anyone.

I left the plane, went through a door into the main hall where I found a pay telephone. I called Don to tell him of the problem; it was the first time I had had an emergency call to make, and was able to get my party — Allah was with me. Don would telex to David Broome who in turn would phone the four horse owners. I would telephone them from England when I knew the day and time of our arrival in Dublin.

'I think that captain is planning an extended vacation from the way he spoke, so we may not get to Ireland until the end of the week is my guess. I'll see you around! It could be another Iranian fiasco!'

'OK, love. I will expect you only when you walk in the door. Is that right? Take care.'

I walked directly through the door by which I had entered the terminal. No one even noticed that I was walking directly to the runway from the main terminal building without having to go through any security checks or customs. I was, frankly, amazed.

Once again aboard our ELF I buckled myself into the seat in the cockpit next to Robin. I had never taken off in the cockpit so it was a very exciting experience to see the runway whizzing along in front and finally to fly above it. Once we were airborne the captain signaled me to come forward where I could stand beside him and get a wonderful view of our desert country. The ghanats, underground channels which supply the bulk of the water to the country, looked like molehills or bomb craters that dotted the land in long lines that stretched for miles and miles. Everything was of varying shades of brown. I remembered when I had first visited Iran how brown and same everything seemed. It had depressed me but now that I had lived in the country for some time I found so much difference in the shades of brown that it had become beautiful to me.

I once again settled down to read my book on the seat at the back of the cockpit. If you are familiar with the C 130 you will know that there is a long undivided seat across the back of the cockpit upon which three people can strap themselves in with seat belts very comfortably. Above this seat is a bunk. I actually spent a lot of my time lying in the bunk reading on flights in these planes for one was comfortable, out of the way and had the most spectacular view out the windows in the front of the plane.

Dr. Cutler kept disappearing and by the way that he staggered up the stairs from the back of the plane I knew that he was taking nips from his scotch bottles.

By the time the six hour flight had ended Robin had had a chance to sleep off his morning and early afternoon bout. We arrived in Athens late afternoon. We flew over the Aegean which looked sea green and tempting before landing. Even though the temperature would not really be conducive to swimming I was sure it would be warmer than Tehran had been when we left.

Tehran doesn't actually get terribly cold in the winter. It may go below freezing at night but the sun comes up almost every day and warms the air to the fifties and often sixties. There is some snow most winters but it does't usually last for more than a day or two except up in the very high mountainous areas.

Once the plane had landed we helped the crew close it up for the night. We would have it refueled just before we took off the next morning. We joked around taking pictures of each other and getting to know the crew a little better. As they were to be our companions for the duration of our journey it was a good idea to become as friendly as possible. They had all been to Athens on previous flights; the captain was bold enough to admit that he loved coming to Athens especially because the girls were so nice. It seemed that he had a special lady friend in Athens and he tried to delay his take off from Tehran every time he left in order that he might spend a night in that romantic old city. I thought of the incorrect papers trick they had pulled in the morning! Everyone was talking excitedly as we walked from the plane to the terminal building, which was a beautiful new modern building that contrasted strikingly with the ancient hills and olive groves around it. The navigator, Ali was whispering to Dr. Cutler that it was too bad he had Mrs. Rose tagging along for he too, could have a good time in Athens. Laughingly Robin told Ali that he really didn't mind taking care of Mrs. Rose as long as Ali would see that the two *djelodars* from His Majesty's stable did not get into trouble.

We cleared customs without any problems and as we walked through the door we were approached by two well-dressed men, obviously Iranians from the Embassy. They informed us that they had had a call that day from His Majesty's Imperial Court that we were to be taken care of for the evening. I noted that the faces of our Iranian crew fell considerably. They did not want to be harnessed by Embassy people. Robin and I had thought we would get a quick look at the Acropolis and then take a tour of the Peta or old part of Athens. We hoped to have a good Greek dinner and to listen to some Greek music. Now this Embassy fellow was along, and he probably was from Savak.

We were ushered into three awaiting black limousines. Robin and I were in the car with the senior Embassy man and the crew and our two boys were split up in the other two cars. Our man pointed out the sights as we sped towards the city. Piraeus was that way; there was the Colosseum; there was the Acropolis in the distance on the hill. Most of what we saw were fleeting glances but fun to see. The cars stopped in front of what looked like a very exclusive hotel. It was, and we were told by our 'leader' that it was the best and most expensive hotel in Athens, the King George. After registering which consisted of signing our names only to a sheet of paper, no questions to be answered or passports to be handed in, as we were guests of the Iranian Embassy. We all hung around indifferently not knowing quite what to do. I could tell that the boys from the stable and the crew were rather overwhelmed by the hotel and our embassy officials who seemed not too inclined to spend the evening with us, but politely asked if we wanted to be escorted here or there. We were all so vehement about the fact that we needed no escorts they quickly and happily left. Robin and I were in a hurry to take in our sightseeing so agreed to meet in the lobby in a half an hour. I wondered about my partner for he was still showing some of the effects of his binge. I checked with Davoud and Abdula to see if they wanted to come with us to see the Acropolis but they sheepishly said if I did not mind they were going to see the town with Hossein, the load master, and his assistant. I told them to behave and not to take much money with them.

'You know, Mrs. Rose, I have been abroad before,' Davoud replied to my advice. A bachelor and very attractive, I was certain that he knew how to handle himself.

'Khonume Rose, *Naurahat menishi* (Do not worry).' was Abdulla's answer. I was a little troubled about Abdulal though; he was older than Davoud, about thirty-five and had a wife and three children; I always found him very naive and innocent. He had never been outside of Iran save to go to Kiesh Island with the horses that were taken there for his Majesty to ride during his Now Ruz vacation. I again warned them to be careful and went up to my room.

I was surprised when I returned to the lobby about forty minutes later, to find Robin all ready and chipper as could be. He had never been in Greece before either so was as excited as I was to get out to see this historical place. We thought we might be able to walk to the Acropolis so started walking in the direction we thought it would be. We stopped at a little street corner kiosk where we bought a map and guide book and some strings of worry beads. These were my only purchases in Greece and very inexpensive. They were, however, a great success as small gifts when I got back to Iran.

Having checked over the map we decided we had best hail a cab which at that time of late afternoon proved a problem, for most of the people had not come out of their houses from their afternoon nap and thus not many cabs were cruising the streets. A cheerful old fellow finally picked us up but when we said that we wanted to go to the the Acropolis he shook his head and indicated that it was not a good idea. We insisted however, and in a few minutes we were let off at the main gate. By now it was almost dark and we were not going to get a very good view of this world famous tourist attraction. Due to the fact that it was winter there was no sound and light. We had hoped that we might strike it lucky, but no. That must have been why our taxi driver was negative about taking us to our destination. As we walked up to the main entrance the moon began to climb into the sky and shortly the whole hill was illuminated almost as well as if it had been day. It was fascinating for us to see this ancient ruin having read so much about it and having seen Persepolis in Iran. The Greeks were the ones who had destroyed the Summer Capital of the Ancient Persians and the Persians had been to blame for much of the ruin of the Acropolis. The Greeks had been much more efficient in their destruction than had the Persians —it was obvious. But of course the Acropolis was strategically much more difficult to capture or plunder, being on the top of a hill. Persepolis was built into the side of a mountain with a great view on one side but with only the side of the mountain on the other.

As we walked and discussed this great wonder of the world we heard muffled giggles and sighs in the bushes of those young lovers who were taking advantage of the warm moonlit night. Unfortunately we were not able to bribe the guard into letting us inside, but we did spend three hours nevertheless, at this phenomenal place. Later we went to the Peta to listen to the haunting, yet gay music of the Greek guitars and finally to have a marvelous dinner. I introduced Robin to Retzina, Greek wine that I have loved from the first taste I ever had and he too took to it; we finished off the evening with yet another bottle of Retzina and finally weaved our way back to the King George.

The morning came much too quickly. My head hurt and my mouth felt stuffed with cotton wool. How would poor Robin feel? The call came that the Embassy cars were waiting and I was barely awake. I had a hasty cold shower, dressed and arrived in the lobby to find that the crew were still having their breakfast. I never ate before noon unless it was forced upon me but I did like a glass of juice and a black coffee. Robin was already seated eating a hearty breakfast so I joined him and choked down my libation. How could he look so chipper and healthy when he had had such an alcoholic time the previous day? I was in dreadful shape and had just had a little too much wine with and after dinner.

The crew of the plane went through a special gate agreeing to send a messenger to us at the duty free shop when they had refueled and were ready to go. Robin and I approached the immigration control and of course were immediately asked for our boarding pass. We had none! The little Greek man could not understand us and we could not understand him. He would not let us through.

'He's bloody wasting my time in the duty free shop!' complained Robin when the man signaled another, who came over. He spoke a little English. We could not enter through the control and into the customs hall until we showed our boarding pass, he reiterated.

'No pass! No need pass! Own plane. My plane! ELF 95. We go to England.' was how Robin tried to explain it. 'We have a private plane. It belongs to the Shahanshah of Iran.' he said.

'Iran?' questioned the other little man.

'Yes, my plane Shah plane! Eeraan. You know oil, benzine. Shahanshah! Eeraan.' continued Robin. Our two *djelodars* were in stitches behind us seeing the antics and trouble we were having.

'Oh, yes.' said the little man. 'You may go. We know your plane. You go to England.' He gave our passports a glance and a quick stamp and we were through.

In the customs hall Robin made a bee line for the alcoholic section. He bought a case of scotch. I was aghast.

'Robin, how are you ever going to get that back into Iran? You know the customs will never let it in duty free!'

'Use your head, girl. Why do you think I brought all those tack boxes? They certainly are not full and most of what is in them will be put on the horses.'

I had wondered why Robin had had three large baby blue tack boxes put on the plane. Actually the color should have been called Persian blue, or Royal blue, for it was the color of His Majesty's Royal Standard and the Stable color of the Imperial Stables. I now realized that our veterinary who had flown the horses to Kiesh Island several times before, knew what he was doing. When he had been in Kiesh he had been able to go to Dubai for shopping each time. Dubai was a free port in the Persian Gulf, and many things that were very expensive in Iran could be purchased reasonably there. Robin had mentioned that he brought a few things back from Dubai but I had not clued into the fact that he had smuggled them into Iran. I as-

196

sumed it was "diplomatic immunity" being a part of His Majesty's entourage.

I now decided that I too, had need of a few items that I would not be able to obtain in Tehran. Being a wino at heart I bought two cases of Retzina! The boys bought perfume for their lady friends asking my advice.

When Ali came into get us, we were laden with parcels to take out to the plane. It took us two trips to get the cases of wine and liqueur on board. Robin carefully took the horse blankets out of one of the tack boxes and packed our purchases in them, then replaced the blankets on top of the cartons.

It would be a five hour flight once we were in the air. Take-off was smooth and more or less on time, that is, Iranian time. I was just about to go up to my berth that I had secured for my reading and resting when Robin signaled me that he wanted me to look at something in the back of the plane. By the time I had crawled down the narrow ladder he was opening his Air Lingus luggage that he had been carrying with him —what a clever fellow! Two bottles of champagne sitting in plastic bags of ice. He handed me two clear plastic glasses to hold while he popped the cork of one of the bottles. The cork hit the ceiling of the aircraft but the pop was barely audible due to the racket of the engines in the aft section. He carefully poured out two glasses without spilling a drop, then set the bottle back in the ice in his hand luggage.

'Here's to the first Imperial Iranian Champagne Flight!' he toasted. We soundlessly clinked our plastic cups and each took deep gulps. My, it did taste good! I am a true lover of champagne even if it is not my usual morning libation.

'This will clear up that wine headache I am sure you have; mine is killing me!' admitted my companion.

'I never would have known that you were feeling poorly, Robin. I have been in agony but you looked so well this morning; I was sure you had no bad effects from our last night's escapade.'

We chatted and sipped until the bottle was finished. True, I began to feel much better; however, when he opened the second bottle I was not quite as enthusiastic. I could only think of how I would be feeling at the end of the trip if I shared a second bottle. Also there was the problem of having to use "the ladies room". When I drank champagne it always went right through me and on this military plane, facilities for the lone lady aboard were less than adequate. At the back of the plane there was a hole, part way up the side; this was where the men relieved themselves. After having taken their relief there was a wire handle that was pulled which emptied the tank into the air outside I presumed. We had joked about this system on our previous flight to Russia and I was still not sure if this was what really happened to the waste. Nevertheless, I could not picture myself sauntering up to the hole in the side of the plane, pulling down my panties and putting my little bottom up to the toilet. I hadn't actually measured it but I was certain that I wouldn't be able to reach it anyway. Too high for my short legs.

I said to Robin that I would just have a half a glass as he poured from the second bottle. 'What do you mean?' he questioned. 'We have to finish off the two bottles to make certain our cure is successful!'

'Well actually Robin, my real problem is that if I drink much more of this stuff I'll definitely have to relieve myself. Now can you see me putting my lily-white ass up to that hole over there in the back of the plane? I just don't think I could manage it. And I don't want to spend the next few hours crossing my legs.'

He doubled up with laughter. 'I'd never thought of that problem. It's so easy for a man to take a quick piss. I guess these planes are not made for the ladies of the air force. I wonder if the women's libbers have got a load of that yet. Couldn't they have a ball getting after the aircraft builders?'

After a few more moments while the two of us were chuckling away he came up with a solution.

'No problem, at the moment anyway. You can just hop in one of the horse crates; they're empty and no one will see you in there. If they do they'll know what you are doing so will give you your privacy. Now, drink up!'

I sipped, but slowly. Robin got way ahead of me on this bottle. I was beginning to feel a little light headed anyway. Eventually the champagne was finished. My companion looked rather wistfully at the empty bottle. 'I'll remedy this,' he commented and headed for the tack box that we had filled with our purchases. I took the opportunity to sneak up into the cockpit and climb into my bunk. I had my book but soon was nodding and eventually fast asleep.

A jolt awoke me! I could see the captain was very busy talking into his microphone and both pilots were adjusting levers and buttons. The navigator was working with something on his table. My ears were popping and in a few minutes the good veterinary doctor appeared up the ladder from the back. I could see that Robin was none too steady on his feet. As he walked forward into the tiny cockpit he bumped into the chief engineer who sat behind the two pilots. Eventually he was standing right beside the captain; however, as he leaned over to ask him a question he banged his head against the window. He was mumbling something and rubbing his forehead when the captain said, 'Mrs. Rose, would you please come here.'

I slid myself across the bunk to the ladder and cautiously climbed down. For some reason my balance was off and my ears were still popping. 'Are we descending?' I asked Ali the navigator. He nodded in assent.

'Khonume Rose,' started the captain in Farsi. 'I think that your horse doctor is drunk!'

'*Bali*' was my only reply. He obviously was.

'What are you going to do about it?'

'*Heech*.' What could I do about it? Nothing.

'But it is your responsibility, Khonume Rose. He must go and lie down in the back of the plane. You must take his whisky bottle away from him.'

Now how could I do a thing like that? He had about thirty-six of them. 'I will see what I can do.' Robin had been oblivious to the conversation for even though he did speak Farsi, in his state he had no comprehension. He very gladly went down to the back of the plane with me and when I took out a couple of horse blankets and fixed up a resting place for him he was only too cooperative to lie down and have a nap.

When I got back into the cockpit I told the captain not to worry that Dr. Cutler would rest most likely until we landed in England. I then asked why we were flying so low for it was obvious to me now that the reason I had been awakened was we had been descending and rather quickly.

'We have a slight problem. You see, our IFF is not working for some reason and the French authorities asked us to descend so that they could identify us.'

I had no idea what the IFF was so Ali explained that it is some sort of device that transmits a certain signal to the radar that is on the ground. Every country monitors all the planes that are flying over its territory and because the signal from our IFF device was not working on the plane we were asked to descend so that we could be identified. It was not enough to identify ourselves on the radio. There was nothing mechanically wrong with the plane, I was assured.

'Now, Mrs. Rose, what are we going to do about the doctor I have been told by my friends and others,' (probably the SAVAK information people) 'that the doctor likes his whisky but we cannot have him in the state he was in today when we have horses on the plane? I don't like horses anyway. I am very frightened of them. What if something happened?'

'Don't worry, Cyrus,' (I decided to use his first name to make him feel that I was really with him.) 'When it comes to his business, and that's horses, you don't have to worry about Dr. Cutler. You see, he will be very busy during the time that we have the horses on board so he is having his relaxation now. I can assure you he will not have a drop of whisky the day we are to pick up the horses.' I went back up to my roost where I read for some time before I heard the captain and copilot anxiously calling to me. They were pointing to something below the plane out of the window. My heart began to beat rapidly, what could it be? The adrenalin was rushing. When I got to the front window I saw that they had wanted me to get a good view of the White Cliffs of Dover. We were still flying very low and the view of these chalk white cliffs was spectacular. I had never seen them before. It must have been mental telepathy because a much improved Robin came up to the cockpit and too, got a good view of our first glimpse of England. Shortly thereafter we landed at Lynam Air Force Base.

The customs officials had to inspect the plane and made a big deal about the fact that we had straw in the horse crates. We were not allowed to let one piece of straw touch English soil. They actually wanted to burn it but somehow we persuaded them to let it go by. We all had our passports stamped and were hustled off to the visiting air force quarters. It was a dismal grey Second World War frame building that smelled. We were informed that we could have lunch there and sleep there until we left on the continuation of our flight. It was then that Cyrus informed us that it would most likely be a day or so before we could leave because he had to get the IFF fixed before we could pick up the horses. Robin obviously had no intention of spending the extra day or so in Lynam, thank goodness. He took me aside to say that the two of us should go into London where he could pick up veterinary supplies and drugs from the company that usually ships them to the Imperial Stables in Iran. Excellent idea, I thought, for I could also arrange to buy some tack that was dearly needed.

We quickly conned Ali, the navigator, into taking care of Davoud and Abdula and grabbed a local taxi that just happened to be sitting in front of the door of the barracks. We would call Cyrus the next evening to see what time our departure would be the following day. If there was to be a departure! Cyrus seemed doubtful that we would leave that soon. As a matter of fact, as we stepped into our cab he let it be known that perhaps it would be three or four days. We were positively gleeful as the taxi sped away to the train that would take us to London.

Our sojourn in London started with a stop at the Veterinary supplier. We arrived just before closing at about four-thirty in the afternoon so we were the only people in the place. There was a room about sixty feet long and half as wide that was filled with shelves in library fashion except that upon the shelves were drugs. I had a great time poking in amongst the shelves. I was able to get a huge supply of phenelbutazone, which we used for the jumpers and which was at that time difficult to obtain in Iran. Robin bought large quantities of the drugs he needed that were not available in Iran and all sorts of vitamin supplements. By the time we had spent three hours in the place we had spent thousands of pounds of Imperial monies.

After having arranged for delivery of the supplies to Lynam we took the subway to the center of town, got ourselves a couple of hotel rooms and went out for a fantastic dinner of seafood at Bentley's, a place we both knew.

The next day we went shopping for my tack. We had called Mr. Afshar, the ambassador from Iran to England, and arranged that the bills from Giddens,where Kambis had always done business in London, be sent to the Embassy. What fun we had in Giddens. We bought out the six or seven beautiful jumping saddles they had in stock. There were bits, reins, breast-plates and many other gadgets that I thought I needed. I recall that we topped the drug bill by thousands. But what fun we had doing it!

We called every evening and finally were informed that the plane would leave for Ireland the following day. We had four full days in that wonderful city of London, visiting galleries, eating delicious food, going to the theatre and shopping.

Before heading to the station I called the people in Ireland and told them to have their horses ready for us at Dublin Airport the next morning. Robin and I checked out of our hotel to catch the train for Lynam. It was a bit touch and go, for we made the last evening train for our destination by exactly two minutes. The will of Allah!

We had had no dinner but thought we could perhaps get something like a sandwich at the barracks. When we arrived however, we were to discover that everything in the kitchen was shut tighter than a drum. We could use the coin operated dispensing machines that were in the mess hall. They were all empty. We finally were able to get two cups of lukewarm chocolate. We had been eating such fine fares that past few days that we certainly could afford to skip a meal.

I had a tiny little room with two small twin beds and child's crib. It made me think of my own sweet children at home. I wondered how they were getting along. Don had been right to expect me when I arrived. We had already been gone for six days and would not be home for two more if all went well.

I was wakened twice by people banging on my door. I once got up to find that someone was looking for a Captain Jones. The second time I didn't bother to answer. About seven Robin knocked to tell me that if I wanted to use the shower it was free. All the crew had had theirs and so had he. There was no seperate facility for ladies in this army barracks so I had to wait my turn and hope that no one came in while I was taking my shower! I had never been in such a situation but was certain I would be less embarrassed than the man or men who might surprise me. Luckily I didn't have to find out.

I walked by the row of toilets that included one "Persian Version". There were so many flights of Iranian military personnel coming into Lynam that they had a Farsi toilet installed. This is a porcelain fixture that sits right over the drain hole. On this fixture are two foot rests. The idea is that one places one's feet on the appropriate spots, then squats right down to do one's business. For a westerner it takes many long months to adapt to this position but they say that the Iranians have the same problem using a western toilet. The rough concrete floor of the wooden shower stall reminded me for some reason of athlete's foot. I guess some subconscious memory from childhood which caused my feet to itch for weeks after this cold morning shower in England.

I gratefully accepted a glass of watered down orange juice and a cup of tea in the mess hall. That was about all that I could down in that barren looking place. I noted that Robin and the crew, sitting on their metal folding chairs, were picking at rather greasy looking fried eggs.

As we were being bussed out to the runway I could see that there were two more Iranian C 130s sitting next to ours. There must have been a reunion of some sort with three full crews in town. The Iranian planes could easily be distinguished from the British ones because they were painted like the desert, whereas the British were a true camouflage green.

'Oh yes, our friends came two days ago. We had a very good party in the town that night. We took the two boys from the stable with us. They did not drink very much Mrs. Rose, you don't have to worry. I took care of them.' Ali told me to my inquiry about the planes.

When Iranians are away from their homeland they seem desperately homesick. For some strange reason they all miss their desert country. Even well educated people who perhaps never expect to live in Iran again have an inner longing for the homeland, so when a group of Iranians happen to meet away from their own environs they get on as though they had been friends forever. There is a comradery amongst them that I have not seen in any other nationality. I could imagine what a party they had. Being Muslims they were not supposed to drink but when they got away from the eye of Mohamad in Iran they all tried their hand at it. They loved to party and they all loved to talk; in order that everyone got his turn at talking, the parties usually went on all night. I was sure they had had an all-night party two nights previously; no wonder they were all asleep when Robin and I arrived at ten the night before.

'Is everything all set to go, Ali?' I questioned.

'*Bali*, Khonume.'

'Did you get the IFF fixed, finally?'

'Well actually Khonume we were not able to find the part so we will fly without it.'

'But Ali, that's why we spent so much time in England. You were supposed to be having it fixed. How will we manage without it?'

'Not to worry Khonume. We will fly very high but if we are requested we will have to lower our altitude.'

'Well, I hope you know all about the way horses travel in a plane at a low altitude when we are hitting all those bumps the way we did when we flew over France on the way here. They don't like it. You will have the horses of His Majesty on the plane and he will not like it if they arrive injured.' I was laying it on a little thick but it was true that the horses worried about the air pockets that were often hit in these big planes when flying low. I really did not relish having four horses scrambling all day long.

Ali went over to the captain who was busy with the instrument panels; when he came back he said not to worry, we would just fly high no matter what. That sounded logical. I could imagine a squadron of French Mirages coming up to have a look at us because our pilot would not lower his altitude due to the fact that he did not want to disturb the horses of His Imperial Majesty the Shahanshah.

'Don't tell Dr. Cutler that the IFF is not in order, it will worry him and he will have enough problems today.' It was agreed.

It was a quick hour hop to Dublin and as we circled to land I was able to count four horse vans waiting at the side of the runway. I had been expecting some kind of slip-up due to the fact that we had to delay from the original time and date. I guess I had lived in Iran too long; the Irish, where horses are concerned, were super-efficient.

The plane landed without problems. We lowered the tail opening and jumped out to greet those expecting us. The only people were the owners of the horses and the Irish Agricultural Inspector who had arranged the health papers for the horses. No welcoming crew from the Irish government!

The load master with the help of Robin arranged for a fork lift truck to unload the pallets upon which we had the horse crates and I went with the boys to put the protective bandages on the horses. I ended up doing two horses myself and Abdula the other two because Davoud was ill. He said he could not bend down without being sick at his stomach. That was some hangover! Two days old.

A friend of Robin's from schooldays came out to the plane and the two of them disappeared inside the airport for some time. By the time they returned we had the horses on the plane and the captain was supervising the refueling and doing his routine check. Robin and his buddy, Johnny suggested that I then go into the airport terminal to have breakfast as Robin had. Aha! Good idea! I checked with the captain about our departure time and discovered that all the boys wanted to have a few minutes in the Irish duty free shop as they had never been to Ireland before and they were sure that there must be some Irish souvenirs they could take home to their families. I had time for breakfast.

The captain wanted to know what I was going to do about lunch for the crew. I hadn't a clue. Johnny suggested that there was an Air Lingus truck loading one of their planes just next to us so I went over there and asked if they could sell us some box lunches. For thirty two pounds we were able to get the eight lunches we needed; they would be delivered in just a few moments. It had now started to pour. When we had landed it had been misty; as we were doing up the horses it was drizzling; as we were loading it was raining and now it was a real downpour.

I had a very good breakfast of home baked Irish rolls and butter and then went to the duty free shop to get the boys moving. Ali was in there and came up to ask me a favor.

'You see Khonume, I'm not allowed to bring any liquor with me when I enter Iran. I noticed that you and the doctor have packed your big trunks with liquor. I was wondering if I bought a couple of bottles if you would get it into the country for me and then I can pick it up from you after we get back.'

'Of course, Ali. Get what you want and I'll take care of it for you.'

Robin had made another purchase, a case of Jaimeson's Irish. I bought some cognac for Don. I was looking forward to the duty free shop in Yugoslavia. One of the crew had been there before and had told me it was especially good. These Iranian flight crew were comparative shoppers in the duty free shops of the world.

Back in the plane, almost ready for take-off, I was relieved of my thirty two pounds and had eight lunches plunked on my lap. Having had to get up to stow the lunches I decided to go down to Irish soil one more time to have a final look. The sun was shining through an opening in the clouds and the Emerald Isle looked beautiful, even on the runway of Dublin Airport. As I was about to climb back in the plane for the final time a security policeman came running up to me.

'Hold on, hold on a minute now, Maa'm!' he shouted as he approached with mincing steps.

'Yes?'

'Do ye know tha'yer plane hasn't the proper clearance to leave this airport? To tell you the truth we didn't know you were even coming. We are going to have to take care of things in the proper manner now. Go in there and tell your captain that he will have to come to the office with me.'

'I know that he has filed our flight plan so there should be no problem; if anything had been irregular it should have been taken care of by the tower.'

'The flight tower doesn't ken whose here legal or illegal. Now you just go in there and tell your captain to come down.'

I could not believe that we had just merrily landed in Ireland without the proper clearance. My heart was beating fast as I climbed the stairs into the plane. Everything had gone so smoothly so far, now what was to happen?

'Cyrus, there is some little uniformed man down there who says that we do not have clearance to leave Dublin. As a matter of fact he says that we didn't have clearance to even land here. I think he is some sort of military security.'

'That's interesting,' Cyrus replied with a grin. 'You just strap yourself in, Mrs. Rose, and I will take care of that problem.'

I did as I was told and heard Cyrus give the orders to close the door of the plane and we began to taxi out. I couldn't see the little elfin man but I was sure he was shaking his fist. Cyrus was in contact with the control tower so we weren't flying blind. I just guessed we had decided not to take care of all the formalities. A typical Iranian trick.

We had no troubles on our nine hour flight to Belgrade. They would start when we landed. The French did not make us lower our altitude to identify ourselves, so the horses all rode as though this was an everyday affair and the grooms were able to catch up on their sleep. Robin and I took turns checking the horses every fifteen minutes. We had both bought the James Herriot books about the Yorkshire veterinary and were buried deeply in them. We chuckled and laughed until the crew had to ask what we were reading that was so funny. It was hard to explain and when we did they didn't understand what was so funny anyway.

Everything was meant to have been taken care of by the Imperial Court as far as giving our Irish horses stabling for the night so we expected to see a horse van near the runway when we descended, but there was nothing. We had been directed to park the plane at what seemed a long way from the terminal buildings and no one seemed to be around or to have taken note that we had arrived. The "Follow Me" car had disappeared and there we were waiting by our plane not knowing quite what to do.

'What happens now Khonumc Rose? You said that the horses would be taken care of when we arrived and it looks as if they are trying to pretend that we don't exist.' Cyrus was tired from the long flight and obviously wanted to close up the plane for the night and have a look at Belgrade. Actually, as most of us had never been in Yugoslavia, we were all quite anxious to have a look around. There was not too much we could do until we got the horses off the plane. We waited and waited until finally Cyrus said that he would go to the terminal to announce our arrival and ask what the procedure would be.

No sooner had Cyrus left on foot to take the long walk to the terminal building than a black security car appeared followed by a military jeep with four armed soldiers. There was much commotion and hustle and bustle as the military got out of the jeep and proceeded to scan us all, with the automatic rifles cocked under their armpits. One signaled with the barrel of the gun that he wanted to go into the plane. Our Iranian crew and stable help were frozen with fear! It was up to either Robin or me to escort the officer inside the plane.

'You had better go inside, Gail. I think that I should stay out here with our Iranian friends. They would feel safer with a man!' There it was again! But what about poor little me going inside that dark plane, for Cyrus had turned off the lights to conserve on power, with this mad Yugoslav?! I put on my most foreboding expression and walked in ahead. I turned and with my hand signaled for him to come in. We entered by the side door which was just to the rear of the second pallet. My guard began nosing around our luggage, that we had put on a pallet behind the two that contained the four horses, and was about to ask me to open the tack trunk that held our contraband liquor when one of the horses snorted! I have never seen a man look so frightened. He was so terrified that he cocked his gun. I pointed to the horses and he saw what had made the noise. I could tell that he was not at ease when he saw that our cargo was live horses. I ushered him closer and by sign language suggested that he walk up the aisle in front of the horses towards the cockpit. It was a rather narrow passage as the crates were as long as the pallet and the horse's heads hung over the front a couple of feet. We travelled with the horses facing sideways as it made it easier to get to each horse to attend to it if there was a problem. Also we were able to hang the hay nets from the side of the plane and eating always kept the horses quieter. My guard could not get out of the plane fast enough. He jumped down not waiting for me and I heard him shouting loudly to his compatriots. At least we had diverted his attention.

When I found my way back to the ground I saw that there was a third car parked beside the jeep; it bore the seal of the Imperial Embassy of Iran. I felt quite relieved. There were two little men well dressed in black business suits who spoke very good English and Yugoslav. Robin said that from the gist of the conversation there was no stabling for the horses and they were going to have to be kept on the plane. I groaned; the poor animals had already been on the plane for more than nine hours; the crew needed twelve hours off before they could fly on to Tehran.

It would be awful for them and the risk of them contracting shipping fever was good.

I tried to explain to the Embassy men that this was not good enough. We were here with His Imperial Majesty's horses to pick up a horse that His Excellency President Tito had given our Shah and there was no arrangement for these Imperial horses to rest for the night! This was ridiculous!

The problem turned out to be one of health regulations; we showed our papers but they were not looked at. There was no way that our horses were going to be allowed off the plane.

It was then I discovered that the Yugoslavs expected us to lock up the plane which they would guard for the night. No one was allowed to stay on the plane. I hit the roof! My fiery temper took over and I, in no uncertain terms, told one little man from the Embassy that it was his responsibility to see that we were able to leave the two grooms on board to care for the horses. We would also need a water supply to give the horses. If one animal became sick due to this mismanagement of the Iranian Embassy in Belgrade I would personally tell His Majesty about it. I also said that I would hold this man personally responsible. I took down his name, number and position in my little red book that looked quite official.

After some discussion amongst our Iranians and the Yugoslav officials we were informed that the boys, poor Davoud and Abdula, would be allowed to sleep on the plane. A water truck would be summoned immediately in order that we water the horses. There would be all night guards around the plane and one of these would escort our grooms separately to the restaurant in the terminal to have dinner.

Cyrus had returned and we began to close up the plane for the night. It would be cold for Davoud and Abdula so I suggested that they use the heavy wool horse blankets that were on top of our contraband. I also told them to blanket the horses, which were not used to this cold in their native Ireland. The two boys looked crestfallen but there was nothing more I could do. We waved them a fond farewell making certain that they had money for dinner and were whizzed off in the two waiting black limousines to the immigration.

Everyone was allowed through without any ado save for Mrs. Rose! Being a Canadian I needed a visa for Yugoslavia and Mr. Mehran had neglected to obtain one. Our Embassy officials smiled taking my passport, leaving me on the other side of the bars, and disappeared. My friends disappeared. Isn't that typical! I would have to spend the night with the horses too!

About ten minutes later a man approached me, obviously a Yugoslav official. He handed me my passport and proudly pointed out my new visa.

I thanked him profusely.

By the time we left the airport it was already deep dusk so there was no chance to see downtown Belgrade. Our Embassy officials told us there was not much going on in the city at any rate. The drive to our hotel, which was at the edge of the city, took about twenty minutes over a very good highway. The hotel stood within a complex of very modern office and apartment buildings. This we were told, was the type of center that was being developed in the country to take the place of the old antiquated office buildings that were being torn down. From the outside the atmosphere was austere and antiseptic at once.

As it was still early and we were told that dinner was not served until about nine we decided to take an hour and then we would all meet for a before-dinner drink. When it came to the time Ali the navigator was the only one to appear for cocktails bringing tales of tired and hungry associates whom we would see later at dinner. No matter, we had an interesting time talking about life of a young man in the Iranian Air Force who had signed up for twenty years.

Looking out the huge plate glass window at the stark view of lawns that looked bluish with the illumination of the mercury lighting and the very modern buildings nearby Ali explained that as there was conscription in Iran each young man was compelled to serve at least two years in the military; actually, there was spot conscription for the women as well. They took about twenty-five per cent of the female population. When conscripted you could sign up for the two year stint which was the usual, or sign up for twenty years. As a twenty year assignee there were a lot of advantages, over the two year people, and there was the guarantee of a secure job for the duration of your stint in the military.

Ali had been a twenty year man and was now becoming slightly dissatisfied after ten years of his obligation had been filled . . . granted, he was given air force housing at Mehrabad, but it was not very attractive being in a concrete compound of apartment buildings. He did not have a telephone and was not allowed one. He had to share a communal bathroom with another family. The main thing was, that now his pay seemed very poor. When he had enlisted, a young ignorant boy, it seemed good but as time went on with inflation and no hike in pay to offset it, Ali could not live the way he would like to without the help of his wife who was working, and what would happen if she became pregnant and her income stopped? There was no way he could ask for an early retirement and his life was totally controlled by the Air Force. He was even told who could be his friends. Cyrus our pilot, he told us, had been in the air force for twelve years and was a very good pilot. He had been offered a job with Iran Air that would have paid him about twenty thousand dollars a year (a lot of money in those days). Often Iran Air could take military pilots out to fly as civilians for it too, was a government organization. The Air Force would not let Cyrus out because he had flown the F5 from which he had ejected safely three times. Now due to his back which had been injured, he was on the more sedate C 130 but for security reasons the air force would not let Cyrus go. Later in the evening he himself told us how bitter he was.

The three of us finished our drinks and went downstairs to join the others for dinner. We were told that the supper club was open and served a delicious gourmet dinner, as well it had dancing. I don't recall what it was we had to eat but I do know that we had nothing but champagne to drink. Ali who was forbidden alcohol twenty-four hours before flight joined in! As the evening lengthened we ordered more champagne and all toasted the wonderful trip we had had with a great crew. The music was very good so I was on my feet dancing in turns with the group until the band stopped playing for the evening. Then waiter brought us the bill. When Robin calculated how much it was in dollars he sputtered slightly. 'It is about five hundred dollars, Gail. Who is going to sign it? You or me?'

'Why don't we both sign? No sense in putting the responsibility on one

213

set of shoulders.' I suggested.

We had originally agreed that we would meet for breakfast at seven, but due to the lateness of the evening we had told Cyrus to call everyone when he awoke and we would then get ready. It was after eight when the call came but I was still feeling fuzzy from all the champagne. It was after nine by the time we got to the plane and a bedraggled group it was at that. Davoud and Abdulla were also looking a little worse for the wear after their night in the plane, complaining that they were unable to sleep due to the cold. I did feel guilty, especially when we had had such a sumptuous evening.

'For heaven's sake, Gail. This is their job. We'll take them to the duty free shop. That'll make up for it.' That duty free shop certainly took care of everything!

Our Lipizzaner was waiting on a blue and white horse van so as the loadmaster got himself organized to put the horse on the plane Robin and I went over to have a look. It was a very pretty animal. Well made with lovely intelligent eyes but . . . it was a stallion! My orders said that we were to pick up a mare. Robin and I looked at the horse and then at each other and burst into laughter.

The trainer of the horse came up to me with a dossier neatly typed up that gave all the information we would ever need about the horse including a long document about his training to date. It was all written in Slav!

Through an interpreter we did learn quite a lot about the horse but no one would give in when we kept insisting that this was the wrong horse. Even our Embassy officials who knew nothing about it insisted that we were incorrect; we should have been expecting a stallion.

I remember that once the horses had arrived in Iran Agha Bozorg, Kambis' father, came to the stable one afternoon to look at all the horses we had brought back. I purposely kept the Lipizzaner until the end to show him. When we brought Neopalitano Streaka out his first comment was,

'Mrs. Rose, you have brought me the wrong horse.'

'I know I have, sir.'

'Why did you bring the wrong horse?'

'Because this is the horse they brought to the plane. I told them it was not the horse you were expecting but they refused to budge. It was either this one or nothing.'

'So you brought this one. Good! Though I cannot see what good one Lipizzaner stallion is going to do us?'

'But Aga Bozorg, he is not here for a purpose; he is here to be shown to guests as a gift from President Tito. He is to be ridden and enjoyed, that's all. You should take him yourself to ride. Maybe even His Majesty would like riding him.'

'Yes, yes, we will see.' But I could tell he was not pleased with the gift.

Later on he did ride the horse but didn't like it due to the rough high stepping gait. His name became Taj and he became a hack for guests. Poor Taj, his talents were never realized.

After a final shopping in our last duty free shop before returning to Iran we took off with the Lipizzaner stallion unhappily scrambling around his crate. He was a problem the whole trip but did make it safely. We were not able to land in Doshuan Tappee near the stables because it was dusk and there were no landing lights there, thus we had to go to Mehrabad. As we had radioed ahead the truck from the stable was waiting for us. So were Khanlakhani and about twelve of the boys from the stables. They all wanted to see the new horses.

We were able to unload quickly without being approached by anyone from customs. Our stash of goods from the duty free shops across the world was safely put on the *vanette*, (pick-up- truck) and driven to the stable by my friend Mizapur. He had strict orders not to let anyone touch the trunks until either Dr. Cutler or I arrived. We had locked them and kept the keys but it was amazing how often someone would take a hack saw to a lock to get into something that might be of interest.

I ran into the VIP lounge to call Don to meet me at the stables before I got in the car that had been sent to drive Robin and me back to Farahabad. We had not even had to go through immigration. We had given our passports to a little man who said they would be returned the next day. And they were!

We had arrived safely. Everyone who counted seemed to be well pleased with the Irish horses. The trip was a success.

The only aftermath of the trip that rather saddened me was that about a week later Ali telephoned me to say that the air force had forbidden him and any other of the crew to see Robin and me socially. In the military if you wanted to socially see a foreign resident of Iran you needed to first apply for clearance. It had not been granted. Ali himself would come to my house two evenings later to pick up the things for himself and the other boys of the crew. I asked him to bring his wife and said we would have the Cutlers for dinner. One last party! It turned out to be a really enjoyable evening. Ali's wife was a fun loving person with a great sense of humor. I was sorry that this would be our first and last such evening for I was sure we could have become good friends. But it was not to be.

Robin had a telephone call about two months later from Cyrus, who was rather upset. The air force usually allowed them a small amount for hotel rooms the nights they were in foreign countries. On this trip, in Athens and Belgrade, the crew had been taken with Robin and me to the best hotels and been put up by the Embassy. Somehow the Embassy had forwarded the bills for the rooms to the Air Force which had deducted the amount from the crews' pay. I felt this was completely unfair as the crew hadn't had a choice of going elsewhere. They were ushered by the Embassy staff to these hotels and told to stay there. Cyrus wanted to know what Robin or I could do about it.

We talked it over and finally decided that we had not better interfere.

We ourselves had far exceeded our expense accounts and it was common knowledge at the stable that we had brought in a lot of contraband liquor; Kambis must know all this for he was that well informed. We decided to do nothing.

I felt badly when Cyrus called me a few weeks later to see what we had been able to do. I decided to mention it to Kambis and he told me he would take care of the problem.

It was about a year later that Robin and I were trying to get money out of Kambis for some project or other when he said, 'You two certainly know how to spend my money. I'm still getting over the shock of your dinner in Belgrade!'

We got the money!

LEBANON

James Underwood was probably one of the biggest single boosters of Show Jumping in Iran. He was an Englishman who had spent many years in the Middle East. As a very young man he worked for the British Show Jumping Association getting out their press releases and so forth. His true love was of racing but somehow he was not able to land anything in that field, so he took a position in the lesser sport of show jumping; at least it was still to do with horses. Being young and adventurous he soon grew tired of the job at the BHSA and decided to see the world. He spent quite a few years in Egypt working for the big English newspaper there however, when things began to get tense he moved on to Lebanon. Soon he decided that Beirut was not for him, becoming a bit too explosive! That was when he answered an advertisement for a reporter needed on the staff of one of the two English newspapers in Tehran.

In 1967 James arrived in Iran and took the Tehran Journal by a storm. He was very successful and his bold way of writing about the most delicate matters in the Iranian news made him a respected and popular columnist. He very quickly graduated from reporting the very mundane happenings about town to being asked to attend and report some of the most important social functions. To have a trusted newspaper man who was thought well enough of to report happenings in the social life of members of the Imperial Court was almost unheard of! James did occasionally stick his neck out and get his fingers wrapped for making some critical remark about the Imperial family or not praising enough some social reform or other. I remember one article in which he was discussing the five top families of Iran and of course included in this article was the Pahlavi family, that of His Imperial Majesty. James had put the names of these top Families in Alphabetical order thinking this would be the fairest way and would cause less ire amongst the people about whom he was writing. The Khalils and Khosroshahis came before the Pahlavis. This created a storm from the press office of the Imperial Court. Pressure was brought to bear upon the paper for which James was working and he was refused permission to do any further reporting until notified. This unexpected holiday lasted only two days, for Her Majesty heard of the misjudgment of the press office and made an apology about the incident.

The papers were all heavily censored , but as well as the censorship the Imperial Court press department carefully read every line in all the papers in the country and if it was found that anything whatsoever was out of line with the guides put out by their office, disciplinary action was taken. Either the paper itself or the individual reporter needed to account for the error in protocol.

I met James for the first time when I went to the "Pony Club" instruction that was held at the Imperial Stables when we first visited Iran. I had found him very pleasing and extremely informative. He was a man who could pass for an old thirty five or a young fifty five. No one knew exactly how old James was and that was the way he wanted to keep it. We became very good friends over the years and I have James to thank for a lot of the good publicity I received.

That first day we met, there were many people hanging around to get a glimpse of the Crown Prince and his sister as well as His Majesty himself, but amongst the crowd two peculiar men stood out. One was wearing a beige leather cowboy jacket with fringes and a pony skin Stetson hat; he was a fairly attractive Iranian sporting a small mustache. He would have been about thirty five. Next to him was a rather large, both in height and breadth, man also wearing a cowboy jacket but his was brown. He had acute features that showed that he must have been very good looking in his day which now was obviously over. The two of them were be leashed with three apricot miniature poodles. A most unlikely sight.

'You see those two funny looking chaps over there.' James pointed them out. I nodded. 'They are a very interesting couple. The older one is Prince Davelou, he is the Imperial Court landscaper. Educated in Paris and all that. He is actually a Khadjar but well favored by the present regime. He was just caught in Switzerland smuggling drugs. Do you know that they put him in jail there and the Shah paid his bail and brought him back here? The younger fellow is his "friend". They have been living together for some time. He was a bus driver for the Tehran Transit before he was selected for a better life! This is all very hush-hush so don't mention it!' I did question Louise Firouz about it, who said that she was not sure if it was the same Prince Davelou that had been brought back after having been caught for drug smuggling but she could verify the story about the bus driver.

James covered the Pony Club happenings and every event that had to do with horses in Iran. When we started having the friendly competitions at Nowruzabad and Dashte Beheshte that summer James attended each one and gave such good publicity that we began to have quite a number of spectators at the events. When we commenced the Show Jumping Schedule in 1973 James wrote something almost every day on the sports page.

Thus, it was not surprising that James should come to Kambis with the information that at a party given by the Lebanese Ambassador, James had been quietly informed by his host that the Lebanese were very interested in coming to Iran with their horses to compete in a Show Jumping competition. At this time General Khosrodad was actually president of the Riding Federation so Kambis passed the word on to the General. Kambis had been Riding Federation President but when he was given the title of President of the Football Federation pressure was brought to bear and eventually he did relinquish the post for about a year, when he again took it up because General Khosrodad was unable to continue due to his military commitments.

Correspondence flew back and forth between Iran and Lebanon and things seemed to be going very smoothly. A group of Lebanese came over to visit us in Iran to check out our establishment and see if our standard of jumping was close to their caliber. It was felt that the Lebanese who had competed in Europe were much stronger than the Iranians. I was put in charge of escorting the three man delegation around the Farahabad complex and showing them where their horses would be stabled, which was to be at the Farahabad Club. The men were most impressed with our facilities. Our three big sand rings were more than adequate and they thought well of the obstacles we would be using in the competitions. They stayed on through Friday to watch a competition in which luckily every event was won by an Imperial Stables rider; I myself actually won one and was second in the only other event I had entered.

Everything seemed to be set up including the dates which would be mid-April.

At The Royal Horse Society and The Riding Federation we were working hard on schedules and getting the rules and regulations for the competition completed to send to Lebanon.

Then the disappointment came! The Lebanese informed the Iranian Federation that they had decided they could not afford the transportation for their horses. It was to happen again! But, no! General Khosrodad got on his wagon and went directly to the Shahanshah to ask him if he would lend planes to transport the horses to and from Lebanon. His Imperial Majesty did want Iran to become international in every field possible but he would not lend two military planes to transport the Lebanese horses. He would lend ONE plane. It meant that the Lebanese would only be able to bring eight horses with them but it was certainly better than none.

We began a program of intensive training that was to last two months. The date of the competitions would be in June due to the change of transport plans. In June due to the heat, the competitions would have to be held at night. In our training program we included our weekly shows some of which we had at night to give the horses experience at jumping under the lights.

I had decided that as I was the National Trainer I would stick to that job and not compete myself. I continued to ride my little horse Roshan but would turn him over to Kambis for the Lebanese events. Included on the team were Ali Rezai, Ezat Vodjdani, Reza Tarash Kashani who would ride his Moroccan Barb Shehey, Reza Hadavand, Hossein Karimi Majzoob , Kambis Atabai and General Khosrodad , all from the Imperial Stables. As well there was Hushang Tehmouri from the Imperial Guards. Ali Reza Soudovar fielded Freddy Elghanian, Goli Bakhtaar and Marion Haratunian, all whom kept their horses at his Dashte Beheshte Stables in Karadj. General Djahanbani who had his own stable but trained with Ali would be the final member of the team. Our team of thirteen riders would be fielded with two horses each so it made for a rather uneven match if you were going to count numbers. The Lebanese were bringing five riders and eight horses.

When the day of arrival for the Lebanese came everything seemed in readiness. The Farahabad Riding Club had emptied eight of its stalls to make room for the visitors.

The day the Lebanese horses were due to arrive in Tehran, Robin was called upon to make an emergency call in Karaj so it was I who was sent to meet the plane. I would meet the veterinary from the Department of Agriculture who would be there to check the papers of the incoming horses. I took along four of the djelodards from the stable to help unload the horses.

Naturally the plane was late and we had to sit and cool our heels in a dusty little Quonset hut at the edge of the runway. It was about a hundred and ten in the shade and the seats were of plastic imitation leather. Even though there were fans tirelessly stirring the air it was a very uncomfortable wait.

When we heard the loud roar of the C 130 despite the heat outside, we all rushed to watch the plane taxi to a stop about a hundred meters away. All were consumed with curiosity to see what these great Lebanese horses looked like.

The first thing that caught my eye as I saw the first pallet lifted off the plane was that the two horses were poorly groomed and their mares untended. I was surprised, for to me it showed slovenly horsemanship to let the horse's mane get long, thick and shaggy. The other six horses were slowly off-loaded and even though they were a good strong looking bunch of horses not one of them really caught my eye. I felt assured that we would do very well during the few days of competition.

The Lebanese speak Arabic and the Persians speak Farsi but the two languages, though written with the same basic alphabet, are no more alike than Spanish and German. The veterinary who had come along with the horses gave me the veterinary papers for the animals which I in turn passed along to the Iranian government vet. He surreptitiously glanced through them and then said to me that he really didn't understand them. That sounded par for the course! I had never had to read such papers with results of tests for Dourine, Glanders, African Horse Sickness and other diseases. I questioned the Lebanese vet whose English was not very good. He said that he spoke much better French. Just what I needed! Some of the papers were in Arabic but others were in French. He explained as best as he could and I in turn went carefully over them with our Iranian vet. We looked at each horse and checked its markings with the papers and as our Iranian veterinary read off the list of diseases immunizations and tests I cross checked with the papers. It all seemed to be in order so the official stamp was placed on the papers of each horse and they were handed back to their grooms.

There was of course, the usual round of parties given for the visiting team which took up every evening that there was not a competition, and during the day I was busy making certain the parcour was set up and keeping track of my usual jobs at the Imperial Stables. We arranged for the visiting team to have a schooling under the lights the night before the first competition and the horses went very well though my original opinion didn't change. I felt we had much better horses.

The night of the first competition came. We would have two competitions each of the three evenings. One for the A Jumpers that would be over a course of jumps of up to 1. 40 and a B division for horses that would jump up to 1. 20. It was quite embarrassing for the Lebanese. I felt for them.

The results were as follows:

B Jumpers. Table A:

1st Feridoun Elghanian -Sunshine (Iran)

2nd General Mohammad Khosrodad -Heydarbaba (Iran)

3rd Golnar Bakhtiar -Shapdiz (Iran)

4th Makram Alameddine -Inchallah (Lebanon)

5th Habib Kassir -Von Pappen (Lebanon)

6th Reza Tarash Kashani -Sheyhey (Iran)

A Jumpers. Table A:

1st Ali Akbar Rezai -Shahbab (Iran)

2nd Ezatollah Vojdani -Shabrang (Iran)

3rd Kambis Atabai -Rostam (Iran)

4th Habib Kassir -Zarafeh (Lebanon)

So it continued throughout the three days of competition with the Lebanese getting a placing or two but Iran took all the major prizes

The parties were all enjoyable and the Lebanese guests could not have been pleasanter but we all knew that they were humiliated to have come to Iran and done so poorly. At the final dinner party the president of their Equestrian Federation, Mr. Fauzi Gandour, stood up and made a speech in which he invited the Iranian team to come to Lebanon in the fall of the year to compete there. 'I hope that when you come to our country we will give you a better run for your money. It is not a shame to have been beaten by such good horses and riders.' It was obvious that he had some big plans for the fall and we were to find out what those plans were in the near future. Mr. Gandour was a man of action and he planned to improve his Show Jumping Team.

Gen. Khosrodad and his girls, Bahman Shahandeh at back

225

PRINCESS FATIMAH

Shortly after the termination of the Lebanese competitions I was at the office working out the autumn schedule when I was summoned by my boss. He was still elated at our performance against the Lebanese team and was at any moment ready to discuss it again so when he brought up the subject I was not at all surprised.

'You know, Gail, it has done wonderful things for Show Jumping in Iran. Why, the whole Royal Family is extremely pleased that we made such a good showing. It has certainly endorsed my hiring of you which as you know was a sticky situation at first and it has made Mr. Alam have more respect for me and my "games" as he calls my interest in jumping. As a matter of fact, Princess Fatimah has just called me on the telephone and she is bringing some English friends of hers down to the stable this afternoon. She wants to show them some of our horses. I would like you to have a demonstration of jumping for them. You know what to do. We should show some of our Arabs and perhaps Shahin our new Turkoman stallion and then have a few home breds jump, a Turkoman or two and two or three of the German horses to show that we can take the big fences too. As a matter of fact, I would like you to ask Don to come down as well. This man Bridell I think is his name, is involved in the construction of helicopters and is a very big businessman. Don could fill him in well on some of the business aspects of Iran.'

'If you want to ask Don to come down to the stables you had better call him yourself.' I commented.

'What is the matter? Aren't you two speaking or something?'

'No, no. It is just that I'm home so seldom due to my work both here at the office and at the stable he has the children calling me "Mrs. Rose"! I am sure he will be most honored that you would like him to come, but I do think he would like you to call him yourself.'

Kambis picked up his phone and had his secretary get Don on the line.

'Don, this is Kambis. I have your wife in my office. I wanted her to relay a message to you but she refused telling me that you two are not speaking; she said I had to call you myself.' There was a pause and Kambis chuckled. 'I hear you think I am working her too hard. Well, don't worry, you will be off to Europe in another few weeks for a well-earned holiday.' He asked Don to help out with the princess and Mr. Bridell, then hung up.

'Is there anything else you want to discuss with me before I go on back to the stables?' I asked. There was not; so I excused myself and went back to my office to tidy up my desk and then drove back to the stables.

I decided that I would not ride myself but would put Ezat Vodjdani on Roshan because Shabrang had injured his hind fetlock and Alborz, the young Irish horse, was still too unpredictable to put in a demonstration for a member of the Imperial Family. I arranged for a number of the Iranian bred stallions to be lead out; Kambis could give a little spiel about each one. Then we would have two of the stable's broodmares brought into the ring with their foals; we had a couple of very good looking foals that had been sired by our Thoroughbred Stallion. Davoud Bahrami would ride his little mare Mojgan and Ali Rezai would put Zahak over some fences as the example of Iranian bred Jumper. I picked Hossein Karimi Majzoob on Shabahang and Rezai again on Shahab to jump the bigger fences. The plan all set out, I got Makeki to set up the jumps that I would check before the big performance. I was typing out the plan to give to Kambis when Ezat came into my office.

'Khonume Rose I have a special request. I think you will not say "yes" so I am not sure whether to ask you or not.'

'Fire away, Ezat.'

'Well, I'm not sure you will like what I have to ask. You always say that when you make a decision it must be stuck to.' He paused not seeming to know what to say next.

'Well, go on. What is the trouble? Do you not want to ride Roshan?'

'Oh, yes. I am so happy that you will let me ride your horse; it is an honor because I know how you feel about that horse. It's just that I want to ask you to let me jump Alborz over the bigger fences with Ali and Davoud.'

'Ezat, I think it's too soon for Alborz. He just arrived here from Ireland five months ago and he isn't really ready to jump the bigger fences yet. He hadn't had much done with him until he arrived here and you know yourself how hard you have worked. You don't want to spoil the whole thing in one shot. I'm putting up some big fences for the boys; granted they will be only individual obstacles but they are not going to be small.'

'I know all this Khonume, but I want to show you that Alborz has wonderful ability. I think he is ready to go in the big classes.'

He had been pushing me for weeks to let him enter Alborz in the bigger classes but I had refused wanting the horse to gain some real confidence over the smaller jumps before moving him up.

'Well, I know all that too, Ezat. After all, I bought the horse; do you think I would have bought that ugly looking thing if I didn't think he could jump? I am the trainer and I too know what he can do. So let's forget it.'

'OK, Khonum,' he said with a smile. 'I thought that was what you would say.'

When he left the office I began thinking about the horse Alborz and how well he had done in the shows of late. Why, he had been in the prizes in all but one of the Lebanese competitions. It might be fun to see how he would attack a few big fences. I suppose there was no harm in trying. If we had trouble I would just tell Ezat to pull up. I went over to the door and saw Ezat's slim form dejectedly walking slowly over to the tack room. I presumed that he had made some sort of bet with the rest of the boys. They constantly would bet with each other about how I would accept an idea or if I would grant some special request. I had always told them not to be afraid to ask me something, for all I could say was 'no' and perhaps some of their suggestions would be good ideas that would help. My office door was always open to my riders.

'Ezat!' I called. He turned around, 'I have changed my mind. You may ride Alborz when Shabahang and Shahab jump. We will just put him over the 1. 40 jumps though not the higher ones.'

'*Muchekeram*, Khonum.' He jumped with glee. He let out a war whoop and I saw the faces of his cohorts appear through the door of the tack room. Ezat had obviously won more than the change of my decision that afternoon.

At the allotted time the guests arrived. I waited with Don and Kambis to be presented to the Princess and her friends. I could see that the little tea house by the side of the ring was a bustle and I noted that the Imperial champagne glasses were set out on trays. Champagne and caviar it was to be then. I couldn't wait until my job was completed so that I could have a sip of that wonderful champagne that was especially bottled for His Majesty by some unknown vineyard in France. Each bottle was labeled with the Imperial Iranian Crown in gold and had black lettering "Mohamad Reza Pahlavi". I had once tasted it in the Atabai home and it was truly the best champagne I had ever put to my lips. His Majesty did not drink alcohol but he did enjoy wine and especially his own champagne on occasion.

I found the pretty princess simply charming when I met her. She was about forty but looked much younger. Her hair was blondish brown and she wore a very attractive white pant suit. Her features were that of her older brother but they looked very pretty on her. She had a lithe youthful figure for someone her age. I had heard she was an excellent tennis player and also the only woman pilot in Iran. Her main interest was in flying helicopters and of course the only helicopters in the country were military. It wasn't difficult for her to arrange to use a military helicopter, for not only was her brother the Shahanshah but her husband, General Khatami, was the chief of the Imperial Iranian Air Force. Unfortunately, General Khatami met with a very tragic death in 1975.

When I first arrived in Iran I had visited the country home of Ali Reza Soudovar one afternoon; he had as a guest, a young Frenchman who was giving the first instruction to Mahmadi, Ali's brother, in flying a hand gliding kite. I spent most of the afternoon watching this lesson and listening in. To me it was a terrifying thing to fly through the air on such a device, but it fascinated me. I was reminded of Leonardo da Vinci and his early experiments in flying. Later on in the day I had been introduced to Stephan and learned that he had been brought to Iran by General Khatami to teach him how to fly a kite. It has been said that the General was a real dare devil and wanted to try everything. It was a shock to Iran when General Khatami was killed while flying free on a kite over Dariush Dam near Shiraz in the autumn of 1975. His Imperial Majesty was so angry that one of his most valued Generals and husband of his sister had killed himself in such a foolhardy way that he refused to allow a period of official mourning. The funeral was very quiet and the day after, it was as if Khatami had never existed. There were rumors of treachery, of course. One line of gossip was that the general had not intended to fly free that day but the rope attaching the kite to the boat had been frayed and had severed of its own accord.

I happened to meet up with Stephan again some months after the tragedy and questioned him about it.

'You know,' he said, 'I told the General many times not to try to fly free at that Dariush dam, for there were always treacherous cross-currents of air. I myself, a young man, had many troubles with those currents when

I was demonstrating to the General. I told him that he must never let free from the boat but he didn't listen. A draft came and took him and dashed him against the side of the mountain. *Adieu!'*

After the introductions and a congenial chat I excused myself to do my behind the scene job of getting the show on the road. Kambis and Don both gave comments about the stallions and breeding stock. At one point Kambis commented, 'Your wife certainly has you well educated, Don. I think you know more about the horses than I do.'

'She talks about them in her sleep!' was my dear husband's reply.

I stood in the center of the ring when the jumpers came in, for I always liked to be there to make constructive criticism if necessary, and Kambis felt it made the show look more like an informal schooling. Also the King had liked it that way. Kambis had said, 'Give lots of instructions in Farsi; the princess has heard about how cute it is, from her brother.'

I saw Kambis taken aback when he saw that Alborz was to jump with the German horses. I myself, was very nervous. The Iranian horses had jumped their course very well. Now our imported stock needed to do their part. Shabahang went first then came Alborz. He was all business and jumped the six obstacles perfectly. I heaved a great sigh of relief. When we had raised the fences for Shahab and Shabahang to jump again I saw Ezat signal to me that he wanted to try but this time I didn't relent.

The show had gone very smoothly; when I walked over to where our visitors were seated to get my champagne, the princess told me how impressed she had been with the big bay horse from Ireland.

'Mrs. Rose, I almost told you not to let him jump when I saw that you were putting Alborz over those big fences.' was Kambis's comment.

'I knew you would have a fit, Kambis, but Ezat really wanted to do it and being the Champion of last year he wanted to ride over the big fences for the Princess, so what could I do but let him try. I think it was good for the horse too, and it shows us that he really has gained confidence.'

My champagne and caviar were not forthcoming and everyone seemed to be moving off someplace. I was shattered but could not very well say, 'Hey, where's my champagne?'

'Don had suggested that we take Mr. Bridell, who was a coaching man, over to the carriage house to show him His Majesty's carriages' Princess Fatimeh informed me.

The princess was driving her friends around herself in her late model Chevrolet so Kambis, Don and I got into Don's chauffeur driven car to meet them at the carriages.

'It was a very good show you put on, Mrs. Rose. I want to compliment you on it.' Kambis said as we headed for the other side of the compound.

'I am glad you all enjoyed it. But I have a complaint to make. While I was out there working so hard you were all sipping on champagne and eating caviar and you didn't save any for me.'

'I thought of it,' said Don. 'But when I saw they were on the last bottle anyway I decided that I might as well drink the last glass. You always like to have two glasses, not just one.'

The Imperial carriages were housed in a very small little building that was not really conducive to showing them to the general public. Kambis was having a larger building built where they could be seen by visiting personages but it would not be ready for some time.

The coachman in charge was Abdul Hossein Rezai. He claimed to be seventy years old but he had lived under five Shahs so he must have been at least ninety. He himself had driven four Shahs, the last two of the Kadjar dynasty, Shahs Mohammad Ali and Ahmad Shah, as well as Reza Shah and the present Shahanshah. In between Ahmad Shah and Reza Pahlavi there was a Kadjar Crown Prince who was never crowned but who had ridden in the state coaches. Abdul Hossein had no idea there was any distinction between the Kadjars and the Pahlavis. His father had worked for the Imperial court and his son, Ali was one of the best riders in Iran riding for the Imperial Stables. He was in effect, a man devoted to his job and King. It was seldom that he had visitors in his carriage house but when he did he loved it. I always took my own personal visitors to see the carriages and he told the same story with me translating, word for word, each time. Kambis allowed me to do this for Mr. Bridell.

The commentary by Abdul Hossein went as follows:

'This *deroshki* was made in Russia for Faith Ali Shah. It is 150 years old. This coach was made also in Russia for Mohammad Shah; it is 120 years old.' These first two vehicles were obviously very old but in perfect shape. They had both been repainted just a few months before by an old *deroshki* painter in South Tehran.

'This is the coronation coach of Nasuradin Shah,' he pointed out a lovely small coach the interior of which was a soft cream brocade. As Nasuraddin was crowned in 1848 it was indeed very old. It was one of the first of the coaches that had been made in Austria for the Iranian Royals.

The coach of Muzafaradin Shah who reigned from 1853 to 1907, the year Iran gained its first constitution, was made in England. This coach was also used by Mohammad Ali Shah who reigned but two years after his predecessor. In this coach the faithful Shah had been brought to Tehran from Esfahan where he had been assassinated. The story goes that he rode in a sitting position so that the population would not know that he was dead. It was only after his arrival in Tehran that the announcement of his death was made however, it was never really publicly proclaimed that he had been assassinated.

Sultan Ahmad Shah had a beautiful coach brought from England; its windows were beveled and etched around the edges; there was a beautifully hand tooled cornice of solid brass around its top; it shined like black patent leather and the Pahlavi crest on its door did look very impressive indeed. This coach had been used by Reza Shah for his own coronation in 1925.

Some of the coaches did bear the Khadjar crest which had just been painted on a few months previously. Until recently the name Khadjar had almost been *verboten* in the country but as the Pahlavi dynasty became more and more secure the Khadjars were admitted to have existed for the hundred and fifty years of their reign .

'And this,' said Abdul Hossein with reverence in his eye, 'is the coronation coach of our Imperial Majesty the Shahanshah Aryamehr.'

This coach had been brought from Austria only a few months before the coronation of the Shah and the Empress. It was a huge coach not unlike in shape, the Royal Coronation coach of the British Royal Family. But this coach was painted a baby blue, the Imperial Color of Iran. There was much decoration of gold leaf, the four turrets at the corners being of solid brass, to look like gold. The driver's seat up front was draped in a soft blue velvet with fringe and tassels of gold braid. The interior of the coach was decorated with a beautiful silver blue brocade and upon the floor was a mohair carpet of the Royal shade of blue. The *piece de resistance* however, was the huge crown, a replica of the Pahlavi crown, which adorned the top and center of the coach. In fact it was so gaudy and brash that this coach, in which rode His Majesty and the Shahbanu for his coronation, and in which they rode once a year for the opening of parliament, was simply magnificent.

This Imperial Coronation coach had been ordered by His Majesty for his coronation years before he was actually crowned. He refused to have himself crowned King of all Persia until he had an heir and until the country was in a stable position both financially and politically. The coach arrived a month before the coronation along with its matching baby blue harness and postilion saddles. The eight white German coach horses would be used to pull the coach at the coronation. I can imagine the excitement and fuss that was made the first time the new harness and coach were to be used. It was felt by Abulfath Atabai, who was then Master of His Majesty's Horse that there should be a practice with the coach, even before the rehearsals for the coronation. So the horses were harnessed and hitched to the new coach and off they went around the roads of Farahabad. At that time the stable's roads were not well constructed and the gates were very narrow. As the horses turned the corner up by the main gate there was a misjudgment as to the tightness of the turn and the coach tipped over in slow motion as its wheels caught the edge of the curb. Disaster! Disaster! Abulfath went mad! And so he should have. A team of men from Austria had to be sent to repair the damage to the tune of thousands of dollars.

There were other lesser vehicles in the carriage house. A pony cart handmade in Iran a hundred years ago. One of the first Iranian made *droshkies*, a landau sent to an Iranian prince by a Russian prince.

Mr. Bridell was most pleased to have been able to see all these Imperial vehicles and the princess herself said, 'Why Don, I would never have thought of showing the carriages. It has been a most interesting experience for me too. I really didn't know that we had all these.'

Turning to Kambis she said, 'You know, we should have a proper place to display them rather than this cramped little garage.'

'I am working on another building but it will take time to complete. Eventually we will have wonderful facilities to display the carriages.'

After The Princess and her guests bade us farewell Kambis invited Don and me to his house to have a drink before we went on home to have dinner. He was pleased with the afternoon for he was sure that the Shah's younger sister would make a favorable report on the afternoon's activities.

I was given my glass of champagne after all!

SUMMER VACATION AND TRAVEL

The beginning of August Don and I went off on a much needed holiday to Europe. Actually the first few days we were to be in Rome where Don was to make a report on a big aluminum sheet rolling mill that was to be built in Iran. Don had been on loan from his company Reynolds Metals, to the Iranian Aliminium Company (IRALCO). The mill was to be put into production by a company owned by Princess Shams who was the Shah's older sister. An Italian company was making a bid on the project and Mr. Afshar, the Iranian Ambassador to Italy, who was also the financial advisor to Princess Shams, would give the final OK for the project. Don had felt all along that there had been some hanky panky financially between Mr. Afshar and the Italians, but it was something that was not suspected by those involved. Don had been working on having some developer bring in a sheet rolling mill since he had first arrived in the country and he was just pleased that someone was actually doing it.

When we arrived in Rome we were met by an Embassy car and driven to the Grande Hotel. This was a beautiful old hotel with all the charm and class one expects of such a place. The furnishings and service were true old world. When we were taken to our room we found we had been given a suite with a large sitting area. Our bar was well stocked with scotch and vodka which were Don's drinks and many small bottles of Dom Perignon which were my specialty.

As Don was tied up with business meetings and the presentation of his report during the daytime, the Italian company had made arrangements for the fiancé of one of their executives to take me under her wing and show me the sights of Rome. We spent a morning visiting the Forum with its beautiful Corinthian columns, the many altars, State Archives of ancient Rome and antique temples. I suppose that the Colosseum is the most famous and well-known monument of Roman Antiquity; it impressed me the most! I had studied Latin and knew that this enormous amphitheater was begun in 72 A.D. by the Emperors of the Flavian family and completed under Titus in 80 A. D. It had been destined for gladiatorial contests and wild beast hunts, but with the coming of Christianity, events changed and bloody combats were no longer appreciated. It was severely damaged by earthquakes and stands a ruin today but so full of history that one could spend hours just looking and musing.

Another afternoon we spent visiting some of the more notable monuments of Rome and ended our tour in the Piazza Novena which is the most outstanding square of the Baroque period in Rome. With its Fountain of the Moors, Church of Saint Agnes and the famous Bernini Fountain, it is an awe inspiring sight. The afternoon was very warm so we sat down to have a glass of that icy cool lemonade that one is served in the sidewalk cafes of Rome. We chatted superficially about Rome and Gloria's love for the city and how she would be so sorry to leave when she and Frances were married and would be living in Torino.

'You are Mrs. Gail Rose!' announced a man whom I had never seen before. As I stammered in shock he continued, 'Your husband is with the Aluminum in Iran. He is Mr. Donald Rose. You see, I know very much. I know about you. I know that you work for His Imperial Majesty the Shahanshah. Tell me, do you like Iran?'

'I do not talk with strangers.' I was finally able to blurt out.

'But I am not a stranger, you know I am Iranian. Do you know Chattanooga? It is on Pahlavi Avenue just below the Hilton and just north of the Imperial Country Club on the opposite side of the road, of course. You see I know Iran. I am Iranian.'

'I really don't care who you are. You have interrupted me and my friend and as I said you are a stranger.' By now I was becoming very angry and I could see that my Italian friend was a little on edge. Her English was not very good and she knew no Farsi but even not comprehending the conversation, she could tell that I felt that this man was threatening me.

'Ah, now listen! I also work for the Shah. Do you like the Shah? Do you think he is doing a good job for Iran?'

I finally replied in Farsi, 'I have nothing to say to you! Everyone in the world can see what a great job His Imperial Majesty is doing in Iran so you don't have to ask me such a stupid question. Now leave me alone or I will have my friend call the police.' I hoped that my little affirmative about the Shah would satisfy him and my threat would send him running. I was correct in my assumptions.

'I have been very pleased to meet with you Khonume Rose. I will have a favorable report to make.' I had instinctively known that this was a Savak agent.

I was pleased that I had been so curt with him and also that I had let him know of my admiration for the Shah.

'But Gail, who was that ugly leetle man?' Gloria asked as he disappeared amongst the crowd.

'That was a Savak Agent working for the Secret Police of the Shah of Iran.'

'But why was he wanting to talk to you? Do you know heem?'

'No, I have never seen him in my life. You see, I work for the Shah, and I guess they just wanted to check up on me.'

After having gone to London to shop, see some theatre and meet with friends we decided it would be fun to go to Dublin for the Horse Show

Week. We had tentatively arranged with the Elghanians that we would meet in Dublin so when they called us at the Westbury and said that they had made reservations in Ireland, we were only too pleased to meet them there. Neither Don nor I had been to the famous, legendary Dublin Horse Show before.

We met for dinner at the Royal Hibernian, my old American Express card friends. Having told Freddy and Elian the story Don had heard many times about the pearl and the oysters I ordered oysters at dinner. Everyone laughed at me but wouldn't you know, I discovered two seed pearls in my oysters that night. That time I had someone with whom to share my experience. We drank champagne and decided to go to the races the following day. Maybe our luck would hold and we could arrange to pay for our whole trip from the proceeds of our day's wagering.

It was a beautiful day at the Leopards Town track. We all felt we had the calling and so wagered heavily on the first few races. None of us cashed a ticket! It was while I was mulling over my bet for the fourth race that a man of the cloth came up to me.

'Why yer lookin' so serious, me girl? Could I help ye wit somewhat?'

'Just give me a good tip on the next race, Father, and I won't be looking so serious.'

'Well, ye know I don't really come to the races too often but this track is just too close to miss the chance to put up a wager or two. Mind you I don't do all that well, but I would say I am not all that bad a handicapper.'

He gave me a grand tip for that race, after which I introduced him to the rest of group. We spent quite an enjoyable afternoon with the good father and even though we didn't end up paying for our trip we did have a good dinner that evening on our winnings.

The Dublin Show is of course, a book to itself. We had a wonderful time amongst the horsey people and watching the great jumping contests. Kambis had given me a budget to buy a couple of horses for the Imperial

Stables so when I found two I telexed asking him to call. Of course when the call came I had left just minutes before on my way to visit Lord Darsbury, where we were to spend a few days. When we eventually did get in touch with each other the word was go ahead and buy. I had great hopes that the one horse Ballylea, would arrive in Iran in time to send to Lebanon for the competition. This horse had jumped on the Irish team and I was sure Kambis could become a champion on it. Amazingly the money arrived in a few days and I was able to pay for the horses before I left Ireland!

SECOND LEBANESE COMPETITION

Once back in Iran it was back to serious work. The Lebanese competition was to be the 20th of October and to last for ten days. We were to have four days of competition during that period. The rules and regulations were to be almost identical to those that we had used in Tehran in the spring.

Along with our training schedule we were including a series of six competitions from the first four of which we would choose the official team to represent Iran.

Kambis had to be away with their Majesties for the first two competitions and I had not entered his horses in any events but they had been training well. I knew that he wanted to be on the team, and of course he would no matter what, but it would be much better if he could win his place rather than usurp it.

The morning after his first competition The Tehran Journal contained this article written by James Underwood.

RIDING SHOW HAT TRICK.

A jet-powered performance —that was the only way you could describe Imperial Stables boss Kambis Atabai's brilliant hat-trick in yesterday's Riding Federation show jumping at Farahabad.

For he'd only stepped from the jetliner in which he had accompanied Their Imperial Majesties on their Far Eastern tour an hour or so earlier. He had rushed home, changed into his riding clothes and was collecting his first trophy within three hours after setting foot on terra firma.

Riding the wonderful little Turkoman Shirin, he landed the opening D and C class events. In the first he had to jump off against several others with clear rounds to win the trophy.

In the second he and Shirin went round at such a speed that although they had a refusal their time was faster than runner-up Nader Djahanbani on Jet who had jumped a fine clear round.

Then in the B jumpers class he mounted an entirely different type of horse, the German bred Rostam, who was making his seasonal debut after summer treatment from the vet, and after a thrilling jump-off with his old rival Manucher Khosrodad, on Upa Negrin, landed what I believe is the first hat-trick in senior show jumping in Iran.

It was no wonder the bleary-eyed Atabai, who had barely slept in three days, then called it a day and left his Imperial Stables colleagues, Reza Hadavand on Shabahang and Ezat Vojdani on Shabrang to battle it out with Khosrodad in another exciting jump-off for the puissance prize.

This fine piece of riding by Atabai must put him in fine fettle for the trip to Beirut, when he will be a member of the Iranian team which will compete against the Lebanese later this month. General Khosrodad himself was out of luck, having to be content with a second and then a third behind Hadavand and Vojdani in the puissance.

But, the General who is the president of the Iranian Show Jumping Federation will be assured by yesterday's jumping that he will have a se-lection of competitive horses for the Beirut contest.

Kambis was of course, thrilled about the publicity which was also good in the Farsi paper. It really assured his position on the team.

Good old James, he really knew how to play his cards right. In the final selections we had a team that consisted of eleven riders and sixteen horses. It was quite a group! From the Imperial Stables we had, of course, Kambis along with Ezat, Ali Rezai, Reza Hadavand, General Khasrodad and surprisingly enough Davoud Bahrami. Again James came through with great publicity about Davoud:

"DAVOUD'S SO COOL AS HE GETS TOP HONOUR.

A momentous period in the life of 17 year old Tehran schoolboy Davoud Bahrami starts on Friday. He and the little grey Imperial Stables mare Mojghan will compete that afternoon for the Crown Prince's trophy, the top prize for junior riders in Iran. The following Friday the pair will compete at the Kayhan InternationalKurosh Stores show at Nowruzabad. And a few days later Davoud and Mojgan will fly along with the rest of the Riding Federation team, to Beirut, where they'll represent Iran against the Lebanese team in an international contest.

Davoud, son of a longtime stableman in the Shahanshah's employ at Farahabad, is taking it all calmly. 'Of course, I'm happy to be chosen to represent Iran,' he laconically told me.

He's been given every chance to develop into a top class rider by Imperial Stables boss Kambis Atabai. Hundreds of hours of free instruction culminated in a month during the summer with leading international show jumping trainer Paul Weier in Switzerland, where he went along with the talented Feridun Elghanian children.

On his return to Farahabad both Atabai and Gail Rose, the Imperial Stables jumping instructor, were delighted by the progress he had made. 'Just watch him ride,' Mrs. Rose told me at a show on his return. 'His style, his control of the horse -he's really absorbed everything that Weier taught him.'"

General Nader Ddjahanbani would, of course, be on the team with his imported gelding Versingetorix. His other mount being a stallion would not be permitted to go to Lebanon because the Lebanese had put a ban on stallions coming into the country from Iran. While having been flattered that the Lebanese had held such regard for the Iranian equine species as just as virile as their human counterparts it did cause us some difficulty in selecting the team horses.

Feridoud Elghanian was selected with that wonderful Irish mare Sunshine which had done so well when the Lebanese had visited Iran. Freddy was a problem though. He was Jewish and his family were on the Palestinian Black List for their support of Israel. Freddy and his wife were in a quandary as to how they were going to get into Lebanon without creating some sort of international incident. Correspondence between the Iranian Embassy in Lebanon and the Lebanese government solved the problem in that our host country guaranteed the safety of our Jewish rider and his wife. Actually, there were so many important Iranians on the team that the security was extremely strict and one extra to protect did not seem to bother the Lebanese government.

Goli Bakhtiar, the beautiful Goli, *femme fatale* with those marvelous features, striking black eyes, luscious long black hair and figure to match, had one little Turkoman stallion that had carried her to many victories in the speed classes of the low division in the spring competitions, was going to be one of two women on our team. In early September Goli came to me to ask me a confidential question.

'Gail, you know how badly I would like to go to Lebanon. What would you think if I gelded Shabdiz now? Would he be able, in six weeks, to go to Lebanon and jump?'

I was shocked! Iranians had never wanted to geld their horses; to them it is a crime to take away the manhood of an animal. Dr. Cutler and I had had many a tense moment with Kambis, who was much more lenient than most, trying to persuade him to geld this or that horse. I had heard in gossipy conversations the comment, 'Watch out for that Goli, she would cut off anyone's balls!' She was now literally going to do that to her horse!

'It is really not such a serious operation you know, Goli. The vet just goes in there and cuts out his testicles with a knife and then you have to walk him for a few days, twice a day to make sure that he doesn't swell up too much and the wound drains well. If there is no infection, which there should not be, you could be riding him in four or five days and jumping him again after couple of weeks definitely. Now, this is my own opinion; you had better check with Robin about it —he is the expert.'

'Yes, I'll do that. It's just that I wanted your opinion first because I didn't want to look the fool going to Dr. Cutler about something so delicate if it weren't going to be possible.'

Robin confirmed what I had told her. Poor little Shabdiz had his balls cut off so that he could go to Lebanon and carry Goli to honors.

Marion Hartunian had but one horse and could ride but one horse! Geiran, a grey Turkoman stallion, could be super or terrible. He was no more than 15.2 hands high and carried Marion, who was a very big girl, to some spectacular victories over the years. He also refused to go over the first fence on many occasions but this spring he had won the Kayhan Grand Prix in fine style and the publicity carried Marion to stardom in Iran. Marion's father and mother had been chief supporters of the sport over the years and were always willing to lend a horse or give a party when asked. The Armenian Hartunians were extremely proud of their nineteen year old daughter who was attending college in the U.S. Shahin had permitted his daughter to stay in Iran during the fall, thus missing one semester of school just on the chance that she would be chosen for the team. General Khosrodad, being a very soft-hearted man and a great believer in sportsmanship, said that if a horse could be found for Marion she would be given a place on the team due to her record with Geiran. Ali Reza Soudovar had a lovely Irish Thoroughbred mare which could jump the moon if she were headed towards it so he offered the horse to the girl. So we had Marion!

The final member of the team was Colonel Sohrad Khalvati. "Father of Show Jumping in Iran", he called himself. He was about fifty-four years old at the time of our first international sojourn and I am sure that in his day, he was the best to be found in Iran. He did love the sport and put a lot into it. Unfortunately, he had not kept up with the times so he and Kambis were constantly at loggerheads when I first became the trainer of the national team. At the time of the team selection Kambis hated the sight of this feisty little man.

'He is just like Hitler only much more stupid!' Kambis commented to me one day. It was true, his appearance did resemble the dictator. He had had three wives. The first one was British and with her he had two children. One day for a reason known only to the colonel and her, she disappeared with the children never to be seen or heard of again. His second wife was a Polish woman who it is said was very beautiful. She gave the colonel two more children. One day she disappeared too, but she didn't take the children! His current wife was an America girl much younger than he was but the perfect wife for Sohrab. Kay idolized this man and took all the garbage he had to hand out without blinking an eye. At times she should have blinked or ducked for she was often seen with black ones. She walked into more doors than anyone I knew! She was a very kind woman and a wonderful mother to their son and when Sohrab was not in one of his tempers he was really very good to her.

Even after having three foreign wives Colonel Sohrab Khalvati professed to be a hater of foreigners and all they stood for in Iran. When the Lebanese trip came up he began to bear pressure upon Kambis and General Khosrodad. His daughter had married General Nasiri who was the head of the Savak in Iran. One of the colonel's favorite threats to people, he was trying to bludgeon into doing something for him, was, 'I am not afraid to use my power. You know who my son-in-law is! I will get my son-in-law after you.' Everyone in Iran was terrified of the Savak. Just to have one's name mentioned to the chief of Savak was threat enough to persuade a person to do almost anything requested. So it was that the fine colonel was asked to be on the team. But what horse would he ride? He wanted one of the German horses from the Imperial Stables. Here Kambis put down his foot.

'How can you deny me, the "father of show jumping" one of your good horses? You let those grooms and those stable boys ride those good horses.

Those boys are not worth a hair on my ass!' The colonel's language was colorful. But Kambis did not relent. Thank goodness.

It was Ali Reza Soudovar, the "supporter of show jumping", who came up with a horse. He had a lovely Anglo Turkoman mare that had done very well in the junior classes with his young rider Akbar Kazami. The mare could certainly handle the small division in Beirut.

To my mind there was one rider who had been left out. That was Hushang Temouri who with his horse Ramsar had done very well of late. He was never even considered for the team. And why? General Khosrodad had his eyes on Ramsar. The General wanted a horse for both the big and small division and had only one dependable mount in Upa Negrino. So it was that the General went to Colonel Pakhnidjad, Tehmouri's superior officer. He seconded Ramsar for his use on the Iranian team. It was the only thing that I had ever seen the General do that I felt was unfair or unsporting, but he did it!

Ballylea, my Irish purchase, had not arrived for Kambis. What actually happened was that after having waited for weeks, suddenly two days before we were due to leave for Lebanon the Imperial Iranian Air Force said that they had a plane that had clearance to go to Dublin to get the horses I had bought and it had to be done immediately. So Robin Cutler and two grooms went off on another Irish jaunt. I was sorry that I was not included.

It meant that we were shipping sixteen horses from Iran to Lebanon with no veterinary on either of the planes. I would have to give the tranquilizer shots before we took off and there was one *djelodar* who had just come back to Iran from a year's course at Melton Maubray in England who would be of help. I would fly with one load of horses and he with the other. General Khosrodad had arranged for Don to go on the Military plane with the horses, something he was dying to do! He would be an official in the jury at the competition in Lebanon and it saved the team money by having him travel with me in the air force plane.

It was amazing how smoothly the loading of the horses at Doshan Tappe went the morning we left. The planes were ready; we had the horses on the pallets, gave them a small tranquilizer and loaded them in no time. The only catastrophe was when Shirin, Kambis's Turkoman Mare jumped out of her crate onto the runway as the pallet was being loaded by the fork lift into the plane. We had a few tense moments trying to catch her and were relieved to find that she had done herself no harm.

Off we flew to Mehrabad where there were a few delays due to the fact that some of the passports had not arrived at the airport and then the navigator on one of the planes was pulled off to navigate on a plane going down to Shiraz to take some bigwig general on a mission. We took off with the first planeload of horses but the second one had to wait another hour for a new navigator before it could depart.

Four and a half hours later plane number one arrived safely at Beirut Airport. It had been an easy flight and no problems with the horses; I had travelled with a syringe in my breast pocket in case a horse became uneasy or threw a fit. How I would have managed to get the needle in a fit-throwing horse I am not sure, for I found it hard enough to give an intravenous shot with the horse standing still. Luckily Allah had been on the side of me and my horses.

I had never before been to Lebanon and was most interested to see how the Mediterranean looked from the air as we were making our final approach to land.

The humid warmth that hit us as the plane doors were opened made us feel that we were walking into a sauna. Compared to the dry, cool October air we were having in Tehran, this was an inferno.

A very official group of men walked out to the plane to accept our animals' papers and send the humans to the immigration department to get our passports stamped. We had a problem! The equine papers were on the other plane so we had to wait until it landed, if it ever did, to have the horses cleared through. We decided that we would send the people in two groups for their clearance. We had a problem there too! Aside from Don and myself all the others on that plane were on a joint diplomatic passport given by the Imperial Court. The passport was on the other plane in the hands of Colonel Alai. Don and I went to the immigration leaving the others and the horses to wait for their compatriots. We would at least have a look around the Beirut Airport.

We waited on the hot tarmac for over an hour when we finally saw the C 130 lumbering through the sky towards the landing strip like a fat swallow. The horses on our plane were all broken out to say nothing of the rest of us who were dripping with perspiration. I had no idea that Beirut would be so hot this time of the year. It made me begin to wonder how our horses would handle the change in climate.

Once the import papers for the horses had been delivered to the correct hands we began to off load the pallets. Two by two we took the horses off and two by two they were loaded into awaiting horse trailers. The trailers had been loaned to the Lebanese Federation by the few private individuals who owned them.

It had been well organized. The moment our first plane had landed the people with the trailers were alerted. It was planned, that as the horse show complex was just a ten minute trailer ride from the airport the trailer contingent would be informed as we landed. They had arrived as planned but as the horses could not be offloaded until the papers arrived, unfortunately for the kind Lebanese who were driving the trailers, they had a long wait in the sun due to the Iranian disorganization.

I moved off with the first trailer to the Sports Complex leaving Don to bring up the rear. I was startled by the Palestinian camps that we passed on the way; I had been warned but had not correctly pictured what I was to see, in my mind's eye. We passed three camps and each was identical. A plot of land about two acres in size was covered with tin and cardboard shacks; there were scraggly looking barefooted children playing in small patches of sand between these flimsy homes. Dirty looking remnants of clothing were hanging on the sides of the shacks, obviously laundry out to dry; filthy women with straggly hair were lingering in doorways, many very pregnant. And the stench was indescribable.

The stables of this Sports Complex were of concrete block, sturdy, well built and exceptionally clean. Each block of twelve stalls had two electrical fly killing machines so there was nary a fly to be seen which is most uncommon in any place where horses are kept. The only disturbing fact was that on the corners of every barn there was a ring of sand bags which were used as protection for the many soldiers that were on guard in the area should there be an attack of PLO. Not a hundred yards down the hill was a large PLO camp. Naturally the top of the hill was rimmed like a fortress with sand bags and there were many soldiers with guns resting on the sand bags on duty at all times. As the trailers with the horses drove in the gate of the fenced compound we could see the Palestinian children peering through the chain link to see what was happening. Some of them had the most beautiful faces if one could disregard the filth. The deep brown almond eyes that were most appealing, took in all that was happening.

I had a look at our setup and assigned the stalls giving the list to Sefola Siri, who had arrived back from his blacksmithing course in England just two weeks before our trip. There he had learned not only to shoe a horse but also to speak quite understandable English. I had assigned him as my assistant for the trip and chief of the mission, for the Imperial riders and grooms. All had respect for Sefola who was a man in his early thirties and a very devout Muslim.

Just five months later he was to go to Mecca where he became a Haji Agha. It is a very difficult feat to make the Haj; the believer must go to Mecca where he performs a number of difficult tasks during a ten day period. One of these tasks is to walk the ten kilometers from a religious shrine on the outskirts of the City of Mecca to the most holy Kaaba, or black-robed tomb of Mohamad, and back again seven times in one day. Many of the other tasks are considered too sacred to be revealed to the unbelieving world.

The Shahanshah had completed the Hadj when he was a young man.

I went to have a look around the complex while I was awaiting the rest of the horses and men. The main show jumping ring looked like it was much larger than anything we had in Iran save the grass ring of General Djahanbani upon which we had not yet been allowed to jump. Luckily there was no bank, for we had not had the experience of jumping our horses over such an obstacle as there was not one in Iran. There was one large water jump and a small one over which jumps would be built but I had confidence that these would not give us any trouble. The footing was a fine, yet springy sand of a bright red color; it seemed to me much superior to the heavier sand footing we had in all of our ménages in Iran. The jumps were all in a small storage ring behind the main jumping area and were in the midst of being painted and repaired but what I was able to see of them looked to be very colorful and well built.

After I had finally made sure all the horses were bedded down and arranged for the men to be taken to their hotel, which was near to the sports complex, we were driven off to the Phoenicia Hotel, the most luxurious in the city. In our room was a schedule of the events for the ten days. As I looked it over I realized that we just had a half an hour in which to shower and change for the first of many receptions. Our room was very spacious and the refrigerator was well stocked with champagne and scotch so we were able to revitalize ourselves before the evening's events.

The following morning I was up at six and on my way to the stables by half past six in a courtesy car that was provided for my use during the sojourn. As the days wore on and more and more hangers on arrived I found it more difficult to get one of these cars to take me to the stables and often had to hire a taxi, however the first few days I did enjoy the luxury of the "trainer's car". Don liked to sleep in; the big part of his trip would come in the afternoons when he would be sitting in the jury box adding up faults.

I arrived at the stable before the boys so was able to get an ungarbled report on the condition of the horses from the two men who had been on night watch. All seemed to be eating and drinking well but they were feeling the heat as they were damp with sweat. Once the rest of the men arrived I had the horses all bathed and walked arranging to come again in the afternoon to school them at five when it was cool.

Back at the hotel again, I met up with Don and some others of the group in time to go down to the main shopping district to take advantage of some of the wonderful buys one could make in Beirut.

After a rather informal luncheon Ali Reza and I rounded up all the riders who were staying at the Phoenicia and piled them into the bus; these were the riders with a pedigree! The other riders, the Imperial *djelodars* were staying near the show grounds. Our bus stopped at this less expensive hotel to get the rest of our "International" riders, and then off we went to have a light training session with the horses.

The Lebanese had made available to us many obstacles in the main jumping ménage and all the horses schooled well. We did not overdo it due to the previous day's flight and the heat but we all felt well pleased riding back on the bus to our hotels. The next afternoon would give us our answers. The competition was to start at two in the afternoon.

At noon sharp, the following day the small bus pulled away from the front door of the Phoenicia Hotel. Aboard we had, Goli Bakhtiar, Marion Hartunian, Sohrab Khalvait, Freddy Elghanian and General Khosradad. Kambis had only arrived shortly before and had rushed upstairs to change. He would come to the show grounds as soon as he was ready. General Djahabani, being his aloof self, decided to ride to the grounds in style in his chauffeur driven black limousine.

Just as we rounded the corner of the hotel there was great commotion at the side of the bus and the driver slammed on the brakes. He seemed unnerved as a bearded Arab type swung aboard. It was not a Palestinian Gorilla; it was just Ali Reza Soudovar, late as usual, running for the bus. The general admonished him for his tardiness but he just laughed, shrugged his shoulders and said, 'You should know by now, General, that I don't know how to tell time.'

'You know, Ali, this is a very serious matter. We are here to win the prizes and you are one of the trainers. You must try to be on time!'

'Gorbonetu Timsah. I will certainly try from now on. I do apologize.' The General then took over the bus giving a monotone speech about the greatness of Iran and how we would live up to the Iranian standards by winning for our country.

'You know, Meeses Rose, I theenk that we have a very good chance against these Lebanese. Remember how we annihilated them when they were in Iran. I propose we do the same thing here. What do you say?'

'Timsah, I can think of nothing I would rather have our team do but seriously, I think we must not be too sure of ourselves. It's overconfidence that often causes rider faults. You are here to compete and it will not be a walkover. We haven't seen these new horses that Makran Alamadin and Mr.Gandeur have bought for the Lebanese team. I understand that they are top European show jumping horses. Please don't be overconfident and if you give your little pep talk to the boys from the stables once we pick them up, I beg of you not to make them feel overconfident.'

'Khonume, we are Iranian and we go into battle with all confidence; that is how we conquer.' Answered the General. There is no record of the Iranians ever conquering!

Ali Reza had sat down saying not a word during this intercourse.

'*Teemsah*, the Khonume is right you know. This is not a battle; this is a sporting event. You are a great Iranian sportsman as well as a general.

You must understand what she is saying. We Iranians have a temperament that isn't not really the best for sporting events. We are apt to blow it. So let's not count our eggs before we have bought the chickens.'

By now our bus had reached the hotel where Ezat, Reza, Davoud and Ali Rezai would be picked up. The boys looked very smart in their white britches and red jackets. I could tell though, that they were all very nervous. Davoud Bahrami, the youngest, had been to Switzerland during the summer and Ali Rezai had been sent to England once to pick up Partheon Shaft and Tired Monarch, the two Thoroughbred stallions that had been bought for the Imperial Stables by Mr. Afshar, the Ambassador to Britain a few years ago but, the other two had never left Iran. As well, they had not been included in the previous night's festivities, why I was not sure but it seemed that the general felt they would be an embarrassment to Iran because they were just stable boys. I got up from my seat next to the general to sit with the boys and give them a bit of encouragement.

Just as I had finished explaining to them that we would be up against stiff competition with the better horses the Lebanese had purchased and that they would all have to be just a bit sharp riding in a new place, the general began his monotone discourse about the greatness of Iran and Iranians and that we would no doubt win every event hands down. More than likely we would take the first three places as we had done in Iran the last time we had met the Lebanese. I decided to say no more. What was the use? This was obviously Iranian strategy of which I knew little and was finding more and more difficult to understand.

Once at the stable we checked the horses and told the grooms to saddle them up while we went *en masse* to walk the course. I took my group and Ali Reza Soudovar took his group. General Djahanbani and Colonel Khalvati arrived, hopping from one group to the other.

There would be two classes as we had had in the spring with the C / B horses jumping up to 1. 30 and the A horses to 1.45. We did note while walking, that the jumps were all of maximum height but very few had any spread at all. The widest oxer was just one meter. We had trained over big wide oxers and spread fences. The riders felt this was a real advantage but I warned them that it might pose a problem in the combinations. Our other problem was that we had a speed class in both divisions that first day. In Iran we seldom had speed classes because we were trying to get away from the steeplechase type of riding that had been the norm before I took over the show jumping organization with Ali Reza. Walking the course I cautioned my riders to cut the corners and go slowly rather than race around the course and be unable to make some of the tight turns.

I had everyone warm their horses up early so that all the riders would be able to rest and watch a few horses go before their turn. The first of our team to go was Reza Hadavand who followed instructions to the letter. He cut where I told him and he went clean. To that point he was in first place. Ezat, who had Alborz in the small class, raced around flattening his horse to knock down three fences. Rezai did the same with his Zahak. Davoud Bahrami went carefully and a bit slower than Hadavand but I was pleased. General Khosrodad on Tehmouri's Ramsar was eliminated. Kambis had a dreadful round on Shirin being eliminated when she ran out the third time. Marion Hartunian was dumped at the last fence; Khalvati went like a maniac having some fences down. Goli Bakhtiar was one of the last to go. She turned on the ignition switch of Shabdiz and went around like a demon. She was clean and won the class. Fantastic! Reza Hadavand was third and Bahrami fifth. I was very pleased. It was certainly a good start.

Then came the A class. Shabrang had two refusals and a knockdown. Rezai had three fences down, all in the combinations. General Khosrodad was eliminated again and General Djahanbani had five fences down. Kambis knocked three. We were nowhere with the exception of Freddy Elghanian who was seventh. My Generals and *djelodars* did not get one prize!

It was a very downcast lot that rode the bus back to the hotels. General

Khosrodad had accepted a ride back with the other General in his limousine as had Kambis. Ali Reza Soudovar had gone back in another car with Colonel Khalvati and his wife. It was just me, Freddy and the boys from the stable. I tried to placate everyone including Freddy Elghanian who had had quite a bit of trouble making the turns with his mare though he had gone clean. I set the following morning at nine for a schooling and pep talk session. It was a noncompetition day and the Lebanese had arranged for a sightseeing trip for all the dignitaries. I decided to forego this event as did Freddy and Marion; we would try to get things right with the horses.

As I entered the hotel feeling only slightly dejected I saw Kambis's cloudy looking face. He had obviously wanted to discuss things with me. I had not had more than two words with him since he arrived earlier in the day, and he wanted a report.

'Well, Mrs. Rose, your boys did not do so well today. I must say I am very disappointed in both Ali Rezai and Ezat. They should have done better.' I wondered what he was thinking of his own performance.

'Kambis, you know very well it's not fair of you to judge the boys on one class. What about you? Obviously one of the blabber mouth hangers on has come to you to stir things up. It can only be that informer Bahman Shahandeh; he's nothing but a trouble-maker anyway and how he happened to arrive here for this event I have no idea; he certainly doesn't add anything to the sport, and it is a sport! This is not like you!'

'All right, all right!' he protested with a hint of a grin on his severe face. 'Let's sit down and have a cup of tea. Then you can tell me what has been happening and how everything else has been going.'

I gave him a detailed account of the events up to his arrival and was taken aback when he said, 'I can't imagine how that bitch Goli Bakhtiar was able to win a class; of all the people she is the last I wanted to see win a ribbon in this event.'

'You should be proud for Iran that a member of the team won. For heaven's sake, this is a team event, not an individual competition.'

'Well you know, Gail, that I want the stable to do all the winning, not these others who are part of another organization. To me it is the results of the Imperial Stables that are important.'

'Then you're wrong. What counts is the team as a whole; the Iranian team. People will not remember that Goli came from Soudovar's stable; they will remember that Iran won.'

'Let's not argue that point into the ground. Now tell me, how was the flight yesterday?' I told him every last detail. He was not shocked or angry that we had had to wait due to the whims of some waterskiing general. That was Iran, a country for generals!

'Actually the only problem that I have, other than the fact that we didn't win the big class, is the attitude that General Khosrodad seems to have about the boys from the stables. He refused to allow them to come to the first night party or the reception last night nor did they go to the luncheon yesterday. All the Lebanese riders were at all the events and it must seem very strange that only some of the Iranian riders attend the functions. To me it looks obvious that there is a great class distinction within the ranks of the Iranian Show Jumping Team. I tried to talk to the General about the matter but he wouldn't listen and just told me that they were a bunch of stable boys and wouldn't know how to behave.'

'But that is dreadful!' Kambis was incensed. 'As you say this is a team event. How dare General Khosrodad impute the suggestion that we are not all equals on the Iranian team! You are very right in bringing this up. It will be very bad publicity for our team if this continues. I'll speak to the general about the problem.'

At just that moment who should come through the lobby of the Phoenicia but Manucher Khosrodad. And just the luck of it that I would have to be present while Kambis spoke to the general about something that I had already mentioned to him. It would be so obvious that I had been the one to "tell".

'Manucher?' sung my boss in his most sickly sweet voice. *'Salam ale-com? Chetori agha jun? Chance no dashtid! Che shot?'* (How are you my dear general? You had bad luck!)

While Kambis talked around in circles about the day's event and then back to the receptions and parties that had been held I tried to quietly gather my things and sneak off to my room.

'Mrs. Rose, please don't leave just yet; I have a few things I want to discuss with you. I know that it takes you ladies quite some time to dress for a dinner party but I won't take too much more of your time. I forgot to ask you how the boys from the stable behaved at these parties that the general is telling me about.'

'Well, um . . . actually, they were not at the parties.' I stammered my reply. He was such a bastard was the only thought in my head. He really knew how to put one on the spot.

'Kambis,' the General seemed to be coming to my rescue. He really was a basically kind man and he could see, or thought he could, that Kambis was going to blame me for the exclusion of the boys. 'You see, I was not sure what you felt about it so I decided upon my own, that the boys should not go to the parties. Mrs. Rose did speak to me about having them included but you know they are just stable hands and they don't know how to behave at social functions. Why most of them have never eaten with a knife or fork.'

'Timsah Khosrodad!' Kambis screamed at the top of his lungs so that many heads in the lobby turned towards our little group. 'Are you suggesting that I have not prepared my men for their mission? Do you think that I have not given lessons in etiquette to these men? Why, I even outfitted them with decent civilian clothes to wear to the parties. The riders have tuxedos and the other *djelodards* will wear their uniforms to the more formal functions.'

'But Kambis, you can't mean that you want these peasants included in all the social activities?' queried the General.

'I do! And I will refuse to attend myself it if is not taken care of. How would it then look for your team if the Court Minister did not attend? I know I am not a general but in the eyes of the Lebanese I am as important a figure as you yourself seem to be. I know that you are the captain of the team and all matters must be given your approval, but if you don't give your unconditional approval to having my boys attend these affairs you may be very, very sorry.'

'Don't be so angry, Kambis. Of course I will arrange things so that the Imperial Stables men will be included. I'll arrange everything. Don't worry. Will you excuse me, I have to get this arranged for tonight. This is the night we have all been invited to the Casino for dinner. We're to meet down here at eight o'clock sharp. Not Iranian time.' He chuckled and went off.

'Now what was it that you wanted to discuss with me, Kambis?' I questioned.

'Nothing really, but I wanted you to stay through my argument with the General; it made things easier for me. I'll say that he is a fair man. He could have cast the blame on you but he didn't; you know most Iranians would have.'

'That I've already learned, Mr. Atabai. Now if you will excuse me I must run up and change for the evening's festivities.'

What an evening for our innocent young peasant men to start out their social calendar in Beirut. The Casino was the most luxurious I had ever seen and the floorshow that lasted for three hours the most elaborate I had ever seen or perhaps will ever see. There were dancing beauties, lions and tigers, tight rope walkers, strip tease dancers, every sort of entertainment that could be imagined. Around the edge of the semicircular stage was a six foot wide trough that could be raised and lowered. It was used as a train track, an animal walk and even filled with water and used for boats and water skiers. As our group was sitting right next to the edge of the stage it made things more spectacular. The grand finale was a ride of the Seven

Horses of Destiny. Upon the stage galloped seven white horses with their riders in brilliant red costumes; they ran through clouds of steam and yet never got near us even though one felt they were coming to ride over the audience; it was the most spectacular part of the whole show.

We had had a marvelous dinner before the floor show started and had planned to do a little gambling afterwards before we went home. However when it was finished, we all looked at each other bug-eyed, surprised that it was after one o'clock. We had a half an hour's ride back to the hotel and I noted that none of the Lebanese team members had stayed. They must have snuck away while the lights were out. Ali Reza Soudovar had slept through the whole thing he said, and was still a little bewildered at his place of awakening, so I took it upon myself to squelch the gambling idea and ordered all participants home to bed at once. Our early morning schooling would not be as early as we had planned.

As I was awake early anyway, I decided to go down to the stables at seven. I left Don sleeping like a babe and tiptoed out of our room. I recalled that I had tentatively arranged to drive down to the stable with Marion Hartunian and was surprised to find her waiting for me in the lobby.

'I just could not sleep last night.' she said, 'so I came down here just a few moments ago hoping that I hadn't missed you.'

We had a bit of a problem finding a cab that would take us all the way down to the Sports Complex and the courtesy cars were not due to arrive until nine that morning. The drivers had had a late night!

Marion seemed rather nervous as we chatted about nothing at all. Finally she said, 'Mrs. Rose, why did they choose me for this team anyway?'

'Call me Gail. Actually Marion, you have had some good success with your horse Geiran so you deserved a place just through him. We couldn't bring him as he is a stallion and Ali offered to let you have a horse. He was certain that you woud be able ride the mare Admiration. But another reason you were included was that your parents, particularly your father, have been such great supporters of the sport for the past few years that for them, the team wanted you to come. It's a great thrill to have a daughter on the team and he and your mother are here enjoying themselves being proud of their daughter.'

'But that's just it. I didn't want to be here because of my father. It's not fair. I can only ride one horse and that is Geiran. Everyone in Iran knows that, so why make me come here and make a fool of myself on a horse that I can't handle?'

'Marion, don't think you're of making a fool of yourself. You're here to represent your country. You can get around these little jumps with Admiration. Just steer her and away you go. As long as you do not tense up you will have no trouble.'

'Ali Reza makes me so nervous. Will you help me? He screams at me in the practice ring and then I get scared! I wish I didn't have to ride.'

'I'll help you when we get down to the stable now. I'm sure you can do it, but please don't take a defeatist's attitude. We'll see what we can do and if I don't really think you can do it I'll tell the General and you won't have to ride. OK?'

'Oh, that's great. Thank you.' She was silent for a moment and then rather shyly asked, 'You know that Lebanese rider who rides the little chestnut Arab horse in the small class?'

'What's his name?'

'I think it's Masoud something or other.'

'Oh, yes. I know the guy you mean. Quite a good looking man in an Arab sort of way, but he rides like a sack of potatoes, on a white faced Arab.'

She laughed, 'Yes that's the one I'm talking about. What do you know about him?'

'Nothing, but I'll see what I can find out. OK? Are you interested?'

'Well, sort of. You see, he asked me to go out with him. And I don't

261

know anything about him. I thought you might be able to see what you can find out.'

During the morning all went well. Marion did a good job schooling with Admiration and I felt she now had new confidence to go on and ride the following day. Kambis had an uneventful workout on his two horses and the rest of the crew went as well as I had expected. Just as the schooling had finished Don arrived to go over some things with the other members of the jury. When I had checked that the horses were all done up I went up to the jury stand to find that the meeting was over and all were having a sociable chat. Don and I were the only representatives of the Iranian contingent; Ali Reza Soudovar had slept in and the others had gone on their sightseeing trip.

Amongst those present was the handsome rider, Masoud. Don was already talking to him so I casually sauntered over to join in. I would be able to find out something for Marion. As it turned out he invited us to go to his apartment for a drink on the way back to the hotel so I would certainly have a lot of information by the time I next saw my young friend. From what I understood, her parents were very particular about the young men she dated so she had to have a lot of information to give them should she decide to accept an invitation.

'I'll drive you in my car,' said Masoud. 'I've told the driver you came with Don, to report back to the hotel. My apartment is very close to the Phoenicia so I will take you there when you're ready to go.'

It was very kind of him. He whizzed us along the wide Beirut streets lined with tall apartment buildings. We stopped in front of a soft yellow building of about ten stories. Masoud had the use of a covered parking space right next to the front door of the building. We went through a Mediterranean looking door into a very attractive hall filled with plants of all description. There was an elevator, but just one.

'You see we have the penthouse; I think is how you Americans call it.

This elevator is for our private use. None of the other tenants in the building come in this entrance. Even though we live in an apartment it's like our own house because we never have to see the other occupants if we don't wish to.'

'We?' I questioned.

'Yes, my wife and I. We don't have any children. You'll like her very much. She is Egyptian and very beautiful as well as a very intelligent and interesting person.'

The door to the penthouse was opened by a striking tall woman of about thirty-five. Her black hair was pulled severely back from her olive face accentuating her large black-rimmed brown eyes. She wore a black long sleeved turtleneck pullover and a black A-line skirt; so plain, and yet with the gold pendant she wore, obviously Egyptian, it was a magnificent and extremely ornate look; she wore long gold dropped earrings to match the pendant. She could have gone anywhere in that outfit, shopping or even to a formal dinner party.

We spent an enjoyable hour or so with Masoud and his wife. She, it seemed had the money in the family and the brains. She had obtained her Ph.D.in New York and was working as a journalist for a prominent women's magazine in Beirut, but I had the definite feeling that she certainly didn't have to work. It turned out that Masoud was some sort of salesman, but I never could figure out what it was he sold. All I could think of while we were in his home was that he was definitely a dirty old man to have asked that sweet, innocent young Iranian girl to go out with him. I wanted to hurry back to the hotel to break the news to Marion.

When we finally did get back to the hotel I called Marion's room and found that she was out. Oh well, I would see her later. She didn't come to the dinner party that night and so it would have to wait until the next day and with the competition being that day I didn't get a chance to see Marion alone. She slept in and didn't come to the stable with me as she had planned and we missed each other the rest of the day.

The competition went well for the Lebanese though beautiful Goli Bakhtiar again won the speed class in the low division; gelding Shabdiz had not had any adverse effects on him; Reza Hadavand was fourth in the same event. The Lebanese took the first three places in the A division while our own Ali Rezai placed fourth on Shahab. Kambis rode a disasterous round. Ezat and Shabrang were eliminated. General Khosrodad did get around the course but with two refusals. General Djahanbani had five fences down after making a spectacle of himself in the schooling ring by jumping his poor Versingetorix over too many fences, knocking downing most of them. He should have been reprimanded by the Steward of the show but was not. To me it was a real embarrassment to have a member of the team behave in such a way for not only did the horse knock the fences and become exhausted but the General abused him with whip, spurs and voice in such a way that one could not ignore it; he was even noticed from the stands around the main ring.

Marion, maid Marion! What a wonderful round she had, clear until the last fence which was a double, a small oxer into the triple bar with one stride between. As she approached the oxer I saw that she was off balance and leaning a little to the left. The horse was coming at a breakneck speed and our rider did not attempt to check. The fence loomed and the horse made a quick veer to the right. Marion was hurled over the oxer and landed head first in the triple bar that was seven meters the other side. She demolished the fence and I was sure, herself as well. She lay in a heap for some minutes before the first aid arrived and carried her off on a stretcher. My schooling had not been as miraculous as I had hoped.

Because Kambis had had a bad round on Shirin on the first day, I had put Ali Rezai on her and he had gone around the course but had finished with four fences down. I was sure that Kambis would be happy about that.

General Khosrodad had completed the course on Ramsar even though he had a couple of fences down so he would be happier. But all in all, our record was not very good to date and the next competition in two days time was to be the Nation's Cup.

Each country was to enter two teams of horses that competed in the small division, for the Nation's Cup. The entries for the Cup were to be declared after the second competition so when the events for the day were finished I went up to the Jury room where we would declare our teams. Ali Reza Soudovar met me there to discuss how we would set up the teams.

The A team from Iran would consist of Goli and Shabdiz; no explanation for that choice was needed; Davoud Bahrami on Mojgan had done well; Sohrab Khalvati had taken sixth place on Lady Jane that day so he was selected for the A team. The final choice was difficult in a way, for even though Reza Hadavand had been in the prizes both days of competition with Cobalt, he usually was very unpredictable. Ali and I both felt that Ali Rezai on Shirin would be a good choice, for Ali is a determined rider and Shirin was usually a super jumper. But we could not put Shirin on the A team when we considered her performance in the current competition. So it was Reza Hadavand and Cobalt.

The B team consisted of Shirin and Ali, Freddy Elganian and Sunshine, Ezat and Alborz and General Khosrodad and Ramsar. Quite a motley group, but with a bit of luck they too had a chance. The following day was a rest day which gave the horses a day during which we would just work lightly on the flat. They were all feeling the climatic change from Iran and were a little sluggish.

Ali and I were discussing the problem of the horses as we walked down to the stable to check out the horses before going back to the hotel.

'Well, Gail, I'm giving all my own horses a shot of Vitamin B Complex in hopes that it will pick them up. Why don't you do that to the Imperial Stables horses?'

'I really don't know in my own mind if that'll really help and you know that Cutler disapproves of that needling business. I couldn't take the responsibility of going ahead and doing it, especially with Cutler not having arrived yet. Maybe if you said something to Kambis and Khosrodad they might go along with it.'

When we got to the stable all the riders were dejectedly sitting on the tack boxes in front of the stalls, including Kambis and General Khosrodad. Djahanbani had already left for the hotel.

Ali went over to Kambis and had a long drawn out conversation like only Iranians can do. I, of course, knew the gist of it. Eventually I heard my name called by my boss and walked over to where the two were head to head.

'Gail, what do you think of Ali's idea of giving an injection of B complex?'

'I feel it couldn't do much harm. I'm not convinced of how much good it'll do but there are so many varied theories about this injection that I hate to say. I guess I agree and to tell you the truth, we need all the help we can get.'

'Well then, if you give your approval you might as well get ready and start to work. Seeing as the good doctor has not yet arrived, he's probably on one of his expensive trips around London instead of picking up my horses, you will have to be the one to give the injections.'

'I will go and get the stuff.' said Ali, hurrying off to the tack room. He emerged with two large 100 cc bottles of Vitamin B Complex. I had given many needles in my day but the one I really hated was this B complex. It smelled terrible and if it gets on your skin you smell for days. It had a pungent odor that was very difficult to mask and impossible to be rid of.

'You might as well start with your horses Gail, and then we'll do mine.' I knew what was coming. For sure I would end up doing all of the horses. I had to change the needle on the syringe eleven times for the eleven horses that belonged to the Imperial Stables group. Each time I changed needles I got more stuff on my hands. I was beginning to feel sick. Finally I had finished.

'Would you mind doing my five horses too, Gail?' asked Ali.

'Yes Mrs. Rose, why don't you do the rest of the horses too?' Kambis said. I could tell him why! I was almost sick from the smell. I would be the most unpopular member of the Iranian contingent and mostly because of my smell.

'Gee Gail, thanks a lot.' Ali said as I finished his last horse. 'You know that stuff makes me sick. I just hate the smell.'

'Well so do I and I'm just about to be sick from it. If people start avoiding me I'll know it's not my bad breath! Actually, if things get any worse as far as our performance is concerned, I may be happy that my smell keeps people away.'

That evening we were entertained at a huge sit-down dinner party that was held at the Phoenecia. We were entertained by one of the most famous belly dancers in the world, Shecoufeh. She was like and elastic noodle and danced for what seemed like hours.

I still had not had a chance to speak to Marion about her friend and the following day James Underwood, Don and I were going on a sightseeing trip to some old ruins down by the sea at Byblos. Perhaps I could catch her after I came back from the stable in the morning before we left.

I did not see Marion until late the next afternoon. When the three of us arrived back from Byblos, the Elghanians and Marion were in the lobby having a drink. They asked us to join them, which we did. Before I had a chance to say anything to her Marion had excused herself to go upstairs to have a nap; she was still feeling the effects of her fall the previous day.

'My God, that Marion is quite a girl you know,' commented Elian Elghanian after she had left.

'I think she's really quite sweet.' I said.

'Gaily, you are just so naive.' It was Freddy. He was always complaining that I was naive. 'Do you know where that girl has been spending her time while she has been in Beirut?'

'No.'

'Well, I will tell you. She has been in bed screwing Masoud, you know that crazy guy who rides the chestnut Arab. He picks her up here at the hotel and she makes some lame story up to tell her parents, then they go off to his apartment. She told me just now. She just came out and said that she had been out fucking Masoud this afternoon. She is so cheeky you know. Can you imagine what her parents would say? They would die. And she just told Elian and me out and out like that. Can you imagine?'

I couldn't imagine. I said that Don and I had had a drink with Masoud and his wife, one of the first days and that I was sure that his wife would not like him bringing young Iranian girls home to fuck with. I wondered if Marion knew he was married. Freddy doubted it.

I left the group and went up to Marion's room. She answered and asked me to come in.

'I have been trying to talk to you, Marion, but I haven't been able to find the chance. How are you after your fall?'

'Oh, I'm all right but I don't want to ride that crazy mare again.'

'Well, that's up to you. If you don't want to, that's no problem. I'm sure that we could get Davoud Bahrami to ride her for you and you could say that you're hurt.'

'Actually, I was thinking of that. I've already told my parents that my back hurts.'

'Listen Marion, you asked me about that Masoud guy. I learned a few things about him. '

'Oh, Masoud! He is fantastic! I have been to his apartment and out to lunch with him. He is the most gorgeous man!'

'Uh, ... Well, you know Don and I went to his apartment for a drink the other day and his wife was there. She's Egyptian. Did you know he was married?'

'Oh, yes. He told me. He picked me up after he dropped you and Don

268

off. He took me to his other apartment; the one he keeps just for his lady friends. He took me there and just undressed me very casually and began to fuck me. It was so exciting. He's so gentle and so virile. I've never had such a good fuck in my life. It gives me tingles just to think about it.'

'You should be careful, you know; you don't want to get into trouble here. We are guests of the Lebanese Federation and it would be a dreadful embarrassment to everyone if they thought that we had brought along a young lady who liked to spend her time in bed with a married man instead of riding with her team mates.' As the coach I had to admonish her even though her personal life was not really any of my business.

'For heaven's sakes Gail, don't be so straight. No one will ever find out about this. I just like to have a good fuck now and again.'

I couldn't believe my ears and said no more. It is a conversation that I haven't mentioned to anyone until now. I went up to my room to have a shower and get dressed for the dinner party that was being given by Mr. Fauzi Gandeur, the President of the Lebanese Equestrian Federation.

The party was held in Mr. Gandeur's beautiful penthouse apartment only three blocks from the Phoenicia, but even so the chauffeur-driven cars were assigned to drive us over at nine o'clock. The Iranian ladies were looking their best in beautiful long dresses. They had all been dressed to the nines every evening, always in a new dress. I had felt so inadequately prepared with my standard two little French numbers which were plain and only dressed up with jewelry that I'd gone out that day and bought something a bit more *chique*. A long black and white print with a wide patent leather belt and mother-of-pearl buttons from the waist to the rather low neck line. I was most pleased with my outfit and felt great when as assembling to leave the hotel General Djahanbani came up to me to tell me how well I looked. His own wife was one of the best dressed women in Iran and Goli Bakhtiar with whom at the time he was enamored also wore beautiful clothes.

The apartment was unbelievable. Once again reached by a private elevator from which one entered an oak paneled entrance hall with beautiful *Nain* carpets covering the white marble floor. The antique pewter chandelier was more for effect than actual lighting, for the indirect lights hidden in the ceiling moldings lit the magnificent renaissance paintings to perfection. It gave the impression of being in an old English manor house in that hall. The drawing room was very French and yet comfortable; the soft shades of green and blue blended well with the oyster walls upon which hung some very lovely Impressionist paintings including a Renoir. But the most beautiful part of the apartment was the huge garden that overlooked the Mediterranean. It was on the garden patio that we ate our sumptuous meal at small circular tables set for six. The soft candlelight, pink table cloths and beautiful pink floral arrangements made for a very intimate atmosphere. The party went on until the wee small hours with the Iranian and Lebanese alike enjoying themselves immensely. All were looking forward to the morrow's competition which was slated to be the last. However, during dinner General Khosrodad proposed that there be one final event to be held two days after the final competition. This would be hosted by the Iranians who would provide all the prizes, set the courses and hold a farewell party following. How could the Lebanese refuse?

People began drifting off and we too decided that it was time to get some sleep. Robin Cutler had arrived that afternoon from Iran and was his gay self by the time we said our farewells. Robin had delivered the horses I had bought in Ireland that summer to Tehran the previous day and had flown immediately to Beirut. A group of the Iranian contingent decided to walk the few blocks along the edge of the sea to our hotel. With Robin in the lead we sang hearty Irish Ballads bringing the silent street to life.

The Nation's Cup course seemed quite difficult as we walked it, compared to the previous days; Goli Bakhtiar's little horse would fly over the fences flat out when they were low but some of these obstacles were above the maximum height and I cautioned her not to let the horse get too quick for if she did she would be in trouble. I didn't want to complain about the height because I felt it would be poor sportsmanship; Kambis and General Khosrodad were all for making a formal complaint; however, with the help of Cololonel Khalvati I was able to keep them from doing this.

In the first round Freddy Elghanian had three fences down and a refusal for a total of fifteen faults. Ezat had just one rail down for four faults, General Khosrodad was eliminated and unbelievably Ali Rezai on Shirin was clean. The B team had a total of nineteen faults dropping the score of the general.

Goli Bakhtiar had two fences down for eight faults, Davoud Bahrami had a clear round, Col. Khalvati had four faults and Reza Hadavand had four faults. Counting the best three of the four gave our A team a total of eight faults.

The Lebanese A team also had a total of eight faults and their B team had sixteen faults, so going into the final round the two A teams were tied.

Goli Bakhtiar was first to go for Iran in the second round and incredibly to many she had a terrible fall over the natural oxer. I was not surprised but I was upset that it had to happen in this so important event. She accumulated twenty four faults. We would not want to count her score in the final tabulation, so everything lay in the hands of our last three riders. Colonel Khalvati went clean. Davoud Bahrami had a refusal at the last fence and incurred three faults plus a quarter of a time fault. Reza Hadavand was the last of our team to go and the last horse in the class. The Lebanese A team had had a total of eleven team faults in the final round for a total of nineteen. Reza could go around and hit one fence and we would win the competition; however, if he had two obstacles down the Lebanese would win by a quarter of a fault. Amazingly enough Shirin and Ali Rezai on the other team had again a clear round, the only pair in the whole competition to have a double clean. I could hardly watch as Reza went around; when he hit the natural oxer I wanted to cry but then he seemed to pull things together and went on well, jumping cleanly and carefully. I thought all was won when I saw him just tick the last fence and luck did not keep it up! That top white pole rolled in slow motion to the ground. I was sick! Standing at the out gate I saw the tears in Reza's eyes as he rode through. I could not look at him; I knew how he was feeling and could say nothing. *Bad Bakhte*! (What a shame) We were second by 1/4 of a fault.

In the A Jumper class that followed we fared well. Of the three horses in the jump-off we had two. Ali Rezai on Shahab and incredibly Reza Hadavand on Shabahang. Reza was knocked out in the first jump-off to take third place and Ali jumped against Makram Alamadins' beautiful new European mare to lose by a tenth of a second and take second place.

After the show and the presentation of prizes I walked dejectedly back to the stable area. Before I turned the corner I could hear the noise. There was obviously an argument of some sort going on. I stopped to listen. I could hear Kambis's voice clearly saying that the teams had been chosen on merit of the horses' performances during the current competition. This was fair and there was no other way of doing it. As I stood quietly who should come alongside me but Ali Reza Soudovar.

'What's up, Gaily?' he chided me.

'Sh . . . I'm listening to the Iranian team and followers discussing their loss in the Nation's Cup.' I could hear one irate voice loudly complaining that if the team had decent trainers instead of a foreign woman and a half hippy freak it would do better; I was finally able to place it as that of Bahman Shahanden. Ali and I were gratified when we heard both General Khosrodad and Kambis supporting the team trainers. The discussion seemed to be getting louder and obviously there were two or three going on at once. Shortly we were joined by Cutler and Don who had been im-

272

bibing in a quick drink before coming over to the stable to check things out. Ali and I silenced them and whispered what was going on. They laughed jovially.

'What do you expect, you two? You know you are well loved if your team is winning but it's totally your fault if things don't go the right way,' commented Don. 'Let's get out of here. We want to go back to the hotel to have a rest before we go to that party the Ambassador is giving tonight. We were hoping that everything would be all finished up here at the stable when we got here.'

'Robin,' I said, 'I think you had better take a quick look at all the horses; after all, that's why you are here and you have to put on some semblance of professionalism in front of Kambis.'

'Say, that is a good idea. Perhaps I had better have a look at the hosses.' He laughed in such a way that I knew he had already had one too many.

We four rounded the turn; as we did so silence reigned at the Iranian Team stables. All the hangers on were there as well as the generals, the colonel, the riders and grooms. It was one happy party!

'So the great trainers have decided to show their faces after their ridiculous defeat this afternoon!' It was, of course Bahman Shahandeh. He was a pudgy, sleazy little man with a bespeckled face as round as the moon. His father who owned one of Tehran's newspapers, "The Farman" had founded a large part of his fortunes by writing scathing stories about prominent families and individuals, who were shown them before publication and paid to have them discarded. Bahman at the time was a member of The Majlis (parliament) which was an appointed position. Through his contacts, he had pushed his way into the horse world to become the official commentator for The Royal Horse Society. Thus he had come to Behruit.

We said nothing.

'Well Mrs. Rose, Ali, what have you to say about this afternoon?' Kambis wanted to know.

'I think that we did very well to be beaten only by a quarter of a fault. It seemed to me that most of the riders rode well and we just happened to have a little bad luck.' I tried not to sound flippant.

'Why was Shirin not put on the A team?' questioned General Khosro-dad.

'We thought of it, but *Timsah*, you must admit that until today she had not gone well. She was eliminated the first day and on the second she knocked down four fences. How could we put a horse that had not performed well since we arrived in Lebanon on the A team?' Ali said it in Farsi so that all around could understand. There were no further comments.

'I think I had better have a look at these horses.' spoke up Dr. Cutler. He walked into the barn weaving a little. As he passed the stall of Rokhsar the horse lunged over his door and bit the good doctor right on the head and in doing so knocked him to the ground. There was our veterinary lying on the floor in front of the stall bleeding profusely from the forehead. Everyone rushed over at once almost crushing him so that he couldn't rise.

'For Christ's sake leave me alone you bloody fools!' he yelled at the top of his lungs. The crowd dispersed.

Robin casually got up and took a swab of cotton saturated with alcohol, dabbed his head and again started for the far end of the barn. This time he walked in the center of the aisle where no horse could lunge at him.

I heard someone whisper, 'I think that the doctor is drunk.'

Slowly the crowd of hangers on got into their respective cars and drove off to the hotel leaving the grooms, riders, trainers, doctor and Don and I to go back in the bus. The riders all came up to Ali and me apologizing for not having done better. We reassured them that they had all ridden a good ride that day and hopefully we would win at our own show in two days. We dopped the Imperial Stables boys at their hotel to quickly change for the big party and the four of us went to ours.

When we arrived at the hotel Ali went off to his room while Robin joined Don and me in our room for a quick drink before changing our clothes.

'Listen, Robin,' I said. 'You had not better drink too much more tonight; you don't want Kambis down your neck about it.'

'Kambis doesn't care what or how much I drink. Why I've spent many an evening with him when I polished off a bottle of Jamison's. Don't worry about me, Gail.'

Suddenly there was a loud blast from outside the hotel. The whole building shook!

'What the hell was that?'

'It sounded to me like a Molotov cocktail.' said Don.

'Can you imagine Freddy at this moment? I'll bet he is scared out of his wits. You know how paranoid he is about being here in Lebanon. Let's call his room.' It was Robin's suggestion. We called and there was no answer.

Don and Robin decided to go his room which was just across and up the hallway about ten doors. I decided to take the opportunity to have a quick shower. I was no sooner out of the shower and in my dressing gown when there was a knock on the door. I opened it to Don and Robin with a pale, shaking couple. Freddy and Elian.

'We found Freddy hiding under the bed when we knocked on the door. So we decided to bring these two down for a stiff drink to calm their nerves.' said Don. They both had a scotch on the rocks but it was a few moments before anyone said anything.

'You know, I've been terrified this whole trip that someone is going to bomb us here and when I heard that noise outside I was sure it had my name on it.' Fred was shaking.

'Eet was soo fonny,' Elian was obviously shaken by the episode but she could laugh about it. 'All of a sudden there was that beeg bomb noise so Fred says to hide under the bed and the next theeng I hear someone ees at zee door and Fred, he say, "Don't answer! They have come to get us!" But I get out from under zee bed and who do I find? Not zee Palestinians but Robin and Don. Such a relief!' She laughed heartily and the next thing we knew, Fred was laughing as well.

'I guess I must have looked pretty silly when you two came in the door. But you know during this whole trip I really didn't feel I should have come but I hated to miss the fun. And now what fun is there? Before you and Ali all showed up at the stable there was a terrible row. Everyone was calling the other man something worse! I don't remember who it was that said that I should have been left in Iran for I am such a "chicken rider". They said that Goli was the typical woman letting the side down at the last minute. You would have been shocked. Of course, Kambis and the General were wonderful because they kept saying it was an Iranian effort and we should stick together but it was dreadful. Do you want to know how it started?'

Of course we all did.

'That Bahman Shahandeh the trouble maker came round to the stable and in loud , ringing tones addressed Kambis and General Khosrodad , "I hope you two are now satisfied with your wonderful team trainers . I would suggest that you give them each a congratulatory gift for the great job they have done in botching up the Nation's Cup. You should give that foreign bitch a case of champagne to wet her insatiable appetite for that drink and give the hippy a large carton of hashish!"

'It was really embarrassing and no one knew what to say, so that's when everyone started to argue. I tried to get a word in edgewise but couldn't, however Elian had lots to say!'

Elian would have lots to say. She was one of the most vociferous people I knew. And her piercing voice could be heard for miles. She was a true and loyal friend and I was certain that she had only good things to say about her friends, Ali and me.

I called to Ali's room to ask him if he would come down to have a drink and talk over the problem that I thought we should solve that evening. He accepted and we all decided to meet in half an hour when everyone was ready for the party. We should have plenty of time to hash things out before we left for the Iranian Embassy.

At our meeting it was decided that I would go directly to Kambis and Ali would tackle General Khosrodad with our complaints.

The Elghanians, Roses, Ali Reza and Dr. Cutler arrived together at the stately old Mediterranean home that was the residence of the Iranian Ambassador to Lebanon. It was a lovely big house obviously made for entertaining. Of course, the floors were covered with exquisite Persian carpets and on the walls hung many Old Persian paintings of the *Chai Khoneh* period which were just beginning to come back into popularity. Previously they had been called *Qadjar* paintings and as that word had been a no-no in Iran for so many years, so were the paintings. It was through the efforts of the liberated Sahabanu that these paintings were again admired.

Having made our correct entrance and introductions to the host and hostess, Ali and I each made a bee line for our respective targets. Luckily, they were standing together so we were each able to get hold of one and take him aside.

'Kambis, I am both hurt and disgusted with the behavior of the Iranian contingent this afternoon. So we did not win the Nation's Cup! We lost by a quarter of a fault only. We gave a very good show. I understand our dear friend Mr. Shahandeh has made some disparaging remarks about Ali Soudovar and me. We both take offence at these remarks. It's not only an insult to the two of us but it's a disgrace to the country of Iran and His Majesty that the Iranian representatives cannot stick together for this event. When a team leaves a country to compete in another, the individual people become one. The team is one representative for that country. There may be petty feuds at home but they must be suppressed when abroad. I think that

Mr. Bahnan Shahandeh is a disgrace to his country and should be admonished. We must become united again and with Bahman here putting his nose in the works it will be hard to do. Lord knows how he managed to wrangle his way to Lebanon. He is nothing but a trouble maker and he must be made to understand that he has nothing to do with the Team. So he should keep his mouth shut. If you, however, agree with what he has said you can only fire me because you can't have a trainer in whom you don't believe.'

'You are right, of course. Bahman Shahandeh has no right here and we were wrong to let his little comments get under our skin. Naturally everyone was disappointed that we didn't win, especially since we would have if you had put Shirin on the A team, but I know why she wasn't put on and I do agree with my trainer and have faith in her. Please don't be upset. I will speak to Bahman and to be sure we will ostracize him for the rest of the trip.'

I had of course, known that Kambis would support me and Ali too. It was his duty and he was a man who always did his duty to the letter.

The General and Ali joined us, having had their own private talk. They both agreed that the comments about the champagne and the Hashish were uncalled for, especially in front of all the grooms and the Imperial riders, to say nothing of the "hangers on". The only problem was that Bahman had hit upon two weak spots. I did and always will like my champagne and Ali enjoyed his Hashish!

We all went in separate directions agreeing to make this party of the Ambassador a success and to have a jovial time. We would put on a happy face for all to see.

It was about this time that I noticed that Robin was seated upon a beautiful oak straight backed chair of the Edwardian Period right by the stairway. He seemed to be nodding and I feared he might fall over sideways. Just as I caught Don's arm to point out what I'd seen, Robin did topple to the floor. Don rushed over to help him up. He was obviously drunk. Now he had to be quickly sent back to the hotel before he made a scene or embarrassed himself. It seemed no one noticed the incident so Don helped him down the stairs to the front door and got one of the chauffeurs to take him back to the hotel giving him directions to take Robin to his room. We hoped that no one had seen the episode but such luck did not exist. Later, thanks to Bahaman Shahandeh, all were to talk about it.

By the time the sumptuous buffet, consisting of the typical Iranian fare including Kilos of the best caviar had been put on the table, word had filtered through the Iranian ranks that Bahman Shahandeh was the troublemaker who was causing dissension in the team and was to be avoided at all costs. Lebanese, who were few at this party, and Iranians made their dinner groups around the many round tables that flanked the large reception hall. As all Iranians were avoiding Bahman and his lovely wife Shayesteh, they were not included in any of the groups. It really was shocking to me and yet I enjoyed it in a sadistic way, to see the two go from group to group to see if there was room for them at the table. I was sitting at a table with General Khosrodad, a Lebanese couple and Marion Hartunian's parents; Marion had been feeling ill and had decided not to come; the absence of Masoud of the Lebanese team was evident to me although I think few others were aware. When Bahman came to our table the General curtly said, 'We have a place for Shay but for you, Bahman, there is not a place at this party.'

Bahman seemed totally unperturbed; he chuckled and said, 'Well then, Shay and I will sit over here in the corner by your table so that we can listen in to what you are saying about me.' It was so totally childish, but typical of him. The Lebanese must have thought the Iranians complete fools which at that point I did as well.

A few of us stopped in at the discotheque in the Phoenicia when we got back to the hotel to have a drink and relax. As we went in the door who should come running up behind us? Of course, Bahman and Shayesteh.

'So, you are all having a party. Is it all right if Shay and I join you?'

'Absolutely not!' we all bellowed in unison. The maître de looked up in shock at the noisy group that was entering his domain. Bahman took the hint and the rest of us had an enjoyable hour dancing and talking.

The following day was spent by most of the group doing a final shopping. In Iran it was very difficult to buy anything in the way of clothes, gift items, children's' toys and other imported commodities; there was a three hundred per cent tax on luxury items so we didn't usually purchase them there. Beirut was bliss for us; a shopping haven! All sorts of things imported from Europe and America were available. Don and I spent hours in a wonderful toy shop buying all the children's Christmas presents. That year Santa went to Lebanon. Others of the group bought French shoes, silk blouses, designer dresses and one unnamed coupled spent two thousand dollars on blue jeans and related articles. Everything that had been bought that day was sent to the Roses' room because the Roses were flying back Imperial Iranian Air Force rather than commercial and we wouldn't be checked by the Iranian Customs officials who were very strict with Iranian Nationals when they brought in imported goods. One corner of our room was piled high with boxes and extra suitcases. I hoped we would find room for everything on the plane.

The Iranian sponsored competition was more successful for our team. We had set two Table A classes; the lower division would have one jump off while the higher class would jump off twice. We thought it would make for quite a lot of excitement since there had only been a couple of other jump off classes in the whole competition. Ali Rezai on Shirin won the B competition doubly rubbing the salt in our wounds from the day of the Nation's Cup. The other placings were divided among both Iranian and

Lebanese riders. The A class ended up in an exciting jump-off between Ali Rezai on Shahab and Lufri Tasabeghionhis on Lebanon's Irish bred Persuasion just back from Europe. Unfortunately, Ali had a pole down as he was trying to beat the time of Lufri who had gone clean again on his lovely horse.

Iranians certainly do know how to throw a party. Following the competition which was really to be the last, we held a cocktail party in the reception room of the Sports Complex. The champagne flowed like water, the caviar and hors d'oeuvre were plentiful. Many speeches were made by the Lebanese and Iranians alike.

It was decided that we would have more of these friendly interchanges between Lebanon and Iran; the following April the Lebanese would come to Iran again. Unfortunately, just weeks after our trip things in Lebanon flared up; the Phoenicia Hotel, like so many others in Beirut was almost completely destroyed by bombs and fire. Of our show jumping friends, few stayed in their homeland through this trouble. Many fled to Europe to wait for the anarchy which reigned, to disappear. To date few have returned and unfortunately we did not have another friendly competition.

The day after the final competition we were due to leave. The majority of the team members and hangers on were flying out by commercial airlines in the late afternoon. The plan was that the horses would fly out in the early morning, about nine. I had Sefola organize the packing of all the tack and equipment so that all we would have to do the following morning would be to put the protective bandages on the horses, load them on the trailers and send them off to the airport where we would immediately put them on the awaiting planes. It sounded so simple. My only worry was, would the planes be waiting?

Robin and I arrived at the stable at six to supervise the bandaging of the horses and loading in the trailers. The first trailer arrived about seven and we began loading. It took us about two hours by the time the last pair of horses had left the stable area. During this time little boys from the P 10 camp below came up to sell us trinkets. I bought two lovely long necklaces of bright blue beads which were said to ward off the evil eye; they each had a brass talisman for luck at the bottom and were strung on a leather thong; they were made long enough to go around a horse's neck. An equine good luck charm.

Don arrived and the three of us drove off to the airport. We searched the runways for our two Imperial Iranian Air Force planes to no avail. I went in to one of the offices to find out if they had any information about our planes. None. We called to the tower and there were no flight plans for planes coming from Iran as yet. That meant that the planes had not left Tehran. It would take them at least four hours to reach Beirut from the time the flight plan was filed. Panic! It was already hot and the horses were almost all loaded on the pallets, standing in the hot hundred degree sun ready to be lifted onto the planes.

I called the hotel to speak with the Generals. Kambis had already left so it was either of the two who would have to OK my plan. I got General Djahanbani who was an Air Force General.

'Teemsah, we have a problem. The planes have not arrived and are not expected for at least five hours. Actually, the pilots haven't even filed their flight plans which means that they could be later than that. We have all the horses on the pallets here at the airport and there they cannot stay. I'm sure that if the planes land even by two o'clock this afternoon they won't be able to fly back tonight due to the fly time regulations so I would like to put the horses back on the trailers and plan to leave tomorrow. At the moment the trailers are still here so it won't be difficult. However, if we wait until later they will all have dispersed and it will be very difficult, not only to get them back, but to even ask.'

'Mrs. Rose! The planes will return to Iran today. General Khosrodad and I will be sure of that. We will come to the airport and order them to return.'

'Actually, General, I've flown a few times with the C 130 pilots and it seems to me that they can only fly a certain number of hours in a day. If they have been on duty from early morning they will not be allowed to return until tomorrow.'

'That may be what they have told you, Mrs. Rose, but I am a four star General as is General Khosrodad and they will not disobey an order from us . You will be leaving with your horses today.' He was emphatic.

'You are telling me then, Teemsah, that you really don't mind having the best horses in Iran stand on the tarmac all day in the hot sun after they have had such a grueling ten days. It's a long flight for them and I feel that it would be much better to wait until tomorrow rather than have them stand all that time out in the sun. It's cruelty!'

'I don't care what you think, Khonume. The horses will stay and will leave today. That is an order!' It was also the end of the conversation. He hung up!

I called the hotel again in fifteen minutes, after I had received word from the tower that one C 130 from Iran had filed its flight plan and would be arriving about three o'clock. This time I went through the same banter with General Khosrodad. Unfortunately, he had already talked to General Djahanbani and they stuck together. I was really distressed about the situation. Not only did I fear for the horses standing around all day but, I didn't want to stand around all day when we could be doing something better. I had asked the Lebanese who were so kindly driving the trailers to wait until I found out the status of the planes and now I would have to send them away. But, I knew we would have to take the horses back to the stables later on!

'My generals have told me that the horses will be leaving today so I guess you had better go. I have a dreadful feeling that we'll be seeing you all again later today.' I told the chief spokesman for the Trailer contingent.

'If there's a chance that your plane will not be returning to Tehran today, it would be much better if you would send the horses back to the stables now for they will be more comfortable and also most of these trailers that have been so kindly lent to us will be going back up to the mountains where the people keep their horses at this time of year. It will be impossible to do it later.'

I knew this, so decided to make one more try at the Generals; before I did however, I contacted the tower again and learned that the second Iranian plane had filed to land at three thirty. Once again on the telephone I got in touch with General Djahanbani and again explained the situation. He was firm. I was to send the trailers away. The horses would leave that afternoon.

After doing as I was told I managed to arrange to have the horses stand in a nearby hanger; we got hay and water for them and arranged them so that one groom could hold two horses. That way every hour there would be relief from another set of men. Those who were off duty the first hour went rushing to the duty free shop to spend what money they had left. I had divided the prize money won by the Imperial Stables horses equally among all the Imperial Servants who were on the trip so they were all eager to spend it. I then went to the Airport caterers and ordered box lunches for everyone. These tasks completed I went into the airport in search of Robin and Don who had left me after the first telephone call saying that they would be easily found when they were needed. I knew of course, it would be the bar. I located them where I expected but was surprised to find that they were drinking coffee. The bar had not yet opened! By this time it was just about eleven o'clock which was opening time; I was easily persuaded to join the two of them in having a Bloody Mary. None of us had eaten breakfast so it was a good excuse. We passed the next few hours shopping in the duty free shop, eating lunch, checking on the horses and sitting in the bar. Don and I weakened in buying a television set for Azizeh, our maid, who had hinted many times that this she desperately needed. Many of the stable boys bought tape recorders and transistor radios as well as television sets, all of which were a quarter of the price one would pay in Tehran. I could not imagine where they got the money, but Robin told me they were given money by friends and relatives every time they left the country, for it was known that they could bring in the things they bought duty free. Some of the most astute of the group bought the items to take back to Tehran and sell for double or triple what they had paid for them.

At three fifteen I heard the drone of a C 130 and sure enough, soon it was in sight on the horizon. That beautiful mountainous horizon had given us some interesting sights, for just past noon we had witnessed a dog fight between two fighter jets from Lebanon and Israel. It was a really frightening experience even though it lasted only a few minutes before the two planes were gone from the horizon towards the south.

Our second plane followed closely and the two planes were on the ground and parked by three thirty. At that time a large chauffeur driven car pulled up alongside and the two generals got out. This would be it! Would our powerful generals be able to counteract the orders that had been given to the captains of the planes, if those orders were to return the following day, of which I was certain they were?

There was much discussion but I stayed far enough back so that I wouldn't be able to hear. Robin, Don and I lay bets. It happened to be Don's fortieth birthday and he, Robin and I had laid bets that the birthday dinner would be in Beirut, and we would not be leaving that day.

The crews of the planes were closing up for the night while the Generals were obviously arguing with the two captains. We then saw the captains salute and walk off the field leaving the crew to finish closing up the planes.

Robin and I walked up to the Generals who were both beet red with anger. 'What is the verdict, *Teemsah*?' Robin addressed Khosrodad.

'I am very sorry to say that these captains have orders and we cannot countermand them. They have been on duty for too many hours and must not fly back to Tehran until tomorrow morning.'

General Djahanbani seemed to take over. 'Mrs. Rose, you must get in touch with the Lebanese Federation and have them arrange to take the horses back to the stables, right away. General Khosrodad and I must leave immediately for we are flying with the rest of the group on the four ten flight. I am sure you will have no trouble and we will see you tomorrow.' That was it! Off they went!

Robin and Don went immediately to the Bar. I went over to the load master's office to once again use his telephone. I had a very embarrassing time explaining to Mr. Gandour what had happened; he was most annoyed that we had botched the thing up. It would take hours to get the trailers back and then he might only be able to find two available. He would see that the Imperial Veterinary and Mr. and Mrs. Rose had a room for the night at the Phoenicia. If there was anything else he could do I was to call him. I then told Sefola where I could be found and went to join the gentlemen.

When I got to the building they were not in their usual place. I wandered around the duty free shop and found them standing talking to our Iranian group who had not yet boarded their plane; they had all had a wonderful day shopping in Beirut. They were laden with parcels and hand luggage as only the Iranian tourist can be. I fell upon Colonel Khalvati to tell him our predicament. He had heard nothing of it and was incensed. Then some of the others came by to hear the story as the colonel told it. Everyone was shocked and sorry but what could they do? They had had a wonderful day. Only Ali Reza Soudovar wanted more details as to the condition of the horses; the others never thought of the animals. The flight to Tehran was called so we waved them all a friendly goodbye and went to the bar to have a stiff drink.

With the use of just two trailers it took us until seven o'clock to get the horses back to the stable. That done, all save the poor fellow who drew to be on night watch, crammed into a minibus to go back to the respective hotels. As we dropped the men off at their hotel I went in to check that they did have rooms. The Lebanese had been very efficient; all was in order. We arranged to leave for the stable just after nine the next morning. No point in trying for an early start. The captains had said that they didn't want to leave until noon. They would be partying that evening.

Once we had reestablished ourselves in the Phoenicia and cleaned up the three of us went upstairs to the Rotisserie to have that sumptuous birthday dinner for Don.

'You and I lost the bet, Gail, but I think we will be able to sign for this one like we did for the one in Belgrade, so we really haven't lost. We've all won! I'd like to suggest that we have the dinner to end all dinners to make up for the hard time we had today. It's owed to Don on this, his fortieth birthday.' Robin did love extravagance, especially when he wasn't paying for it himself. Who would pay I was not sure. The Lebanese Federation was our host during the competitions but it was the fault of the Iranian contingent that we were still in Beirut. I just hoped that the bill did not get sent to Iran for then it surely would end up in our hands eventually.

We drank Champagne, ate escargot, oysters and other exotic dishes, and toasted the fortieth birthday many times. At midnight Don gave up smoking; he had been a two pack a day man so we needed more champagne to make other toasts. By the time we were ready to go to our rooms it was almost two. The bill arrived! Robin looked at it and then passed it on to me. I was shocked. We had consumed almost six hundred dollars worth that night. We pulled our usual trick of both signing. It had been a wonderful party and such a good ending to a very frustrating day. We would now have some good memories of that last day in Beirut.

The following day all went smoothly. At noon the engines of the two C 130 planes started up. We were in good enough time to land quickly at Mehrabad, get everyone checked through immigration and immediately take off to fly to Doshan Tappe. It was a very well organized flight.

The two mile walk back to the Imperial Stables loosened up the horses after their five hours in the plane even though the dreadful evening traffic was frightening. Horses, personnel and equipment were all back at the stables by seven. A good time to go down to Dr. Cutler's where his wife Margaret, had prepared a good meal for us. Not quite as sumptuous as the previous evening, but very good.

While we were having our drinks she handed me the morning paper. James certainly had done his job well. He must have arrived home to go directly to the paper with his article the previous evening.

"RIDERS RETURN WTH FEW LAURELS BUT WTH A FUTURE" was the headline.

'The first ever Iranian equestrian team to compete abroad returned to Tehran from Beirut last night without the main laurels, but with the certainty that they have the potential to compete successfully in many other countries. Though they took their full share of place money, the Iranian riders took only three of the eight first prizes offered.' He went on to list the individual wins of the Iranians and, of course, the team loss by one quarter of a fault.

There were pictures of Goli Bakhtiar, the heroine, and Sohrad Khalvati.

At the bottom of the sports page was a small blurb headlined:

OUR RIDERS NEED QUALITY JUMPERS

'Although naturally a little disappointed that Iran didn't win more trophies, Riding Fereation President Manucher Khosrodad couldn't help but be generally satisfied with his team's showing in Lebanon.

Besides the problem of the change in altitude and temperature, this was the first occasion most of the members of the team had jumped abroad. And the experience, he pointed out, will be of immense help.

The Iranian horsemen were able to see some of their weaknesses and could now go on to correct them. "We have to get down to training very seriously", he said, "as well as try to get better horses."

The Lebanese, too, were frank about how much they had learned during the event. They were as delighted with the success of the events as were their Iranian visitors.'

Team in Lebanon: L-R Reza Hadavand, Kambis, Gen. Djahanbani, Goli Bakhtiar, Ali Rezai, , Marion Hartunian, , Author, Gen Khosrodad, kneeling, Freddy Elganian, Davoud Bahrami, Ezat Vodjdani

Walking the course Khosrodad, Reza Hadavand, Ali Rezai, Author, Kambis

Manuchehr and Bahman Shahandeh with spectators

Chai Khaneh painting

SEASON'S END

Now that the International Competition in Beirut was over it was time to get horses and riders ready for the next big event in Iran which would be the Aryamehr Cup. It was to be held at The Imperial Stables on November 13 or Aban 28 of the Persian calendar. That gave us just over two weeks from the time we arrived home from Lebanon.

We had changed the format of the competition so that the team Trophy would be jumped for on Thursday afternoon, in the lower ring at Farahabad. The actual Aryamehr Cup itself, would take place in front of His Imperial Majesty on the Friday in the main Farahabad ménage. The team competition was to be a modified Nation's Cup Competition for C horses; that meant that either D or B horses could also compete; however, a horse competing in the main event on Friday was ineligible for the Team event. Each Club registered with the National Equestrian Federation was permitted to enter two teams.

Due to the fact that I was designing the course for the event and we had enough riders and horses for the two teams without me, I decided not to ride. I had a lot of responsibility in preparing the organization for the following day as well, so I felt even though some people would criticize me, in order for things to run smoothly it was better if I stuck to training and organizing. The horses were all fit and ready to go as the end of the season was approaching but as ever, the riders needed a lot of drill. Paul

Weier from Switzerland had come to Iran in the spring to give a clinic and I was able to employ many of the excellent ideas he had used.

I was sure that he thought us a mad bunch when he arrived early one Friday morning so that he would be able to view the competition of the day. Nothing spectacular happened that day but after the classes were over he commented to me that he had never seen such dreadful hands in his life. He could hardly believe that they had been worse when I had arrived. Actually, things had improved a hundred fold in the Imperial Stables. He did comment that Davoud Bahrami he thought, was a boy with a lot of talent and the only rider that seemed to have a real feel for his mount.

During the two weeks that were to follow we had a morning training session exclusively for the riders of the Imperial Stables and an afternoon session for any other riders in the country who wanted to attend the clinic and pay a fee. Ali Reza Soudovar who was a friend of Paul's, had arranged for him to come so the afternoon riders were almost exclusively riders who kept their horses at his stables.

The first day of the actual clinic he began to work on gymnastic jumping for the horses that would teach the riders to more a part of the animal. The Joint Sports Federation had lent The Imperial Stables an instant replay video machine and I was lucky enough to have my brother visiting who was in the film business. I persuaded him to come to do the camera work for us. We found that once the men got used to the idea that it was themselves they were viewing they were able to see their mistakes and could better understand what Paul was trying to show them.

We had an exhausting four hour period of work from seven until eleven each day; during the training period I was at Paul's side trying to take in as much as I could and translating into Farsi what he was telling each rider. The riders would ride a group of fences then view themselves; ride again and review. There were a few who just could not get over how handsome they looked on television and gained nothing however, the majority learned a lot.

292

Kambis had been unable to attend the first two mornings and when he showed up the third day he was in a fierce temper. The first group of horses were to be the young ones which were just jumping small obstacles. I had thought that Roshan would be a good horse for him to ride. The horse had improved so much since I had him in my program that he now rode like he was a made horse, so I thought it would be a good combination for them to work through the small gymnastic combinations. I obviously made a great mistake because Kambis could not get him to jump over one pole.

'Mr. Atabai! Just relax your hands, sit lightly on your seat and push with your legs.' said Paul calmly.

'No! No! It is not a six foot obstacle; just trot in with cadence. You do not need to gallop! Stop! You must steer the horse! It is elementary! Do you not even know how to steer a horse? Try again. NO! No, no, no, it is impossible! '

Kambis was flying into the series of four obstacles set at no stride, one stride, two strides and three strides. Roshan jumped the first and then threw Kambis right over the second. There he lay on the ground. The Imperial servants ran to his rescue. He lay until they came and then allowed them to help him up and dust him off. His hat had come off in the fall but he refused to put it on so Akbar, his ever present servant, held it for him.

'Mr. Weier,' said Kambis, 'I do not like you or your methods, right now. I will refuse to ride any more today, but I want to watch what you are doing. I want you to know that we are paying you good money to teach us some finer points of show jumping and I don't want you ruining His Majesty's horses.'

Paul was aghast but he pretended not to be bothered and continued the work with other horses and riders. Constantly Kambis interspersed comments of criticism and chastised me for allowing this Swiss to ruin the horses. I was most embarrassed.

'Why is Tala jumping such a high jump? You will ruin her. She is just a young mare. Mrs. Rose, it is your responsibility to see that these horses are not ruined!'

To Ali Rezai, who was riding Tala, he called, 'Ali, you must take that mare back to the stable. I do not want her ruined!' Ali obeyed. I argued but to no avail. It went on like that during the morning.

When the actual clinic was finished I had Kambis's two jumpers Rostam and Rokhsar sent down. The first two days I had asked Paul to ride these horses. I wanted his opinion and felt that by him giving them training rides it would help with their performances. When one is training an amateur rider to ride show jumpers it is necessary to keep the horses sharp and that means that a better rider than the amateur should ride them as often as possible. Thus, I had Paul who was an experienced and accolated rider get on both horses as I wanted to take advantage of his expertise.

Seeing his horses arriving from the stable all tacked up he asked, 'Why are my horses coming? I told you that I did not want to ride any more today.'

'To tell you the truth Kambis, I've had Paul riding them the past couple of days; I felt it would do them good.'

'Akbar! *Begu que asban nayan*.' He screamed at Akbar. (Tell them not to bring my horses)

'Mrs. Rose, understand that I do not want this man, no matter who he is, to ride my horses. It is your job to see that my horses jump and you usually do a good job. I do not want the horses ruined DO YOU UNDERSTAND?'

'Yes!' I was humiliated. I could stand it no longer so walked quickly out of the ring and up to my office. How was I to get through the ensuing days?

There was the day when the driver forgot to pick Paul up at his hotel so he hailed an orange *Toman* taxi which drove him through the dreadful early morning traffic. I never could figure out how he found the Stables, for he spoke not a word of Farsi. He claimed to have pointed right, left and straight in order to direct the taxi driver.

There were parties, of course. Everyone in the horse world wanted to entertain the celebrity. Kambis continued to be difficult but he did finally consent to ride Rokhsar and Rostam in the clinic every morning. Kambis loved to see himself on TV!

We had a competition and constructive criticism following the final day of the clinic; it seemed to both Paul and me that the one person to gain a lot from this clinic was General Khosrodad. Paul spoke with him in French and he listened intently. He did what he was told and it seemed to me that he was really improving.

One day a group of us flew to Shiraz with Paul to show him the sights of Persepolis of which Iran was very proud. We were even able to gain access to the tents in Tent City where all the dignitaries stayed during the 2500th Anniversary of the Iranian nation. The tents were furnished with antique and reproduction furniture of the style which might be found in the country of the guests that were staying in that tent. Thus, there was a Louis XIV tent for the French President, and an early English decor in the tent where Prince Philip and Princess Anne stayed. I will grant the praise of organizing this wonderful trip to General Khosrodad. Paul was rightly, very impressed.

On the final evening of Paul's stay there was a dinner party held at Xanadu, the very best French restaurant in Tehran. The General wanted me to write down a constructive comment that Paul had for each rider that had taken part in the clinic. After we had eaten a sumptuous meal I sat next to our expert and went through the list of riders one by one. Three of his comments stand out above all the others.

Of Davoud Bahrami he said, 'There is a boy with a great talent. If you ever want to send him to me in Switzerland I would love to have some real time to train him.' I did send Davoud to him that summer.

'General Khosrodad was the most cooperative rider in the clinic. He tried very hard to do everything I asked. It is a shame he is not younger.'

'You don't really want me to make a comment about Mr. Atabai do you?' He asked when we got to Kambis's name.

When I nodded in the affirmative he added, 'All I can say, is he has nice hair!'

I was asked to submit to the Equestrian Federation in writing these comments made to me. How could I put down the comment about Kambis? But I did. And he actually laughed when he read it!

Wednesday was the day I spent building the course for the team competition. It was also the day Prince Davalou spent putting the finishing touches on his masterpiece of landscape gardening in the main ring where the Puissance Class for the Aryamehr Cup itself would be held. I think it took me two hours with the help of ten men to set up my course. It had taken Colonel Khalvati a week to set his five Puissance fences and the good Prince three days to complete the decorations. I have to admit that the course was magnificent. The obstacles were banked with flowers and there were small garden patches full of brilliant autumn flowers scattered around the ménage. But what impressed me most about the Prince's course decoration was that he strutted around wearing a beautiful Chesterfield coat with a black velvet collar. At one point he loosened it and I spied the lining. Being bold, I asked him to show it to me. The soft grey silk was hand painted depicting a beautiful French pastoral scene. I have never seen such a work of art on a top coat! He was most pleased to show it off and explained to me that a friend of his in Paris who was an artist had personally done the painting.

Thursday noon arrived a crisp, clear fall day that one only finds in Iran. The ever-present sun shone brightly in the Persian cerulean blue sky. Thursday in Iran is like Saturday in most Western countries. For many years there was only one day of rest in Iran but in the late sixties it was decided that most of the people needed at least one other half day holiday each week. There was much debate as to whether it should be Saturday, a day of rest that would coincide with the Western world or Thursday, the day before the Sabbath. His Majesty and his advisors finally decided that the day before the Sabbath would be much more appropriate. So Thursday became a day on which most offices closed their doors at noon; it was the day people took off for their week-end homes in the country and in 1973 it became a bank holiday which meant that Iran was cut off from the Western world financially, for four days each week. What did it matter? Iran was becoming so important that many felt it did not need the West or the many Western advisors that were living in Iran.

This particular Thursday there was quite a crowd gathered to watch the Aryamehr Team Cup. The trophy itself would be presented to the Captain and members of the winning team by His Imperial Majesty the following day.

Our Imperial Stables A team consisted of Ezat Vodjdani on Alborz, Ali Rezai on the little Torkoman Zahak, Davoud Bahrami on Mojgan and Kambis Atabai on Roshan, which had been jumping very well for me during the season. We really had a good chance I figured, and how I wanted them to win. Our B team was a motley group captained by General Khosrodad who was not at all happy to be riding on this second team. I had explained to him that we needed to win the Cup and that I felt his horse Hedarbaba was not of the class with the first four horses. Being a good sport he was able to accept the explanation but warned me that he expected to have two perfect rounds on his horse now that he had his new spurs. These were a fantastic pair of sharp pointed spurs that were about two inches in length. It would be impossible not to hit the horse with these at every stride and they would certainly be felt by the poor beast.

Two teams had equal eight faults after the two rounds had been completed. One was the Imperial Stables and the other Ali Soudovar's Dashte

Behrht team. I had been criticized for making the course too easy by a few of the riders while they were walking the course. Ali Soudovar himself had laughed at the final fence which was a triple combination of vertical poles with one stride between at the maximum height of 1.20M. I had kept silent knowing that this fence was much more difficult than it appeared and had warned the riders from our teams to ride the combination carefully, for with too much speed the horses would become sloppy and be likely to roll a pole. After the first few horses had gone the riders watching began to realize that the course was not as simple as they had felt while they were walking it.

The first horse in the jump off was General Djahanbani from Dashte Behrht. He jumped the shortened course clear and in a very fast time of forty five seconds. Kambis was second with Roshan. He started out like a bat out of hell; Roshan is a very careful jumper and so cleared all the obstacles well; then disaster hit when Kambis cut too short into an oxer and the little horse ran out for three faults. It was disappointing but we had three more good horses to jump and only the best three out of the four counted for the final score. Goli Bakhtiar had a fast clear round of forty seconds for Dashte Behesht; Davoud Bahrami was clear but in forty-two seconds. The next two horses on both teams had clear rounds but when the total times were added Dashte Behesht had won.

Friday dawned bright and clear again. I hoped that my riders would have better luck than the previous day. The puissance is an exciting class for the spectators to watch. Each horse and rider negotiates the course of five obstacles, some spread and and at least one vertical, and those who complete the course without any faults enter the second round over a shortened course; those clear again jump over an even shorter course and so, until there are just two obstacles left; one is a spread which is optional but is usualy jumped as a warmup fence and the other a vertical, usually a wall which is the last fence to be jumped. After each round the obstacles are widened and raised.

After the first round fifteen of the twenty horses that had competed were clear. Of those fifteen, five were from the Imperial Stables. Kambis was riding Ballylea and I was extremely nervous. The horse had arrived while we were in Lebanon so he had only just over two weeks to train with him. The first week during the training session both horse and rider had done well and seemed to suit each other, but during the first competition in which Kambis had shown Ballylea, the latter had very neatly dumped him in the middle of the brush at the last fence. This made a great front page picture for the Tehran Journal though it was just on the 'sports' page of the Kayhan! The training went well the second week; the horse was noted as an excellent Puissance horse in Europe where he had been a part of the Irish International Team many times.

When Kambis had entered the ring the first time I had been unable to watch.

After the second round many horses were knocked out. By the fourth round we were left with one rider from the Imperial Guard, Kambis on Ballylea and General Khosrodad on Golitussi. I could hardly believe that the big grey carriage horse of the General was doing so well. We'd had quite a time with him the previous two weeks, as we had all season. He was beginning to get more and more careless over his fences, rapping almost everything.

I had tried various devious methods such as poling with a bamboo pole, with a big heavy pole, with a tack pole and even putting a thin wire over the jump that would break if he hit it. This latter device usually frightens the horse and it then begins to really pick up his feet. Not so with Golitussi!

I had finally decided to get brutal with the horse. I had the mechanic from the Imperial Garage come to fix a device that worked on a twelve volt battery. He arrived on a Saturday morning while Kambis was still there so that Kambis was able to describe the technical terms of what I wanted to Aghaye Shariat. Basically, what I wanted was a battery that I would attach to a wire that would run about six inches above the top most pole of the obstacle. This wire would break on impact and would need a ground so that when the horse hit it he would be grounded and get a jolt. This was very difficult to explain to the mechanic who certainly did know about cars and batteries but knew nothing about a horse. He kept saying how danger-ous this would be. The horse would get a shock! That was the idea, but he couldn't quite seem to understand why we would want to do this.

The following day I had a call from the garage that Mr. Shariat had a device down at the garage and if I would go to look at it he would bring it up the next morning if it was what I wanted.

I always loved going to the garage. I am not a car nut but His Majesty had some of the most beautiful cars I have ever seen. The new garage had just been completed at Farahabad which was part of a project to phase out the down town offices of the Court and eventually have them all at the more convenient place for the Imperial Family, Farahabad. In the huge indoor parking building were the cars of the Royal family; there were perhaps seven or eight Rolls Royce; one in particular was about a 1935 vintage; to me its huge wine and black form was very regal; it seemed the Rolls Royce Company decided that it wanted this car for its museum as it didn't have one of this model, so they sent someone to offer one million dollars for this car. Naturally the offer had to go to His Majesty who flatly refused to sell the car; although rarely used, if it was a collector's item then he would col-lect it! There were Lamborghinis, Mercedes Benz of every description and many other types of sports cars and limousines. At that time there was also parked in the garage a car that had caused much controversy, a Stutz Bearcat.

It seemed that an American businessman had bought up the old Stutz patents and name and decided to make this famous car again under the name of Stutz Motor Car of America. The parts would be all hand tooled and the car itself was individually assembled. There had been about ten of them made recently, one of which was in the fleet of the King of Saudi Arabia, another was in Egypt and another in Jordan, it was reported. The president of the company brought his Stutz to Iran for the Industrial Exhibition that year and during the show he met our friend Bahman Shahandeh. Bahman told him that he would be able to get him an interview with Princess Shams, the Shah's sister, who would definitely be interested in buying the sleek metallic grey automobile. The American businessman fell for the story and when the show was over he handed the keys of his $50,000 car to Bahman who was going to take care of the permits for it. For two weeks Bahman was seen around and about the city driving this beautiful machine. He certainly did give it a lot of advertising but what a risk in that perilous Tehran traffic.

Finally our American friend became a bit worried about his car and the validity of Mr. Shahandeh, who when confronted, told him that he would take him out to the home of the princess the next afternoon. True to his word Bahman drove out with the owner of the car to the beautiful home of Princess Shams that had been designed by Frank Lloyd Wright. Its name, "The Pearl", comes from the fact that it had a huge pearl-shaped dome. Bahman got out of the car and was greeted at the door by a woman and a man. Our American did not speak any Farsi but was presented nevertheless, to whom he thought must be the princess and her husband. The couple were taken for a drive in the car and then dropped back at the mansion. After a long conversation Bahman had with this couple he and his friend drove back to Tehran. How excited the American was for he thought it was the princess they had driven around.

How let down he was when he heard that the princess was allergic to the mouflon carpet on the floor and thus would not buy the car. He would be happy to change it but still the answer was no.

Bahman kept the car saying that he would sell it to one of the lesser royal personages if he could keep it a month or so more. Our American businessman decided to leave it with him and went back to the States. I will give Bahman his due. He did try to sell the car and that morning when I was at the Royal Garage it was being looked at by the Imperial mechanics who said what a wonderful machine it was. It was decided by the Imperial Court that His Majesty would accept it as a gift but he would not buy such a car.

Shortly after it was turned down by His Majesty, Bahman was arrested for driving a car without registration, insurance or certification! The American came to get it when he was duly notified and that was the end of the Stutz in Iran.

I heard Bahman much later telling an Iranian friend how he had such a wonderful time with the car. Why, he had even driven the owner out to Princess Sham's residence and taken the housekeeper and her husband for a ride. 'I didn't actually tell the man that it was the Princess who was in his car; why actually she was out of the country at the time, if he had wished to check. I just told him that for security reasons I could not tell him who was in his car.'

Mr. Shariat had rigged up a wonderful device with proper switches and a very unique catch that would hold the wire together over the fence but would break if there was enough impact, such as a horse striking it while in motion. I "OKed" the work and said goodbye until the morrow. The following morning the mechanic and the device were in the ring at six thirty. He had painted the two switch boxes and had the battery enclosed in another painted box; everything was so much more professional than I had needed, but hopefully it would work well.

I had Davoud Bahrami on Gollitussi for I didn't want the General to be the first to try the horse over the electricity. I had heard of cases where the rider got the shock too! The wire hummed when we turned on the switch and the mechanic who wanted to check that there really was current started with a jolt when he touched his finger to it. It sparked too!

302

The first time Golitussi jumped those wired up planks he hit the wire but the next time he really cleared it by a mile. During the week I moved the electric device and wire from one jump to the other so that he would not know where to expect it.

There were just two fences in the fourth round; although the first fence was jumpable it was optional and would not count for any score. I liked that optional fence for it wakes the horse up to what he is doing in the ring before the big wall must be attacked. I heard the crowd groan when Temouri from the Guard knocked a block off the big wall. I had been trying to keep Kambis calm for he was to go next. He cleared both of the obstacles beautifully and so did the general. That meant a fifth round in which both horses and riders were from the Imperial Stables. How pleased His Majesty would be. He was showing little interest in the horses at that time, mostly due to his other commitments, but when he did watch a competition he liked for his own stable, into which he put so much money, to do well.

Kambis went first. This I could watch, though in the previous rounds I was so afraid that Ballylea would dump him that I cared not to watch. He jumped the optional jump well and then he came around and seemed to cut just a little too sharp turning into the wall. The jump was good but Ballylea dropped a hind toe and pulled off a block.

'Now General, it's yours. If you can jump that wall clean you have won the Aryamehr!'

He did it! The applause and roar from the crowd was thunderous. He is a very popular man and everyone was pleased to see him finally win the Aryamehr Cup after trying for these four years.

His Majesty came down from the Royal Podium to present the prizes to the first six places and then he was to present the team prize to the Dashte Behesht Team. All the Team riders were ready and waiting in their immaculate attire but when the call came to ascend the podium their Captain General Djahanbani told them they could not go up; he was to accept the prize alone! There were three disappointed faces. Actually only two, those of Ulrika Von Wulffen, a German Princess who sometimes would come up from Esfahan, where her husband ran a farm in partnership with an Iranian, to compete as a part of Ali's team and Danny Elghanian; Goli Bakhtiar was not disappointed! Her father had been exiled by the Shah and killed years before and she hated him; she had actually not given him the customary salute when she came into the ring for her rounds.

Following the presentations His Majesty and the other members of the Royal Family flew away in their helicopters to the palace in Niavaran.

Previous to the team's going to Lebanon it had been decided to hold a cocktail after an evening event at the Farahabad. There would be no wild music and only finger food so people would certainly not stay long enough to drink too much. By the time I checked out the horses and arrived at the party most of the finger food was gone and so were the people. A small select group, including the Atabais, Elghanians, Shahandehs, the riders from the Imperial Stables and the Roses were left. I was astounded when suddenly Colonel Shaki arrived cursing and swearing at General Khosrodad. Without warning the two men were having a fist fight. It took six men from the Imperial Stables to separate them. Shaki was escorted from the stables. That was to be the final party! No party to celebrate following the Cup!

The next event in the season of Show Jumping was the Iranian National Championship. Due to the Lebanese trip it had been postponed until later in the season and I really was afraid of the weather. It had been planned to hold the competitions on a Friday, the following Tuesday which was a holiday, and the final event would be again on a Friday. The plans were made, the prize list sent out to the competitors, and the sponsors were all arranged. Because Kambis had to go to Gonbad to the races on the Tuesday at the last minute the Championship would be held on three Fridays. That meant it would run into the second week in December and for certain there would be snow. I argued to the point of getting his ire up to a peak that I had never quite seen before but to no avail. If Kambis could not be there, there would be no event. He was the Chief of the Royal Horse Society and things would be done his way. More and more he was becoming autocratic and not willing to listen to reason.

The first event was won by Ali Rezai and handily. He didn't go off course as he had done the previous year. He also won the second event. He would certainly win the title of Champion of Iran.

During the final schooling the Tuesday before the event I had put up a series of obstacles that would pose a problem similar to one I would put in the final event; as I was designing the course I could give this little bit of extra help to my own riders. I had a triple bar with a bending line to an oxer that could be ridden in either three or four strides and then the same distance to a wall; if a rider wanted to take a chance and go for the time it could be done in three strides on the left side of the obstacle but it was safer to jump to the right side in order to land after the oxer, turn left and jump a wall with poles over it in four strides. Everyone did this beautifully. Ali jumped last and decided foolhardily to take a chance. The three strides to the oxer were good but when he landed and turned he had what looked like a distance of two and a half strides to the wall. I saw it coming and in an instant horse, rider and wall were in a pile on the ground.

The horse was up first, rather stiffly, then came the wall; Ali, I was hoping, was playing the Iranian trick of being dead when really there was nothing but a bit of hurt pride. He was the only rider other than Kambis that I had not been able to break of this silly business. After a moment Ezat and Reza Hadavand were off their horses and ran over to him, also the ever present Akbar. They all gasped in horror. I ran over, my heart racing. Ali was just coming to, but what a mess. His face was a mass of blood and there seemed to be no nose. All I could see was blood. I had Reza rush to get his car while Ezat and Akbar carried Ali in sitting fashion across the ring to the gate. But by the time they got him to the gate he wanted to walk on his own. Abdula had brought a bottle of savlon, some warm water and cotton wool. He cleaned some of the blood off the face which made it look not quite so bad but his nose was definitely broken and he seemed to have hurt his knee and left arm. I hoped nothing was broken.

My hopes were in vain. The next morning when I arrived at the stables I saw that Ali's arm was in a cast. His face was much better but he was limping badly and it seemed that he had cracked some ribs as well.

'Ali, you will never be able to ride on Friday. What a shame.' I was sick at heart for I knew how badly he wanted to win the Championship.

'Khonume Rose. I will ride. I will ride today. If I don't ride I will never ride. After the competition then I will rest.' He certainly was a tough one.

He rode all week. He even popped Shahab over a few small gymnastic obstacles on Thursday morning to make certain the horse had not lost his nerve. I was sure that Ali had not lost his, but horses are funny creatures and I felt that Shahab needed a few small fences to give him confidence. Once a horse loses its nerve it can become a real problem, often refusing to jump.

Shahab jumped well over the gymnastics so I had Ali put him over one big oxer of about 1.40M. He had no problems, though how Ali himself was able to negotiate the jumps I wasn't sure.

Thursday noon I started to put up the parcours. Actually, I did very little of the work myself, for my trusty Maleki and his crew were able to do most of it. All I did was give him a drawing of the course and a drawing of each individual fence. It was a far cry from those first days building courses; Maleki and his boys had learned well.

The first course that I had ever seen built in Iran was that Aryamehr Cup course that I did with Colonel Neshati. I had been frustrated beyond all means when I saw that there were twelve men who all worked on one fence. It was impossible. It was like a "Laurel and Hardy" comedy. While one raised one side another lowered the opposite side. Poles fell, people screamed and it took hours to build a whole course.

The first months that I worked at the Imperial Stables I tried very hard to change the system by laying the course out with poles on the ground and then having the crew bring the various pieces of equipment for each fence one by one. Once the pieces were there I left some men to put the fence up to a specified height and width and got another group of men to bring the components of the next fence into the ring. This was a bit better than the usual Iranian method but it still was not good enough. I needed one man who could organize the whole thing.

Maleki became my number one course builder in a very roundabout way. The first few times that I built courses at Farahabad I noticed that there was one man who really seemed to know the obstacles well. He was the most energetic and very willing to help me. He was a good looking Iranian of small stature, a neat little Hitler mustache, big brown eyes and a very high forehead. I attributed the extra intelligence he seemed to have to that high forehead. My mother had always told me that the high forehead denoted high intelligence. As the months went on I began to rely upon Maleki to take care of the obstacles; at that time there was not a specific person denoted as keeper of the jumps. He, like every other *djelodar* at that time had to ride every day and take care of his four or five specific horses. He was a relatively new member at the Imperial Stables; that is, he was a first generation employee. He had been hired after he had finished his stint in the army which had been about ten years previously. Now there were certain old guard *djelodars* that did not like this upstart and would very often tattle tale to Kambis, something that my boss really liked. He loved to be informed of irregularities that had taken place in the stables, then he would interrogate the culprit in the presence of the other *djelodars*. Kambis's punishments were harsh.

One time Mashed Ali had complained that he was working too hard on days of horse shows, because he had to take care of four horses. He had to have them all groomed, tacked up ready for the rider at the correct time, bathe them when they were finished and do them up. For his impudence he was fired from his job. He was actually not fired from the employ of the Imperial Stables, for it was impossible to fire an Imperial Servant however, he was taken off horse duty and put on night watchman's duty at one of the building sites. This was sad indeed, for Mashed Ali was one of the *djelodars* that really did love his horses.

Maleki's turn came. Kambis had been out hunting in the mountains one day and on the way back he stopped in Jajaroot, a little village, to telephone for a car to come pick him and his guests up; he then telephoned to the stable to have the reserve duty officer of the evening take a mule and ride seven miles to the designated rendezvous point to meet the other six men with the horses and mules and help bring them back to the stables. Now Maleki who was on duty, had a friend who lived in Jajaroot, and that friend happened to be visiting him so when the order came his friend, who had to go home anyway, offered to drive him to the meeting place. This seemed a sensible enough idea so Maleki put on his warm winter hunting gear and drove with his friend to the appointed spot where he got on one of the spare horses and lead a couple of others back to Farahabad. About two hours were saved by this move and Maleki was quite pleased with himself.

The next afternoon Kambis stopped by the stable to see that all the hunting horses had arrived safely and to find out what time they had arrived. He was rather shocked that the train of horses and mules had arrived by seven o' clock. He had just called the stable at five so how had Maleki ridden the seven miles and returned with the others in such a short time?

'Well,' said Akbar, 'Hossein happened to be visiting him so he just drove Maleki up and that way he was able to save time.'

Kambis hit the roof. Maleki was called up and given the tenth degree.

Then and there, Kambis demoted him to *metar* or groom. He would from that day wear groom's clothes and do groom's work. He was no longer a *djelodar*. This was a terrible shock to Maleki who was very proud of his job and had really no intention of disobeying orders; he had just thought for himself and in Iran sometimes that is a worse thing than disobedience.

Poor Maleki. He was not really a very good groom and he hated it mostly for the social disgrace that he was going through. I began to realize that there were many things that Maleki had been doing for me that now were left undone for he didn't have the time to help me. After two weeks I went to Kambis to explain that I felt this was a wicked punishment for such a ridiculous offence and that I also felt that Maleki could be very useful in the position of general handy man around the stable. He would be in charge of the jump storeroom, make certain that any repairs around the stables were done, change the jumps for our training sessions, keep the rings in shape and do any other odd jobs that needed taking care of; there were hundreds of things he could do.

We had two full time carpenters at the stables who made and repaired jumps; as well they did many jobs that came up around and about the stables and at the homes of the Atabais, both senior and junior. They needed to be supervised.

'But Mrs. Rose, every man who is a *djelodar* must ride. Maleki must ride and be made to ride hard.'

'That is fine with me, but let's face it, he is never going to be a great rider of show jumping horses. I know he is good in the mountains, but there is a lot of work for him to do here at the stables.'

'Mrs. Rose, if I grant you your wish of getting your dear Maleki out of the salt mines, so to speak, you must make him ride two horses every day. And all winter I want him drilled to death so that his bones ache. If I let him off this punishment for insubordination I will turn him directly over to you and if there is any problem you will be responsible. He is very lazy and that is the only reason he took a ride to Jajaroot that night. There is nothing I hate more than laziness.'

'Kambis, I will certainly accept that responsibility readily because I think he's a good man and shows initiative and intelligence. That's rather refreshing to see.'

'Are you trying to tell me that the men at the stables are stupid?'

'Oh! For heaven's sakes no! But there are many who are so afraid to act upon their own initiative, that it makes me sick. You can't run an operation successfully unless the help are able to go ahead and get things done. Most of the men are afraid to eat lunch without asking permission. Maleki isn't and I like that!'

'I'll let you know in a few days what I have decided. Now let's discuss more pleasant matters.'

A few days later I had my reply. Kambis arrived at the stable about seven thirty and immediately called me and Maleki to talk to him. He did not meet with us in his office but right there in the stable yard he told Maleki in a tone loud enough for all to hear that I had saved him from his horrible punishment. He said that Mrs. Rose was to be his unconditional boss. He would answer to me. If he got into any trouble it would be Mrs. Rose not him, who would be punished. This was very good psychology, for by that time the majority of the men at the stable liked me because I had brought some sort of organization into their lives. Maleki was beaming from ear to ear. Of course he would cause no more trouble. He kissed Kambis's hand as was the custom and when dismissed ran home immediately to tell his wife, who was also in disgrace, and to change back into his *djelo-dar* uniform.

From that day Maleki became my right hand man; he took complete charge of the rings, jumps and anything to do with repairs around the stables. He changed our gymnastic lines of fences to my specifications at least twice a week. The stable looked in much better repair. Those broken hinges were all fixed. He checked the automatic watering bowls so there were very few spillages which was a relief. He was always around when I needed him. Each morning after the riding sessions were finished I would go into my office to do my daily paperwork and at that time he would come in to make his report for the day.

The first month after his run in with Kambis I did give him the responsibility of four horses but two were young three year olds and I had one of the young boys working with them. Maleki was obliged to ride in the class with the group on two horses, and he actually seemed to derive some fun out of it. Gradually, however, I was able to phase out his riding obligations.

Several months later he came to tell me that he had a problem and through much embarrassment and guess work I realized that he was explaining that he had a hernia. So I was not surprised one morning when Kambis drew the subject to my attention.

'Mrs. Rose, I have just had a medical report from the court hospital and your handyman Maleki must go into the hospital for a hernia operation.'

'Yes, he has already told me about it. I have had him working doubly hard to get things in shape here so that we will not miss him for the time that he will be laid off. He informs me that the doctor told him that he would be able to be around the stable in about ten days, though he will be unable to do any hard labor or lifting for some time after that.'

'Well, I guess you are going to have your way after all. You will have to give his horses to someone else as it seems he has been advised against further riding activity.'

'I hate to tell you this, but Maleki has had no horses for over a month. I sort of phased him out of them when his work load around the stable became heavier. I hope I'm not in trouble for this; you know how I hate being in your bad books.'

'I don't know why I have a woman in your position. How can I be angry now that the thing is a *fait accompli*? I don't think I will ever learn to understand women. I have to contend with you, my secretary, Mary Gharagozlou and Louise Firouz, not to mention my wife. I really think that you will drive me crazy if I'm not already there by now! So we don't have a problem, you have taken care of Maleki's horses. I guess it's time I got on my horse.'

'Indeed it is.' I called the grooms to bring out our horses. We were taking a string out that morning to work up the long sand track in the desert. Once Kambis and I were mounted the others followed in behind and we set off.

'I hope you don't think that I deceived you about Maleki and the horses, because I did not. If you ever took the time to read the stable charts you would see that under Maleki's name there are no horses. I have explained that if there was ever a doubt in your mind as to which groom a horse belonged, you only need look at my chart. It's the most up-to-date record. Khanlakhani sometimes does not get the information of changes from me for a couple of days and then it takes him a week to redo his lists.'

'You needn't worry, Gail. I know all women are naturally devious and what can I do about it? One poor lone male!'

When I had first arrived at Farahabad there were three donkeys, a pair of white Andalusian donkeys that belonged to Princess Fatima and a regular Persian donkey. These donkeys were used in turns to pull the drag that leveled the ring. This drag was like a small harrow made of welded steel with three inch prongs that were dragged through the sand. In Farsi it was called a *shenkesh* (rake). There are many different kinds of rakes and in English we have different names for them but in Farsi there is only one word and it takes in any kind of rake.

Naturally these donkeys had to be driven from behind by a man. The names of all the *djelodars* were on a roster for such things as night watch duty, lunch duty and *shenkesh* duty. To drag the three rings it took a whole day using these little donkeys and it seemed to me that it was a waste of the time of a rider or anyone to spend a whole day *shenkeshing* the rings. I had them divide the roster up so that each ring was done twice a week but not by the same person. This was better but it was still a boring job, hard work and to me a waste of time. I decided that we needed small tractor for this job.

My first letter to Kambis on this matter was received with horror. 'Do you know how much one of those tractors costs here in Iran? About five thousand dollars, probably a lot more. Do you think I have a limitless budget? There is no way I can provide you with this machine. I can't see what is the matter with the donkeys? You'll make the men too soft with your tractor riding.'

'I have no intention of having the men use this tractor. It would be strictly under the jurisdiction of Maleki. As well, the tractor could be used to haul a large wagon in which the manure could be put every morning instead of having each individual groom wheel his manure a quarter of a mile away to the manure pile. Think of the time that's wasted! The grooms would have more time for grooming and doing other things.'

'They would have more time for lazing around!' was his reply.

Shortly after this, one donkey that belonged to the stables died and the two that were Princess Fatimeh's were taken away, so we had to use a little Caspian Pony for the job and he kicked and fussed so much that it became a real problem. I would occasionally make snide remarks that it was a shame there was not enough money in His Majesty's stable budget for a tractor to keep the ring in shape for his expensive horses but Kambis didn't budge on the subject.

One morning when I arrived at the stable what should I see but a beautiful orange tractor sitting proudly in the middle of the stable yard? I was astounded! This became known as the Maleki Machine and on pain of death did anyone else touch it. The rings were in much better shape once the tractor was put into use. The manure transport was much more efficient and the wagon was also very useful for moving jumps around. I never thought I would be so happy to see a tractor. When I profusely thanked Kambis for our new piece of stable equipment he was rather elusive about its origin but I gradually was able to piece together the fact that it had been part of an order of small tractors for the various palace gardens around Tehran and I guess the Imperial Stables qualified as a palace garden.

To get back to my Championship course, Maleki laid out the poles for the eighteen obstacles that the regulations called for and then gave the *djelodars* diagrams of obstacles that each was to build with the help of three grooms. In less than an hour Maleki who had been supervising called me from my office to check the course and take the final measurements of each obstacle. I had only to change the heights of two or three jumps; meanwhile, I had one of the men measuring the course and we were finished. It gave me such a sense of accomplishment when I was able to complete a job in such a short time without all the confusion and hassle that had been the norm when I first arrived at Farahabad.

As I stood out on the top step of the Imperial Box to make my final observations a first flake of snow landed on the tip of my nose. Within ten minutes the ménage was covered with a white blanket. I looked at the ominous sky and had the sinking feeling that this was not a quick snow; this was the beginning of winter and we were probably in for a few days of it. I was almost certain that the final event would be either cancelled or postponed for a week.

By the time I drove home the roads were already slippery and the radio reported that the freezing temperatures expected for the evening would make conditions hazardous.

I awoke early the next morning to see that it was still snowing. It was just six but I could already hear the *Barfis* calling their haunting chant. These men went around with wooden pallets with which they shoveled snow off the flat rooved houses. If the roof was not cleared of the snow it would melt and the water would seep down through the concrete and brick roofs causing water damage and sometimes the roof to cave in.

I called Kambis who suggested that we postpone the event until the following Friday. He would take care of the formalities of calling the press and so forth. It was disappointing but at least it gave Ali Rezai another week to recover from his fall. Our telephone never stopped ringing all day. Friends, the press, acquaintances and strangers wanted to know what would happen. Then late in the afternoon the telephone went dead and dead it stayed for three days. It continued to snow for two more days. On Sunday I tried to drive down to the stable but the roads were so bad that the traffic was barely moving and the accident rate in Tehran during a snowfall was very high. I got as far as our local taxi office where I was able to make a few telephone calls. Kambis felt that if the snow did not stop that day we would have to cancel the final leg of the Championship because the ring drainage was not good enough and the chances of it drying by Friday were slim.

The snow did not stop and on Tuesday there was an official notice of the cancellation stating that the leader to date Ali Rezai, would be declared Champion of Iran. I was able to get to the stable on Saturday and found a very dejected group of men. They had been clearing snow for days and there were huge piles of it in the middle of the stable yard. I started off a snowball fight and then ran into the sanction of the tack room. Nasser would not let snowballs be thrown into his domain. Everyone seemed in better spirits once the white bullets had stopped and I suggested we start to get the horses out. We could do three lots before noon if we hacked them out for just an hour each.

We had some beautiful riding that morning in the virgin snow. We spotted hundreds of mouflon that had come down from the mountainous terrain for protection and fodder during the blizzard. We all galloped and frolicked about until everyone was exhausted. It was the end of the show jumping season but we would soon be working with the season's three year olds; the men would have lots to keep them busy in the months to come.

Kambis and Khosrodad walking the course, Rajab and Abdula far left

Davoud Bahrami

316

Reza Hadavand on Shabahang

Floral decorations by Prince Davalou

Kambis on Rostam, Khosrodad on Upa Negrino, Ezat on Shabrang

Goli Bakhtiar receiving prize from Princess Shams

After the show party

Princess Shahms' Pearl Palace

LEFT: Fred Elganian, James Underwood, Col. Shaki, Ali Reza Soudovar seated (bearded)

19 CROTCH GRABBERS

When I first visited Iran I noticed that many of the men walking on the streets walked along holding on to their crotches. I was certain that they were uneducated peasants who didn't know any better or perhaps had a bad case of the crabs. However, the longer we lived in the country the more I realized that Iranian men were a race of true "crotch grabbers". I decided to make a secret study of the various types of "crotch grabbing".

Ali Rezai was the first one I noticed at the Imperial Stables and most likely it was because he seemed to spend more time standing around gossiping than did any of the others. He would walk into Khanlakhani's office which I shared during the early months of my employ, holding on to his crotch; as he talked he would move the hand up and down the side of his leg, actually hanging on to his penis. It was so obvious that I was afraid to look at him directly fearing he would feel my stare. I classified him a "perpetual crotch grabber".

Ezat Vodjdani was not as obvious as Rezai but he was a "telephone crotch grabber"! I would see him standing up in the stable yard by the telephone talking on it and grabbing onto and playing with what he had between his legs.

I noted that many of the riders would dismount from their horses and immediately grab their manhood before even putting up the stirrups or starting to untack the horses. They were the "after riding crotch grabbers".

Well I thought, these men were only Imperial Servants and surely the more educated of the race were not so rude.

But then I noticed that my boss himself would rub his hand up and down his leg. I wondered about his conformation for he slid his hand almost down to his knee. He did it while giving orders to the Imperial Servants at the stable, while standing talking to colleagues at a horse show and even when at a dinner. He fitted into the same class as Ali Rezai, "perpetual".

General Khosrodad was not an active grabber in that he didn't move his hand around as much as most, but just held on. He usually did it just after getting off a horse so I wondered if it was hurting him, until the day I ran into him on the ski slopes at Deszine and found that he did it there too. He was a "sporty crotch grabber!"

Amir Pahldad, my assistant at the Royal Horse Society, would sit at his desk with one hand on his pipe and one in his lap; the lap hand moving rhythmically. I couldn't actually see him grabbing from across the front of the desk but I decided he was a "sitting crotch grabber." I don't know how he ever got any work done with both his hands busy; most times it was evident that he didn't get anything done but one thing I would say for him is that he didn't grab on while standing up. He must have learned something from his education in France.

I only met one "riding crotch grabber" in my time in Iran. He was a boy who rode for Ali Reza Soudovar, Ali Akhbar Khazami. He spent a lot of his time on horseback riding with one hand and doing you know what with the other.

In all the time we were in Iran I never saw a female crotch grabber so decided that it had to have something to do with the manhood syndrome that the Persians have, or perhaps they were all so glad that they had not been castrated as was the custom years ago in Persia that they wanted to remind themselves of their maleness at all times. Be that as it may, if you ever have the fortune to visit the "Land of the Great

Sophie" do not be disturbed by this preoccupation with the male genitals; it is just an unconscious mannerism of the race.

ALI REZAI

It was just a few days after Christmas that I arrived at the stables around nine o'clock, my winter starting time, to find Ali Rezai dressed in civilian clothes.

'Ali, what are you doing wearing those chic clothes during working hours?' I presumed that he was about to ask me for the day off to go to the doctor or to take care of some business in the city.

'Khonume Rose, I not work at Imperial Stables more.' I could not have been more shocked if I had been told the Shah had resigned.

'What do you mean? I've heard nothing about this.'

'Yes, I go to see Mr. Atabai today. I tell him that I is finished.'

'But Ali, why? You have a good job here. Where else in Iran would you go to get such a good job working with horses? And also, if you leave the Imperial Stables it'll be very difficult for you to get a job elsewhere; there are certain people who could make it very difficult.'

'I know all of this, Khonume, but you see I am a human also. I cannot take all the debasing language and hard treatment that is customary working for Kambis and Agha Bosorg.' I had never before heard Ali speak of Kambis by his first name.

'Ali! I know you better than you think. You're lying to me. What is the real reason that you are going to resign?'

'Khonume, I have lost my nerve. After that fall I had I was very fright-

324

ened. When you made me go over those jumps to see if Shahab was scared, it was me, not Shahab that needed the test.' He continued to lie to me. I had seen Ali have numerous falls and I had heard the amazing tales of his youth when he was said to have nerves of steel. He would jump any fence, ride any horse and accept any dare. Obviously there were plans that Ali was not going to discuss with me at present. He was going to the office of Kambis.

Of all the men who were *djelodars* Ali was the best educated; not in years of schooling but in experience. He had been given opportunities that most young Persian men of his station would never dream of and his experiences made him want more than he was expected to want.

Some years before, he had had a dreadful accident in which he had broken his back. He had tacked up a rank stallion and mounted it in its stall. As he was riding the obstreperous animal out through the stall door it reared. In so doing Ali was caught at the small of his back between the horse and the steel door frame. This blow broke a vertebrae in his back and then as he slid down towards the ground the outward protrusions of each of six other vertebrae were injured. When he hit the ground his head snapped back and he thankfully was unconscious. It took nine months of hospitalization before he was released just barely able to walk with a cane.

It came to the attention of His Majesty that Ali had had the accident and when the Royal Family went to Austria for their annual check-up Ali was taken along as part of the entourage to have his back looked at by European experts. It was quite an experience for such a lowly man to be part of His Majesty's group but Ali observed well and learned much about social graces as well as the ways of the Europeans. He was not hospitalized there, so was able to see Vienna and a way of life he had never dreamed existed. The doctors found that the nerves of the spinal column had healed well but there was still muscle, ligament and cartilage damage that could probably be improved by therapeutic treatment. It would be advisable, they claimed, to have an operation to smooth the surfaces of two of the vertebrae but otherwise Ali could be expected to live a normal life.

Ali refused to have the operation and was sent back to Tehran to report back to work. Kambis and his father had gone with His Majesty to St. Moritz where the Imperial Family spent their winter vacation. When Ali got back to Tehran he did not report back to work and when his boss arrived a month later to discover this fact, he gave the delinquent *djelodar* a year's vacation without pay as punishment.

During that year Ali wangled the use of a stable belonging to the Imperial Court from Agha Bazorgn, Kambis's father, much against Kambis's wishes. There Ali set up a riding school which prospered as such small establishments do, enough to keep him and his family fed and clothed.

By the end of the year Ali had acquired four very good Turkoman stallions that were jumping very well so when his establishment was closed, which Kambis made certain of, he came back to the Imperial Stables with these horses. He again wangled a small stable from Agha Bosorg about one kilometer from the Imperial stables where he was able to keep his horses until he could sell them. Eventually two of them were bought by the Imperial Stables and the other two he sold to private individuals making him a nice little profit. The rumor was at the time, that Ali did not really want to go back to work at the Imperial stables but he was forced to because he was still under Royal Contract.

Ali never seemed terribly bothered by his back during the time that I had been working with him except that he claimed that it hurt him to ride without stirrups and do a sitting trot. I compromised allowing him to post while he was riding without stirrups! Very occasionally he would complain of a back pain and excuse himself from riding but generally he had ulterior motives and I learned to keep one jump ahead of him. I am sure that he did have some pain, especially in the winter when he complained bit more.

The winter before our abortive Championship which he won by default he began complaining frequently about his back problems and finally when it came time for the Imperial Family to go for their winter vacation and medical check-up he was again taken along. This time he wanted to have the operation. He was being given a second chance. Kambis didn't go that year due to more pressing business in Tehran so he entrusted Ali to the care of Prince Davelou who was part of the entourage. All of us at the Stable were worried about the outcome but Ali seemed determined to go to Europe and be cured once and for all. His close friends in the ranks of the *djelodars* were most emotional and all insisted on seeing him off at the airport the day of departure. For their primitive minds, going off to an unknown land for such an operation was like brushing with death. For the next two weeks all the discussion was about their comrade who was in such danger in Europe, then gradually things died down. In Iran experiences and people are forgotten very easily so Ali was dropped from daily life.

Now, Ali was leaving the employ of The Imperial Stables where he had been a fixture most of his life; I didn't know if Kambis would accept his resignation but as it turned out he did and Ali moved into a new civilian life.

One noontime while I was in my office on Pasteur Avenue I was summoned from across the street; Mr. Atabai needed to speak with me at once. As usual I dropped what I was doing to answer the call. There were two or three people waiting in the ante room to see my boss but there was no one I recognized. It didn't surprise me that I was ushered in by Mrs. Nazami immediately.

'Rose, go right on in. You will be hearing some shocking news!' She never could remember my first name. Actually many of the Iranians called me Rose; it never really bothered me and it was easier for the Persian tongue to pronounce. Don however, became most annoyed when we received invitations addressed to Mr. and Mrs. Gail Rose. A bit too much for the American ego.

327

Kambis was on the phone as usual but when I entered he had only one up to his ear; hopefully, he would not get another call before he had a chance to talk to me. I was apprehensive about this news.

'Good morning, Gail. I have some news that will be a shock on your system so you had better come over here and sit down.' He pointed to the chair to the right of his desk. The tea boy brought in tea for me, and lemon water for Kambis; his gout had been bothering him so he did not take tea which is full of tannic acid. We sipped our drinks in the small silver teacups passing pleasantries of the day and discussing stable business. It is the Iranian way to keep one in suspense as long as possible.

'Well, I guess I had better tell you my news. Ali Rezai has run away from the hospital in Austria and no one knows where he is. It seems they were giving him drugs for his pain and he went berserk; he kept saying that he was imprisoned and he was being uncooperative about having his back examined. This happened during the first week. The second week they stopped giving him the drugs and he seemed to settle down but it seems what really happened is that he got on very friendly terms with his night nurse who let him dress and slip out of the hospital so he could go gallivanting around town to return in the early mornings. But one morning he didn't return so the nurse had to confess her folly.'

I had to laugh. 'It sounds just like Ali. He always was a cheeky devil.'

Kambis seemed to feel there was some humor in the incident, but he was worried about the whereabouts of his charge. 'It's partly your fault you know, Gail. You were all for the operation if it could fix his back. When I suggested we send your "golden boy" you were very enthusiastic so I pursued the project. And now look what has happened! I hate to think where he will turn up. Maybe with luck he just won't ever be found!'

A few days later I was making a late afternoon stable inspection when Kambis arrived for his daily check. During the winter months he didn't ride on a regular basis so he would make a point of visiting the stable at some point almost every day.

'I was going to call you this evening, Gail.' he said after we had greeted each other. 'I've had news of our world traveler.'

'Well, tell me! Where is he?'

'At the moment he is in London being taken care of by Mr. Afshar, our ambassador there. He really is an amazing man, that Ali. He flew from Vienna to London, who knows when or how, and it seems that when he ran out of money he went crying to Mr. Afshar at the embassy. The Ambassador is a soft touch anyway, and as you know has always been interested in the Stables and the boys here so he believed Ali's ridiculous story which I can't comprehend yet. He told Mr. Afshar that he had been forced to go to Austria and that the doctors told him after the first day that the operation would relieve the pain, however he would never be able to ride again. He had not wanted the operation if these were the conditions so he told this to the doctor who then had him sedated and forced him to sign the paper of release permitting the doctor to do the operation. He claims that he had to escape from the hospital in order to prevent them from doing the operation against his will. This is of course, totally ridiculous. I have spoken on the telephone with Davalou who says that the doctor had arranged for Ali to have therapy and in order for his back muscles to relax they had given him tranquilizers. He did say that Ali seemed to go berserk from the injections and they were discontinued. The story about the operation preventing him from riding again is nonsense as well so he told me, but I'm being sent the medical report and will know more then. In the mean time we have Ali being flown back here at the expense of the Imperial Stables and I now must decide what to do with him. I have a good mind to fire him. I have put up with so much from him but I really hate to. You know that his father, old Abdul Hossein has been working at this stable for seventy years and it would kill him to have his son fired. You have no doubt heard many stories about the year of absence I gave him and I'll not go into that now, but I can't do the

329

same thing this time. What do you think should be done?'

'Frankly Kambis, I think it would be a mistake to fire him. You were the one that gave him the opportunity to go to Austria for the operation. He is actually an ignorant man, despite his cunning, and he was probably frightened in a hospital where he didn't know the language and panicked. You have to face the fact that even though he's rather unorthodox and must constantly be reprimanded he's the best rider in Iran. You want the Imperial Stables team to win as much as we can; His Majesty likes to see that the Imperial Stables is at the top of the list and I feel the same way. If we had a lot of depth we could chuck Ali tomorrow without worrying about him coming along and beating us on other horses, but as things stand we have that threat over our heads. It might or might not happen, but I'm sure he could ride for Ali Reza Soudovar who has only mediocre riders and very good horses; with a good jockey like Ali he could give us much tougher competition than he does now. Not that I'm afraid of competition but I feel at the moment for our image we must keep him. Therefore, we need to think of a disciplinary action to make him understand that he betrayed your trust.'

'I totally agree with you, but what will this be? I have been wracking my brain since I heard the news. All I can think of is to give him extra duty time and whenever a job that's not very pleasant comes up give it to him. You know the problems we have when "guests" come to the stables to ride. Someone has to take care of them as they're usually friends of some dignitary or other. No one wants to do that so we'll give him that responsibility as the only name on the roster and no, absolutely no, days off!' was Kambis's solution.

'That sounds like a good plan to me. I'll give him all sorts of extra jobs to keep him really busy so that he has hardly time to take a breath. And I don't think we have to say that he's being punished. You'll probably want to talk to him about his behavior. I personally won't mention that I know anything but he'll get the idea.'

'You know Gail, I should never say this and please don't ever repeat it, but I have to admire that Ali. There he was, a poor Iranian peasant who through the years has had some exposure to a better life and he took the opportunity, even though it wasn't his to take, to go off for a week some-where in Europe to have a good time. I hope he had fun. I wish I'd had as much spunk when I was away in England at Sandhurst, but I was afraid to leave the grounds.

'You know when I was a young boy Ali and I were best friends. I was the son of the Master of His Majesty's Horse and a Court Minister living in the big house at Farahabad and Ali was the son of the carriage driver, but the two of us got along well. We rode together every chance we got. Whenever my father took me hunting in the mountains, and that was often, I always begged to have my friend come too and my father, who was once a stable lad himself, always consented. Even when His Majesty went out the two of us were allowed to tag along. We became inseparable. Then I went off to school in England, then to Sandhurst and eventually into the Military and to training college in the States and I came home a Major.

'I have of course, told you of my finagling to get out of the military and when I did, I took my father's position as Master of His Majesty's Horse. When I first came back to Farahabad Ali came rushing over to my father's house to see me but I wouldn't allow him in the house. I told the servant to tell Ali that he was a *djelodar* and if he had business with me he must come to my office in the stable. I had to do it, for if I was to be suc-cessful in my job here I couldn't have friends among the *djelodars* for they must all respect and fear me.

'The first time I went to the stable and saw Ali, I wanted to rush to him and hold him and kiss him as is our custom but I wouldn't allow myself. I had a lump in my throat when I spoke to him but I spoke to him as *Agha*. And when I let him kiss my hand as all the others did, I debased him and it was finished between two dear boyhood friends.

'Over the past six or seven years that I have held this position, I've tried to show him that I still love him but he always does something for which I must reprimand him, as if he is trying to punish me for not keeping the friendship . I suppose in America we could have remained friends, but it's not the Persian way and we're in Persia.'

Now as I looked at Ali I knew that his story of lost nerve was a lie; he was constantly looking for a way to hurt Kambis, to get even with him or perhaps even to become his equal. I knew Kambis would let him resign and I knew that it would be good for Ali, for he had enough moxie to make a success of his life.

His resignation was duly accepted by Kambis who then proceeded to blaspheme the man to all and sundry. What else could he do? He Kambis, had been hurt that Ali had finally made it a two way break. Ali went to work for Ali Reza Soudovar but that only lasted a few months for Ali Reza had no boyhood friendship to remember, and he would not take the insubordination. He found that Ali didn't follow instructions and he was always late to work; as well, the horses seemed to lose condition after Rezai took over as manager and rider for Dashte Behesht.

Ali Rezai then had some marital problems when he was trying to take on a second wife. In the Muslim religion if a man wants to take a second wife he must have the consent of the first, but his first wife would not consent to this second girl whom she said was a "painted lady." The girl friend then threatened to sue Ali for breach of promise. Eventually Ali did divorce the first wife to take the second but it lasted only a short time and soon he was back knocking on the door of the mother of his three beautiful children.

After three years on his own Ali became successful in the horse business. He was the first true professional horsemen by Western standards, in Iran. He set up his own club in shoddy conditions at first but he was able to sell horses to a lot of wealthy people from the new middle class that was developing in Iran. He took a trip to Ireland to buy a few show jumpers there and then a year later bought another ten European horses for his clients. He was ultimately considered an equal to Kambis economically and socially; in most countries the successful horse trainers are successful socially. Ali became about as equal as he could ever expect to be in Iran and I know that he was proud of his accomplishments and personally considered himself an equal. Just before we left Tehran I heard Ali call Kambis by his first name in public.

Ali Rezai winning at Championships

Ali Rezai schooling Shahab

MASHHAD

The winter time was a period that I found trying. The weather was most often unpredictable. Even though there was usually not a lot of snowfall in Tehran, when it did snow it snowed hard and long. The temperature, which usually was above freezing, during the day quickly melted the snow making the riding rings at Farahabad quagmires and totally useless for many weeks on end. After my first winter at the stables, during which we did little more than take the horses out for long hacks each day, I decided that I would have to do something about this problem.

My first suggestion was to have one of the three rings completely re-built with adequate drainage. This suggestion was accepted but was not acted upon for two years. My second suggestion was to build an indoor ménage which would be useful both in the winter and during the heat of the day in the summer time. Also I felt that when breaking young stock an indoor ring would be most helpful.

About the time I was trying to persuade Kambis to build an indoor ring Dr. Cutler was pressing for his new X-Ray machine. One wintry afternoon he and I both approached Kambis as he came into the stable yard. I'm sure he felt the vultures were descending upon him.

'Now look, you two, you both want something for the Imperial Stables that will cost us a great deal of money. The X-Ray machine has been on the list for quite some time but has not been ordered mostly Dr. Cutler, be-cause you would not tell me which one you want us to order. Now just two days ago I received your official request for a $50,000 piece of equipment and the same day I find a request from Mrs. Rose that will cost me considerably more. First of all, I don't know where I'll get the money for these projects and secondly, I wonder if they're necessary. You Dr. Cutler, have been working on this hospital of yours since you came here; I guess that was three years ago although it seems forever, and it's still nowhere near completion. I'll not order your X-Ray until I see that the operating room is near completion.'

'But Kambis,' interjected Robin. 'You're the one who has held up my project. I can't do the work myself you know, and every time I talk to Arseli, he tells me *Farda* (tomorrow). Then *Farda*, he tells me that you won't give him the men to do the work and so it goes.'

'I have a lot of projects you know Robin, and I really feel that you're the one who is being lax here. You'll recall that the operating table you ordered was delivered about six months after you arrived here. It was your choice and when it arrived you seemed to be very excited about it. You put it in that corner in front of the pharmacy covered it with canvas, where it has sat for about two years. I haven't heard of any operations that have been performed using the table and I see the thing just rotting away there. You'll probably do the same with the X-Ray machine.'

'Kambis, you're not being fair. I can't use the table until I have the operating room completed. I have designed a place for the table but the door to the recovery room is not ready yet, so I can't put the table in the hospital.'

'I'll speak with Arseli this afternoon and your hospital recovery room door will be complete in two weeks; at that time I wish to see the operating table in place. Only then will I order your X-Ray machine.' He began calling for Arseli, "*Mohandess Fardah*", as I always called him (Engineer of Tomorrow). One of the *djelodars* went running like a chicken with its head cut off to find Arseli, the engineer who took care of all the construction at the stables.

'Now Mrs. Rose, about the indoor ménage. You may speak with Mohandess Keymadat. He's the one who is doing the work down at the Farahabad Club. Give him your ideas and a plan of what you want. I'll have him draw up an estimate for the work. You both might just get your way.'

As things turned out we got neither the X-Ray nor the indoor ring. The X-Ray was ordered but we were informed there was a two year delivery date and by that time Robin had left the employ of the Imperial Stables. The operating room was finished within the two weeks but when they put the operating table in it, there seemed to be some problem with the motor of the table. One day when Robin had been called away to attend an emergency, the electrician arrived at the stable and I was the one who had to tell him what was wanted as far as the tilt on the table. It had to rise up to the level of the elevated recovery room door and then tilt up so that the horse could be easily rolled off. I wasn't really sure myself what Robin wanted but was pleased to find that my guess had been correct. The operating room was completed except for the lighting and the X-Ray machine.

My other suggestion had been to enclose a piece of high dry land that was behind the new carriage house, with a fence so that it could be used for turning out the three year olds before they were lunged each day and also it could be used as a place to lunge them, as it would be the only dry enclosed piece of land that we would have during the wet times. This was done almost immediately so we were able to keep the young horses in work during the winter months.

During our long rides out, I was able to reflect back on some of the things that had happened during the year. One of the most memorable experiences of the past few months had been my trip to Mashhad.

One morning about two weeks before we were due to leave for Lebanon. Kambis asked me, 'What are you and Don going to do this Friday since there is no horse show?'

'I hadn't really thought of it. I guess we will spend a quiet day around the pool with the children.'

337

'As long as you have nothing special planned maybe you would like to come to Mashhad. I have to go up with the Crown Prince who will be presenting his trophy to the champions of the Youth Soccer Association. The Khorasan team is last year's champion and will defend its title against the team from Azerbaijan; it should be a very interesting match. Also, you will be able to visit the Mosque there and the tomb of Imama Reza. I know how interested you are in our religion and it's almost impossible for a non-believer to enter the shrine, but as a guest of the Crown Prince you will be able to go in. We are taking two 737s up, one for the Prince and his entourage and one for the press and some of the overflow of officials. Do you think you would be interested in going along?'

'Oh! Yes, definitely. That sounds really super. I don't even have to ask Don because I know he'd be as excited to go as I am. Thank you very much. We accept with pleasure.'

We were to be at the VIP Pavilion at Mehrabad at nine on Friday morning. When we arrived we saw many of the high government officials, some of whom we knew and others whose faces were familiar but we had never met. We spoke with Mohandes Sadeg, one of the Shah's closest personal friends and some of the others. Coffee and tea were being served to the guests awaiting departure along with delicious Persian Pastries.

I was happily munching on a delicious *baklava* that had been soaked in buckwheat honey when Pulad Mansapur strutted in. Pulad had been recently made Managing Director of the Royal Horse Society and was a long-time acquaintance. He and I had developed a love hate relationship because I was the complete westerner in the office and expected things to be done in the Western way, quickly and efficiently. Pulad, on the other hand, even though he had been educated in the States, Colorado to be exact, was a total Persian; nothing was ever done if it could be put off for some other time; he filed away all reports and letters to be forgotten forever; he sat behind his desk talking on the telephone looking terribly busy when everyone knew he was doing nothing; he never made a decision himself, leaving things either at loose ends or for someone else to follow through with; he was totally charming making all who dealt with him feel that he was a very concerned and efficient executive. With all these characteristics which totally went against my grain, I couldn't help but be fond of Pulad.

I had travelled with him to Shiraz to set up a Royal Horse Society Riding School that was a part of the Equestrian activities sponsored by General Hossein Djahanbani (Nader's brother) who was the head of the Tank Division and Tank Training of the Iranian Army. The facilities were rather primitive but the General was amenable to any changes that I would suggest and did make the changes once I had given him a report. Pulad and I had had great fun on this trip. Don had come down to make a marketing study for Iralco so the three of us spent some fun evenings eating out at the few good restaurants one found in Shiraz. Pulad had recently broken his leg playing polo so while he was hobbling around on a walking cast his trademark became, "I don't dance."

'Hey, Pulad, what are you doing?' Don greeted him.

'I don't dance.' We all laughed and joined together to spend the day in each other's company.

We were like the Three Musketeers. Standing on the steps of the Pavilion we watched as the Crown Prince and his party arrived. Kambis got out of the long maroon Mercedes limousine in which the prince was riding along with two of the body guards. There were three or four other official cars out of which stepped many important Court figures and secret service men. They all entered the plane and it taxied off, at which point we were ushered into the other Iran Air 737 that was parked on the runway. I had never been on one of the planes fitted for officials and press so was surprised when I saw the interior. Up front the seats were as one usually sees on a commercial plane but the back half was fitted out into little compartments similar to those on a train. The seats were comfortable plush covered arm chairs with a card table between. The press was ushered to the front and the rest of us who were a part of the official party were seated in the back.

The three of us sat with Mohandes Sadeq and had a most interesting trip. He explained that Mashhad was the fourth largest city in Iran, lying in a broad green plain bounded by mountain ranges. Though it is a thousand feet lower than Tehran the climate is harsh and changeable; it is said to have less mud or dust than anywhere else in the country. He told us what the protocol would be and then filled us in on some of the history of Mashhad and the shrine. I had read The Land of the Great Sophy by Roger Stevens in which he writes:

"Meshed owes its site and size not to its commercial importance or its position on great trade routes, but to accidents of religion. Had Imam Reza not died here in 817 in the little village of Sanabad, there would be no city on this site. The very name means the place of martyrdom. The first shrine on the site was built by Haroun al Rashid's son, and the history of the town is largely the history of the shrine. It may be summarized briefly. A new shrine was built by Mahmud of Shazna in 1009. The town was sacked by the Mongols in 1221, but the shrine was restored by Oljeitu in about 1300. The city grew as a result of the destruction of Tus by the Mongols in 1390; it was favored by Shah Rukh whose wife Gwadar Shad built the great mosque which bears her name in 1414. It became increasingly a place of pilgrimage under the Safavids, and the shrine was further enlarged by Shah Abbas. Mashhad was the capital of Iran under Nadir Shah from 1736 to 1747; further additions were made to the shrine by Faith Ali Shah. By now Mashhad had become an important point on the trade route between Turkestan and the West, but it was adversely affected by the Russian advance into Central Asia and the building of the trans-Caspian railway. At that time, as capital and commercial center of the relatively fertile province of Khorasan -the largest in the country —and as the terminus of the eastern

railway, Mashhad was a thriving place but its main source of income and prosperity was still the pilgrims. The shrine is the most important institution in Mashhad; moreover, it is the largest owner of land in Iran, not excluding the Royal Estates and government lands. The process of acquiring property started nearly a thousand years ago when a certain rich man presented his land to the shrine in order to salve his pricking conscience —for what crime history does not relate……

The shrine as an economic entity dominates Mashhad and is without rival in Khorasan; furthermore, it owns property or villages in Azerbaijan, Kerman, near Karaj, and even in Afghanistan.

For the non-Moslem visitor, Mashhad is a tantalizing place. With one glorious exception, it is totally lacking in buildings of historical or archi-tectural interest………everything is concentrated in and immediately around the shrine and, with certain very limited exceptions, is barred to the non-believer. Reza Shah built a great circle of avenues round the central com-plex of buildings, which enables them to be seen from without, but any attempt to enter any part of the great circle, except the short alleyways of the old bazaar, without proper authorization, is emphatically not recom-mended."

I asked the Mohandez if Don and I would be able to gain entry to the Shrine for I had read that it was impossible for the non-believer to enter.

'Why of course, you are a guest of the Crown Prince and will certainly be allowed in. We have arranged for a *chador* for you to put on when you get inside the gate so there's nothing to worry about. You must take off your shoes at the door of the shrine itself, but you'll go with us and just do what we do. You'll be surprised at the beauty,' answered the Mohandez.

Once we were on the ground our plane taxied in and parked next to the Crown Prince's plane which had already landed. We disembarked and were ushered into a large air conditioned bus that would take us immediately to the Shrine. The ride seemed too short, for I was fascinated as we drove along watching the activities in the streets. We drove down the Khiabani-Pain which Stevenson so aptly describes:

"A magnet which draws pilgrims from far and near, Mashhad is also the border town of Turkmenistan,

the gateway of Central Asia, the capital of what is racially the most variegated province in Iran, and

a neighbor to the desert. The heart of this secular Mashhad is the Khiabani-Pain, the long avenue which runs east from the Shrine. It is not a beautiful street; the buildings, with the exception of a few set back in

alleys, are modern and tawdry; it has nothing of the glamour and mystery of the covered bazaars of Isfahan, Yazd, Tabriz and elsewhere. But it is pulsating with activity and full of color and contrast. For once the women with their uniformly blue chadors, provide less variety than the men. White-turbaned Baluchis with swarthy features jostle with high-cheek boned Turkomans, wearing not the fur caps of the steppe but dashing yellow turbans. The green bandana, too, the hallmark of the sayyid, is much in evidence, covering, many, a bearded face, whose owner strides arrogantly through the crowds with an impatient sweep of the shoulder. Donkeys or camels jog wearily out of side streets, and merchants fill the air with cries of their wares. This is not the place for hidden treasures or the finer fruits of the Persian artistic genius; but the Khiabani-Pain provides a dazzling display of local homely objects of a kind which, divorced from their home surroundings, look exotic; textiles, hats, beads and ropes."

All this I was able to view as we drove along, for the traffic, both modern and ancient, was such that our bus crept along.

When we finally stopped in the place cordoned off for us beside the gate of the Shrine, the crowd was immense! People were crushing each other to get a glimpse of the Crown Prince as he came out. The police were numerous as were the secret service which were meant to be plain clothes men but their western dress was more like a uniform amongst these people in the native dress of their tribes or region.

The limousines of the Crown Prince and his entourage drove out the gate just as we were getting out of the bus so we were almost unnoticed as our group of about fifteen people walked in the gates. The security had cleared a path for us and we entered without being jostled by the crowd. It was just as I was putting on the *chador* that was waiting at the gate for me, that I heard some rather uncomplimentary remarks about the foreign woman being allowed in the Holy Place. I quickly bowed my head and hid my face in the customary manner and followed Pulad and Don up the beautiful garden walk; the garden itself was said to be more than two acres in size and was planted with beautiful roses for which Persia is renowned. There was a proliferation of buildings within this 400 yard diameter circle which was like a small city in itself. It is said to be one of the greatest concentrations of religious buildings in the world, if not the greatest, including Mecca itself. The great golden dome of the shrine itself glittered in the brilliant sunlight standing out amongst the other domes of turquoise and green tile.

We were the only people in the shrine at the time, its doors having been closed to the general public for the visit of the Crown Prince. I took off my shoes at the entrance to the shrine, leaving them with the others on a beautiful Persian carpet. At first I looked only down at the huge floor covered with layer upon layer of exquisite carpets, but then I cast my eyes up to see the walls and ceiling covered with a mosaic of mirrors; I had seen this mirrored effect in the Golestan Palace in Tehran but it was a mere preview of this mirrored hall with all its stalactites. There of course, is no furniture in the mosques; the Mullah mounts a pulpit from where he gives his lessons while the people squat, sit or stand on the carpets below him.

The inner chamber was decorated with newly fitted mirror work which glittered like silver in the brilliant light. The floor and dado, as well as the balustrade in the hall, were made of a local yellow marble.

Pilgrims pass from the Chamber of Salutation into the Holy of Holies, the *Haram*, or tomb chamber of the Eighth Imam. Three doors lead into the *Haram* -one of silver given by Nadir Shah, another of gold plate studded with jewels given by Faith Ali Shah, and a third also of gold plate. A dado of early 13th Century Kashan luster tiles lined the tomb chamber.

We went through to the *Haram*, or the shrine itself. There was a huge filigree silver cage about twelve feet long by six feet wide and perhaps eight feet tall. The workmanship of this silver filigree was very intricate for so large an object. Inside the cage are the remains of the Martyr Imam Reza, encased in a marble casket. When I came close to the object of the shrine itself I was startled to see money strewn all over the floor around the small tomb. It seems that the worshippers poke coins, paper money and pieces of jewelry through the slats in the grillwork when they make their pilgrimage to Mashhad hoping their prayers will be answered.

Just before we left Iran I read in the paper that the grillwork around the tomb of Imam Reza had been replaced with a solid gold grill that had been fifteen years in the making. This new grill was the gift of His Majesty the Shahanshah and had cost seven million dollars.

We left this awe inspiring shrine to have a quick look at some of the other buildings in the complex which were not equal to the shrine but in their own way beautiful and interesting in that they came from such a jumble of periods and styles.

Our time up, we rushed off to our awaiting bus which had pulled up directly in front of the gate so that we would not be bothered by the faithful who were by now pressing to get into their shrine. Our bus took us to the outskirts of the town where the new Hyatt Hotel was found; there we had a very pleasant luncheon in one of the small private reception rooms.

Lunch finished we again boarded the bus and headed for the football stadium; as we got closer to our destination progress became very slow as the streets were crowded with snarled traffic and pedestrians.

It turned out to be a rather exciting game and the victors were the team from Khorasan again so the crowd went wild. The Prince presented his trophy and it was over for us save an uneventful trip back to Tehran.

Mashad

HIRMAND

I missed not having Kambis come to ride with us as often in winter, for he always seemed to have some interesting little story to tell me as we would walk our horses from the stable to the ring. I remember one morning he started his conversation with what seemed an odd statement. 'Did you have a good dinner last night, Gail?'

'Why yes, we did, as a matter of fact, we ate at Xanadu with the El-ghanians.'

'I wish that I could say the same. I was expecting a delicious dinner. We had been invited to the palace for a rather informal dinner with His Majesty and the Shahbanu and the fare there is usually the best one can expect in Iran.'

'I'm sure it is, but what happened?'

'Well, you know His Majesty has a new dog, a Great Dane puppy, which was given to him a few months ago. The dog is now almost a year and you can imagine quite large.'

'Yes, I had one once, so I certainly can imagine how big it would be.'

'As this was an informal affair, just ten or twelve of us, the dog was present as well. Before dinner he kept putting his big nose all over the fruits and sweets that were placed around for us to eat so, as you know how we Iranians have a slight distaste for dogs as house pets, no one seemed inclined to eat what was offered. Then we went into the dining room where what smelled like a delicious dinner was being served. But again the dog came. No one dared say anything to His Majesty who didn't seem at all bothered by the dog's sniffing at the food. Well, as each person was served the dog followed along behind and he was just big enough to get his head right on the table, so he would sniff at each plate after it had been served. We were afraid to hit the dog so we were obliged to eat some of what was on the plate but all the time the thought that the dog had breathed germs on the food was there. I could hardly touch a thing. I came home simply starving and intended to raid the refrigerator, but when Avid and I went down to the kitchen, the servant had locked it and we couldn't find the key. Can you imagine?' I could and was really tickled. It made His Majesty sound so much more human than I had ever imagined him to be.

Another morning I had been telling Kambis that Don and I had met the Minister of Education at a party given by the German Ambassador; he of course, knew the man whose wife was chief of all university education in Iran. Talk about keeping it in the family! This discussion got Kambis off on a tangent about education, for it had just recently been decreed that all elementary education would be free, from that date. Up until then, even though it was compulsory, it had to be paid for, which meant that in actual fact there were a great number of children who did not go to school, for the lack of funds.

'But you know Gail, I personally am against this free education. It's a terrible burden to the taxpayer and also a little education is a bad thing. If you look at many of the Latin American countries you'll find that the dissatisfaction came from the student groups. I think in our case here in Iran, it's better to keep many of these people uneducated for then they'll be more likely to stay content; once they get a little bit of education they'll begin to see more what they're missing against what they have. People in this country have been given so much in the past fifty years since Reza Shah came into power but it's human nature to become dissatisfied; they forget what they have gained and only see what they don't have.

'I fear for this country when these children that will be given free education start university, for then they become the dissidents who will cause a great deal of anguish for our regime. As it is now, the people must work to give their children an education or the children must work to put themselves through school, but when it becomes the right to be educated the attitude will completely change.

Many of His Majesty's advisors feel as I do, but at the moment Iran must take care of her international image and to be a nation that gives its people free education seems to be more important to most than the consequences that may follow.'

'It was broadly publicized that education would now be free to all Iranian children. The government was nationalizing all the schools in the country whether they were private institutions, religious or parochial in nature. Many of the neighborhood schools were already subsidized by the government but they were not totally supported by these funds and needed the private fees in order to operate efficiently; now the government would totally pay for the schooling. The process would take some time before it would be totally implemented, but it was to happen.

And yet two years after this took place my own maid had to continue to pay a fee to the principals of the schools that her two children were attending; granted the fee was considerably smaller than previously, however it did exist. I was not able to discover whether this was an official cost to the students or an under-the-table handout to the staff of the schools.

I had been finding my work load increasingly heavy each ensuing month since I had commenced as a full time employee of Kambis and at the end of the Show Jumping season of 1974 I had decided that I could not continue for I felt that I was neglecting my duties as a wife and mother. Shortly after Christmas I had written Kambis a letter of resignation in which I explained in full my reasons for wanting to resign.

Just a few days after I had sent him the letter I was called into his office at the Court, just as I was about to leave my office for home. I went in fully expecting to find that I was once again an unemployed woman living in Iran; I was having pangs of remorse for ever having written the letter because I really did enjoy my job and knew that I would be bored without something challenging to keep me occupied.

'Gail, I was very disturbed to have received this letter of yours; you really don't mean that you're not happy with your work both here and at the Imperial Stables do you?'

'Kambis, it is not that I'm unhappy as I explained in the letter, I just feel that I'm working too hard; during the show season I get to the stables at six o'clock or earlier and by the time I have finished there and then come into the office to do the Society work I don't get home until three-thirty in the afternoon. Some days, on an average of twice a week, I have to go to the stables in the afternoon and am not home until six thirty or seven. I just don't have enough hours in each day to get everything done that I want to do. This time of year is slacker because I seldom get to the stable before eight thirty or nine but I still do have to come into town almost every day. No, I'm happy with my work, there's just too much of it.'

'Well, I think there are ways that we can relieve you here at the office so that you do not need to come in every day and I'm sure you can afford to take off two days a week from the stable, especially at this time of year. This is the slack period as you said, so you should take some time to go skiing which I know you enjoy very much. I'm going to take this letter of yours and rip it up because I know that you didn't mean it, and you know that it's impossible to say that you will no longer work for His Majesty in Iran, especially when you have a job that no one else in the country is able to do. So it is settled. You won't resign and you'll take it a little easier than you have been. At this time of year it shouldn't be difficult.'

I agreed to this and went out much happier than I had been when I entered his office.

It wasn't very long after the episode of my resignation letter that Kambis began to be very cool and to the point. There was nothing tangible in

his personal manner towards me but I felt it in the replies to my letters deal-
ing with stable matters which I sent to him once a week.

One day, I received his reply to my report, which he had scribbled in
the margins. He informed me that there was a paper shortage in Iran; would
I please not leave such large margins in my reports; where he would then
put his remarks I wasn't sure.

Robin Cutler too, was finding Kambis not only cool but curt with him.
Robin and I were two extremes. I put everything down on paper; that way
I knew I wouldn't be accused of doing something without having first obtained permission in writing; to me word of mouth permissions in Iran were
not valid, for it was so easy to refute them. Robin on the other hand, could
not be bothered with scraps of paper and the official channels. He felt it
was a waste of his time to sit down for hours writing reports and letters of
request, so his business encounters with Kambis were more often face-to-
face than were mine.

'You know, Gail,' he said one morning, 'I don't know what's the matter
with Kambis at the moment, he seems so completely disinterested in any
of my suggestions or projects. I'm having a devil of a time to get him to
order that X-Ray machine and you were there when he said he would order
it as soon as the hospital was completed. He seems to be most disinterested
in what's going on about here; he lacks his usual enthusiasm. It's getting
to be a pain to work for him.'

'I've noticed that myself Robin, that he's very cool, but I think that he
has other pressures that are upon him right now and once the good weather
is here he'll be back to himself.'

'Well, I certainly hope so because my contract comes up this July and
I have a lot of things I want to present to him if I'm going to stay in this
place.'

One morning when I arrived at the stable Maleki came running up to
my car as I got out. He had obviously been waiting for me.

'Khonume Rose, you are in terrible trouble!'

My heart sank, 'Why? Maleki what have I done now?'

'Agha came down to the stable last night and noticed that the light in your office was on. He wondered if you were here, but when we went to look we saw that you were not in the office, but had left the light on. Khahlakhani was not here either, and no one knew where the key to your office was so the light had to stay on all night. Agha is very angry and told me to give this to you.' He handed me a note.

Dear Mrs. Rose:

Where you come from in Canada I know that electricity is not expensive for you have an abundance of hydroelectric power. We in Iran do not have this abundance and our electricity is very expensive. I find it most lax of you to have left your light on in your office overnight and I intend to take more severe action if I find this happening again.

Sincerely,

Kambis Atabai

I felt rather stupid for having left the light on and would certainly not make the mistake again but I was slightly annoyed by the tone of the letter and the signature was so formal and so unlike my boss. What was troubling him?

One of the horses that I had bought in Ireland had caught the eye of Agha Bozorg and His Majesty. Hirmand was the tall seal brown thoroughbred three year old that had been a little more expensive than I had planned to pay but when I got him back to Iran everyone felt that he was a magnificent animal. I decided to work with him myself as I just didn't want to turn him over to any of the boys. He was built to be a jumper and with him I would enjoy working and proving that the Thoroughbred was the most athletic jumping horse there is.

One morning while I was hacking him in the ring early in his training Agha Bosorg came to watch. When I went over to say good morning, the

351

old man said to me that he felt this was the most beautiful horse in the stable. I agreed. He then asked me what I thought about training him to take the place of Azar, His Majesty's parade horse. His Majesty must have a very beautiful horse to ride each year at the Azerbaijan Day Parade when he reviewed the troops. Azar was now seventeen and it was time to think about a replacement. Did I think that this horse had the temperament to do such a job? I wasn't really keen on the idea but the horse did belong to His Majesty and it wouldn't hurt him as a jumper if he had to go on a parade once a year; also he did have a very placid disposition, so I said that I felt that he might be able to do the job. It was decided between us that I would commence going down to the Imperial Guards Parade grounds one morning a week to see if the horse would be a likely prospect for the job. He would arrange for it; all I had to do was go down there, which was a fifteen minute walk on horseback, to get him used to music and the marching of troops.

So it was that the following Sunday morning I rode down to the parade grounds with Akbar, who was on the old horse Azar. Each morning in the *Podegon* the troops assembled at the beginning of their day to parade and be reviewed by the officer of the day and to be given their orders. The three thousand troops began to assemble at six fifteen for the inspection which started at six thirty. Akbar and I left the stable at six and arrived just as the troops were assembling. There I was, one lone woman, riding the Shah's horse, amongst thousands of men. Hirmand followed behind the calm Azar and never flinched a muscle. I was really pleased that he took so little interest in the troops and the band that was playing marching tunes during the inspection.

I decided that this routine should go on for the horse every day for two weeks and then we could work down to the once a week schedule. After the first four or five times I decided that we should be standing in the parade grounds as the troops came marching in. This didn't seem to upset the horse. The only time he shied was one morning when we were walking

352

amongst the troops before the ceremony had started; a jovial platoon commander arranged for his platoon to "Present Arms" just as I was passing on Hirmand. At the clicking together of heels and slamming of the guns he scooted out from under me like a cat. It was just the will of Allah that kept me on. The whole throng of men then broke into a roaring laugh. Talk about being laughed at by thousands. I laughed too!

We stood beside the flag during Flag raising ceremony; we walked around the band as it played the marching music; we stood for twenty minutes at attention during the inspection and order of the day; we marched in amongst the troops; we took the salute with the Colonel; we did everything we could do that might frighten a horse in the circumstances without getting in the way of the proceedings. By the time Azarbaijan Day was upon us Hirmand was well schooled.

There had been some problems with Azar the two previous years due to the fact that the Imperial Guard had had a few mares in their ranks which rode directly behind His Majesty. Now Azar was a very virile stallion and had become quite agitated, as a matter of fact erect! This was most embarrassing to Kambis, the Master of the Horse, whose responsibility it was to provide a suitable horse for the Shah. They say though, that His Majesty really didn't mind; as a matter of fact, he thought it quite appropriate!

The previous year Robin had ordered a ring that is put over the stallion's sheath which is meant to prevent this indelicate act in public, but when it came the day to put it on no one seemed to know how to fit the thing.

The year of Hirmand, the guard had been ordered not to bring any mares so that Azar would not be tempted to display his "stallion hood". It had been decided by Kambis, his father and I that if Azar in any way acted up during the dry run that Hirmand would be used; however if Azar behaved well, Hirmand would not be used but would attend the ceremony and be ridden as a part of the parade. I was of two minds, for it would be a great honor to see my beautiful Irish Thoroughbred ridden by the Shahan-shah of Iran; however, it would be a terrible disgrace if for some reason the horse didn't behave well, and after all, he was just a four year old. His Majesty did not tolerate disobedience no matter whether it be man or beast.

The day of the Parade dawned bright, crisp and clear. The 21st of Azar corresponds with December 13th of the Western calendar, so it was cold but not unduly. Kambis picked Don and me up on the way to the ceremony. He had arranged for us to have front row center seats at this prestigious event. Jafar, Kambis's chauffeur, was driving with Kambis sitting in his customary seat in the front; sitting in the back made him car sick.

When we arrived at the entrance way to the freeway the police were there checking the cars, for only cars with special security passes and peo-ple with official invitations were allowed on the highway where the cere-mony would take place. Kambis had an official court car however, when we were stopped by the policeman who asked for the special pass and the passes of the occupants of the vehicle, there were none. The policeman re-fused us entry.

'Listen!' said Kambis, 'I have His Majesty's sword and cape in the back of the car. You see them? I am Kambis Atabai!'

'I am sorry sir, but I have orders to let no one in who does not have the correct official passes. You do not have any so you may not go in.'

'But I am the one who issued the order, don't you understand? I am Kambis Atabai!'

'As I said before, sir, I cannot let you through.'

'Just one moment.' said Kambis. He told Jafar to dial a number on his car telephone. When he was connected with his party he said, '*Teemsah*, this is Kambis Atabai. Your men are doing a fine job this morning. As a matter of fact, they are doing such a good job that they will not let me in.' There was a pause. 'Of course, I don't have any passes with me. I com-pletely forgot them. Thank you, *Teemsah. Ghodafez.*'

We watched the policeman who was eyeing us suspiciously. In a few moments he reached for the telephone on his Harley Davidson Police Bike. He listencd on the telephone, said a few words, and then hung up. He came over to the window on Kambis's side of the car and saluted. *'Behbakhshid, Agha.* But you know I was just doing my job. I might have made a mistake that would lead to serious consequences, if the wrong people were let through you know. You may pass now.'

Jafar let Kambis off behind the stands then drove around to the front of the Royal Box where he let Don and me out. Our seats were directly to the right of the Royal enclosure where the Shah and Shahbanu would be sitting.

We were the first to arrive so we took up our seats and watched as the guests arrived. It would have been an assassin's paradise. Every military and diplomatic official in the country was issued an invitation to this ceremony which was nothing but a display of the arms of Iran, and an impressive one. All those invited were expected to attend. The Russians arrived in full dress, the Red Chinese, the Japanese, the Americans, the Germans, the Turks, the Yugoslavs, the French, the Canadians, the British and on the list went. By fifteen minutes to ten every seat in the stands was filled.

Horses were parading up and down the road; I saw my beloved Hirmand, named after an Iranian river; there was Azar with a checkerboard imprint on his golden rump; the Guard's horses were having a final rundown. Then came the whirr of the two Imperial helicopters. They could be heard as they were taking off from Niavaran palace and ten minutes later they were landing at the far end of the Parade Grounds just out of sight.

The big maroon Rolls Royce drove up to the Royal Box and out stepped the Shahbanu, Court Minister Alam and Premier Hoveda; then it silently drove up to the far end of the asphalt. Soon the sound of horse's hooves could be heard and His Majesty appeared at the head of the parade riding . . . Azar! It was a spectacular sight to see this beautiful flame-colored

Anglo Arab, carrying His Imperial Majesty in full military dress proudly, to review his troops. The band played, His Majesty saluted, and the crowd cheered as he rode past.

It took about twenty minutes for the reviewing of the troops, little of which was visible for the invited guests; they were left to stare at the empty road in front and the Aryamehr Stadium beyond. The maroon Rolls Royce drove up again and His Majesty was ushered out; when he had ascended the box the band played the Azerbaijan and Iranian Anthems while all stood at attention. Then the show began.

For two hours we watched the parade of troops. It is impossible to describe it all, so I will insert the list of what we saw as it was printed in the English program given to all the guests.

Supreme Commander's Staff

In the presence of

HIS IMPERIAL MAJESTY

SHAHANSHAH ARYAMEHR

SUPREME COMMANDER

Review and Parade of

Azerbaijan Ceremony

Thursday, Azar 21, 1353 at 10, 00 hours Tehran

The Typical Infantry Units

Of the

IMPERIAL ARMED FORCES

1. Command Staff of Parade and Review
2. Military Academy
3. Imperial Air Force
4. Imperial Navy Force

5. Cadre Training Centre

6. Revolutionary Corps (these are like the marines)

7. Police Headquarters

8. Gendarmerie

9. Special Force, Brigade

10. Imperial Guard

The Typical Armoured, Motor
And Transportation Units
Of the IMPERIAL ARMED FORCES

1. Police Headquarters

2. Gendarmerie

3. Imperial Air Force

4. Imperial Navy Force

5. Imperial Guard

6. Imperial Ground Force

I was disappointed that there were no fighter planes swooping over but I was impressed to see the missiles, tanks and other military vehicles on display.

The show over His Majesty, the Shahbanu and other officials drove off in their Rolls Royces and other luxurious limousines to the helicopter pad and then flew away. We more mortal, waited for Kambis who himself opted for a helicopter ride in the second shift, leaving us to ride home with Jafar alone. Once on the road we realized why. All the military vehicles that had been on parade were wending their way through the center of Tehran to their various bases leaving scant room on the streets for other vehicles. It took two and a half hours to get to our home from the parade, a ride that had taken fifteen minutes earlier in the day.

Hirmand had not made the parade the first year but his training was not lost for he continued to be held as the reserve horse for His Majesty at such events and in due course would be ridden by HIM.

During the winter the horse became quite full of himself; he was able to buck me off on numerous occasions when I was riding him out; it was not meanness, just his way of saying how good he was feeling. After the third fall I decided that he would be turned out into a paddock each morning before I rode him. He could have his bucks when I was not on his back. This worked very well indeed, and he once again became his docile self. Whenever the footing permitted we would jump him over small fences in the ring or over some of the cross country jumps that were on the grounds. He was continuing to show an amazing ability.

One afternoon in early February I had a call from Ghassem at the stable. 'Khonum Rose. *Hirmand yek cam del daar mikone.*'

'How bad is the colic, Ghassem?' I questioned rather startled. 'Not too bad, Khonum. I just thought that I should tell you. Do you want to talk with the doctor?'

'Yes, yes. Is he there? Put him on.'

Robin confirmed what Ghassem said, that the horse seemed to have a mild case of colic. He wondered if he had eaten some frost bitten grass and that had caused it. He would keep me informed.

I had never heard of a horse getting colic from frost bitten grass. In Canada our horses ate frost bitten grass all winter. If it were the grass that had caused it, I must be to blame for if I had not turned him out in the paddock he would not have eaten it. Yet this was ridiculous. Anyway, Robin said it was not serious.

Later in the day I was called again. The horse was no better but the doctor was taking care of him. The boys at the stable would keep me posted.

About eleven o'clock the telephone rang. It was Robin. 'I thought I had better tell you myself, Gail. Hirmand just died.'

I cried! I hadn't cried over the death of a horse since I had been a little girl but I cried for that beautiful Hirmand. There are certain horses in one's life with which one has a true rapport and he was one of those with me; I was heartbroken.

'I did everything I could to save him Gail, but it was so quick there was little hope. I had him under anesthetic when he died; I was going to operate hoping to find the torsion so that I could save him, for that's what it had to be. I'm doing an autopsy in the morning, if you'd like to come, be at my house at nine o'clock.'

I went. Robin and I drove out to the piece of desert where he did his autopsies. They were not clinically antiseptic affairs but it was by far the most practical thing to do; once the autopsy had been performed the animal would be left in the desert where the vultures would pick its bones clean within a number of hours; in a country where the meat was not used for dog food and the bones not used for glue it was the only answer to the disposal of carcasses.

I didn't know whether I would cry or be sick when I saw the big tractor bringing the wagon upon which lay my beloved horse. It was when my eyes began to well up that Robin said, 'You know it's a funny thing, but I did my first autopsy on a horse that I was attached to and I was afraid I would cry through the whole thing, but when you see the dead animal you realize that it's not your animal, but just the shell of what your horse once was.'

It helped me and it was true. When I saw the carcass there was no resemblance to my near perfect horse; the eyes were lackluster, the glossy coat was gone; those vibrant muscles were still; it was not Hirmand.

After much searching in the intestinal cavity Robin finally found the twist or torsion in the large intestine; it seemed to have been caused by an old adhesion in the wall of the colon that was probably the result of parasites years before. The gut had burst in front of this volvulus which had been the cause of death. At least it had not been caused by the frostbitten grass!

WINTER OF DISCONTENT

One bitter cold morning after having ridden the first lot of horses out in the drizzle I went into Khanlakhani's office to warm my feet and hands by his gas fire. The usual routine was that when the first string of horses and riders came back to the stable yard the old tea man, Ali Akbar, brought the silver tray with small silver cups to wherever I happened to be at the time. But this morning he did not appear.

'Where could Ali Akbar and my tea be this morning?' I asked the secretary.

'Read this, Khonume Rose!' Khanlakhani pushed a very official looking piece of paper in front of me laughing as he did so.

It took me some time to read the paper as I was not the most proficient in reading Farsi but I did understand that from the indicated date, tea was not to be served in any Imperial offices during the working day, with the exception of when official guests or foreigners were present. The paper was signed by the Court Minister Mr. Alam, and handwritten at the bottom, a note added by Kambis who had indicated that it included the Imperial Stables. 'You see, Khonume, you can only drink your tea during special times and in the cafeteria.'

'But Khanlakhani, this is my special time and we have no cafeteria here. Also you are forgetting that I am a foreigner; I may not be an official guest but I do qualify under the other heading.'

'Bali, Khonume! I didn't think of that. Of course we can have tea in your presence. ALI AKBAR! *Bia inja!*' When the old man put his head in the door Khanlakhani told him to make a big pot of tea; everyone would drink tea with Mrs. Rose, the foreigner. And thus the routine continued each morning or whenever someone wanted tea, it had to be in the presence of "the foreigner"!

During the winter Kambis became more and more surly; he was most curt when I was with him, barely being bothered to be civil and his sarcastic and critical remarks in reply to my letters of request and reports were beginning to get me down. Robin and I would often compare notes at his place where I often had lunch with him and Margaret. We had many a laugh about our situation but underneath it all we were both rather unhappy. I had sent in my resignation which had not been accepted so I knew I was wanted and needed in my job but I just couldn't figure out what was causing Kambis's fury. Robin was about to tender his resignation but was persuaded by his wife to wait until his contract came due in July just a few months hence.

Every time I received an envelope from Kambis's office there was something I was doing wrong. I was using too much paper; I was spending too much of the Imperial Stables' money on things that were not budgeted for; the mountain horses were not fit enough so I was to personally supervise the work of these ten horses and five mules; the stable was becoming sloppy so I was to inspect after the weekly cleaning sessions; I was not to park my car by my office; it must be over in the lot in front of the new carriage house; I must be certain that the carriage horses went out two days a week instead of the one that I had suggested for winter routine; my typing was not improving, and on and on. I sometimes thought that he must have been lying awake at night thinking of nasty things to write to me.

One rainy Thursday afternoon when I had given the *djelodars* the afternoon off I was about to get in my car that was parked in front of my office when Khanlakhani hailed me from the door of his room across the stable yard from mine. I walked over to meet him in the doorway of the main stable which was about midway between our offices. In his hand he held a large white envelope. It was from Kambis's office I could tell, without even looking at it; my stomach had butterflies as I turned the envelope over and over in my hands.

Khanlakhani knew things had been rough for me with my boss for he had been having similar problems. 'What do you think? Should I open it now or put it in my desk and look at it after the weekend? If I open it now I may spoil my whole two days off; however, if I don't open it I will worry about it all weekend.'

'You should open it now, Khonume.' The ever faithful Khanlakhani would not dream of leaving unfinished business. Why, it would be on his conscience if I didn't open the letter.

I slowly broke the seal and pulled out the double folded paper. As I unfolded the letter a piece of blue paper fell on the ground. Khanlakhani stooped to pick it up.

'I think this is a check Khonume.' He handed it to me without looking at the face of it. I accepted it and was shocked to see that it was made out for about two month's salary. I was afraid to read the letter for I was certain that this was my payoff and that I was fired. It read:

Dear Gail:

This is in appreciation for all you have done here at the stable. We would have a very hard time indeed without you. Thank you for bearing with me and thank you for everything you have done.

Kambis

'Well, Khonume, is it good or bad?'

'Oh, Khanlakhani, it is wonderful! It is a bonus check and such a nice letter. I hope that *Agha* is now in a better mood. Have a wonderful weekend.

363

I won't see you until Sunday morning.' I danced to the car; for certain Kambis's black mood had broken. And it had.

**Author winning, Gen. Khosrodad 2nd
at Djahanbani's grass field**

NOW RUZ

Now Ruz is the big holiday in Iran; it is as its name denotes the New Year. To most Iranians it is like a rebirth or new life. During this holiday His Majesty took his family and many friends to Kish Island in the Persian Gulf where they would water ski, swim, lie in the sun, gamble at the casino and ride his horses which were shipped down by military planes to the island for the two week period. He himself would do a lot of business with his Arab neighbors, inviting separately the Sheiks of the Emarites, King Hassan, King Hussein, King Faisel and other leaders of the Arab World.

From the beginning of February, we at the stables would concentrate on the legging up and readying of twenty or so horses for the trip to Kish. Sixteen animals were taken but usually four or five would develop leg trouble or some other problem that would duly knock them off the roster for the trip. We had to send horses that would stand galloping for long periods over the sharp coral that is found on this Gulf Island. Naturally none of the foreign horses would be suitable for such punishment and the majority of the Persian and homebred jumpers were too big or did not have legs that would stand up, so we selected from the mountain horses and the many hacks that were kept for the purpose of visitor mounts. Three and preferably four strong, forward going horses had to go for His Majesty who rode, more often than not, twice a day while he was there, that left twelve horses for people like Kambis, Mr. Alam, Kambis's father Agha Bozorg, the two royal children who rode and the many visitors.

The horses would invariably come back just before the thirteenth day of *Now Ruz* exhausted, thin and most of them lame. I hated to see them go but after all, they belong to the Shahanshah and they were for his pleasure and by that time the vacation on Kish Island was almost the only time he would ride his horses regularly. Most often the problems that came home with the horses were not irreparable so people like me and Dr. Cutler had to just grin and bear it.

From about the middle of February until the trip to Kish His Majesty and the Royal Children would come to Farahabad two afternoons a week in order to get themselves fit to ride while they were away.

His Majesty would ride out with Kambis and his father and ten or twelve of his body guards who were mounted on Imperial Guard horses. They would leave the stable lickety split and I'm sure never stop until they returned about an hour and a half later.

When I first arrived at the stables Colonel Neshati took the Crown Prince and Princess Farahaz for lessons the times that they came to the stables; however, he gradually left and there was no one to teach their lessons.

Kambis himself would often take them for lessons foregoing his ride out with the Shah. I had assisted him in these lessons trying to make them interesting and yet not giving the children any really difficult exercises to do, for their French governess was always present and she hated horses and riding. She would use the faintest excuse to curtail the activities. In her mind riding and jumping were very dangerous and the Royal Children should not be subjected to such unnecessary dangers.

Little Prince Ali Reza would sometimes ride the Caspian Pony Khorma or be put on the lunge line mounted on one of the quiet hacks. Kambis loved to have the boy on the lunge for he was an incorrigible child and while he was going round and round on the lunge was the only time he was under the complete control of anyone. Kambis could be merciless in making him do all sorts of callisthenic exercises and I am sure that he often went home with sores on his little bottom. He would scream to Kambis, '*Basta! Basta!*' (Enough! Enough!) But the more he complained the more Kambis would make him work. I would have a dreadful time keeping a straight face while I was supervising one or both of the other children.

Eventually Prince Ali Reza was send down to Colonel Neshati at the Farahabad Club where he took his lessons with Kambis's two children. This was much more fun for him and the colonel was a wonderful teacher of children with his good sense of humor.

The Crown Prince began spending his free afternoons taking flying lessons and had no time for horses. At the age of fourteen he gained his pilot's license. In the newspaper interview which was published just a few days after he had accomplished this feat he was quoted as saying, 'Ever since I was a little boy I wanted to fly a plane.' To many he was still a little boy but he must be an amazing one to have learned to fly a plane at such a young age. It was said that he was the youngest pilot in the world.

One afternoon during the winter of Kambis's foul mood I was working with Hillbrow, a horse I had bought in Ireland at the same time as Bally Lea, when I looked up at the end of the ring to see Princess Farahnaz and her governess sitting watching. I rode over to greet them when who should come along but General Khosrodad. We all chatted for a few moments and then I excused myself to continue my work so that I would be free to help the princess if she wanted to ride. She had not mentioned riding and protocol was that she must make the suggestion; it was the Persian way.

The General knew that we had been having troubles with this horse; he was young and fresh and became a little rank when jumping a line of obstacles. I was just about ready to go back to the stable when the General called me over to where he was still standing with the princess. 'Mrs. Rose, Princess Farahnaz would like to see you jump some fences with that horse.' Of course, it was the General himself who was consumed with curiosity and he knew that I could not refuse the request of the Princess.

'As you know Teemsah, we have been trying to settle him down because he tends to rush into his fences however, if the Princess would like to see him jump I will take him over these few small fences that you see here.'

I was able to jump what was in the ring without any trouble and Hilbrow seemed to stay quite calm; the princess was very impressed with the horse.

'That's what I would like to be able to do. I never have had a chance to jump anything that is higher than this.' She held her hand about eighteen inches off the ground.

'Well Your Majesty, I would be very pleased to help you learn to jump if that is what you would like to do.'

We parted and I figured that this was one of the days that she was not going to ride so I took Hillbrow in and got aboard Ballylea. I had no sooner started work with him when Rajab, the fat old *djelodar* who was one of the favorites of the Royal Family came galloping into the ring calling my name at the top of his voice.

'Khonume Rose, the Princess wants you to ride out with her. Come, follow me. They have just gone up the road at the back of the stables.' We went out and cantered up the sand road that lead away from the stables towards the mountains. When we caught sight of the princess, her body guards and a couple of the other *djelodars* who were riding with her, I turned to Rajab. 'You will have to take Ballylea back to the stable for me because I don't want to take him up the mountain; I would be afraid that he might hurt himself. I'll take your horse,' and so I climbed aboard Badpehma, the tongue-less horse, for the first time.

Badpehma had at one time been a very good mountain horse but for some reason he lost favor with the Shah and was now only used as a hack for guests or in the mountains by one of the *djelodars*. He was a very pretty pure white Turkoman and a very beautiful mover. I felt his fluid movement as I rode toward the group ahead of me; it was like riding on a rocking chair, it was so smooth. Badpehma had gotten loose one night about three years previously and by the time the night watchman heard the noise, he had fought with one of the other stallions in the stable, which somehow had also become loose. Badpehma was the loser however, for in the course of the fight the other horse had bitten off his tongue! According to Robin it was amazing that the horse had lived; he had to be fed a liquid diet and intravenously until the tongue, or stub of a tongue, had healed and then he had to learn how to eat without that so important a part of the digestive system.

The princess was riding Khatun, a little anglo Arab mare that I used with the junior riders at the stables. There were seven young boys between the ages of eleven and thirteen who road with me a couple of days a week. Actually, it was Rajab's son Mahmad Reza who rode the mare and had done such a good job of training her. When we had started working with her she would not jump over a stick and by this time she was a certain contender in every competition in which she was entered. The mare was quite difficult to jump and would not make an ideal horse for the Princess to ride in shows, but she was quiet enough out on the trails.

During the ride the princess talked of how she wanted to learn how to jump and even enter the competitions. My heart cried out with joy for I could think of no better boost to show jumping in Iran than having Princess Farahnaz a competitor in the junior classes.

I explained how she would have to come to ride as often as possible on a regular basis and that it was hard work, not just a half hour fooling around in the ring the way she was used to riding. She seemed to understand and said that she would start coming two days a week from that day. She was a very pretty young girl who, at the time was about thirteen years old.

I was very enthusiastic about teaching her; she was quite vibrant and intelligent and she loved horses. She began to come regularly and seemed to me to have a talent. After riding we would go into the main stable where she liked to give the horses carrots and apples and to learn a little about each one.

My main problem was to find a horse upon which she would definitely win in the show ring. Khatun was good for practice but when the jumps got higher she was apt to refuse unless ridden by a strong, knowledgeable rider, so she would not do. Of all the horses in the stable I figured that my Roshan was the best. He had become an easy ride and was a super jumper that was really able to go in the ring and do it all himself. His only problem was that he was a stallion and he tended to get studdish around other horses. I discussed this problem Kambis and was able to persuade him that we should geld Roshan; it would do him no harm and most likely improve his manners in the show ring and he would forget his studdiness so he would be safe if it should happen that the princess did ride him in competition. So poor Roshan lost his manhood.

After the *Now Ruz* holiday the princess stopped coming to ride and so it was the end of my plans to make a Princess Anne of Iran. I hoped that someday she would take up riding again, for she did have the talent, but of course there were so many other things in her life that I am sure it was hard for her to choose which was the most important.

I found that Roshan did improve after having been gelded and he continued to be a winner at the shows.

Now Ruz is the time that servants and employees were given a monetary bonus similar to what is given in the Western world at Christmas time. However this *Now Ruz Aidee*, as it is called, was definitely expected and it would at least match the amount of one month's salary. It started out centuries ago that landowners and noblemen would go about their holdings throwing gold coins to the servants and slaves on New Year's Day, but it had become big business. As well, the *Aidee* would be given at least one week previous to the actual *Now Ruz* holiday so that it could spent on new clothing and gifts for members of the family.

At the Imperial Stables each man received his one month's extra salary, a new set of working clothes which was the uniform that must be worn every day, riding boots for the riders, and the traditional box of *Shirinee* or sweets. As well, a number of sheep were killed and each member of the Imperial Staff was given one kilo of meat per member of his family.

Before I arrived at the Stables the riders of the horses which received money prizes in the horse shows also received this money at Now Ruz; however, at that time the prize money was very small and there were only four shows a year.

Towards the end of my first show season at the Stable, I had a talk with Kambis about what we were to do with the prize money that had been won by the stables. The riders such as Ali Rezai and Ezat Vodjdani were making noises about how rich they were going to be after this show season, for the Stable's horses had earned close to fifty thousand *Toman* which was a little over thirty-two thousand dollars. I personally felt that it was unfair that the show riders alone should receive the money; what of the older *djelodars* who worked so hard with the mountain horses and the hacks? What of the grooms who fed, cleaned and generally cared for the horses? I put forward a suggestion that we take the lump sum of money that had been earned by all the *djelodars* who had competed and the amount Kambis, General Khosrodad and I had won and devise a method of dividing that money amongst the staff of the Stables. Kambis thought that was a great idea; however, he left the method of division up to me. In other words, I was to submit a feasible method for this plan.

I wracked my brain for two weeks fussing and fuming over the most fair method of parceling out the money; finally, I handed in a most complex financial statement which basically gave the riders who had won money, fifty percent of the prize money they had earned personally; it then portioned out the remainder of the money, including what Kambis, the General and I had won, to all the other *djelodars* and grooms. Kambis thought this a rather brilliant method and I myself was rather pleased.

One morning at the end of the show season I had come across Ali Rezai, Ezat, Reza Hadavand, Davoud Majzoob and two or three of the others in the tea room after riding. They were all adding together figures on small pieces of paper.

'What sort of high finance are you people up to?' I questioned.

'We are figuring out how much money we won in prizes this year. It is quite a lot, you know.' answered Ali.

'Yes, I too have figured it out and was much surprised to see that the stable won over fifty thousand Toman. Why, we could buy a nice new European horse for that.'

'Meeses Rose! That money does not belong to the stable. We the riders, get that money! It has always been so.' Ezat was quite vehement.

'But you forget that in years before you didn't win nearly this amount of money. The rider who won the most last year received just over one thousand Toman and what about the other men like Rajab, Akbar, Jamshid and the others? I think that everyone should have a share in the money because the stable is a team you know.'

They were aghast! What right had I to meddle in the division of the prize money?

'But Meeses Rose, those others do not risk their necks jumping the way we do and we always give a tip to the groom who rubs the horses that won the most.'

'Do you forget that many of the men work as jump crew for nothing on the show days and the day before when the jumps must be set up? Do you forget how the grooms must have your horses at the right place at the right time during every show? Everyone here helps on show days. You men who have the chance to ride in the shows have the fun of riding and the glory of it too. Why, think of all the publicity you get in the national newspapers! You become heroes but the others who work just as hard in another way get no recognition. To my mind the money from the prizes should be divided up amongst everyone.'

'Oh, no!' they all cried. 'That is not fair! Maybe in Canada it would be a good way but not in Iran. No, no, it will not work here.' Everyone was speaking at once and they were all extremely agitated.

'Khonume, you have not mentioned this to *Agha*, have you?' It was Davoud asking the question. 'I would not mention it to him because it would make him very angry.'

I figured that the conversation had gone far enough. The reaction was as I had expected. It was not up to me to tell the men of this new change in policy and I was now afraid to do so for they would surely stone me. I hated to think what would happen when they found out the facts.

A few days later when I arrived at the stable I saw a white Mercedes that I didn't recognize in the parking lot. It was not the most recent model but I knew it was an expensive car. I wondered if we had some guest at the stable to be shown around so I went directly to Khanlakhani's office. I saw no one other than the secretary himself.

'Khanlakhani, I was expecting to find a guest. Whose car is the white Mercedes out in the parking lot?'

'Oh, Khonume,' he chuckled. 'That belongs to Ezat. He thinks he's a bigwig now that he won so much money in the shows this year so he bought a big car.'

'But Khanlakhani, he has not been given his prize money yet. Mr. Atabai wants to wait until *Now Ruz*.'

'He always does, Khonume, but Ezat borrowed the money to buy the car; then he will pay it back when he gets his *Aidee*.'

Obviously Kambis had not sent Khanlakhani the plan yet, for he did not know that Ezat would not be getting all of his prize money and now the stupid man had borrowed money to buy a car that he could not afford. And on top of that Kambis did not like the *djelodars* to have cars. I would have to speak to him immediately about the mess it seemed I was creating by my new-fangled ideas.

It was a few days before I was able to see Kambis as he had gone to Germany for the International Football Federation meeting in Munich. In the meantime I saw two other new cars in the parking lot. One was a souped up Volkswagen that looked like a space ship with its fiberglass body; that belonged to Ali Rezai. The other one was a beige Volkswagon that belonged to Reza Tarash. Then I discovered that Reza Hadavand had bought a new motor bike. I was becoming more and more worried for I was certain they were all borrowing on their prize money but I dared not mention a thing to anyone.

I was thrilled when Kambis arrived to ride in the morning the day after he got back from his trip.

'I'm so glad to see you, Kambis. How was the trip?'

'You won't believe how terrible it was. Do you know that the first night I was there I went down to the cocktail party, leaving my room locked of course, and when I returned I discovered that everything had been stolen? My cuff links, some of my clothes and all my money, which was three thousand dollars American, cash! I had a dreadful time getting things straightened out; it just spoiled the whole trip for me. But let's not talk about that. How are you and how have things been here at the stable?'

'Everything has been going smoothly as far as the horses and work are concerned however, it seems there is a problem. I don't know quite how to put it to you but here goes. You approved the plan for distributing this year's prize money, right?'

'Right.'

'You told me that you were going to inform Khanlakhani of the plan in order that he might get all the payments straight, right?'

'Right.'

'Up until this year the riders all received their own prize money won and so it was not wrong of them to expect the same thing this year, even though the amount would be much greater. Am I correct in this assumption?'

'No, they should expect nothing! But go on.'

'Well, I came across some of the boys adding up all their monies won and tried to diplomatically put the idea that it wasn't fair for them to receive all the money this year because it was so much, and they all had a fit. They thought I was crazy. So I left them however, letting them know that I thought the money should be divided up amongst everyone. Shortly after this conversation I noticed that some of them had bought cars and motor bikes and I'm pretty sure that they've borrowed money on the expectation that they'll be receiving their total prize money. Those who won the most money seem to have bought the most expensive vehicles. I'm really worried because I don't want them to get into trouble because of my new-fangled idea and perhaps we should just leave well enough alone and take just the money that you, the General and I won and divide it up amongst everyone else and let the boys have their own prize money.'

'Nonsense. It seems there is an English expression, "Don't count your chickens until the eggs have hatched." We have a similar expression in Persian and those boys should not be counting on something they don't have. No, we will go on with our plan; I think it is excellent, and they'll just have to pay the consequences. And now I think that I'll not even give them any warning of the new system. It will just be a surprise when they are given the money by Mr. Baharpur the week before *Now Ruz*. I'll tell Khanlakhani that it's top secret and not to let anyone know of the method of distribution.'

Fat chance there was of that! Khanlakhani had a marvelous way of letting the cat out of the bag without really telling anything and I was sure that he would make a point of telling all about the prize money. There would be many who would be happy but those few who would be receiving less than they expected would cause havoc, I knew.

When I detected no undercurrents of dissatisfaction in the atmosphere I could only imagine that Kambis had not yet let Khanlakhani in on the news. However, I didn't have too long to wait.

I arrived at the stable one Sunday morning after having taken off my customary Friday and Saturday, to find Ali Rezai, Ezat , Davoud and the two Rezas standing in front of my office . I knew that they had been told the dreadful news. The other boys who had competed had not really won enough to be affected by this distribution method, as a matter of fact, they would more than likely benefit, and so it was obvious that they didn't appear on my office steps. Instead of going to the office I went immediately to the main saddle room where Nasser greeted me with a smile. Mahmoud his assistant, to whom I had given a bonus just recently for the excellent job of repairing some saddles, laughed out loud.

'Khonume Rose, you are a tricky one. You told these "Great Riders" a month ago what you were going to do but they didn't listen. Now it comes from Khanlakhani's mouth that you were talking seriously. For the rest of us it is a wonderful thing that you have persuaded Kambis to divide the prize money amongst us all, but those "Heroes" over by your office are really angry. Last year it didn't matter, but this year when we all realized that those *prima donnas* would receive so much money, most of us at the stable were very upset because we felt that in our own way we did help. I know that I can't jump over the big fences, but any time one of the show jumping riders has trouble with his tack or breaks something who is the one to fix it? Me.'

Nasser coughed so he added, 'Or Nasser. Why, he made those shipping bandages for all the horses without any help from any of the riders.'

'Khonume Rose,' said Nasser. 'What are you going to do this morning?

376

All the boys have said that they are going on strike and will not ride their jumping horses.'

'I think Nasser, I will ask you to take my saddle over to Abraheem and have him tack up Roshan. I think I'll ride down to the Farahabad Club to see what's going on there. Maybe if I sneak out the back way the strikers won't see me.'

I safely left on my horse planning not to return for an hour or two.

When I returned, as I figured the boys were still sitting on the steps of my office. I got off Roshan, gave him to Abraheem, and decided it was time to be brave.

Everyone started talking at once when I got near the little building that served as my office and had a classroom where lectures could be held and movies were shown whenever we had them available. When I finally got them to stop their fanatical dissertations I asked for one person to tell me what they all had to say.

As usual Ali Rezai took the stand. 'Khonume Rose, you cannot do this to us. We were counting on the money that we had won this year. That's why we all have bought new cars and motors and we had other things that we wanted to do as well. We've decided that all of us are not going to ride the jumpers any more. If you will not let us have all our prize money why should we risk our necks?'

'*Gush con*! (listen)! I warned you all that I was planning to do this. I gave you reasons then, so I won't repeat myself. Even if you were to get all the money you individually won, you don't go out and buy things on borrowed money! It is very bad. What would have happened if *Agha* had decided that you wouldn't get any money? So it is finished. Now, get to work with your horses. You have wasted half the morning as it is, and will all have to step to it to get all your horses finished today.'

'Meeses Rose. We decide that we do not work with the jumping horses.' said Ali in English.

377

'What do you mean by that? And Ali, you had better say it in Farsi so you don't get it mixed up the way you sometimes do when you speak English. I want to have this right.'

'Bali Khonume. All of us who are standing here have decided that we do not want to ride the jumping horses any more. We will not do it for nothing which is what you expect. You give us mountain horses, old horses, young horses, but not jumping horses.'

'Is that the decision of all of you?' I questioned.

It was a unanimous 'Yes!'

'All right then. Just give me fifteen minutes and I'll draw up a new roster of horse distribution and I'll tell you which horses you have under your care. It seems to me that you are an ungrateful bunch and don't deserve to have jumpers anyway. I wonder that you would give up the horses that you seem to love and that have carried you to victory to people like Akbar, but that's your decision. Ezat, go to Khanlakhani's office and ask him to round up all the *djelodars* in his office; we will have a meeting there in fifteen minutes. Now please excuse me! '

It took me no time at all to assign those cheeky devils the mules and all the uninteresting horses in the stable. I had given over most of the jumpers to three or four of the younger men who were aspiring to be jumper riders but few of which had much talent. Just to be nasty, I had given one of Ali Rezai's best horses to Akbar, whom Ali felt to be the worst horseman in the stable and able to lame any horse he got his hands on.

With everyone assembled in the secretary's office I announced that because of the fact that our show jumping riders had decided to retire I was going to reassign most of the horses in the stable. I stated that this might not be a permanent assignment because some of the men might change their minds, but it would stick for at least two weeks to start with. Regular training would be starting very soon and it was important that the jumpers, most of which had been laid off for the past two months, be well legged up and ready to start their programs. Of course, the majority of the men who were being assigned the jumpers did realize that the situation dictated that it would be unlikely that they would keep these horses during the season, although some of them had hopes that maybe one would remain in their hands.

The faces of Ali, Ezat and the others were a study as I assigned each one a mule and four or five other of the worst horses in the stable. Not that the horses were bad, it was just that they were not popular due to the fact that they needed long slow work every day if they were mountain horses, and the horses going to Kish needed to go out twice a day at this time. They would be riding from early morning until dark.

'Now that everything has been fixed, Khanlakhani, would you type up this list for me and give each man a list of his horses just in case he should forget? It's almost ten thirty so I suggest that everyone gets a set out immediately, before lunch.'

During the week one by one the riders of the jumpers came to me individually when they were certain that no one was looking. Each one had the same story; he did not want to stop show jumping; it was the idea of the others. They thought they would force me to give them their money because they all knew that there was no one else who could ride his horses the way he could. What would I do if we did not win as much in the coming show season? Each rider missed his own horses and wanted them back. Would I please reconsider? The last to come to me was Ali. He was very humble and went on in detail about how it was Ezat and Reza Hadavand who had made the plan; he, of course, had nothing to do with it! I did nothing until the following Sunday.

After a week they were all very dejected. I called a meeting first thing in the morning and took out my old roster, explaining that I had decided to make some changes in the list of horses each *djelodar* had to work with. Silence reigned as I read off the old list. 'It seems as if our "Jumping Team" has decided to come out of retirement so as you note, everyone has the same horses back that he had this time last week. I do want to thank all of you who put up with this nonsense that certain people caused; it certainly will not be forgotten by me and I have arranged for an additional bonus to all of you who were so good about it. Now let's get to work.'

With the advent of spring and the improved temperament of my boss, life at the Imperial Stables was enjoyable. Everyone seemed very happy with their *Now Ruz Aidees* when they were received. We stuck to the same formula for dividing the money each subsequent year while I was in charge of the stable. The big winners had accepted the fact that the new system was a much fairer method of distributing the money, especially when I had informed them that first year that if there was any more grumbling about it I would make certain the money was kept by the stable itself to offset some of the operating expenses from then on.

On the eve of *Now Ruz* the sixteen horses left Doshan Tappe Airport for Kish Island. Each year, for some reason it took all the *djelodars*, save the duty man of the day, and most of the grooms to take the sixteen horses to Kish. Those who did not go with the horses would be on the roster for the return trip. It was a fun trip going down on the planes with the horses, especially as it was usual, that the planes would not return to Tehran until the following day. Each year I had been invited to go on the trip but had turned it down, for I liked to be left alone to ride as many of the horses as I could to see how they felt and if there were ways in which I could improve their training. As expected, the men didn't return until late the following day, so within the two days I was able to ride about fifteen of the jumping horses. I was exhausted, but knew where to smooth out rough edges with my training program.

The riders of the jumpers didn't stay in Kish for they would spend the two weeks of the holiday working to get their horses ready to compete in the first competition of the season which was held the week after the thirteenth day of *Now Ruz* or *Siezdah Bedar* as it is called. I gave the men two full days vacation on *Now Ruz* and the day after, as the thirteenth was National Picnic Day. I knew that Kambis didn't go along with this, for I had off handedly asked him about giving days off the first year and he said that while the other men were in the Island working he felt that everyone else should be on duty full time. I decided though, that there would be no sense in working with the men when they wanted to be with their families celebrating the most important holidays of the Iranian year. I also, for selfish reasons didn't want to work those days; what Kambis didn't know wouldn't hurt him as long as we accomplished what was necessary; a couple of day's rest would not hurt the horses or riders.

Once everything was back to normal after the holiday the competitions started and I was pleased to see that again the Imperial Stables horses and riders dominated the placings. Kambis won a good class with Ballylea early in the season but he still professed not to like the horse.

MY GUESTS

I very seldom invited guests to come to ride with me at the Stables, mostly because it interfered with my job to have to spend a couple of hours riding with someone and also because I felt that if something happened it was a terrible responsibility to have had one's guests injured on a horse of the Shahanshah. The recriminations could be far reaching. I did have one friend, the wife of a German Army General, who had a lot of experience with horses, ride regularly helping with some of the younger horses which needed work in basic dressage, but that was a different matter. Her husband was the chief advisor to General Tufanian, head of the Imperial Iranian Army, and so she had the security clearance that was needed.

Because of my policy I was disturbed when I had a telephone call from Susan Khaki one morning. Susan was English and a good friend, who was married to Don's friend Bahman; they had lived in Virginia while Bahaman was an intern at Reynold's Metals, when Don was in Richmond, some years previously and the four of us were very close. When Bahman had resigned his job with the Iranian Aluminum Company and was having such a hard time getting another job, Don was a great consolation to him. Finally, when Bahman was hired by the government to work for IDRO at a very low salary I helped Susan to get a job at the Imperial Country Club teaching riding, which was a good source of additional income for them.

'Gail, it's Susan. How are you?'

'Well, what can I do for you?'

'Actually I was calling to ask a favor of you. You remember Stanley? The President of the company that Bahman is helping to set up an Iranian subsidiary.'

'Yes, of course I do. We had dinner with him the last time he was in town. A charming man.'

'Well, he is in town with his wife and his thirteen year old daughter. I have been taking them around the last couple of days and I had the little girl riding at the Country Club yesterday. She's really a good little rider and is just dying to see the Imperial Stables so I was wondering if I could bring the two of them down for a little tour tomorrow and perhaps you would let little Sarah ride a horse.'

'Lister, Susan, I'll have to check with Kambis about it. I never have people down without permission and I don't know about the ride thing. I would be afraid that she might get thrown off or something.'

'No, really, she's a very good little rider. You wouldn't have to worry about that.'

'I'll check things out with Kambis and then get in touch with you later today. I hope I can work things out.'

Of course that was the day that Kambis was going to Shiraz with His Majesty. When I called his office Mrs. Nazemi said she would try to remember to have him call me before he left but not to count on it. Naturally the day went by and no return call. When I arrived home from work there was a message that a Mr. Stanley Wilks had called to invite us to dinner and would I please call him. As much as I liked the idea of going out to dinner with this charming man and his family, I was a little worried about the fact that I felt I couldn't have the child down to ride at the stable the next day.

On the way to the Hilton where we were to meet for dinner I was explaining my predicament to Don.

'Oh for heaven sake, Gail. You can have them down to the stable without having to personally talk to Kambis. You can tell him when he gets back. You have more authority than that, and how's it going to look to everyone at this party if you're having a good time enjoying this man's hospitality and you won't let his wife and kid go to the Imperial Stables where you are the manager and trainer! I think that you have to go in there and say that you will be expecting them tomorrow morning. What could happen? You're not going to get fired for something like that, unfortunately!'

'I am not bloody worried about getting fired! It's the responsibility of the whole thing. What if I let the kid ride and she falls off and hurts herself?'

'The chances of that are pretty slim, I would say. You don't get asked too many favors from our friends, mostly because they all know that you don't like to take personal friends down there. Everyone respects your wishes. God knows you have made it clear to everyone. So unless this was very important to her, Susan wouldn't have even dreamed of asking you. There is rumor that Stanley's going to offer Bahman the job of Managing Director of Agrosaz Iran and that would be a great feather in his cap; it would also mean a lot more money which you know he certainly could use.'

With these thoughts in my mind I was greeted at the door of the Wilks's suite by Stanley himself and introduced to his charming wife and very pretty daughter. During the course of the evening I did mention that I would be looking forward to having them come to the stable the next morning about eleven.

The next morning I was just finishing up my work sheets when I was told that I had some guests. I called to Jamshid, one of the younger *djelo-dars* who had three of the quieter hacks under his charge, and asked him if he thought the little Apollo would be a good horse for this girl. He said the horse was pretty quiet and so I had him saddle up two horses and told him to take the child for a quiet walk around the stable grounds for about fifteen minutes or so. I had thought of having her ride in the ring but the previous night she had said how she hated ring work and loved to ride out.

I took my three guests, Susan, Sarah and her mother on a quick tour of the two main stable blocks and into the "show tack room" where they were able to see some beautiful pieces of horse artifacts. There were a number of antique saddles and bridles from Royal Families of two hundred years ago. The collection of antique stirrups was the most complete and unique I have ever seen, with stirrups dating back four hundred years. The Shahanshah's parade saddle with his matching bridle and breastplate that were incrusted in gold were items that visitors were always interested in seeing. There were also many gifts that have been given to various members of the Imperial family over the years that were of interest. A beautiful silver encrusted charro saddle from Mexico, a Vaquero's saddle complete with its llama saddle pad from Argentina, an incredible hand carved elephant about three feet tall covered in ivory and encrusted with semi-precious stones which was a gift from the Maharaja of Baroda, the skull of a tiger set in a golden holder that was to be used to hold cigars, were just a few of the things in this marvelous display.

When we came out of the saddle room Jamshid had the two horses saddled and ready. I helped Sarah up, adjusted her stirrups and told her that she was to ride behind Jamshid who would take her on some of the paths that were around the grounds. I had her put the chin strap of her hat under her chin and told Jamshid to just go quietly walking and little trotting. She seemed to have a decent seat and looked relaxed on the small Arab gelding, so I had confidence that all would be well. I did have a thought that I should ride out with her myself but dismissed this as I thought I should stay with her mother and Susan. We went to look at the yearlings which were turned out in the paddock behind the new stable and to see some of the Jumpers.

Suddenly Rajab came running and puffing as his fat frame usually did,

'Khonume Rose! Khonume Rose! *Bia! Khord zamine! Daukhter Farengi khord zamine.'* Sarah had fallen off!

I rushed into the stable yard to see the two horses but neither Jamshid nor Sarah were mounted. It took me some moments to find out that she had fallen off on the road in front of the old gate to the hunting lodge and Jamshid had stayed with her sending the two horses back with a groom who just happened to be in the vicinity. Just as we were about to get into the car to go and pick them up Khanlakhani drove up to the yard in his car with Jamshid and Sarah in the back. She was lying back against the seat and looked like she was unconscious but when we spoke to her we realized that she was not, though she was rather confused.

When questioning Jamshid I learned that she had been knocked out when she fell even though she had her hard hat on. Susan and I transferred the child to her car and she and the mother drove off to the Tehran Clinic to have the poor child checked in at the Emergency Room.

Jamshid was very pale and still shaking when he told me the story. The girl kept passing him and wanting to ride faster. His English was very poor but he could say no, which he did. However, she continued to taunt him laughing all the time. Finally they came to a wide path so she kicked her horse on into a canter passing him. She didn't realize that after about a hundred yards the path turned into the paved road which leads to the stable and when the horse arrived at that spot it turned quickly right, slipping on the tarmac and going down, throwing the girl off to the side where she hit the ground head first?

The outcome of the accident was that Sarah had to spend two days in the Clinic under observation, for she had sustained a severe concussion and she lost her sense of smell, which she never regained.

I was very lucky, for her parents never mentioned that I might have put her on a difficult horse; they both did say that she was a headstrong child and had admitted to taunting the man who was riding with her. I swore never to have another guest ride at the stable.

Helga, my German friend, had often mentioned that she would like to be able to take her husband out for a ride in the desert beyond the stables so I had agreed and said that we must do it someday. One sunny spring morning was the someday. By that time Helga had bought one of the Imperial Stables horses and was keeping it down at the Farahabad Club but was still coming every day to ride with me.

I certainly could not refuse.

Peter had been a good horseman in his day riding in the German Army and having entered Three Day Event competitions many years before. They had horses at their home in Germany where they would be returning at the end of his two year stint in Iran. I had no doubt that he was a capable horseman. As he was a big man I decided to put him on Malek, a Trakhener gelding that was a really quiet hack as well as being a talented jumper and one of my hopes for the coming year.

The three of us set out from the stable in the brilliant Persian sunshine; in that spring time of year there are beautiful colorful desert flowers and the barren mountains take on a hint of green when observed from afar. On close observation they are still brown but there is enough vegetation to give some color to them when seen from afar. We were going to stay out for a couple of hours so we would be able to go up the sand track right into the mountains.

Peter was about sixty-seven years old at the time. As a young man from a very poor family, he had joined the Hitler Youth Organization and then graduated to the the army. He spent much of his time during the Second World War training the German Ski patrol even though he didn't ski himself. He tells the story of how he was raised in Bavaria, and of course everyone from that area of Germany skis. He however, never learned to ski for his family was too poor and he had to spend all his time doing odd jobs to augment the family income. Just before the outbreak of the Second World

War he was called in by his commanding officer who read out his file. Peter listened, and heard the part about expert skier but didn't mention that it was not true; he figured it wouldn't matter.

His commander then informed him that he was being promoted to Major and he would be going to a desolate place on the Yugoslav border where he would be the commander of the Ski Training Division. Somehow he managed to survive his post by hiring local boys to do the training and during his two years there he never once put on skis!

He became a Colonel in the SS and at the end of the war he spent six months in a prison camp in Siberia where he claims to have played bridge most of the time. When he finally returned to his homeland the government helped him to go to college and he graduated as an engineer four years later. But he could not get a job! He was a military man at heart so he signed up to join the army again. There he gradually made the rank of General. When he was fifty he met and fell in love with one of the members of the German Diving Team. She was twice European Champion Lady Diver. He married her in 1960; that was my friend Helga.

I was fascinated to know someone who had been in the SS. During my life there had been so much propaganda against the Germans, and especially the SS that I could not believe that I actually knew someone who had been a part of it all. When I got to know Peter well, I was able to ask him about it but he seldom said much. He did tell me however, that for a poor boy in Germany in the thirties there was not much hope. The only hope seemed to be with the Hitler Youth Organization; the young men got caught up with it. Once caught up with it, one had to go along with things in order to survive and there was no other survival by then. He often would bemoan the way he had wasted his youth. I guess that is why he was able to enjoy his later life so much and why he had married a girl so much younger than he, to reclaim his youth. And youthful he was. A fitter man I had never seen.

We were all cantering up the sand road at a leisurely pace enjoying the cool but vibrant spring air when all of a sudden Malek passed me rider-less!

No, no! Not again so soon after my other fiasco! How could I have been so stupid as think that I could put someone on a horse and have him stay aboard? Helga and I both pulled our horses up and turned around. About a hundred yards back was Peter trudging up the trail! He was obvi-ously not hurt and as we approached him having caught Malek, we saw that he had a sheepish grin on his face.

'When you two girls took off at a canter I was sitting enjoying myself very relaxed. Too relaxed for sure, because when the horse gave a little buck I just fell off. I'm sorry. I hope you don't think me too much of a fool.'

I sighed a sigh of relief that there was no injury; once he was again mounted we continued on our way. I never again had a guest come to ride with me. It was far too nerve wracking.

THE HORSE VAN

Every time I saw the horses loaded on those big open Army trucks my heart was in my mouth and every time I watched the unloading of the trucks I expected to find multiple injuries to the horses, but unbelievably there were seldom any problems, only the odd scratch but nothing more. Nevertheless from the moment the first load of horses was trucked to a horse show with me in the trainer's seat, I harped to Kambis that we needed a couple of real Horse Vans. He agreed, of course, but at first claimed that the cost was prohibitive and then there would be the 200% duty that was levied on such luxury vehicles when they were imported into Iran.

Finally one morning Kambis came to ride with a big grin on his face. He had received permission to order a nine horse box from England. Robin and I were elated. Kambis asked us both to write down the specifications we would like on the vehicle and he would try to get us as close to what we wanted as possible. This we did and were in due course informed that a Mercedes truck had been purchased in Germany, some special deal for the Imperial Court. This truck less the body was shipped to England and there the Lambourne people were building us the van. Like such special orders it took close to six months to build and was finally completed in November, 1974.

Because the truck would have to be driven from England to Iran it was decided that it would be left until the spring when the roads through the mountains in Turkey and Northern Iran would be safer. Those roads were said to be the most treacherous of the world. They were steep and for the most part the pavement was in poor repair or non-existent.

Jahanguire was the Imperial Stables truck driver. Our big army truck was in his care and how he kept that old decrepit thing going was a mystery to all. It was mostly tied together with binder twine and bailing wire! Jahanguire picked up the feed in that truck, went to the Turkoman Sarah for loads of straw and as far as Esfahan for hay and of course he was on call to drive the horses to the horse shows every time we had an away from home show. We usually took four or five truckloads of horses but he became the leader of the convoy of trucks we commandeered from the army. The army drivers had great respect for this man who worked for the stables and followed his orders to the letter. He had, at one time been a regular army driver who was on call to the Imperial Stables. When it was decided that the stables would have its own truck and we needed a driver full time it was asked of Jahanguir if he would like to have the job. He wanted it so he was given a special release from the army and became an employee of the Imperial Court, a position that was considered a great honor by most anyone in Iran.

Our other driver was Mirsa Poor, who was the *vanette* or pick-up truck driver. He had once been a taxi driver making very little money driving through the crowded streets of Tehran from early morning till very late at night. Allah had Mirza Poor under his sight, for one day his taxi was called to the VIP lounge at the airport. He had been waiting to pick up a trip when the next flight came and seeing as he was at the front of the line of the many orange taxis he was waved over to the Government Pavilion. It seemed that some special visitors had arrive in Tehran and Mr. Alam had greeted them as was customary for the Court Minister. But there had been a mix-up and there were not enough official cars to take the guests to the Palace. Mr. Alam and his wife would have to follow the procession of official cars in a taxi! All went well, but as Mirza Poor was driving away after having let his official passengers out he saw in the back seat, the official gold chain of Office of the Minister of Court with its medallions, that the *Khonume* had been carrying for her husband. It must have slipped from her lap and she had then in her confusion at arriving at the palace in a taxi, left it. Mirza Poor thought how much this chain could be worth. If melted down he would be a rich man. However, he was a man of honor and he would not dream of cheating anyone connected with His Imperial Majesty. He therefore turned back towards the palace where he stopped at the guards' gate to return the chain. He had to give his name, *shenoslame* (sirname) and serial number then wait to be released by the guards who were very suspicious as to why this taxi driver would have the important Chain of Office of the Court Minister. As things turned out when Mr. Alam heard the story he was so grateful that he gave Mirza Poor a job for life as a driver for the Imperial Court. He could have chosen almost any job, but he loved to drive trucks so he asked to do that and so he became the driver of one of the pick-up trucks that belonged to the Imperial Stables.

At the beginning of April, just after the *Now Ruz* vacation Kambis decided that the roads would be clear enough so he would send Jahanguir to England to pick up the truck and drive it back to Iran. The journey would take him about two weeks but during that time we would be able to commandeer our usual army trucks and drivers to transport the horses to the shows as usual. Robin was very excited about the truck coming because he thought that the horse shoeing equipment that he had ordered for the blacksmith's shop could be sent on the truck thus saving a lot of money that it would cost us to ship the new shoes and modern farrier tools.

We all bade Jahanguir goodbye and a safe journey. The only thing that I could not figure out was why he was not sent with another driver to help him. He himself did not speak one word of any foreign language and also couldn't read! How in heaven's name would he be able to find his way from the middle of England to Tehran, Iran? Perhaps he had some sort of built in homing device!

The first word we had was when Kambis had a telex saying that the truck and driver had left the factory in Lambourne and were heading towards Melton Mowbray, where the horse shoes and so forth would be picked up at the Military Dispatcher's Office attached to the Equestrian Unit there. It was about a week later that we heard that the license for the vehicle did not permit the transportation of anything other than horses over international borders so Jahanguir'd had to take Robin's supplies back to Melton Mowbray.

Then we heard that the truck had gone on the Ferry from England and had landed safely in France. I could picture Jahanquire driving through Paris! We then heard that he had had some difficulty with the truck and had gone to Germany where he was waiting for it to be fixed. Finally he left Germany and that was all we heard for two weeks. By now our driver had been gone for about a month. What he had done during that period of time Robin and I could not figure out. The only saving grace was that the longer the truck took to get to the treacherous mountain terrain the better the conditions would be. After five weeks we were informed that driver and truck had arrived safely in Ankara, Turkey. That meant that within a few days we would see our Horse Van.

A week went by; what had ever happened to Jahanguire everyone inquired? He still did not arrive. Kambis wired the embassy in Ankara but they replied that he had already left that city. Finally, after another week we learned that he had arrived at the Turkish-Iranian border. We all breathed a sigh of relief, for within two or three days he would surely be in Tehran.

And he was. One bright sunny day around noon as I was driving out the Farahabad gates, a beautiful light blue horse van passed me entering and at the wheel was Jahanguire, who blew two long blasts on his air horn. I stopped in my tracks, reversed and followed the van to the parking lot.

News must have come from the court garage that the truck was coming, for everyone on the staff at the stables was standing in the lot awaiting the arrival of the van. They cheered and clapped as he pulled to a stop. The "oos" and "aahs" were deafening; I had to admit it was a very beautiful vehicle. The main cab was equipped with seating for at least eight people, more if it was filled in the Persian fashion. The floor of the van itself was a thick corrugated rubber and each stall divider was padded heavily to insure that there would be a minimum of injury to the horses. Dr. Cutler complained that the nine horses would be quite cramped and that if there was trouble it would be hard to get to the horses but I personally, felt it was a very efficient vehicle. Robin was disappointed that the cab only, was air conditioned, but what does one expect for a mere thirty five thousand pounds! Jahanguire took us all for a ride demonstrating the stereo sound system, the air horn and many other of the comforts and modern equipment of our van. When he finally drove away to take it to the garage all of us clapped and cheered as we would have for the Shahanshah if he were on an official visit.

The next morning came the sad news; we would not be able to use the horse van for the competition on Friday because it had been found by Mr. Abraheemee, the chief mechanic and manager of the garage, that the clutch was going and needed to be replaced before the truck would be able to be used to carry the horses. He would try to have it ready for Friday morning but he was doubtful it would be available for use. Robin and I were just as pleased because we wanted to have a trial run loading some of the horses to see how they reacted to their new means of transportation and also to figure out what was the best method of loading. Also we wanted to familiarize the men who would be assisting, with the nuts and bolts and idiocincracies of the van.

The next week there was to be a competition at the Nowruzabad Riding Club; it was a show sponsored by the Tehran Journal Newspaper and Pakdis Wines jointly and had been well publicized so there would be a very good crowd, no doubt. What better time to bring out our new truck? Both Tuesday and Wednesday we loaded the horses we expected to transport in the van and took them for a little ride. We found that one or two of them did not seem to like the claustrophobic atmosphere of the closed van and so decided to ship them as usual in the open trucks to which they were used. We ironed out the kinks of loading and were all very excited about using the van for the show on Friday.

I arrived at the show grounds early to supervise the unloading while Robin was to be in charge of the loading end of things at the stable. I saw the first of our army trucks driving in the laneway followed by another army truck and by the time I counted five army trucks it seemed to me that all the horses had arrived. What had happened to the brand new horse van? None of the *djelodars* seemed to know and Jahanguire was not driving one of the army trucks; he would surely have had the answer.

It was Robin who clarified the mystery upon his arrival. 'His Majesty came down to the stable to ride this morning and wanted to see and drive the new horse truck so we couldn't use it to bring the horses to the show.'

It was a disappointment but the following week there was to be a show at the Imperial Country Club and we would be able to use the truck then. Actually we were taking only seven or eight horses to that competition due to the fact that it was open to members of the club only and the *djelodars* would not be able to enter. Kambis, General Khosrodad and I would ride two or three horses each as we were all members.

When I arrived at the Country Club the van was already there and the horses had been unloaded and tacked up in readiness for the commencement of the classes. We had been able to obtain special permission for Davoud Bahrami to enter the junior classes at this exclusive show. He won both of them. General Khosrodad won the C Jumper competition; I won the B competition with Roshan, his first time in that division, and Kambis and I were first and third with our two teams in the relay competition. The

Imperial Stables won all the events!

I went up to supervise the loading of the horses after the show and was shocked to find that none of the horses had been bandaged on the trip over and therefore there was nothing to wrap the legs for the return journey. I ranted and raved at the grooms to whom I had given specific instruction about always putting on protective leg wraps when transporting the horses. I had checked to see that we had all the cottons and bandages for the nine horses the previous day. Why had they not been used?

It was Reza Tarash who finally was able to get a word in to tell me that the doctor had told them that the horses did not need bandaging in the new truck. That was utter nonsense, I complained, but if that is what the doctor had prescribed at least I would not have to take the responsibility of any injuries.

When I arrived at the stable on Sunday morning Abraheem came running up to me. He seemed worried as he told me I had better take a look at Roshan. They all knew how much I liked Roshan and he was the horse that I rode in the competitions with so much success. When Roshan was taken out of his stall I could see at once that he was dead lame. It took only a moment to see that he had a very severe injury on the inside of his left fore coronary band. I examined it carefully and saw that the wound was deep that the coronet was badly damaged. It would take months for this to heal, I estimated.

'How did this happen, Abraheem?' I asked him sadly; it was not going to do any good asking questions; the injury was there and the horse was out of commission for a long time.

'Khonume. He stood on himself in the van on the way back from the horse show Friday. You were right. He should have been bandaged. I told Dr. Cutler when we were loading the horses for the show; I had already bandaged Roshan's front legs, but he told me to take the bandages off so I did.

396

Now look what has happened. I knew you would be very angry, Khonume.'

'I'm not so much angry, Abraheem. I'm sorry for my horse and now I won't have my Roshan to ride in the shows until the injury is healed, and that will be months.'

I decided to go to have it out with Robin. I was furious that he had countermanded my order about bandaging without asking me. Even though he was the vet, he obviously had not done a lot of transporting of horses in his day or he would have known that it was stupid not to bandage when vanning horses. I must say that he was very nice about it and profusely apologized to me about Roshan.

'I promise you, Gail, that he will be sound for this Friday. I know that you have a really good chance so don't worry, he'll be able to go as planned.'

I was very dubious but left things in his hands and sure enough, the horse was rideable by Wednesday so I had two days to work him before the competition on Friday. It was an evening competition under lights and as well as the lighting factor the course was stiff. It had been designed by Geoff Chandler, the new manager for the Country Club, a well-known English horseman and trainer. Roshan was one of three horses to jump clear in the first round and the first to go in the jump-off. The little horse jumped beautifully over the first four jumps; they were high and wide for such a little horse but he had a big heart. The fifth fence was a combination of three oxers with one long stride in between each. Roshan attacked the first of the three with gusto but on landing he crumpled under me. I was unhurt but when he got up I could see that his coronary band was bleeding profusely and he was dead lame. No wonder he had fallen. I should never have tried to show him; I should have done as my own instincts had told me, laid him up for three months to let the injury heal. As it was it took six months and I never did get to ride him again.

GLANDERS AND ARABS

Glanders was a feared disease in the Middle East and Africa. In Iran, thanks to the work of the Royal Horse Society and the Department of Agriculture, it had been almost completely stamped out; however, there was always the fear of it in the back of the minds of the horse people. It is a highly contagious disease of the lymphatic system manifesting itself in the respiratory passages or in the skin. The form which affects the skin of the animal is called Farcy and is not as common as the form which affects the respiratory system and is commonly called simply Glanders. It is a very dangerous disease which is almost incurable and can be transmitted to human beings. A discharge from the nostrils of a gluey, sticky nature, snuffy breathing, ulcertaions on the nasal mucuous membrane, swelling of the lymphatic glands and fever are some of the symptoms of the disease. All affected animals must be destroyed and every animal in the stable where the disease is found must be Mallein tested and if found to have a positive reaction to the subcutaneous injection in the eyelid which is the test, must be destroyed at once.

When I first arrived in Iran I was told a story by Louise Firouz about a case of suspected Glanders in the Imperial Stables. According to her, a horse had come down with Glanders but as it was a favorite horse of His Majesy, Kambis did not dare have it put down, disregarding the great danger there was to the Imperial Family itself. What would happen to Iran if the Shahanshah died? Eventually the horse died and had been buried at the stables and no mention ever made of the incident. Louise was convinced that most of the horses at the Imperial Stables had latent cases of the disease. What a shocking story to tell a newcomer to Iran! Louise had a tendency to become dramatic I learned later, but this story she told me I didn't ever forget. During my first year in Iran I questioned people about the story; all admitted they had heard it but were noncommittal; they all said that they felt it could not possibly have been Glanders. Kambis would never have subjected the Royal Family to such danger even at the risk of angering His Majesty by having to put down one of his favorite horses.

Every new horse that ever entered the Imperial Stables at Farahabad was Mallein tested. We usually would tie the horse up down in the pine woods about half a mile from the barn; later as things became more westernized we had a shed in which the tractors and equipment were stored where we built a quarantine stall. In the time I was at the stables, we found one horse to have a positive reaction to the test; it was a horse that had been given to Agha Bozorg as a gift from one of the chiefs of a certain influential Turkoman tribe and could not be refused. It was suspected that the horse had been stolen by this man from Turkomans in Afghanistan and he had only given it as a gift to get it out of the Turkoman area. It was a very beautiful big chestnut stallion; I learned that it had been put down because of the positive Mallein test.

When the first new horse came into the Imperial Stables after I started working for Kambis, I used it as an opportunity to ask him if he had ever had a case of the disease since he had been Master of His Majesty's Horse.

I saw the twinkle in his eye when I asked the question so I knew that he knew I had been told the story by Louise who at the time was feuding dreadfully with Kambis and the Royal Horse Society.

'I don't know why you don't come right out and ask me a question, if you are looking for an answer to something that's puzzling you, Gail.'

'Perhaps I am learning the Iranian way,' I answered treading a little dangerously for at that time I didn't really know Kambis very well.

Luckily he laughed. 'You have obviously heard the story Louise Firouz has told hundreds of times about the horse of His Majesty that had Glanders and I wouldn't have it put down for fear of the ire of the Shah. Now, I will tell you my side of the story and you can believe whichever one you'd like to. You already know the story of how after many years of training and the support of His Majesty I came home to Iran as a well-trained Army Major. And I have told you how I hated the army and begged to get out. It was only through my wonderful father's sacrifice of this job and the kindness of His Majesty that I was allowed to leave the army to become The Master of His Majesty's Horse. I've had many plans and ideas for the stable which His Majesty kindly has allowed me to implement. What I started with was a run-down mud barn and a couple of paddocks fenced with steel piping. What you have to work with today, my dear Mrs. Rose, is one of the most beautiful stables in the world. You yourself have told me so many times, unless you were just being kind.'

'Kambis, you know that I wouldn't be frivolous in my compliments. I will reiterate that I do think this is one of the most beautiful stable setups I have ever seen, if not the most beautiful.'

'So I will go on. I'd been in my job only for a few months when a horse came down with a high fever and a runny nose. In those days we didn't have a veterinary for the stables but relied on the kindness of the German Army who had a vet stationed here in the embassy. I immediately called this man who came down to Farahabad. I told him of my fears of Glanders and he examined the horse and gave it the injection in the eyelid which is the Mallein test and promised to come back to read it the next day. I had a sleepless night, but it seems that he went to a dinner party and in confidence mentioned the fact that we had a horse with suspected Glanders. Many people in the upper social circle at the time were very jealous and critical that I had been appointed to such a prestigious position, especially when I hadn't fulfilled my obligation to His Majesty by staying in the army, so naturally the talk started. Louise, who for some reason has always had a hate for me, had the story around town in no time.

'When the vet came back the next day the test was negative, so he began treating the horse for strangles, but it seems that we had let it get away from us and had not begun treatment soon enough, so the horse died shortly thereafter. As much as I refuted the story that was being publicized it never really died out.

'His Majesty heard about it and was very angry that the veterinary had spoken of private things in his stable and that was when the idea of having our own private veterinary was born. And that's the story. Now, next time you hear some suspicious things about me just come right out and ask me. I'll always be truthful and if it's something I don't want to tell you then you may believe what you want.'

From then on I always was able to get an answer and there were very few things that I was afraid to ask about.

One day during the autumn of 1974 Robin came to the stables very distressed. It was a rainy day and so I had decided not to work the horses hoping that the afternoon would be clear.

'Good morning, Robin. What are you looking so down in the mouth about?' I greeted him when he walked into the saddle room.

'It sure as f——is not a good morning!' I was startled, for my colleague was usually in good form in the early part of the day; it was as the day wore on and his frustrations caught up with him that he began to get frayed at the corners.

'What bad news have you heard so early in the morning to put you in such a frame of mind?'

'These f————g Iranians will never learn! A horse gets sick and they try to treat it themselves; only when things get out of hand do they think to call in professional help and then they expect some kind of miracle work from the newfangled doctor and if they don't get it, who's to blame? Why the doctor, of course! He's not a good doctor! My life would be much easier if Kambis had not been so good to me. I thought that by allowing me to have my own practice as well as working here at the stables it was a great deal; what a fool I was; it's been nothing but a headache to treat horses for these ignorant peasants.'

'What about all that nice fat money you get? You have to work for your Rials, Robin. People won't give them to you for nothing.'

'The money's not that bloody good you know, and on the lousy salary I make here I need the additional money to survive in this God forsaken country. '

'Why don't you just calm down for a minute Robin and tell me about it. Things can't be that bad.' We worked well together for there were many times that Robin had been the buffer for my anger due to some frustrating incident.

'You're not working horses this morning, Gail. Why don't you get in the car with me and come and see something of what's eating me up and making me hate this country with such intensity. '

Well, why not? Obviously Robin was in need of someone to talk to. In Iran the minor frustrations seemed to build up to a crescendo after a time; when the explosive time arrived it was necessary to have a friend who would listen, understand and consol. I would do that for Robin on the way to wherever he was going in such an obvious hurry.

I hopped into his battered little Peykan, the trunk and back seat of which looked and smelled like a pharmacy, and off we drove at a blistering pace. The pace would slow down when we got to the edge of the city; we would crawl through Tehran with the traffic.

'Where, may I ask, are we going?'

'We're off to my favorite place in Iran! That badly run and filthy stable of Khargushdareh.'

It had been the home of the spring and fall racing meets in Iran for years, but rumor had it that no longer would there be racing at the dusty track. It was still the home of the Tehran Polo Club which held its games two or three times a week in the infield of the race track; the water trucks would spray their way up and down the field of sand between each chucker to allow for visibility during the games. As well, there were two riding clubs that had stabling in the complex. I wondered where and what the problem would be today.

I had heard the story of the race horse trainer who was a big chief of a Turkoman tribe calling to Agha Bozorgh to beg the important man to allow His Majesty's veterinary to cure his most valuable race horse. Robin had been informed by the office of Kambis's father that he was to go out to the race track where he would meet the old Turkoman and his horse. It was not during the racing season so the man had had to truck his horse some twelve hours down from Gonbad e Kavous. When he arrived at the track the chief and all his family had pitched a tent in which to keep out of the sun and the obviously sick horse was tethered nearby swathed in Turkoman horse blankets. Luckily for Robin it turned out that the horse had a not too severe case of colic which he was able to take care of after a few doses of Yogurt into the stomach of the horse by tube. Robin became the hero of the Turkoman people and all those with influence would truck their horses down to the track when they seemed to be off color, where Robin would be called upon to treat them. I wondered if it was another case from the Steppes; it always troubled Robin to treat these horses because most of them were so filled up with opium and other drugs that it was a little tricky.

'May I ask what is happening at Khargooshdareh that has put you in such a tizzy?' I queried.

'Kambis's office had an anonymous caller who said that there are five cases of African Horse Sickness out there. There has not been any of that in the country since Madjid Bakhtiar lost most of his herd sixteen years ago but there was a rumor that some of the Turkomans have illegally brought some horses into the country from Pakistan, where the disease is still evident, so of course panic has set in at the Imperial Court, especially now that the World Arab Association is about to arrive to check the Iranian Arab Horses for registration with them. Foreign visitors always seem to hear the gossip and surely they would hear that gossip, especially since Mary has so many enemies; any rumor of the disease could jeopardize our chances of being registered even though the disease has nothing to do with our Arab horses and their conformation and performance.'

'Oh, Lord, I hope the rumor is false.' I said, reflecting my thoughts on the disease. Mary and her horses!

Mary Garagoslu! It would take a book in itself to depict her properly. She was the daughter of a very prominent Persian doctor who married an American woman in the days when it was not an accepted practice; Mary was educated in America and France and returned to Iran a well-educated beauty, desirable socially because of her Garagoslu name and mentally due to her foreign education and physically because she was truly beautiful. Of all her many suitors she fell madly in love with the thrice married Madjid Bakhtiar, the wealthy head of the Bakhtiar clan and by many years, her elder. He was a sportsman and playboy who had traveled the world. His lands were extensive in the southwest of Iran and he was said to have the greatest Arabian horses in the world. Mary was a beautiful plaything to him at first but when he discovered she could also keep up to him riding horseback in the desert and seemed to have a very good knowledge of the equine he decided that she would be the very woman for him to marry. After the great social wedding feast Mary and Madjid moved to Khuzestan where he kept his herd of hundreds of Arabian horses during the winter months. For a number of years they lived the winter in the southwest and moved north near Hamadan for the summer months. Each year she drove the majority of their herd north to Hamadan where the weather would be cooler.

Her family had a lovely farm and many hectars of grazing land just north of the city. Madjid began to spend more and more time away leaving her to tend the responsibilities while he became the gay playboy again in Tehran and foreign cities. She heard the rumors of course, but she loved her life and her horses. When the African sickness struck the herd it was Mary who tried to nurse the animals back to health, but after it was all over there were only sixteen mares and three stallions of the famous Bakhtiar herd remaining. Mary exhausted, went to France to rest for a couple of months. When she returned Madjid was down in Khuzestan; she left Tehran immediately to go down south to be with her husband. When she arrived however, he introduced her to his newest concubine. For Mary it was the last straw! It was the end of her life with Madjid. She left him. Only months later Madjid killed himself in his airplane; they say he was flying while intoxicated. After Madjid's death, Mary went down to the place in Khusistan. All that was left to her by her husband was a very small piece of land with a mud hut and what was left of the herd. She decided to dedicate the rest of her life to these few horses and to make them famous. She was reputed to drink too much, to have love affairs with the stable men and to steal if necessary to keep body and soul together. She built the herd back up to about fifty horses always being careful to cull when it was evident a horse was not of the best quality. She smoked opium with the Arab sheiks and slept with them in order to get services for her mares to the few good stallions that were left in the Persian Arab belt. Eventually, in 1972, the herd was looking promising but Mary was totally out of funds and could no longer afford to feed the horses so she went to Tehran where she thought she could get some backing. The brothers of Madjid, who had inherited all of his money and most of his lands would not help. The Royal Horse Society was in its inception so as a last resort she went to Kambis Atabai, to see if the Society would help. Kambis was vehemently in favor preserving the Persian horses and had been waiting for an opportunity to get hold of the Arab stud of Mary Garagoslu. He bought the whole thing in the name of The Royal Horse Society and hired Mary as the manager. Her problems were solved! She could go on with her work. His Majesty loved international recognition and thus it was decided to have the herd recognized with the World Arab Association which was sending an inspection delegation within a month. It was very important that nothing should spoil the visit of the officials and this scare of African horse sickness was something that was not needed at the time.

When Robin and I pulled up to the stabling area of the Polo Federation of Khargushdareh three disheveled looking grooms sat squatting on their heels beside the mud walled barn waiting for us.

'*Asb kojast?*' Robin barked at them. They all started talking at the same time as they lead us to the stall of the sick horse.

The horse was indeed sick. It lay prone, breathing very hard and giving the occasional moan. Robin began to examine it quickly and efficiently. After just a few moments he stood up.

'There is some fluid in the lungs and there are some signs that might make the layman believe it was African horse sickness but I think it's a very advanced case of colic, hopeless as a matter of fact. Have you ever seen one like this, Gail?'

I shook my head; I had seen acute cases of colic and I had seen horses operated on for colic and eventually die but I had never seen a horse in such a desperate condition.

'Why do you think that this is "the sickness"?' he addressed the groom.

'Doctor, there is more than one horse that is in the same condition. One does not get so many cases of *deldar* (colic) at one time.'

'How many others are there? I want to see them.' Again I heard the worried tension in my friend's voice. There were four others in a barn where the horses were tethered in standing stalls, the men told him.

'Gail, there could not be four more cases of colic like that at one time.

That horse had no movement in its digestive system. I would give it only a few hours more. It must be in dreadful pain.'

He really hated to see horses suffer but I wondered why he didn't give it some kind of medication or pain killer. I kept my mouth shut though because I guessed he wanted to see the others before he was conclusive about the diagnosis.

The other four were in as bad if not worse shape. When asked, the grooms said that they had all become sick at more or less the same time and that was two or three days ago.

'What are you going to do, Robin?' I questioned desperately; I was sick from looking at the agony in the eyes of the horses.

'Nothing!'

'What do you mean, nothing? You must do something! They are in pain! Agony! You must give them something to relieve the pain, or put them down.'

'I can't do anything. I was told to come out here by Kambis. He heard the rumor and told the head man here that I was coming to check on whether or not it was "the sickness". That was all. I don't have permission to treat the horses. I suspected that they were advanced cases of colic. Have you seen the feed they give these horses here? No wonder five of them have it at the same time.'

'But Robin, you must do something. It is not humane to leave them like that.'

'Get in the car and let's just get out of here! I can't stand the smell!' He got in and started the engine. I jumped in the passenger side fearing he would drive off without me.

We were totally silent for some time. I was bitterly thinking how cruel and inhumane my colleague was, and he was probably hating the Persians and their stupidity.

'I can imagine what you are thinking of me right now, Gail', he finally broke the silence. 'But now you see what I have to deal with. I was ordered by our boss to check out the rumor. I was not told to treat the horses. I must report what I found. All of those horses are owned by ignorant men. If I treat them and they die, which they most certainly will, treated or not, Kambis will be blamed for sending me out and I will be blamed for killing them. If I do nothing to them and they die, it is the will of Allah. If I put them humanely down, which is what should be done, I am blamed for killing the horses that might get better. I have my neck in a noose. I will make my report that the horses do not have African horse sickness and I will suggest that the Khargushdareh veterinary practice euthanize them but this will not happen and I can do nothing. Why do you think I am in such a pissed mood?' We were passing the Hilton Hotel and I was surprised when he turned in.

'I need a bloody big scotch. What about you?' We went in to have a drink and a sandwich.

Two days later we heard that the last of the five sick horses had died. We had a drink to those poor creatures.

A delegation of three came from the World Arab Association to inspect the Iranian Arab horses; two of them were English and one, John Ford who was at the time president, was an American. During their first couple of days in Iran they stayed in Tehran and were shown around some of the stables in the area; the final stable they visited before going to Khuzestan was the Imperial Stables. I was put in charge of displaying our best and most interesting horses.

I decided to show a few of our breeding stock which were Turkoman and Thoroughbred-Turkoman cross, three of His Majesty's personal horses which included an Arab Thoroughbred cross and a Cheneran which is also a type an Arab Turkoman cross and finally the very few actual Arabs we had in the stable. The Arabs included a Jordanian Arab stallion that had been given to His Majesty by King Hussein of Jordan about five years earlier; he was not an especially good representative of the breed I didn't think, and was interested to hear these people say that they also thought he was less than perfect. They had just come from Jordan where they had been inspecting the stable of horses for one of the prominent sheiks and in confidence they told me that they had not passed the herd as a viable breeding herd of true Arab horses.

They were not very impressed with our three year old Arab stallion, a rather pretty roan with a white face and black mane and tail, because of his very weak hocks and narrow stature. I was rather surprised, for I felt he was a typical Arab type with the lovely dish face, crested neck and high tail carriage.

The horse I thought to be the *piece de resistance* of the Imperial Stables Arab horses was a solid black four year old stallion that had been bred by Mary. He had a good solid body, strong legs of good conformation, a high but proud carriage of a rather plain head; he was however, very typical of the Persian Arabs. He was the type of horse that could probably go all day in the desert without ever tiring. His sire, Azar, was said to have won many cross-desert races of the old days; these races were as long as thirty miles. I had seen the old stallion in Khuzestan at Mary's stud; he was indeed a beautiful animal even at the age of thirty. This young animal and his proud carriage made me feel that we did have hope of getting the herd recognized, for the majority of the horses in Khuzestan that they would see, were of a similar type and they seemed very impressed with this horse.

Once the show was over my part was done.

They would fly down to the stud farm with Kambis where they would sleep in the old fashioned Arab goat hair tents decorated with beautiful carpets, huge cushions and low tables for the furnishing. They were to have a taste of the true Arab life.

I had gone down to the stud farm a few weeks earlier to help Mary and her staff with the training of the young stock to lead for inspection, and to help her decide where and just how the horses should be shown for the Inspection Day. I just hoped that these people would be the type to enjoy a bit of the primitive life. If not it would certainly not help the cause. Mary had planned some excellent meals, strictly of the Arab flavor, and had arranged for Arab musicians and belly dancers for entertainment. I would have loved to be a part of it for surely it would be a wonderful experience to see the old Arab world way of life. Many of the local sheiks had promised to come on the day, in their dress robes which were very colorful and of course they would all arrive on horseback which would add to the atmosphere.

The reports were that all went well but it would be some time before the final decision would be made. Mary, who had been working on pedigrees for years, would have to submit her final stud book which had not yet gone to press, but once this was done and sent in for approval it would be decided whether or not the herd was worthy of recognition. Months later the word arrived that The World Arab Association had recognized the Iranian Arabs and the Stud book.

KHALVATI AND ESFAHAN

Colonel Sohrab Khalvati was a cocky little colonel. He looked very much like the pictures one sees of Hitler with the exception that his face had been smashed a few times leaving rather bad scars. His beady eyes seemed to go through people rather than look at them. He was born the younger son of a good Persian family, sometime around 1920, although no one really knew exactly when because he was very secretive about his age. He was sent into the Iranian military when he had finished his schooling. He chose the cavalry and proved to be adroit in his work. He also knew on which side his bread was buttered and cottoned up to his superior officers in order to win brownie points. When Iran was given the opportunity to send cavalry officers to Saumur, which was the be all and end all of military riding in those days, Sohrab was one of those chosen to leave Iran for a full year's training in France.

Khalvati was a powerful figure in Iran, even though he was thought to be a doddering old fool, due to the fact that his daughter was married to General Nematollah Nasiri the chief of Savak. (The Secret Police) Naturally there was more to his power than that, but he used this fact as his trump card. His son-in-law, who was the same age as Khalvati, at least thirty years older than Khalvati's daughter, which was not an unusual situation in Iran, was the head of Savak from 1965 until he was assassinated in 1979. Many people believed that Colonel Khalvati himself was in the Savak, which was possible; he would be the Iranian version of Inspector Clouseau of the Pink Panther movies.

I had a minor run-in with him when we first arrived in Iran and had tried to keep out of his way as much as possible. I was not in the country to make enemies and instinctively felt that he would be the worst sort to make. When I was offered the job as manager of the Imperial Country Club I had refused to touch it, for at the time they were trying to hire me, Khalvati held the reins of the riding sector of the Club; I had no intention of stepping on his toes.

He hated me with such a total passion when I was given the job at the Imperial Stables, he went about the horsey society calling Kambis a traitor to the country for hiring a foreigner when he, an Iranian, could have done a better job. He ranted and raved and bated people every chance that he got. It took him over a year to let up on his tirades about me and when he declared a truce no one was more surprised than me. He held a horse show in Esfahan which he organized for the Iranian Steel Corporation. A beautiful stable, riding rings and jumps had been built there as part of the recreational facilities of the *Sorbahan* as the steel company was called. The mill itself was forty kilometers outside of the city of Esfahan and most of the executives and foreign employees lived in and around the mill area, which though quite desolate, had been developed into a modern satellite town with all the conveniences such as shops, restaurants, hotels and all types of sports facilities. The mill had been built by the Russians in exchange for the rights to transport Natural Gas across Iran by pipeline to Russia.

The horse show that Sohrab Khalvati put on each summer was without equal in Iran at the time. The competitors and officials were housed in the very luxurious and attractive hotel near the Steel Mill that was used for visiting officials and businessmen; many of the big Russian technical experts lived in it while the plant was being built. All meals and entertainment were free of charge to the participants of the competition. The stabling could not accommodate a great number of horses so each club was given a limit as to the number of horses that could be entered.

Since the competitions were held at night under lights, the night pre-vious to the first competition the ménage was open for schooling; there was always a party that night, which was an introduction for all to the two days of show jumping.

The Russians who worked in the mill, that as of 1976 had not yet pro-duced any steel, were bussed out to the show grounds to watch the compe-titions both nights. There were always many of the local Esfahani officials present as well as the president of the steel company and many big Iranian officials, so the crowd was usually large.

It was after a wonderful party held at the Boat Club during the show in 1973 following the competition that Khalvati decided to make amends with me. I had been told by Kambis that I had to take horses to the show and I personally must ride. He had extricated a promise from Khalvati that he would not so much as look at me the wrong way; it was important to His Majesty that we send a team, and without me Kambis would not sent it.

The Imperial Stables had had a very successful first evening; Davoud Bahrami had won the junior class; The Imperial Stables took first place with Ali Rezai and Shahab, second with me and Roshan and third with Ezat and Shabrang in the main event, the Esfahan Cup.

When we got back to the hotel from the Boat Club, where there had been a post-show party, one of our friends invited us in to his room for a night cap, something that none of us really needed, but in which all partic-ipated. We were laughing and carrying on when from the hall, loud raucous singing in Farsi was heard. Suddenly Colonel Khalvati banged through the door of the suite. My heart was in my mouth, for it was obvious that the fine colonel had had too much to drink and that was usually when he could be the most cutting. In he came, poured himself a drink and began to run at the mouth.

'I am Colonel Sohrab Khalvati the Great. Did you see what a wonderful

413

show I put on tonight and what a superb party? I am the one you can thank for that. Do you know that I really hate foreigners? Yes I do! But you see that the great Mr. Kambis Atabai told me that I must be nice to his little chickadee here, Mrs. Rose. Isn't that correct, Khonume Rose?'

I was about to get up and leave when his wife Kay walked in the door. 'Sohrab, what are you doing? I hope you're not getting into trouble. We have one more day of show; please don't spoil things.'

'Kay, my dear chickadee,' he sipped his whisky and chewed on the end of his cigar, 'I am being a good boy. I have come here to tell something to the world! I know you all think I'm going to behave badly and say nasty things but I'm not. I have come to tell a story. You all know that I have said many bad things about Mrs. Rose. You know that my son-in-law is the chief of Savak! Hush! I should not mention that word! It is too secret! I hated my son-in-law because he refused to have Mrs. Rose and her family kicked out of my country. I told him he would be sorry. But do you know, that now I am sorry because I have seen that Mrs. Rose is a very good person. She does not say bad things about me and she minds her business not meddling in my affairs; I will say that I'm sorry not to have her job but I admit that she does it well. I want to say to Mrs. Rose and her husband here that I'm sorry and I hope that we can be friends.'

I was so flabbergasted that I could hardly speak. Don came to the rescue and shook the old Colonel's hand and we all had a drink to seal our new friendship, a friendship that lasted until the day we left Iran. We were even invited to dinner at his daughter and General Nasiri's home.

Khalvati decided in 1975 to add an international flavor to his competition. Every year he went to Aachen where he presented a tray on behalf of Sohrab Khalvati or the Iranian Federation, I am not sure which. While there he had persuaded two French riders to come to Iran to ride in the Esfanah Show. These two riders were at the time at odds with their own Federation but that had nothing to do with their coming to Iran.

Jean Michel Gaud and Pierre d'Oriola arrived just two days before the competition. We had loaned Alborz for the competition and each of the other clubs loaned the best horses they could find. The two foreign riders would have two horses to ride in the competitions each evening. They had just two days to prepare themselves on these unknown horses and at the party the night before the first competition they seemed not to be very pleased with their mounts. After the two days of competition it was a rather different story though, for they had both ridden beautifully and had done very well. Jean Michel had won two of the four competitions and d'Oriola had placed well in each one. My Imperial Stables riders were outshone by the stylish riding of the two foreigners; however, Hossein Karimi Majzoob did win the puissance with Rostam at 175 meters. Second was a two way tie between Jean Michel Gaud on Alborz and myself on Ballylea, which Kambis had finally decided not to ride ever again.

Sohrab Khavati

Spectators at Esfahan

Author on Roshan at Esfahan

THE HOSPITAL

Many strange things had happened while I had been on vacation for a month. One of them was Kambis's decision to no longer ride Ballylea; I was most disappointed about that for it was most certainly a failure on my part to teach him how to ride the horse and also proved that I had picked the wrong horse for my boss.

The other disappointing thing was that there was no longer a Doctor Cutler, the Irishman and dear friend. His contract was up for renewal during the month of July when we were in America and it had just not been re-newed by Kambis, is what I was told. The Shah had sent a C130 to Ireland with all of the Cutler's effects which was a kind gesture, but for me it was a sad day when I heard the news. He wrote to tell us that he had bought a big old house just outside Dublin where he started up his own practice.

In residence was a veterinary who would be interim it turned out, be-cause he had decided that he did not really think his family would like the life in the Middle East. He was a charming young English fellow who was a part of a practice in New Market, England and was on loan to the Imperial Stables until someone more permanent could be found. Nick Wingfield-Digby took his job very seriously. As a contrast to Robin, he would be at the stable most mornings when we started working the horses. He said it was a good way for him to become acquainted with the animals and to see what type of work they were doing in case there was ever a problem. Kam-bis very much liked having his vet leaning over the rail of the ring observing his horses; he thought that it was a wonderful idea; I too liked the idea but I didn't like the interruptions, for Kambis would start one of his ridiculously confusing conversations and I would always have to go over and interrupt to get my delinquent pupil back to his lessons.

Kambis changed his mind after only a few weeks. 'You know, Gail, when Nick first came and started watching the horses work in the mornings I thought it was a wonderful idea but now I don't like it because he uses this time to bother me about problems he is having in that pharmacy of his or in the work that is being done on the operating room. I wish you would tell him not to come to watch.'

'You see Kambis, in the beginning you thought it was great, but now that he has realized that once you leave the stable in the morning you are gone for good, he wants to confer with you early in the morning; you don't like it because he can corner you. He is not so dumb. I personally think it's a good idea to have him watching the horses work but I can see your point in not wanting to be bothered about problems when you are training. However, I can't tell him not to come around. He works for you, not me. I just work as his colleague. You tell him if you don't want him hanging around.'

'Couldn't you just give him a little hint that I don't want him bothering me with things?'

'I don't think so. It is your problem!'

Nick himself, had a big problem in that he was expected to get the operating room finished. If he could do that he deserved a medal of honor.

One morning before Nick had come to the stables I was riding Roshan in the main ring when a tall, heavyset, but attractive man with a full head of wavy steel gray hair walked to the rail and when I trotted over to see what he wanted he introduced himself as Carroll D'Arcy-Irwin, the representative of General Electric Hospital Equipment Division. He had been trying to get hold of Dr. Cutler regarding the X-Ray machine that had been ordered for the Imperial Stables Veterinary Clinic. As he had been unable to reach anyone that would talk to him about it over the telephone he decided to drive down to the stables where he hoped to corner someone.

I was obviously not the one to corner on the subject because I had wanted an indoor arena rather than an X-Ray however, I did give him some time. It seems that this mammoth machine that would be able to X-Ray every part of the horse was ready for delivery, but G .E. had not as yet received any of the promised money from the Imperial Court. All they had was a contract signed jointly by Dr. Cutler and Kambis Atabai.

I informed him that the doctor was not coming back, but that we would be having a new veterinary to take his place who was the one he would have to talk to about the project, along with Kambis. I knew that the possibilities of pinning Kambis down for such discussions would be nearly impossible; he would have to wait in that crowded little ante room for hours in order to get ten minutes of my boss's time.

'While I am here I would like to have a look at your operating room. Do you think that would be possible?' Carroll asked.

'Certainly. I've just about finished with this horse so if you would just go over past the rose garden and through the opening in the wall there, I'll meet you in the stable yard in about five minutes. I walked Roshan back to his stall and gave him to Abraheem then went to Khanlakhani's office to get the keys for the operating room.

'Khonum Rose, you don't need the key; it is open. The men have been working there on the floor. We put all that equipment that came just before Dr. Cutler left, in the new pharmacy. I thought that once the doctor left the hospital idea would die but it seems that Agha is planning to have it finished. Why do you want to go in there anyway?' Khanlakhani had to know all that was going on.

I explained about the X-Ray and told him to call to Kambis's secretary to tell him that he would have to find some time to talk to Mr. Darcy-Irwin.

When we went in Carroll was very impressed with the set-up. There was a large prep room where the animals could be disinfected, operating areas trimmed of hair and any other preoperations could be done. The horse would then be led into the operating room itself which was about fifty by forty feet. There were windows on one wall so that drugs and small instruments could be passed directly from the pharmacy where they would be kept and on the other side was a large window that looked into what would be the padded recovery stall. The operating table which I had helped with one day so long ago, stood where it had been for over a year. It was an obsolete monstrosity, it turned out, and would probably never work in the Imperial Stables set-up. My acquaintance commented on this. The whole theatre and prep room were covered with a soft blue mosaic tile walls and ceiling; the floor was in the process of being covered with a special hard rubber anti-skid material. There were wires hanging down here and there that would be for electrical equipment and lights that had not yet been put in. We found the corner where we thought the X-Ray should go; there were no drawings of the plan, for it was all in the head of Dr. Cutler.

'This will be a fabulous theatre when it is finished, I dare say. There are a few rough edges that need fixing but they shouldn't take much to smooth them out. With our X -Ray you will have the most modern veterinary clinic in this part of the world. When do you think it will be completed?'

'I have no idea. It has been under construction for years. Dr. Cutler blamed Kambis and Kambis blamed the doctor for the slowness of the project; I would figure that it will be completed when the work is finished.' It took him a minute to digest that one but he finally laughed.

'Do you think I could bring my installation expert down here later today or early tomorrow to check out the building as to strength for mounting the machine?'

'Yes, of course. I think though, tomorrow morning would be best. We sometimes have official visitors in the afternoon and we like to keep the place clear of foreigners. If you know what I mean? You probably don't. Anyway why don't you plan on coming down in the morning?'

He planned it and came the next morning just after I had finished schooling the jumpers. He said that he didn't need to bother me so I went about my business. In an hour Carroll sought me out in my office.

'There's a real problem in your operating room,' he said, looking worried.

'Oh, really.' I was not too concerned.

'You see, there's not enough strength in the overhead beams to support the equipment we plan to put in. There seems to have been a major error in planning. You'll have to have the roof of the building totally reinforced which is quite a big job.'

'Actually, Mr. Darcy-Irwin, I won't have to do anything. I would suggest that you arrange to see my boss, Mr. Atabai, and talk things over with him.'

We parted on friendly terms after discovering that our daughters were in the same class at school. We hoped to meet again socially. In the meantime we would both talk to Kambis about the X-Ray problem.

I personally still thought it was a rather big unit for us to have at the stables, especially seeing as most of the work we would be doing on horses would concern the legs and feet, and for those the small portable machines that cost about fifteen hundred dollars would be perfect. I made my opinion known to Kambis but emphasized that I really knew nothing about the Veterinary end of things and was sure that it would be better to get the qualified advice of the good veterinary.

It so happened that a team of vets was coming to Iran from Australia to discuss the proposed race track and Kambis said that he would get them to look at the project, which he hoped would be used by the race track veterinarians seeing as it would be so close to the racing complex, which would just be on the other side of the mountain from the Imperial Stables. I suggested that while he was at it, why he didn't wire the Australians to ask them to pick us up one of the portable X-Ray machines and bring it when they came. Great idea, he would do it. And he did!

So, I had maybe put a bit of a fly in the ointment but I had wanted the portable machine to check on lamenesses that we'd had that I was convinced were in the foot and could only be detected by X-Ray. I hoped that it didn't kill the sale of the big one for Carroll D'Arcy-Irwin.

We saw Carroll and his wife a number of times socially before he came to me one night at a cocktail party obviously troubled. He just couldn't get along with that new veterinary. Due to the fact that he would be in Iran only temporarily had decided to keep out of the hospital project. I knew there was no way, but wished him luck when he told me. The Australians had said that although the big machine would not be necessary, if there was Fifty thousand dollars in the budget for it, it would be a shame not to have it. Nick was of the opinion that it would be as much a monstrosity as the operating table and that there was no one who would be able to operate it nor develop the film properly; an X-Ray technician would be needed, for he himself couldn't do it and not many veterinarians he knew did their own work. As it was, with the small machine, we could take the plates to the Military hospital that was just a couple of miles away near Doshun Tappe and have them developed in a matter of a few minutes as well there was a simple kit for the small plates that we could operate at the stable, if we decided that we wanted to do our own developing.

Kambis loved the idea of saving fifty thousand dollars, so he used the above as the excuse for cancelling the X-Ray equipment. Every time Carroll called the office to speak to Kambis he was told to call the vet. The vet informed him that he didn't think we needed the big machine but if it was on order he had better speak to Kambis. And around and around it went.

I filled Carroll in on what had happened telling him that I had persuaded Kambis to buy the small machine and perhaps it was partly my fault.

'It's actually just as well, because that roof would need so much work, and I know that it would be very bad to try to install such a sensitive device in that place where you work; they can't even decide who is to cancel the order. Can you imagine them trying to take X-Rays?'

'I am really sorry and shouldn't be the one to say so, but I really do think that Kambis will cancel the order sooner or later. It isn't my department but if I were you I would look for another place to sell your wares.'

'That is the problem, Gail. If they would just cancel, I would be happy, because we do have another market for it but, we can't sell it elsewhere until we get the official cancellation from Mr. Atabai's office. You see, he finally put down some money in a letter of credit and that is binding the machine.'

I would see what I could do about it and did the following morning when Kambis was riding. I told him the whole complicated story.

'Why that's wonderful, Gail. Now I can cancel the order without feeling badly that the man doesn't have anywhere to sell the big X-Ray machine. The reason I was afraid to cancel was that I didn't want the Imperial Iranian Court to get a bad name for welching on contracts. I'm glad you told me all this. I will take care of things today.' And he did!

Every morning when Nick came to watch the horses work Kambis would cheerfully ask, 'Doctor, how is the operating theatre coming along? You know I have given it precedence over all the projects at the stables.'

'Mr. Atabai if you expect me to get the project finished you will have to keep the workers moving on the building. That Arseli takes the men off to do other things every day; you will never have an operating room if you don't get the construction work completed!'

Kambis didn't like to hear complaints; anyway he had lost interest in the hospital; it became a joke to Nick, who had been used to working in one of the best equipped hospitals in Europe. While he was at the Stables the operating room did not get finished.

One morning after my work with the *djelodars* was finished, I was riding Ballylea quietly on the flat when into the ring rode a very attractive young Persian man and a pretty, auburn-haired girl.

'Good morning, Mrs. Rose. I hope my sister and I won't disturb you by riding in here?' asked the tall aquiline featured Greek God-like man.

'No, no! Of course not.' Who was this? He was so familiar and yet I couldn't identify him.

'I have been dying to meet you, Mrs. Rose. I am so glad that you happened to be here this morning. I am Kamiar Pahlavi, the nephew of His Majesty, and this is my sister.'

'I am honored to meet you. What do I say? *Valasrat? Gorbaneh shoma?*'

'Oh, no, not for me!' he said in perfect English. 'I don't go for all that stuff. On official occasions OK and for the older generation. I will be most upset if you don't call me just Kamiar.'

"Just Kamiar" and I walked our horses side by side passing pleasantries of the day. He had returned from America with a Princeton degree just a few months previously and had been given a fact finding job by his uncle. He was to infiltrate the new industries in Iran to see if they were really operating as successfully as the reports that were being given to the Shah. He would become acquainted with executive types and workers alike socially and try to find out things that would not be on the obviously trumped up reports that the Shah received.

From there the conversation got to aluminum! It seems that the Shah had told him that Mrs. Rose's husband was Mr. Aluminum in Iran. Anything there was to know about that industry could be found out from him. So Kamiar thought that Mrs. Aluminum might have some behind the scenes information that she had been told. I definitely did, but didn't tell him anything on our first meeting. I suggested that he talk to Don in his office.

'No, I would rather do it at the Horse Show on Friday. Would you let him know that I want to talk to him and then we can make it a very casual, off the record sort of thing?' It was arranged and only when I got to know him better did I let out some of the secrets that Don would never tell. I after all, did work for the Shah and why should he not know of some of the totally stupid things that happened which cost him a lot of money. Kamiar could filter the wheat from the chaff.

We became quite friendly when he began coming to the stable four mornings a week to get into shape. He asked me for pointers which I gave him happily. He was planning to take up polo for his father, Prince Golam Reza, had been a good player and was president of the Polo Federation and he thought it would be fun to learn to play. He had been taking lessons in the afternoon from one of the old colonels at the Khargooshdareh grounds.

One morning he came to me to ask my opinion. His uncle had told him that he could have any horse in the Imperial Stables with exception of the jumpers and his own personal horses, to have trained as a polo pony. Which horse, in my opinion, was best suited?

'Actually Kamiar, the best one we have is already at Khargooshdareh. It's Apollo, a lovely little chestnut Arab stallion! Kambis has lent it to Pulad Mansapur who had it trained; I have seen it in a game and it's super. I think that technically it still belongs to your uncle; I would try to get my hands on it if you can. Pulad doesn't play very often since he broke his leg that time. The best one here at the stable I think, would be that black Persian Arab stallion, Mahmal. He was passed for the stud book but I don't think he is classy enough to breed from, so no one should be too upset if you took him. He might make a good mountain horse but that takes almost as long as it does to make a polo pony so why don't you try for him.' We went to look at him and Kamiar was very impressed with this jet black stallion.

The next morning I was told by Kambis that Mahmal had been given to Prince Kamiar and I was to have one of the *djelodars* start getting him used to a polo stick. He would be stabled here for another month before being shipped to Khargooshdareh where he would be trained by one of the old time polo players.

425

I hated the thought of Mahmal being sent to that dreadful place but hoped that the horses of Royalty would be better cared for than the others. Kamiar brought another horse to the Imperial Stables to ride every day and practice his polo shots, a little bay Kurdish stallion that was slightly unruly when there was a mare in the ring. After a week of being confronted with problems with this horse he came to me in my office.

'Gail, I would like your opinion.'

'Fire!'

'You know that bay horse of mine is a little studdish. If I'm going to play polo I don't want to have to worry about having my mount attacking other horses, especially as I have a hard enough time trying to stay on and hit the ball at the same time! What would you think if I had him gelded?'

'I think that's a great idea. And while you are at it I would have Mahmal done as well. It will be easier to train them and they will be steadier.'

Two days later Nick did the operations with Kamiar assisting.

During that fall I rode Ballylea in the Competitions. Roshan was still out of commission with the coronary injury and so I was glad to have such a good horse to make my appearances on in the B and A divisions. I was lucky in that I did fairly well. Most often I was in the ribbons and when I didn't win it was usually one of my riders that beat me which was better than a personal victory. One competition that comes to mind was held at the Dashte Behesht show grounds belonging to General Djahanbani. He riding Oatfield Hills and I on Ballylea were the only two to go clear in the second round that day over a big course on the grass. I had the disadvantage of jumping first in the jump-off but luckily went clear and careful. If the General turned on the speed he would easily beat me but I felt sure he would have a fence down. He did and I won. The prize was presented by the General's nephew, my friend Prince Kamiar.

426

Robin Cutler

THE CARRIAGE HORSES

When I first started to work at Farahabad there were fourteen carriage horses. Eight were horses that had been imported to Iran from Germany shortly after His Majesty's forced but short exile during the Mossadegh takeover in 1953. These big beautiful snow white Holsteins had pulled the Imperial Carriages at all state functions including the Shah's own coronation since that time, but they were all over twenty years of age and although they were seemingly healthy their age was beginning to tell. When Abolfath Atabai had gone to Germany for the jumping horses the winter of 1972 he also bought ten steel grey Holsteins to replace old Rostam, Ghesar and the others. These young horses were not totally trained when they arrived in Iran however, the Germans sent a skilled trainer to help get them acclimatized and started.

These new greys were all over 16.2 hands and very well matched save one which was a big flea bitten grey named Ghesar II; he looked out of place with the other nine; Aghah Bazorg was not pleased with him and within a few months sent him to me for my jumping string. Of the other nine seven were geldings and two were mares. The ideas was that the two mares would be brood mares as well as doing their work in front of the carriage in hopes that the Imperial Stables would be able to produce their own carriage horses in the future.

For the first few months of my employ I had nothing at all to do with the carriage horses with the exception of the four that we were also being ridden as jumpers. I understood that they worked the carriage horses two or three days a week in the afternoon, but as I was not often at the stables at that time, I never really thought much about what was going on with them.

'Gail, I have a very big problem that I want you to help me with.' said Kambis one morning at the usual early hour of six o'clock. I really didn't want an extra responsibility but I could sense that Kambis was about to give me another job.

'If I can I will, but I hope it isn't something that's going to take a lot more of my time. I am really snowed under these days and hardly ever get home at a decent time.'

'No, no, this won't take much time! You know that President Tito is coming to visit His Majesty in two weeks' time. We are going to need the carriage horses at the ceremony at the Golestan Palace. I found out yesterday that the lazy *djelodars* have not been working them at all for two months. Did you know that, Mrs. Rose?'

'I understood that they took them out in the afternoons.'

'I did too but I checked with Abdul Hossein yesterday evening when I was walking over to the mares' stable and he said that they have not harnessed them since the summer. His Majesty wants to use his new team of eight grays and we have only two weeks. The horses must be taken out every afternoon with one of our carriages into the streets, so that they are used to the traffic. I want you to be certain that it gets done. I also want you to make sure that the horses are behaving well enough at the end of the two weeks to use in the ceremonies for the Yugoslav Premier. Abdul Hossein will tell me they are going well even if they aren't; as you know he only tells me what he thinks I want to hear.'

'Kambis, I know nothing whatsoever about driving horses or how they should behave. You're asking me to do something that's really out of my line.'

'You can tell if they are pulling well; they have to move quietly, evenly and by no means shy at things on the street. You can go in the carriage with Abdul Hossein a few times to see. It will only be for two weeks. You must do this for me Gail, please.'

So it was that the Carriage House became part of my domain. Each afternoon at four o'clock I would drive through the back gate of the compound to where the carriage house was situated to check that the horses were being hitched up and that the boys were doing their job. I usually took my children down with me to ride the ponies at that time, so while they were being lead around or having a lesson at the Farahabad Club I would check in at the Carriage House to make sure that the horses were out with the carriage. When it came back into the yard I would ask for a report on how it went and then would pick up the kids and go home.

About a week later Kambis asked me if I had been supervising the work with the greys so I told him just what it was that I was doing. It wasn't good enough; he wanted me to go with the carriage. So the next day I rode around the back streets of southern Tehran beside Abdul Hossein. I hated every minute of it; the traffic was terrible and the cars came much too close to the carriage, honked their horns and the horses shied and I felt totally insecure riding so high in the wobbly landau. The horses did behave quite well I thought, considering all the distractions they had but I noted to Abdul Hossein that he was only working six, whereas he would need eight horses the day of the big ceremony. He replied that there were only six horses that would pull together. It seemed that one mare would not drive; she went crazy and he refused to put her in harness; one of the geldings Tavous, tripped all the time and threw the others off their rhythm; Ghesar was the wrong color and it would not do to have an unmatched horse in the team so with only seven horses that would pull, six was the most he could hitch up.

There was always an excuse and of course he had been telling me all along that it was going very well. I informed Abdul Hossein that as of the next day he would have to either hitch up the crazy mare, or one of the two geldings so that we could have eight horses. He was most upset that I should interfere but said he would do as I commanded! Reluctantly!

The next day after the carriage horses came back Ali Rezai came to me most upset. 'My *baba*, (father) Abdul Hossein cannot drive eight horses. You see, we don't have eight good ones. General Khosrodad says we cannot use Ghulitussi. Ghesar is not good color, Tavous —he falls —there are three others that are crazy. We had very bad time today so we will use six from now on.'

'I am sorry, Ali, but you will use eight! That is the order!' He went fuming away but for two more days I didn't get any complaints and I watched to make sure eight horses were being used.

Two days before the big welcoming ceremony for Tito, Kambis came to me; 'Gail, my father saw the carriage horses yesterday afternoon and has decided that we must use the old ones this time; he said that they were shying and not going in a straight line. He was very angry at the mess! He will tell His Majesty himself, but for the next official ceremony we must have the new horses ready.'

So two carriages went to welcome Tito: The old white horses pulled the Reza Shah Coronation coach while the team of four black mares pulled the other one that was being used; however, all did not go well as Her Majesty the Shahbanu became very nervous when one of the black mares shied while she was riding in the carriage. No wonder, those mares had not been harnessed for months and months. So more pressure was put on me make certain that the carriage horses were in work. Naturally it fell on my shoulders to get things organized, for I was now considered the stable manager. I set up a schedule to have the black mares, which were seasoned horses, worked twice a week for a month and after that I thought that once a week would suffice as long as they got some exercise in between. The new greys would go out three times a week and every day for a week before any type of ceremony which might be planned.

The old greys were fast leaving Farahabad. Two had to be put down because they were suffering from cancer and two were pensioned off at the Razi Institute where they could be turned out to pasture. The other four were fast becoming very feeble and arthritic.

Months went by before the next event at which the carriage was again needed. The opening of parliament was held in the spring right after *Now Ruz*. The everyday schedule came into effect. I began harassing Ali and his father who still had not been able to do anything with the mad mare Goli. They said that all the others were going quite well though, even Tavous and the flea bitten were not problems. One afternoon when I had lunched with Dr. Cutler and his wife I called up to the stable to say that I would be up to watch the harnessing of the horses.

'Meeses Rose. You come weeth us today to see how good they ees now. You come ride weeth us.' Suggested Ali over the phone.

'OK, Ali, I will do just that.' I had never ridden postilion and thought, it might be fun now that the horses were better trained.

I got to the Carriage House just as the horses did. I never would learn how to sort out all those traces and bits of harness but I pretended to be checking out that everything was being done correctly. The boys were all smiling.

When all were harnessed I was boosted up by Ali onto Ghullitussi; my lead horse was the flea bitten Ghesar. I was the third pair which made me feel truly sandwiched between four horses in front and a pair and the carriage behind. Off we went. I rode the horse on the left, leading the other with my right hand. All was simple as we drove out the back gate and along the half mile drive into the Imperial Guard compound. Once through those gates we were on the streets of South Tehran filled with five o'clock traffic. Ghullitussi began to lean into the bit so that my left arm felt like it was being pulled by a train, while Ghesar was shying at people on the sidewalks and banging into my right leg. I would lose hold of his head and have to crabwalk my hands up his reins to get better control. My back began to ache with the strain. The *djelodars* all knew that I had never before ridden postilion but I had to do it as well as I possibly could because I expected the highest performance from them when on the jumpers; they should expect a good performance from me when they were showing me how to do something. When we arrived back at the carriage house I waited while Ali Karadjbani took the reins of Ghesar and then flippantly and lithely jumped off. God I hurt!

All the boys including Abdul Hossein began to clap. I was just slightly confused. Then they began to laugh. 'Khonume Rose, I am sorry!'

'Why are you sorry, Ali?' more confusion. Now the men were looking very sheepish.

In Farsi the old man explained to me that they had all been so fed up with my complaining and pushing them about the carriage horses that they decided to teach me a lesson. When Ali had hung up the telephone he had jubilantly contrived with the rest of the boys to give me the two worst horses in the carriage. Two horses that had never been paired together before; they felt sure I would not be able to handle the situation! They wanted to see me beaten. But I had surprised them! Only he, Abdul Hossein, trusted that I would be able to do the job and that is why he let these foolish men have their fun.

'You have had your fun, *Baracalah*!' I laughed. 'You don't know how close you were to seeing me give up. I am exhausted and I will tell you that I now appreciate more why you don't really like to ride postilion, but we have to get the horses ready for the opening of the *Majlis* so we have to keep working on it. I too, will ride more often so that I can learn to do it better but you have to give me easier horses.'

Over the next few weeks I did learn, but I never found it an easy thing to do.

By the time the opening of parliament came I wanted desperately to dress up in the red uniform with its gold braid and brass buttons of the Imperial *djelodars* and ride with the carriage; Kambis and I planned it but Security refused to let me do it. Instead I rode right behind the coronation coach in a chauffeur driven Mercedes and from there watched my horses and men perform to perfection.

It was an awe inspiring sight to see that beautiful blue and gold coach topped with a reproduction of the magnificent Pahlavi crown being borne down the wide avenue in front of the Senate building by the beautiful team of matched, save one, greys. His Majesty descended wearing his gold braided medal laden uniform and the Shahbanu was dripping in jewels in a flowing off white satin gown. True opulence that is of days gone by.

There was no cheering crowd lining the streets. Only soldiers carrying guns. The streets had been cleared of people and all the buildings lining the streets as well, for security reasons. The Iranian people could only see their king on television, if they had one.

Carriage training

Pahlavi Coronation Coach

THE GAME PRESERVE

One of Kambis's titles was Keeper of the Royal Game Preserves. Farahabad was actually officially called *Shicar Gar Sultanateh Farahabad* or the Farahabad Royal Hunting Grounds. It was at the western edge of His Majesty's personal preserve which was fifty miles by fifty miles square. When I first arrived in Iran I had hated the brownness of the countryside; it seemed so desolate. The stark brown rugged mountains seemed to hover over me and engulf me. They were so barren and seemingly devoid of vegetation or life. Their oppressiveness totally depressed me. It was Kambis who taught me to love the mountains and appreciate the beauty of the topography and countryside of Iran.

One afternoon shortly after I had signed my contract with The Royal Horse Society and the Imperial Court I was at the stables schooling some horses. Kambis was there and soon I heard the Royal Helicopters. They came into view and soon hovered over the pads and landed. Out popped Princess Farahnaz and little Prince Ali Reza. The Princess was to take a lesson with me and Prince Ali Reza was to be in Kambis's care. The children rode for about a half an hour and as soon as they dismounted the nannies whisked them off into the awaiting helicopters and back to Niavaran palace.

Kambis asked me to come over to his house to have a cup of tea with him and his wife Avid. Mahmad was waiting at the door to pull off our boots. The ever faithful man was Kambis's valet and at his beck and call twenty-four hours a day. In the short time I had been associated with Kambis I had learned how devoted the man was to his employer and to anyone that was a friend; I was always treated with special care when I came for tea in the afternoon or coffee and *nun* (bread) in the mornings. My boots would always be polished when I came down from the upstairs sitting room where we would have our tea.

Avid was waiting for us in the comfortable room that was used exclusively by the family. They would use the large formal reception rooms downstairs when they had visiting dignitaries. Hassan came in with the tiny silver tea cups; tea for Avid and me and hot lemon water for Kambis who was so worried about gout and afraid that the tannic acid in the tea would activate the infliction that both he and his father bore.

'Kambis, Reza the Game Keeper called while you were out and said that he would expect you about six thirty tomorrow morning. He said to tell you everything is ready.' Avid coolly gave the message to her husband.

'Oh, good. I had forgotten that I was to go out with him in the morning. I'll have to call Pulad and tell him to cancel the meeting with Farzine. Gail, what is your schedule for the morning?'

'Oh, the usual. I have about five horses that I want to school over fences and the boys will get some gymnastic drills which I hope to give you as well. I have quite a bit of paperwork that I have to do in the office too. Why?'

'How would you like to forget all the work for the day and come with me to the mountains? I have to go with Reza to count some of the herds and maybe I'll get some shooting in; I think you should see some more of Farahabad. It will be a good chance for you to see what is expected of our horses when they go on a hunting party as you'll be in charge of making sure the boys keep up the training and fitness regime.'

'I haven't yet set up the schedule for tomorrow at the stables. Maybe I could do it another time when I have more time to plan, Kambis.' I had heard stories about riding up in the mountains and was actually slightly nervous, as well here was another responsibility that was being put on my plate!

'No, no. I will give a message to the stable. I have decided that you must come tomorrow.'

'Yes Gail, you wouldn't believe how beautiful it is up in the mountains especially now, in the early summer. It is so green and the flowers are unbelievable.' Avid encouraged.

'Have you gone up often, Avid?' I questioned.

'Not many times because I get a bit nervous about the heights but I have been up with Kambis a few times and I was thrilled by the beauty and the views from the mountainsides. You really must go.'

So it was decided that I would be at the house in the morning at five thirty.

When I arrived early in the morning I was surprised to see that Kambis's Range Rover was parked by the door of the house and that Mahmad and Hassan were putting large suitcase like leather boxes in the back. Mahmad told me to go into the breakfast room where Kambis was having a meal of *nuna lavash*, the flat unleavened Iranian bread, fruit, butter and Iranian goat cheese. I joined him for a cup of tea and a piece of the delicious bread with the tart salty cheese that I could never decide whether I liked or not. Shortly, we were off in the car with one of the uniformed game keepers, who it turned out was the infamous Reza *Shikareh*. (Reza the Hunter).

Reza talked and talked as we drove off towards the mountains. It seemed to me that he was repeating himself but still Kambis laughed and joked with him. They tried to include me as best they could but at that point my Farsi wasn't excellent and I had a hard time with Reza's mountain accent.

On the way home that afternoon Kambis told me about Reza. He had been a game warden for the Imperial Reserves for many years; he was about forty-five years old. Ten years previously he had caught some poachers hunting on Imperial property and had gone into the nearest town to get the Gendarmes to arrest the men. However, he had told them what he was about to do, so before he could get into town they ambushed him, beat him and left him for dead by the side of the road. Many hours later someone found him and took him to the local doctor who cared for him until he regained consciousness and finally contacted Kambis. The poor fellow was never to be the man he had been before the accident; it had made him quite simple but he was a loyal employee and thus Kambis listened to his stories that had been told hundreds of times before; he wanted to keep his employee happy.

'Actually, I even know when to laugh without listening now; I can tell by the intonation of his voice.' Kambis told me.

After about a half an hour's drive up into the mountains to the north, northeast of Farahabad we stopped the car at the end of a dirt track. Awaiting us were some of the older *djelodars* from Farahabad on horseback, horses for Kambis and me, and four pack mules with their colorful pack cases laden down with provisions. The car was unloaded and the leather cases were loaded onto the mules.

As we were waiting for the men to finish loading the mules we had mounted our horses and Kambis pointed to a huge mountain that hung over us.

'We are going to climb to the top of that and then down the other side and again on up the next cliff to the top; that's where I'll be able to count the herd of Mouflon that Reza says has grown tremendously this year. You know the Mouflon were hunted so ruthlessly for years that there are not as many as there should be here. It has just been in the past four or five years since I took over this job that we have been able to build up the herd. It's mainly that I am prosecuting the poachers who come here to shoot, so now they are beginning to fear the reputation of the Imperial Game Wardens. When we start to climb we cross diagonally from one side to the other of this steep grade; you'll see that we have to stop often because it takes a lot out of the horses to climb such a precipice.' He told me.

I looked up with terror. The side of the mountain seemed to be almost perpendicular and it was covered with loose gravel, most of it about the size of a man's fist.

All was ready, so Akbar went to the lead, with Kambis following on his beautiful chestnut Jordanian Arab. I was close behind on Dakht, a Kurdish horse that I learned through the day was very sure footed. We climbed back and forth for about ten minutes and then stopped. My horse was panting hard as were the others. On and up we went. I followed behind Kambis about two horse lengths back trying to trace the exact route he rode. Dahkt was very good and obviously knew his job well for he never took a wrong step. Onward and upward we went slowly; when we looked down from the top of the first ridge we saw a beautiful lush green plateau filled with magnificent desert flowers below. As we edged our way down the steep rocky side of the mountain to the plateau, the green became sparse shoots of chartreuse sticking through a bed of rust colored gravel but the flowers became more brilliant. Bright red, yellow, blue and purple flowers gloriously ordaining blue-green prickly stalks.

Once on the plain Akbar raised his left hand and shouted, '*Berrim*!' Digging his heels into the horse's sides he began to gallop across the plateau; Kambis and I followed suit laughing and racing with each other stopping finally where Akbar was waiting for us on the far side of the field. Looking back we could see the mules still making their way down the steep side of the mountain that we had just descended. We stood taking in the beauty of the scene while catching our breath for we were all three winded, as were the horses. The sweet desert smell tingled at my nostrils tempting me to breathe deeper. There are desert smells and desert smells! There is the acrid smell of the dry badland in the desert that I never learned to like; there is the musky desert smell that is present as the snow melts in winter;

there is the dry desert smell of the hot summer; there is the putrid desert smell, the dead smell that is evident around the gnats; but this new desert smell I loved; it excited me.

When Rajab and Reza caught up with us Kambis said, 'We'll start up this ridge but when we get close to the top Akbar and I will go ahead on foot to the peak, for usually there is a herd of Mouflon just over the other side; I would like to check on the size of the herd and maybe I'll see something close enough to buy us lunch. If you want to stay back with the horses Gail and wait, that is all right, but if you feel you are up to it why not follow closely behind; it will be one of the most beautiful sights you'll ever see.'

The climb was steeper than the first; I was afraid to look back; in places we followed a narrow trail that must have been made by the wild sheep; in front of me Kambis's horse stumbled and its outside hind leg missed the path slipping down the edge of the cliff; I held my breath while I saw the horse lurch forward and pull the slipping leg up; Kambis turned and smiled sheepishly at me; I patted Dakht on the side of the neck; we stopped for a breather. It was cool at the altitude and yet I was perspiring profusely.

'That was close, did it frighten you?' Kambis turned to ask. I was afraid to speak but nodded my head; when would we get to the top? I felt I was hanging on the side of a cliff!

We continued until we came to a spot where the horses could stand side by side. Here Kambis dismounted as did Akbar. They handed their horses to Reza and Rajab. I sat vacillating wondering whether I should try the climb to the top or if I would be safer sitting comfortably on my horse.

'Don't you want to come?'

Silently I dismounted and handed my horse to Rajab who was grinning from ear to ear; he saw the terror in my eyes and my hand was shaking as I gave him the reins.

'*Mobazeh bashid, Khonume. Ba Khoda berid*! (Be careful and go with God.)' Luckily I had had the sense to wear a sturdy pair of rubber soled, lace up boots that were comfortable so I had a good traction on the rocks as I cautiously followed my leaders. The peak was perhaps a hundred meters ahead but that hundred meters took such a long time! I climbed behind not wanting to be left; my lungs felt as though they would explode; how could Kambis and Akbar move so fast?

Finally, Kambis threw himself on the ground at the peak; Akbar just stopped behind, poised for a command. I could see that my handsome boss too, was panting as he lay there peering at I did not know what. He turned and signaled me to creep up to him. When I reached the top and lay crouched beside him he put his hand on my shoulder.

'Look through my glasses straight down towards the river.' he whispered.

I looked and saw nothing but rocks and a few scrubby bushes.

'There are about a hundred in that herd.'

'Kambis, I don't see anything but a lot of rocks.'

'Put down the glasses. Now look where I am pointing. Do you see that big boulder half way down the side of the mountain?'

'Yes.'

'Now follow it straight down to the river. Do you see the sheep between it and the boulder?'

'No.'

'Take the glasses and look at that same spot. Your eye has to be trained to see them I guess, because they are the same color as the rocks. '

I looked through the powerful binoculars and miraculously saw that the rocks had turned into brown animals with large horns; they seemed to be grazing and had not sensed that the enemy was near.

'Yes, that is quite a beautiful herd. Do you see what good shape their coats are in? When the herds begin to grow we have to make certain that they stay healthy; if we find that there are animals that look unhealthy we send out our game wardens to kill them off, for disease spreads like fire in a herd of wild animals .'

Suddenly Kambis, who had been surveying the view in front of us, froze. He grabbed the glasses from me and looked off to the left. Part way down the northern slope there was a patch of snow not yet melted by the spring sun. I saw the faintest movement, I thought.

'That's him!' He turned to Akbar whose blue eyes lit up. 'Is my gun ready?' Akbar nodded in assent.

I waited on the ridge afraid to move a muscle for fear I would give away a signal of danger to the animal, whatever it was, while Akbar and Kambis slowly crept towards the patch of melting snow. I saw them stop and heard a loud report of a rifle. Then they both jumped up cheering. They signaled me to follow them. As I started down the side of the mountain I glanced in the direction of the herd we had been watching, to see it moving *en masse* across the stream and up the other side of the mountain.

Kambis and Akbar waited for me and all three of us started towards the snow which was still a hundred meters away. Suddenly I saw it. Writhing, twisting, rising, falling, slipping down the side of the mountain was the huge mouflon. As we got closer I could see the bloody foam coming out of its mouth. It was so beautiful with the huge set of horns. It made me want to be sick.

'He is tough! Look at him, Akbar! He is trying to escape me even in death! Gail, I have been trying to shoot this prize ram for two years but he's a wily old fellow and was always able to escape me. What a beauty!' Akbar went ahead and grabbed the animal that now lay still, by the horns; he had a good look and then casually took a knife from his belt and slit the jugular vein neatly; blood spurted out like a fountain.

By this time Reza and Rajab arrived on foot to see the trophy. It was decided that they would take care of the animal and take the mules down to a spot they all seemed to know while Kambis, Akbar and I would continue checking the herd. We would meet them at the aforementioned place at lunch time.

We started back up the mountain to get our horses. Over the ridge where we had left them were the horses as well as the mules and their keepers that had arrived at the spot. Kambis gave orders to one of the *djelodars* while the three of us were mounting and we then began to climb up to the right.

'They have left the spot where we saw them so I want to check to see how far they ran when they heard the shot.'

We crept down the side of the mountain and up the side of the next before we finally spotted them in a valley below. Satisfied, Kambis decided it was time to think of lunch. It was difficult getting to our picnic spot, for it was down in the gorge of a small river. At one point we had to get off and lead the horses, the descent was so steep. We came to a slide of shale; I saw Kambis trip and fall.

'Be careful!' He turned to warn me, 'This gravel is very deep. Put your heels down first and lean back.'

I did as I was told but still managed to tumble a couple of times. With the reins of Dahkt I regained my balance; poor animal. When we finally reached more solid footing we stopped to rest. My legs were shaking from the strain as I looked up to the place of our descent in awe.

'Are you all right, Gail? I've never had a woman come up with me and stay with me like this. Usually when Avid comes she stays with the mules.'

'Of course I'm all right. Did you think I wouldn't be able to keep up with you?'

'To tell you the truth I wasn't sure, but now I know!'

We continued down to the grove of trees beside the stream. Rajab came to take the horses from Kambis and me.

'*Har Cheez auzershotid*?' Kambis asked. Yes, everything was ready. We walked into the grove of trees and there was a most beautiful and welcome sight. The ground was covered with beautiful Persian carpets and two huge camel bag type pillows were propped up against the side of a large rock under the shade of a thorn tree. The crystal clear mountain stream gurgled along beside us as we sat sipping a welcome hot cup of tea. It was like a fairy tale, for there was no one in sight, just two exhausted people with only the sounds and feel of nature.

Shortly, the *djelodars* brought huge plates filled with saffron rice, *khoresht* or stew and the liver and heart of the killed mouflon. Kambis called to them to come to eat with us and they brought another plate that had the grilled tenderloin of the animal. I was very unsure of eating the meat of the game but after warily tasting it, I found I was eating one of the most delicious meals of my life.

Once the repast was finished, Kambis and I lay back on the pillows relaxing and talking while the *djelodars* packed up the picnic and made ready to move on.

'These trips into the mountains are the best part of my life.' Kambis admitted. 'I would love to be able to do it more often but then if I did, perhaps the delight would lessen'.

'I think that's probably true. You know the old proverb, 'Far away fields look greener.'

'We have a similar expression in Iran; the mountain looks green until you get to it, is the gist of it.'

'I think that it's just human nature to want what's not readily available. I know that I'm a person who strives desperately to get something that I think I want and then often I find once I have it in my hand , so to speak , I'm not interested anymore.'

We chatted on in this vein, touching on things that were happening at the stable, my summer trip to America, the prospect of taking the team to Russia and finally drifted into a comfortable silence. As I wandered in my imagination I felt Kambis take my hand and hold it; I was brought back to reality and yet did not stir.

'Are you still with me?' he asked.

'Yes.'

'Why is it that the trick of fate brought you and me together now, at this time in our lives?'

'I don't know.' I replied unemotionally afraid of what was to come next.

'Oh Gail! If we had only met sooner. We have so much in common; we could have such a wonderful time together; I would like to become close to you.' his hand was caressing mine. 'You attract me more every day I'm with you.'

'Kambis!' I sat up with a start. 'Kambis! What are you doing? Please don't say another word!'

He lay there smiling his true Persian smile at me.

'Kambis, you tell me that you have gone to considerable trouble to get permission to hire me to do the job you want done at the Imperial Stables, isn't that right?'

'Yes ... but.'

'Just hang on now and let me say my piece.' I interrupted him. 'For me to be able to work for you the way I know you want me to, we can't have anything other than a good friendship. There can't be any underlying secrets, desires or relationship. I find you very attractive to me both physically and mentally; I would love to be able to say let's forget the rest of the world and have The Great Love Affair. I can think of nothing that would be more romantic or fulfilling to me . . . But let's be realistic; it would not work! We would have to live a life of lies. We would hurt people. We would fear discovery. We would most likely end up hating each other. And we certainly could not work as well together. I have been at the Imperial Stables now for about two months and during that time I think you will agree that there have been a lot of changes, for the better. You and I have learned to cooperate with each other and we have accomplished a great deal both at the stables and in the Show Jumping end of things. I think that I'm right in saying that we have become really good friends. And as far as I'm concerned that's how I want it kept. I want to be your friend and a good friend but I don't want to be your mistress!'

'Mrs. Rose! Mrs. Rose!' He smiled that Persian smile and then laughed. 'I have never met anyone like you. You are so right. I know it wouldn't work but I had to try. I thank Allah that you are the way you are. Yes, I think we will be good friends for a long time. Let's shake on it.' We shook.

Shortly, Akbar came to say that everything was ready to continue on our way so we mounted our horses and started off. During the afternoon we were to see a herd of Ibex which are very hard to find, not only because they were not plentiful but also because they are very shy and hide amongst the rocks. I had never believed that an animal could climb such precipices; I was fascinated by them and spent a lot of time watching their lithe bodies and long spikey horns through the glasses. We counted a herd of thirty which at that time was the largest in Iran.

We saw more mouflon and did some more climbing eventually ending up at the spot where we had left the Range River about ten hours before. It had been a truly memorable experience.

During the time I worked with Kambis I learned to love these trips into the mountains. They were like a total vacation; I always arrived home exhausted but thoroughly elated.

One winter morning when the snow was falling softly at Farahabad we left directly from the stables on horseback at seven in the morning. We were walking along the road past the modern palace that had been built by Agha Bosorg, when a small *vanette* sped past us at a good clip and turned into the palace driveway.

'After him, Akbar!' shouted Kambis. Akbar galloped ahead mindless of the bad conditions of the road. A couple of minutes later the *vanette* drove up to us and stopped. The driver got out.

'What are you doing here?' Kambis questioned him.

'Sir, I was delivering some paint to the palace.' the driver answered him in an obsequious manner.

'Do you realize that this is the property of His Imperial Majesty the Shahanshah and these are his horses? You do not speed by them. You stop and wait until they have passed. There is a sign that reads 15 kilometers. You were going much faster. Give me your keys!'

The man handed them to Kambis gravely. He was then told that he could walk behind the line of horses until Kambis decided to give the keys back. We continued along at a walk past the field where the students at the officer's staff college played war games, past the old cemetery, up the sand track and began to climb into the mountains. It was Pulad Mansapur who was with us that day, who finally called Kambis's attention to the fact that the man was still following. Kambis had forgotten him!

'*Ba Khoda*, tell the man to go back. He's had a long enough walk'

Pulad called to the man that he could turn back. We continued in the silence of the falling snow. I suddenly felt a tug at my leg and looked the *vanette* driver in the eye. *'Khonume! Khonume! Swicham nadadam!'* Kambis had not given the man his truck key; how was he to drive his vehicle without his keys? I trotted a few paces up beside Kambis who was draped in a dark brown waterproof poncho to keep him dry in the melting snow.

'Aghaya Atabai!' I addressed him formally. 'The *vaneete* driver is still following us.'

'I told the bastard he could go back. What is the matter with him? Is he enjoying his walk?'

'Swich.' I said simply.

'Oh, for God's sakes!' he laughed heartily as he put his hand under the poncho to get the keys which he handed to me. I halted my horse and waited for the poor fellow to catch up to me and handed him the keys.

'Khonume, gorboneh shoman, muchekeram, kheli muchekeram!' Obse-

quiously he bowed his head 'til it almost touched the ground in gratitude. I moved on again trotting to catch up to Pulad and Kambis who were laughing at the incident; I turned once to see the man's dark form disappearing into the snow on his long walk back to the palace .

'Kambis, you were so mean to the poor man. Couldn't you have just admonished him or something?'

'Admonish, that's a good word. I haven't used it since I left school in England. No, I wanted him to remember not to drive fast around the Farahad roads; that man does a lot of work for the Court so he had to know I meant business. These Iranians don't respect just words; they need concrete punishment to instill it into their thick heads.'

As we climbed higher and the air got colder the snow turned to powder rather than the heavy packing snow that balls up in the horses' hooves. We began to trot on as we were going to a hunting area that was quite a distance. I was riding Tuffan, a Jordanian Arab that had been given to the Shah by King Hussein; it was actually the Crown Prince's horse and he was a perfect mountain horse! He never made a mistake. I had dropped back behind Kambis, Pulad and Ali Monazamee the court jester, who was also a part of the day's party, because I wanted to watch Akbar's horse, Majid, which was in the mountains for just the second time. It was a lovely black Arab that I had been most interested in since we had begun to break it two years before; I had felt it was a little early to take it into the mountains on a full day's hunting but I had been overruled by Kambis who said that it was time. The horse was trotting along well and seeming to be careful where he put his feet.

'*Khub mireh*?' I asked Akbar, who smiled and said that yes, the horse was behaving well. I noted a twinkle in Akbar's eye when he asked if I was enjoying the snow; a twinkle that made me wary for Akbar loved to play a joke and often his jokes proved disastrous! It looked to me as through he was up to something.

I remembered the day he came into the main jumping ring, while I was schooling some of the boys over fences; he was riding Shetune, which means devil in Farsi. The horse was a total rogue and had no place in the Imperial Stables but he was a favorite of His Majesty, so he stayed. Akbar went over to one of the boys, I think it was Jamshid, to try to cut him off as he approached a fence, as a joke, of course. But Shehtune tried to attack the other horse as he passed and Akbar fell off. The horse started to run heading straight for me standing in the middle of the ring.

'Mrs. Rose! Run! Run!' Ali Rezai had screamed at me. For the horse was known to savage people. I ran to the nearest jump which was a brush oxer and crouched behind the brush box. The horse struck the box snorting trying to get at me. It was the form of Dr. Cutler who diverted the horse and saved me. It took quite some time to catch Shehtune. As usual, Akbar's joke was a flop.

When I saw him canter on ahead to speak to Kambis and Pulad I was sure he was up to something; Kambis nodded his head and Pulad let out a laugh. Akbar was about to play a joke on either Monazami or me or maybe both of us.

As we climbed, the snow was deeper. When we came to the first little plateau the horses were well over their fetlocks in snow; there was a lovely white expanse ahead that looked soft as cotton wool. Had it been summer we surely would have galloped across. I was quite surprised when Kambis began to canter. Akbar cantered up beside me laughing in his usual jovial way.

'Khonume Rose, *cours mireem*?' he wanted me to race with him. Was that all the twinkle was about? I assented and off we went past Kambis, Pulad and Monazami. I just kept head in head with Akbar for some sixth sense told me not to pass him; he was yelling and laughing and urging me on. Suddenly I felt my horse tense up so I began to slow down. I could see that Akbar was having a hard time containing his young, inexperienced mount so I pulled up gradually; on went Akbar and suddenly he disappeared in the snow. Then there were hooves flailing as Majid struggled to stand, obviously in a gully that had been covered over by the soft snow. Next a form looking like the abominable snowman appeared.

Everyone was laughing! And I in particular, could hardly contain myself for I knew that the hidden gully had been meant for me, not Akbar. Little Tuffan had warned me with such a subtle move and had saved me.

'Gail, I knew you would outsmart Akbar. That's why I gave him permission to try to dump you in the snow.' Akbar too, was laughing as he started to lead the horse out of the snow filled ditch. He suddenly went white and stood frozen.

'Akbar! What is it? Are you all right?' Kambis sounded worried.

'Agha! I dropped your rifle that I was carrying over my shoulder.' He started rummaging around in the snow, and in a minute or so held up the long leather case containing Kambis's gun.

'Now I will have to check the sight, Akbar. I want to make sure it isn't damaged with the fall.'

Hossein the twenty year old apprentice game warden, walked a hundred paces and placed a round tin plate against a rock. The boy had backed off not more than eight paces to the right of the target when Kambis fired!

'Kambis! You could have killed Hossein, shooting when he was so near the target!' I shouted, my heart was in my mouth.

'All the better if I did!' Kambis laughed. Hossein had been a real problem getting into trouble with the police for stealing and being generally lazy in his job as an apprentice. A year previously he had been sent to ride with me for two months. My order had been to give him all the punishment I possibly could.

Hossein inspected the target and signaled that the bullet had gone right through the center. This time he stepped back only two or three paces.

'I will try for the left corner of the target this time.' Kambis declaired, and when Hossein again checked, the hole was where it should be. Kambis was loving his success and also my fears that he might shoot poor Hossein. There was no doubt that he was a good shot and now that he knew the sights weren't damaged he had total confidence in his aim.

He told Hossein to kneel down and hold on to the side of the target while he took his next shot.

'Kambis! Don't! You terrify me!'

'That's why I'm doing it. To show you that I am the perfect shot,' he laughed.

'You don't have to prove anything to me. I believe it. Now please, don't!' I pleaded.

He fired as I knew he would. I watched Hossein to show signs of having been hit as I heard the shot but he did not move.

'Barakala, Agha! Barakala!' All who were with us were cheering. I was lost in wonder, admiration and yet repulsed when I thought of what could have happened.

Even though it snowed the whole day Kambis got in some good shooting and killed two fine specimens; he also shot five or six mouflon for meat; animals that he said needed to be culled. One of these he gave to me to take home for supper. Azize and Nahid were extremely happy when I got it home and cooked it to perfection, though they saved the head for their breakfast the following morning.

When we finally arrived back at the Imperial Stables it was eight o'-clock in the evening. I had never spent such a long time on horseback, for that day we had stopped for only a short time at lunch due to the fact that Kambis had wanted to cover a lot of territory, which we did. My bones were aching with tiredness and yet I had loved the excitement of being up in the mountains as always.

Poor Monazami had to be helped off his horse he was so sore. Later that night he was taken to the hospital to be treated for exhaustion. He did not return to his home for three days and when he did, swore that he would never go on another of Kambis's hunting parties.

Akbar, Rajab and Reza, the game warden always went with us on the hunts, but as well we were accompanied by at least four other *djelodars* who led the mule train, would prepare our lunch, would butcher the game, go ahead as lookouts or do any other manner of service that they were called upon to do. Often one or two of my show jumping riders would come along to help; they usually were told to ride the mules.

'Just so they don't forget their place.' Kambis would say or, 'to keep them tough.'

I would often ask them what I should do in a certain situation in the mountains and they loved being able to tell me or show me. It helped keep a really good rapport amongst us. I knew though, that they respected me for the fact that I could keep up; whenever Kambis climbed on foot I would go with him with my movie camera and binoculars; they were amazed that I was as swift and surefooted as I was on the steep rocky precipices. In all the time I worked at the Imperial Stables no other woman went out with a hunting party.

There was the day when Kambis, Pulad and I were sitting at the mouth of a shallow cave protected from the snow having a cup of tea to warm up. The mule train had fallen behind but as the tea was being served, small dark objects were seen to be slowly descending the narrow trail on the side of the slope opposite us. Suddenly a black object started to roll down the side of the slope.

Faster and faster; larger and larger; finally the mule lay in a heap in the gorge of the river. Luckily it was dead, poor beast of burden

The most exciting day I spent in the mountains with Kambis was a day when we went up to the reserve that belonged to Prince Abdul Reza. There was a large ram, the leader of the herd, which the prince had been trying to get for years. It was said to be about fifteen years old and had been the obsession of the prince and many of his friends who had tried and failed to bag it. In order to hunt on the Prince's property an invitation had to be given, even to Kambis. No one, save the prince and his personal guests, was allowed to hunt there. In actual fact, there was quite a lot of poaching by American military in particular. Somehow the Americans had become friendly with the head and trusted game warden that worked for Abdul Reza and he was known to let certain groups go up to hunt, for a small fee, naturally!

Kambis had many times told me about this magnificent ram but until I actually saw him I could not realize the magnetic draw of the animal. We were crouching behind a rock near the peak of one of the lower mountains in the Alborz range having climbed at least a half a mile on foot. He put his hand to his lips, touched my shoulder and pointed way down to a trail hundreds of feet below; I could see a herd wending its way along a narrow trail seemingly unaware of the danger that was so close.

I had learned how to spot the animals easily by this time but didn't have the discerning eye of my teacher as to which animal was a good trophy and which was not. This time it was so obvious that the animal in the lead was much bigger than the others, that even with my naked eye I could see that he was the prize. Through the glasses I saw a magnificent mouflon or Urial Sheep, with horns that seemed almost too big for his body; I had never seen such horns on any of the other sheep even some prized ones that Kambis had shot. While we squatted watching the route of the herd, Kambis planned his strategy; naturally we would stay downwind so it meant a lot more climbing.

I was totally excited by the chase; we humans had such difficulty with the terrain over which the sheep could fly, and yet had a weapon that could fell any one of them in an instant! I didn't like the kill but had become used to it and knew that it was inevitable. But that beautiful ram with his shiny taupe coat did not deserve to be annihilated. As we circumvented the herd I kept hoping that the ram would sense the danger and run. We had several glimpses of him and always he seemed unconcerned.

We were finally upon them; the sheep were grazing in a small patch of stubble only a few hundred yards ahead; within a few moments Kambis would have his chance.

Suddenly, this beautiful lead ram raised his head. We dared not breathe! Again he began to graze. Then without warning he took flight; the rest of the herd followed him up, up, up to the top of the ridge and over.

The sight that thrilled me angered my hunting mate and I could tell from his eyes that we were about to go after this animal that had almost been his. We climbed for hours, sending the game warden on ahead many times to scout in which direction the herd had run. Search as we might, we couldn't find the herd. About three thirty Kambis finally decided to give up and stop to have lunch; he was totally disappointed and spoke hardly a word as we were served the usual sumptuous meal by Akbar.

After our lunch it was decided that we should start towards home; we were still quite high up in the mountains and as we made our slow descent we just happened upon the herd of mouflon once again; we were close enough for Kambis to fire. The animals lifted their heads startled! But Akbar was carrying Kambis's gun and by the time he moved forward to hand it to his boss the old ram had darted off leading his herd up the rocks again. I was afraid to speak for I feared that Kambis would be in a rage. We continued our descent in silence for some time.

'You know, I am glad that I wasn't able to kill that ram! He was so beautiful that I would have hated to be the one to shoot him!'

'Kambis! You don't know how happy I am that you didn't. Today when we were climbing over the rocks trying to get close enough to shoot him I kept praying that you wouldn't. I even thought of tossing a rock if we got near, to warn him,' I admitted.

455

'Gail, I knew that's what you were thinking. I could actually feel it. I kept asking myself why I wanted to fell such a kingly looking beast that had lived a wonderful fifteen years. I didn't have the chance though; he was too clever. When we came upon him just now, I knew he had planned it; he knew we had given up and were on our way home and would not be ready for him. One day, of course, he will be ready to be killed, when he gets old and decrepit, but I still hope it's not me who gets him.'

In all the times I went up into the mountains, I only one time saw a dangerous fall. It was early in the morning when the ground was still frozen that we were going through a tunnel over which the Ab Ali highway runs. The floor of the tunnel was sheer ice and Kambis and I were contemplating whether we should dismount and lead the horses through.

'I will go ahead and test it.' offered Akbar who was riding the sure-footed Dahkt. As he entered the mouth of the long tunnel the horse slipped with its hind feet but righted itself. After a few steps, Dakht again began to slip; as he did, Akbar lost his balance and pulled on the reins; this action caused the horse to completely lose its balance and down they both went. At that moment a huge truck went over the highway bridge, the noise frightening the horse. Suddenly we saw the horse clamber to its feet and begin to gallop! Akbar had his foot caught in the stirrup which did not release, and was being dragged behind banging his head against the concrete wall of the tunnel as he went. At the far end of the tunnel the horse finally stopped. Akbar's form was still as it hung from the stirrup. I somehow found myself running through the tunnel. When I reached the other end I cautiously went up to the horse for I didn't want to scare it and have it take off again. I grabbed the bridle. By this time Kambis was with me. He grabbed Akbar's foot and pulled it out of the stirrup.

'Akbar!' Kambis bent over to his friend, fearful the man was dead or at least unconscious. Akbar sat up, opened his eyes and smiled. *'Ba Khoda, Agha, che chance dashtam!'* (What luck God gave me!)

We then began to laugh with relief, at the funny spectacle of Akbar being dragged through the tunnel. As we continued on our way I thought that Akbar would certainly be giving a good stipend to some lucky beggar later that day.

The main game in the Imperial Reserves is mouflon, gazelle and the shy ibex. Up until the early nineteen sixties there had been so much unnecessary hunting, a lot of which was poaching, that the herds had diminished. During the time I was in Iran, Kambis's control had allowed the animals to multiply again and the mouflon were almost too plentiful. In the winter when there was snow they would be so bold as to come for shelter in the pine forest around the Farahabad stable. Many a time I almost came off due to a horse shying at a wild sheep.

I had heard stories of how there had been tigers in the Iranian mountains and leopards too. When I first visited the Imperial Stables there were two leopards caged in a small building beside one of the internal gateways. I had read a story in the newspaper of a leopard attacking a construction worker who was eating his lunch on a job at the outskirts of the city. So naturally the subject of the leopards came up when I began to go into the mountains with Kambis.

'What has happened to these leopards?' I asked.

'When I was a boy there were many. But now as you know there are not many. Maybe there are three here in the Farahabad Reserve.' Kambis told me.

'If there are three why do they not multiply?'

'It is very hard for the female to raise a family in this climate of ours. When she has the cubs it's the time of year when the ants devour everything. The ants get into the cubs and devour them when they are newborn. Then there is mange, other diseases as well. '

'But what happened to the many that were here?' I wanted to know.

'There was a time when His Majesty was what you would call a playboy. I know you have probably read that he used to go out to kill the leopards just for the sport of it. He would invite his friends to shoot these handsome animals to take home to their countries to show the beautiful leopard and tiger skins of Iran. It became harder and harder to find the cats and finally he could no longer shoot them because there were none left.'

'Kambis that's a terrible story! Why didn't someone tell the Shah what he was doing?'

'In those days everyone was so looking out for his own skin that no one would dare tell His Majesty to stop shooting,' he answered. 'You know Hossein, the old man with one arm who tends the old Farahabad gate?' I nodded. 'Well, did you ever hear how he lost the arm?' I shook my head.

'He was a *djelodar* at the time and was on a hunting trip with His Majesty and some visitors. They had just shot a splendid male cat, very large, and Hossein was to cut its vein and gut it. As everyone stood watching, Hossein went up to the cat and as he put his hand out to cut the vein, the cat which was still alive, went after Hossein's arm and totally mutilated it. His Majesty Himself, was the one to dismount and shoot the leopard and thus saved Hossein's life. As you see the arm was amputated but Hossein claims he owes his life to the Shahanshah and Allah in that order.

When I questioned Kambis about the two caged leopards that I had seen at Farahabad, he laughed; that was another story he wanted to tell me.

'It must have been just a few days after you left Iran to go back to Canada that we let them out. I remember because the Crown Prince and the Princess had looked at them in the cage the day you had given them the lesson, so I remember the conversation. The children felt sorry for the animals in the cage and asked me to please let them out. So we did. We made a caged litter that could be carried between two mules and went way up into the mountains to let them go. They seemed so happy to be set free; they romped and played and yet they didn't go too far from us. We all watched for some time and then started back to the stables. They followed us a little way but finally stopped. I was worried that they would have a hard time finding food because they had been in captivity since they had been cubs so I planned to check on them every week or so.'

He told me of how he and the usual entourage of *djelodars* went out to search a week later. They spent the whole morning looking for traces of the leopards and found none. Finally it was decided that the party would split up and meet again in the gorge where Kambis and I had had our first mountain picnic together. Kambis and his group arrived at the appointed place before Akbar and his men; they waited some time and when the others did not come Kambis began to worry. He scanned the sides of the mountains and finally his glasses found the men halfway down the mountain; they were silently signaling Kambis to come up to them. Kambis was not about to go up there when he had planned to have a leisurely lunch by the sparkling brook but it was finally evident that Akbar was being stubborn for some reason. They mounted their horses and began to climb up the side of the mountain. When they eventually reached the rest of their party they discovered the problem.

Looking back to the gorge they could see the two leopards were prowling around. It seemed that the pair must have been following the hunting party that was searching for them, the whole time. Satisfied that the animals were making out on their own Kambis and the group went on. He had the warden of the area keep close watch on them and report any irregularities in the behavior pattern; he feared that because the animals were so tame they might prove to be a public menace or a danger.

'When Don and I first moved into our house I remember reading in the paper that a worker had been mauled by a leopard and had hit it over the head with a two by four and knocked it out. Was that one of the pair?'

'Yes, unfortunately it was. I don't think that it was really going to maul the man; I think it was hungry and was after his lunch, for they had lost weight and we were finding that they didn't know how to feed themselves properly. I was very sad when I learned the workers had killed the leopard, for they did actually beat it to death. Then we had the problem of having one lone animal which was much more dangerous. We tried to recapture it but couldn't so we finally had to shoot it.

The last time I went up hunting with Kambis there was a lot of leopard talk; one of the reasons for the day's hunt was that it had been reported that there had been some sightings of leopards. He wanted to try to find some trace of these leopards himself as he was always dubious of these reports.

We covered a lot of territory that day and did find what Kambis said were leopard stools and as well some paw prints in the soft sand by a stream. I never did see a wild leopard but heard that a pride had had a litter. Before I left Iran one of the *djelodars* told me that there were three known pride in the Farahabad game reserve at that time.

Mouflon on the plateau

The wiley ibex

ARYAMEHR CUP

In September, 1975 Ali Reza Soudovar imported ten Irish horses. Three of these were to be for Kambis, one for General Khosrodad, and the others Ali would keep for his own stable or sell. Two of the horses that were to be for Kambis were fairly well seasoned horses while the third was a young animal that would need a long training period before it would be shown. General Khosrodad was going to keep his horse out at Karaj with Ali Reza because he and Kambis were having some minor disagreement and he was told that he couldn't keep the new Irish horse at Farahabad unless it belonged to the Imperial Stables. The General had paid for the horse with his own money, and he was not a rich man, being one of the few big wig generals who had the reputation of being totally unbribeable. The General didn't want Kambis to get his hands on this new prize possession.

Shortly after the arrival of the horses there was a show at Nowruzabad. The General couldn't wait to ride his new horse. As always he waited until the last moment to warm up for his round so I didn't see him until he entered the ring.

'*Teemsah Manucher Khosrodad ba aspe* Tenderly. From the Imperial Stables General Manucher Khosrodad riding the Irish horse Tenderly,' announced Bahman Shahandeh who was back in the good graces of the horse world again after a long period of ostracism following the Lebanese trip.

I almost fainted when I realized that the General was not riding his new imported horse, but he was riding the horse that Goli Bakhtiar had bought from Ali Reza, which in my opinion was a much better horse. Goli was standing next to me as we watched the General ride a perfect round.

'That horse that the General bought seems to be quite good, Gail. What do you think? It looks a little like the mare I bought, very pretty.'

'Goli that is your mare. The General is on the wrong horse!'

'What?!! It isn't! Are you sure?'

'As sure as I am standing here.'

'Why the stupid———-! —————him!'

'Teemsah! Manucher! Manucher!' she went running screaming after the thrilled general oblivious to anything save the fact that he had had a clear round!

Kambis had again taken over the running of the Iranian Equestrian Federation as well as the Royal Horse Society and so it was that I became involved in more meetings. Saturday was my day off but now the Federation had the meeting on Saturday at five in the afternoon so I couldn't call it a total free day. I was again spending more and more time working from early morning until late afternoon. Don was once again complaining so I decided that it was time to have another talk with Kambis. I really didn't want to leave the stables, but thought that maybe I could stay on and just work with the young children every afternoon and he could hire another full time trainer from either America or Europe who would take over the rest; there were rumors that Don was to be transferred soon anyway, so I wanted to talk to Kambis about that as well.

As I sat waiting in his ante room a mousy little old lady in a very tattered mink coat styled for the forties, stomped straight into his office accompanied by a middle aged army officer. The door slammed and the noise started. This woman was giving Kambis a real piece of her mind; the sound was muffled so I couldn't really hear the conversation but it seemed to be about money. I could faintly hear Kambis's obsequious replies.

'Boy is she giving it to him today.' commented Mrs. Nazemi. I was about to ask who "she" was when the woman and her aide came out the door and again, stomped through the little office. This time she had left the door open.

'Gail, come on in.' I heard Kambis call to me as he sat behind his huge mahogany desk with his head in his hands. I went in and sat in my customary place at his right not wanting to be the one to initiate the conversation. He picked up the phone and ordered some tea for us.

'That woman will be the death of me. I can't stand her tirades. I don't know why I'm the one who has to deal with her. She is totally impossible. Do you know who she is?' he asked me.

'She looks very familiar but I must say I don't know. Should I?'

'No. Luckily not many people know who she is. A most hateful woman. She is His Majesty's sister.'

'But Kambis, it couldn't be. I know what his three sisters look like and she is not one of them.'

'Oh, but she is. You see, before Reza Shah became Shah he was just a little army colonel. He was married to a Kadjar princess; not an important one but she was one. She had a daughter; the woman you just saw was that daughter. She is officially no-one for when Reza Shah made himself king he decreed that no Shah could be married to a Kadjar, a member of the previous dynasty. He had divorced his Kadjar wife but there was still the daughter Hamdamsultaneh. His Majesty still provides for her financially but she is not recognized. She does nothing but complain; I can't stand her. She gives me one of my headaches every time I talk to her.' He held his head in his hands.

'Now what did you want to see me about? I suppose you want to resign or something to give me another headache.'

'No, I just wanted to talk about maybe getting some help at the stables; I'm finding that I'm never at home; even my day off, I now have to go to the Federation and often don't get home from that meeting until nine o'-clock. Don gets rather upset.'

'I don't want to hear about your personal problems. If you can't take care of your personal life that's your problem. Don't come crying to me. Everyone seems to be bringing their stupid problems today. Now do you have anything sensible you want to discuss?'

It was definitely not the time to say any more so I gave a quick report on things at the stable and the list of the current show jumping competitions and left.

Shortly after this meeting one noon I was called into Kambis's office for "something important!" I was told to go right in which I did.

One of the big body guard type men I had seen around many times was reporting something to my boss. They both said their "*salams*" to me and the man went on.

'I am very sorry but there is still no trace and we have exhausted all of our resources. I think you will just have to write this one off, Agha.' The man was dismissed.

'Do you remember when I was in America two summers ago I told you I had bought a car for His Majesty? The summer that I went up to Canada and visited you at your family's farm.' Kambis started the conversation.

I remembered that he had bought a very special light blue station wagon with everything that could ever be put on a car including bullet proof glass. It was a special order that would take months to fill and had cost twenty five thousand dollars. I also recalled the day that I was in Kambis's office when he received the bill of lading for the car after it had arrived in the port of Khoramshah. He had called in one of the trusted Imperial Court drivers, given him the keys, the bill of lading and orders to pick up the car. Weeks later Kambis had laughingly told me that the driver had not been able to find the car at the port, but that it was surely somewhere to be found; now it was a year later and still no car!

'It is a shocking thing that a car for His Imperial Majesty would be either stolen from the docks to be taken to another nearby country where we can't trace it or was maybe sold for parts here in Iran, Gail. It makes me wonder what this country is coming to. How could the port authorities lose a car?' Kambis was quite dismayed.

Another time the "important something" he wanted to discuss with me was the fact that at ten o'clock the next morning the King of Greece would be visiting the stables and I was to get together with Dr. Cutler to organize a good show of the horses of Iran. He was sure the King was not interested in our jumping horses but if he was, we could just lead them out to be shown in hand.

I went back to the stables that afternoon so that Robin and I could get together to plan our strategy for the following morning. We always had fun, for it really was never anything more than a promotion job that any public relations man would be excited to do.

The following morning I expected Kambis to show up to ride but when he didn't come I figured he had gone to the palace to accompany the deposed King to Farahabad. Shortly after ten a single helicopter landed at the pad. Robin and I were waiting at the gate to the heliport to welcome our guest in case Kambis was not with him. Kambis was the first to descend and then the handsome King Constantine alighted. He was truly tall, dark and handsome; one of the most handsome men I had ever met; much more so than his pictures.

The King was a totally charming, easy going man who seemed to be truly interested in what was going on at the Imperial Stables. He wanted to see the mares' stables where we kept the breeding stock and was most interested in the horses we had raised out of our own mares. Mashed Mahmad was all a tither at showing the King of another country his stock; we never did tell him that the king's country had decided that it would be better to do without him.

Of course, there was my favorite stop at the carriage house with Kambis this time doing most of the talking. Abdul Hossein kept making asides to me that he wanted to tell our foreign visitor who I had explained was a shah like our Shahanshah. I did the best I could apologetically interspersing comments by saying that, 'Abdul Hossein wants you to know that this is the carriage that carried Reza Shah the first time he met the parliament.' And Kambis would say, 'Oh, yes, I forgot to mention that fact.' As we left the cramped quarters of the Imperial Carriages I made a point of showing King Constantine the small gallery of personal photographs that the old man had displayed just to the left of the door. There were pictures of him driving five different Shahs, three of which had been Kadjars; there was a picture of his father driving an Imperial carriage; there was a picture of Abdul Hossein in a boxing costume obviously having won a match; he claimed to be the Iranian champion of the day; there was also a picture of his son Ali Rezai riding one of the first jumping horses at the Imperial Stables.

The King was very kind and listened attentively to the stories of the old man; such a diplomat. He told Kambis later that one of the most important things to running a loyal staff of royal servants was to spend a moment to listen to their stories and give them an opportunity to have a little international fame by being a part of visits of people from abroad. Kambis kindly gave me the credit for including people like Abdul Hossein and Mashed Mahmad in the tour; it was a very un-Persian thing for him to have done.

Before the tour was completed we even went to see the incomplete operating room which Robin described so deftly that one felt it was ready for the first operation.

By the time we said our fond farewells to this kind, vibrant man we'd spent over three hours with him; Kambis was making noises that they would be late for an official luncheon so off they flew in the Imperial Bird.

Over the years at the Imperial Stables I was involved with entertaining

467

through the horses, all manner of foreign personages. There were more European princes and princesses than anything, though we did have our fair share of counts and countesses and many Middle Eastern dignitaries. I always enjoyed meeting these people who were for the most part truly interested and most congenial.

I was able to invite some of my husband's business associates from the United States who were interested in horses and of course various members of our families came to visit and wanted to see where I spent my days.

I was most surprised one morning to have a call from an acquaintance I had met at a party given by a Kadjar Prince several months previously. Mrs. Souter's husband was the managing director of the Ciba-Gigy Corporation in Iran. They invited us to dinner a few days hence.

During the dinner party it was brought to my attention that one of the major shareholders of Ciba-Gigy and president of the Swiss company was coming to Tehran; the president was bringing his wife Pat Koeklin-Smythe. It was the same Pat Smythe whom I had met as a teenager when I was in Mexico riding with General Umberto Mariles, who in his day was reputed to be the best show jumping rider in the world. She had been the first woman ever to enter the Olympic Games in the Equestrian Event of Show Jumping. I had admired her since I was a young girl drooling over her horse stories.

When I saw Kambis the following morning I blatantly started the conversation by telling him all about the woman I had so much admired during my early life. He seemed passably interested in my talk but I could tell that he had other things on his mind.

'Well, anyway, what I am trying to get at Kambis, is that Pat Smythe is coming to Tehran to visit with her husband. I'm sure he will be busy with his business commitments so I was wondering if I could perhaps invite her to see the stables and take her out to lunch or something.'

'That's perfectly all right with me. You know that I have always wel-

468

comed your guests here and I know you have been discrete. But this woman sounds like someone who is rather a celebrity. Perhaps we should have a luncheon in her honor out at the Nowruzabad Club that has just opened. Yes, that's it! I think we will invite the horse world to meet this famous woman, who could perhaps give a short talk, and we will get the press to come and make a big deal out of her. I want you to organize the whole thing. Get together with Pulard, and we must not forget to give her some sort of little token gift from the society. You know what to do. I will be a host in name only; it's totally your project.'

I was really thrilled that he had become so enthusiastic about my guest and set about to do the best I could. I knew that the publicity would be mainly for the Nowruzabad Club but I really didn't care and I was sure that Pat wouldn't either.

The day dawned with the usual beautiful Persian blue sky. The KoeklinSmythes arrived at Farahabad at the appointed hour. The tour was a great success. It turned out that Sam, Pat's husband, came to see the stables too and I learned that he had been a member of the Swiss International Three Day Event Team years gone by. He and Pat had first met at the Olympics in Helsinki. The Royal Horse Society luncheon was a great success and Pat's informative talk was received well by all.

During the first week in October I heard a rumor that Jean Michel Gaud, the French rider, was to come to Iran to train the horses of the Imperial Stables. When I asked Kambis about this he sheepishly admitted that he had been discussing the matter through Colonel Khalvati and thought there was quite a good chance that the man would come for a month to help me. I thought it was a great idea to bring someone with more expertise than I had, but I wondered at the choice. I had enjoyed meeting Jean Michel and his beautiful wife when we were at the Esfahan Show in August but I found it very hard to communicate with him for his English was very poor;

knowing how limited Kambis was with French made me more puzzled. Perhaps Kambis was fed up with people like me who would talk back to him. At least if the man didn't speak either English or Farsi he wouldn't be able to stir up trouble.

In due course Jean Michel arrived. I soon learned that he really didn't have any interest in training the *djelodars*; he was a true French aristocrat and wanted only to teach Kambis and General Khosrodad. My boys were very rebellious for they were totally loyal to me and didn't want to take any instruction from this Frenchman, however I insisted that they take advantage of him. I have always believed that there is something to learn in every situation and Jean Michel had been on the French Equestrian Team and certainly had something worth listening to. I began to go out myself to have him school me with the horses that I was working with, hoping to show them by example that they too, could learn something from the man.

It became very difficult, for I could tell that he didn't want to teach the boys and they didn't want to learn from him, but I had to insist that they work together.

Kambis and General Khosrodad were in awe of the man who was very attractive and had a lovely style on a horse. For my thinking he was much too Germanic for the Persian mind but I was glad that they were benefitting from him.

He wanted to reorganize everything at the stables which made me have to keep a watch that things weren't changed too drastically though he did have some good ideas. He thought the *djelodars* were the worst riders in the world but they kept winning in the competitions which totally frustrated him. He decided that Shabrang was the best horse in the stable and took him away from Ezat to ride himself. I was thrilled to see that after two weeks he couldn't get on with the animal and gave him back to Ezat. He then tried Alborz which he had ridden at the Esphahan Show with much success. He seemed unable to get along with this horse either though he did ride him in the Aryamehr Cup, for lack of another mount. He didn't get past the first round. I felt as the month went on that Jean Michel was trying to undermine me.

He was most difficult to work with, refusing to listen to any reason as to why certain things happened at the Imperial Stables. I finally let him do his thing with Kambis and the General and smilingly cooperated as best I could when he was at the stables but I didn't put myself out. I did take advantage of his knowledge by having him school me though as often as I could manage it in my schedule.

Kambis was having trouble with his new horses from Ireland but as Gaud had taken over their training I decided to keep entirely out of it. I learned that Gaud was administering medication by needle to these two horses before schooling sessions and shows but kept my mouth shut.

The first thing he did that really annoyed me was to convince Kambis that the rules to the Championship were not right for Iran. There would be no Grand Prix, just one speed class, a regular table A class with a jump off and a Puissance for the Actual Cup itself. To me this took away the excitement we had with the final competition being a two round Grand Prix.

The second thing he did that really shocked me was to let Kambis go into the main ring and school over the obstacles that were to be a part of the course in the horse show the next day. I went up to him and told him that that type of cheating was something that we had been trying to eliminate since I had been in Iran and I didn't think it was a good policy to let any horses in the ring once the jumps had been put up for the show but he just brushed me off .

I was continuing to ride Ballylea and was usually in the prize with the horse. I took advantage of Jean Michel by schooling the horse only when he was there; everyone needs a ground man in jumping and he was very good at picking out some of my faults and helping me to correct them. I was very anxious to do well in the Aryamehr Cup. I felt I had as good a chance as anyone if luck was on my side. When I rode by the Royal Box in the parade before the commencement of the competition His Majesty smiled at me and I heard him say to Kambis, 'That is the horse I like. Why aren't you riding it yourself?' I later asked my boss what his answer had been, but he was very noncommittal!

The class was a Puissance in which the jumps get wider and higher in the successive jump-offs. I was nervous in the first round but when I made it clear I felt that I had passed the most difficult round; now all I had to do was ride over the jumps as they got bigger. The second last fence in the second jump-off was a vertical plank jump at which I collected Ballylea in order to keep his hind end under him so that he would have the impulsion that was needed. The take-off was perfect but unfortunately for me he dropped a toe and we were out of the competition.

When the prizes were given by His Majesty, I was with my Imperial Stables team to receive the Team Aryamehr Cup which we had won the previous day; Kambis, Ezat Vodjdani, Davoud Bahrami and I had been the winning team. I had been the only rider to have clear round in the final jump-off against the Dashte Behesht team and had clinched the trophy for us. I was glad that I had changed my policy of not riding on the team that year and I can thank Jean Michel Gaud for precipitating my decision. He had told Kambis that the Trakaner gelding that we had been working on so hard was absolutely no good and it was a waste of Kambis's time and his own to bother working with the horse. I had taken the horse over and decided to ride it in the team event to prove that Jean Michel was wrong. I did!

After the prizes had all been given out there were still two boxes on the table that had held the beautiful silver trophies. The commentator who was doing the television coverage of the event then announced that there were two special awards to be given by His Majesty. The first was presented to Colonel Sohrab Khalvati for his part in designing the Aryamehr Parcours.

'His Imperial Majesty the Shahanshah will now present a special award to the person who has done so much to improve show jumping in this country; who has helped us to get on the map internationally, who has given so much time and effort to the sport and who has done so much for the Imperial Stables, Gail Rose.'

There was a lot of applause as I shakily walked up to receive my award from the Shah. He smiled and thanked me for all I had done for show jumping. 'I am at your service, Your Majesty.'

The event was over for another year. The Royal party went out the back of the Royal Box to the limousines that would drive them the few hundred yards to the awaiting helicopters.

I had still not opened the dark blue leather box I held in my hand. Suddenly all of the *djelodars* were around me smiling and shaking my hand. 'Khonum Rose, open your present.'

I did and found a very lovely Rolex watch with an inscription on the back.

When I arrived home late that afternoon, Azizeh and Naheed my house keeper and her daughter, were waiting for me at the gate. They were full of the fact that they had seen me with His Majesty on television. What had he given me? They could'nt wait to see. I think they were expecting diamonds for their faces showed disappointment when they saw it was just a watch. They wanted to touch it though, and they especially wanted to touch the little leather box that the Shahanshah himself had held.

'Azizeh. I will give you the box to keep if you like.' I told her. She cried, she was so happy. After that she made the little blue Rolex box part of a shrine on the bureau in her small house.

Goli on her new horse

Author on Ballylea

MY TERMINATION

The week after the Aryamehr Cup was the first of the Championship Competitions. All entries had to be made by Sunday morning, so Saturday I went down to the stables and went over our entries with Jean Michel who was only concerned that Kambis and General Khosrodad be entered correctly. I took care of the rest of the *djelodars* and the three juniors that would be competing in the Junior Championship.

That afternoon seeing as I was already so involved in horses on my day off I decided to go out and see my friend Ali Reza Soudovar. I arrived at three in the afternoon just in time for lunch. During a delicious meal prepared by his man Morad, which included caviar to start and one of my favorite Persian dishes *khoresh de feshanjun*, a thick paste like sauce made from wild duck, ground walnuts and chocolate which is eaten with rice, we discussed my problems at the stables with Jean Michel and the fact that Kambis was again being a bit of a pain. Ali was most interested in hearing how the horses he had bought for Kambis were doing.

'Sky,' which was a lovely looking grey, 'has started to stop but I think that Jean Michel will be giving the horse a little help, if you know what I mean, in the Championship. "Cliffs" is going well and is putting up with a lot of schooling, more than I usually do. We haven't really been doing anything with the other horse because he is so green and it's the end of the season. Jean Michel doesn't like him anyway.'

'Jean Michel! I can't stand that man! I don't know how you put up with him, Gail. He may be able to ride, but I don't think he could train his way out of a wet paper bag. I would be careful with him because I hear rumors that he wants your job, though I know he could never do it.'

'Oh, for heaven's sakes, Ali! Why would he want my job? He claims to have too many ties and horses back home in France.'

'Don't let him fool you. He has had a fight with the French Federation and the president will never let him on the team again. He doesn't have any good horses. The last one "Tango", he sold to the Germans. It has done nothing since. No, I think you had better watch out. I would hate to see you hurt.'

'My feelings were already hurt when Kambis brought the Frenchman over without saying a word about it to me; if you will recall, I had already said to you that I thought we should get someone really good to go on with the training of the boys because I was beginning to feel that they were about to outgrow me. But then——Kambis wouldn't give me a chance to tell him what I wanted to do and whom I thought would be good for the job.'

'They have not outgrown you yet; anyway, you're much better than this Gaud. He is such an arrogant ass. I really hate him!'

'Come on now, Ali. He's not that bad.'

'You just watch it, little Gailey. He will try to undermine you…. But, I have another idea. I want you to quit your job at the Imperial Stables and come to work for me. It will be much better if you quit now while you have the upper hand, than later when maybe Kambis will be prepared for you to resign. You know that I have bought a place in Ireland. I'm going to move there and this stable will be kept for my brother Mahmadi's race horses and just a very few jumpers. What I would like you to do is to take over the management, train and show the horses, and then disperse most of the jumping stock. I will pay you well, more than you are making now, commissions on the horses you sell and it will be all cash so that you won't have to pay any tax.'

'Ali, thank you for the neat compliment but you must know that I can't leave the stables now. I would like to cut down on my work load but I don't think that Kambis would let me resign. I tried a year ago and couldn't. If I do leave though, I will certainly consider your offer.'

We talked on until the sun had gone down and as usual I was late getting home.

Two days before the first part of the Championships Ali called me; his voice was very distraught.

'Gailey, you have to try to help me. I have made a big mess.'

'If I can I will. What's the problem?'

'Well, I sent my entries for the championship with Mahmoud you know, my brother's crazy driver, and he got into an accident and then forgot to take them in until yesterday and now the Federation is saying that they won't accept them because they were late. I've entered Tossa Firouz on three horses in the Junior Division and she has a very good chance. Akbar of course, will enter in the Senior Championships but he will do nothing so it doesn't matter for him but, for Tossa I just have to try to get her in. Do you think you could call Kambis and try to get him to let her in; you've always been able to persuade him in such matters.'

'I'll call him Ali, but you know he's been very cold lately; I will do my best. I'll call you later to let you know.' I hung up.

Five minutes later the phone rang again. It was my old friend Louise Firouz. She wanted me to see what I could do about getting dauhter Tossa's entries to the championship accepted because that stupid Ali Reza Soudovar had goofed; probably off on one of his pot parties and the entries went in late and now the Federation was saying that they would not accept late entries. I said I would call her back too.

It was by this time about nine o'clock in the evening so I decided to try to call Kambis at his house. Mahamad answered the phone and informed me that *Agha* was not yet home from work. He had had a meeting at the palace but he would have him call me when he arrived.

'Mrs. Rose,' it was Kambis on the phone when I answered it about an hour later. 'What can I do for you so late at night?'

I explained the situation and persuaded him that Tossa's entry in the Championship would make it a much better spectator affair; after all, she was one of the best junior riders in the country and had the use of the very good horses of Ali Reza Soudovar.

'You are always trying to persuade me to do things I really don't want to do, but I guess this time you're right. I'll let her ride. You call Colonel Ashuri tomorrow morning and have him put her name on the list. But I won't let Ali enter that ——Akbar. He is the worst rider in Iran.' I was shocked at the ease with which Kambis had conceded. I called Ali and Louise immediately to give them the good news.

The day of the competition dawned sunny and clear but it was chilly as were many of the days at the end of November. The course that Jean Michel and I had put up looked very good and fair for this first speed event. I went to check that all was ready in the jury; Don, as usual, was the president for the day.

'Listen, Gail,' he said to me, 'This doesn't seem right. They have Tossa Firouz riding her three horses one, two, three. That's impossible for her. Colonel Ashuri says it's because she made her entries late.'

'Oh! Isn't that just typical! Here, let's change that. We'll put her first, sixth and thirteenth. That should give her time to change her mounts and get her breath and she still isn't getting the advantage of going last because we have twenty two entrants. What do you think?'

Don agreed with me and I took the revised order down to the warm-up ring to the starter at the gate. When I got to the warm-up area I saw Tossa sitting on the big Irish palomino stallion in tears. She saw me and rode over to the fence.

'Mrs. Rose, they're going to make me ride my horses first without anyone going in between. I won't be able to do it. I'll be too tired and they will only allow me sixty seconds in between each horse. Can't you do something?'

'I already have. You will go first, sixth and thirteenth. I'm here to change the order with the starters.'

'Oh thank you! But I have another problem. Ali Reza hasn't arrived and I don't know in what order I should ride the horses. What do you think?'

'I would ride your slowest horse first so that you can try out the course and save the fastest for last. I guess ride Cisco King first; you're on him now anyway, and save Venus for last, then ride that new Irish mare in the middle.'

'OK. Thank you so much, Mrs. Rose. I hope Ali Reza doesn't get mad at me.'

'I'll talk to him when he gets here, Toss.' I went back to the main ring as they were announcing the class and the jumping order. I couldn't believe my ears when I heard the announcement that Ateshe Firouz would ride her horses first, second and third. I went stomping to the jury box.

'What the——is going on, Don? Didn't you tell the announcer of the change in jumping order?'

'It was changed back after you left to go tell them at the gate.' Don answered.

'What for? Why did you let them do that? You know the kid can't possibly' ride three horses in a row. What stupid idiot changed it back?'

'Your boss did it.'

'Kambis?'

'He's your boss.'

'Kambis is a SHIT. He is an absolute SHIT!!!! I am going to find him.' My voice was about ten decibels higher than normal.

'You don't have to go far.' Kambis said as he stepped out of the corner of the jury box where he had been standing unnoticed by me. 'So you think I am a Shit?'

'For doing this to poor Tossa, yes. This is a Junior Competition and let's consider the participants; she is one of them and now that we have accepted her entries we have to treat her equally with the other entrants.'

'Her entries were late. Her mother and that——Ali Reza will be punished by me.'

'But Kambis, do you think that by hurting Tossa you can punish her mother and Ali? Your arguments with them have nothing to do with the girl.'

'I have made up my mind. She will ride one two, three, or not at all. I gave a concession to let her in and I am not changing this decision.' He would not be reasonable.

I decided to make one more stab at it. 'Kambis, I am the technical advisor for show jumping in Iran, and I am head of the Royal Horse Society Show Jumping Committee and I will not allow you to do this stupid thing.'

'You forget, Mrs. Rose, that you work for me and I have made a decision that overrides any powers you may have.'

'You are really a SHIT!' I said and stomped out of the box. I ran down to the ring to talk to Tossa. She was already in tears for Mr. Naimi had informed her of the change of order. I advised her to ride her best and take as much time changing horses as she possibly could. I had tried but failed her.

'You can do it though, Tossa. You're tough enough. Just hang in there.'

I had to school my own three entrants, Davoud Bahrami, Homayun Vodjani and Mahmad Reza Sarbazi. While I schooled them over a few fences Tossa joined in for Ali Reza had not shown up yet.

I ran back up to the main ring to watch the competition. Tossa entered on the pretty palomino, "Cisco King" and rode a perfect round in a blistering fifty-five seconds. The crowd gave her great applause. Sixty seconds later she re-entered on the young Irish mare. She had a difficult time making the turns but the mare went clear until she came into the triple combination; she stumbled on takeoff falling through the jump and throwing Tossa to the ground. Both horse and rider seemed unhurt but I could tell that Tossa was shaken. She went back and again attempted the final combination of the course and cleared it without a fault. When she entered again on Venus her third horse, she was still panting and I could see the tears welling up in her eyes. She rode very badly due to her fatigue almost coming off again but not quite.

As much as I wanted my boys to do well I hoped that Tossa would get in the ribbons with Cisco and as the class went on no one seemed to be able to beat her time. When Davoud Bahrami was unable to better it with a beautiful round on Mojgan I knew that Toss had won the class. Davoud was second.

It was with much delight that I watched Tossa ride in on Cisco King to receive her first place ribbon and trophy. She had the most triumphant look on her face. Despite the obstacles put in her way she had won.

The talk of the party afterwards was the Tossa Firouz episode and I expounded with delight at what a shit I thought Kambis had been.

Due to the fact that Lucinda Prior Palmer was due down at the stables the next morning I decided to forego my usual Saturday off; Lucinda, the world renowned British Three Day Event rider was visiting one of her friends Richard Clifford, who was managing the Nowruzbad Equestrian Center.

I was about to mount Malek when Kambis came stomping into the stable yard.

'Gail, I want to see you in my office at ten o'clock sharp.'

'I doubt if I can make it by ten, Kambis, but I'll be there for sure at eleven; is that all right?'

'No it is not! Be there by ten!' He walked off towards his house.

481

Oh, Oh! I guessed I was really in for it. He had obviously not appreciated my conversation of the previous day. He had not slept well on it.

When I walked into the ante room of his office at ten o'clock on the dot, Mrs. Nazami ushered me in immediately. That was either a good or bad sign.

'Good morning again, Mrs. Rose.' Kambis greeted me in a friendly manner as I seated myself in my usual place. 'So you think I am a shit? Is that right?'

'With regard to the little incident that happened yesterday, yes I do think you acted in a very shitty manner. It was childish and stupid and I was quite surprised at you. Shocked, to tell the truth.'

'I hear that you told everyone at the post show party what you thought of me.'

'I most certainly did. The episode was the talk of the town. No one could imagine why, after you have done so much to improve the show jumping in Iran, you would revert back to the Old Iranian way. What you did was really unfair.'

'So, you're telling me that you still think I am a shit. Is that correct?'

'I think you are a shit as far as what you did yesterday is concerned, yes.'

'It must be very hard for you to work for a shit. If that is the case I think we should terminate our arrangement.'

'If that is what you want, Kambis.'

'Gail, I don't want it; I want you to apologize to me and tell me that I am not a shit.'

'Kambis, I am sorry. I don't think that you are a shit all the time but I think you were a shit yesterday. In a way, I am sorry I vocalized what I felt but I did. And if you ask me in ten years what I thought about yesterday I would say that you acted like a shit.'

'You won't take it back then.'

'No I won't.'

'Well then, your employment with the Imperial Stables, The Royal Horse Society, and The Federation has terminated as of this minute. I want you to have all your affairs tidied up by the end of the week. You need not do anything more for me, for I know I would not be able to work for some-one who I thought was a shit. You may go now.'

I got up and walked out. There were tears in my eyes but I was not sure if they were tears of laughter, anger, relief, sadness or real grief. On my way driving home I cried a little, I sighed a little and I laughed a little.

THE FINAL MOMENTS

In reply to my formal letter of acknowledgement of termination of my contract I received by the Imperial Court Courier the following letter:

Imperial Stables December 9, 1975
Mrs. Gail Rose
Hosseineh Ershad
Sharzad Street
Azar Avenue
No. 14 Marjan Avenue
TEHRAN

Dear Mrs. Rose:
Reference: Your Letter Dated 10 Azar 1354

Thank you for the above letter. I am very sorry that you are under the impression that I fired you. I realized that you were very unhappy and I only came to your assistance by relieving you from your unbearable responsibilities.

It is rather unfortunate that sometimes we lose all proportion of our limits and capabilities. I believe that during the past three years you have done a great job. The problem has been that the talent you were given to work with did not match your great capabilities and your vast knowledge.

*This, I am sure, must have caused you a great deal of frustration and un-
happiness.*

*However, I should also like to remind you that we have always appre-
ciated your services for what they were worth. I would like to point out that
being presented to His Imperial Majesty at the Aryamehr Cup was a token
of our gratitude.*

*I have given instructions as regard to your tack and I prefer to pay you
in hard cash for what you have so kindly given to the Imperial Stables.*

The question of severance pay shall be considered.

Yours sincerely,

Kambis Atabai

It was so Persian and so Kambis! I once again did not know whether
to laugh or to cry.

I went to the second leg of the Championship the following Friday
dressed to the nines in my mink coat. There was no way I would miss it
just because I was no longer working for the Imperial Stables.

Avid Atabai came to sit beside me, 'Gail, you look marvelous but why
are you not in your usual riding clothes?'

'I'm sure you've heard, Avid.'

'Heard what?' she looked truly puzzled and Avid was not the type of
woman to play games.

'That I'm no longer an employee of the Imperial Stables. I'm enjoying
retirement.'

'Gail, I don't believe it! Why?'

'You'll have to ask Kambis. We seem to differ as to why. He claims
that I resigned and I claim that he fired me. It would be better if you got
the story from him.'

'I just can't believe it. You are part of Farahabad. Everyone here loves you so much, from Kambis on down to the *mehtards* (grooms). You are joking with me!'

'Honestly, Avid, on God's Honor I am not joking.'

'I knew something was upsetting Kambis this week but I never dreamed it was this. I know the two of you will patch it up. You have had arguments before and worked things out. After a little time you will be back, I'm sure. Why, Farahabad will not run without you. Kambis will be going crazy in a week. I know because I remember what it was like before you came.'

I did not go back!

The *djelodars* all begged me to come back; they came to me with messages that *Agha* wanted me back. They told me how disorganized things were getting; they had all become so used to my iron hand that they were lost without it.

'Mrs. Rose, soon it is time to start work with the young horses; we need you to help us.' Reza Hadavand came to my home one day to talk to me.

At a party over Christmas General Khosrodad told me that Kambis was desperate to have me go back; all he wanted was an apology. I explained stubbornly that I could not do it for it would be a lie.

'But Gail, it is not a terrible sin to just twist the truth a little.' To my mind it was.

James Underwood told me he wanted to do a blurb in the paper about my departure but he would wait until I returned from my skiing holiday in Italy to make certain I really was leaving the Stables. Maybe I would think things over and return to my old job after I'd had some time out of Iran; I would be able to look at things in better perspective.

The only person who believed I was really leaving my job was Ali Reza Soudovar and he was thrilled about it because he desperately wanted me to work for him. I told him that I would have to think it over while I was away.

I was not back in Iran for a whole day when I had a call from Ali Reza. Would I come out to have lunch with him the next day? I did and agreed to take him up on his offer.

The first person I told was James Underwood who wrote the following Article in the Kayhan:

GAIL LEAVES FARAHABAD

TEHRAN -*The Imperial Stables team which took main honors in show jumping during the past year will have a new trainer in 1976. The team has split with its trainer of the past three years, Gail Rose.*

No name has yet been tapped to fill the vacancy. But well known French rider, Jean Michel Gaud, is known to have offered himself for the job as coach for the National Team, and rumors have suggested that he may take over the Imperial Stables coaching too.

Mrs. Rose, once among Canada's leading show jumpers, is in Iran with her husband. She said yesterday that she had thoroughly enjoyed the job at Farahabad, and was particularly pleased that Stables boss Kambis Atabai had landed the National Championship this year. Members of the team won the title in each year for which it has been competed.

She was also pleased with the progress made by some of the younger riders of great potential, like Davoud Bahrami, who will next year move up into senior competition.

'I really enjoyed working with the youngsters there', she told me. 'And I think one of them, Mohammad Sarbazi, may turn out to be the best rider Iran has ever had. '

Besides her work at Farahabad Mrs. Rose has played a big part in getting show jumping in Iran aligned with international rules and organizations. And she has landed several trophies during the past season.

There was a good picture of me riding Ballylea.

Jean Michel Gaud arrived in March to take on the position I had held, a job that he kept for just four months. He and Kambis could not get along.

The first few times I saw Kambis at the competitions he was very curt with me but as time went on he became his usual friendly self. He personally asked me to go back to work for him but by that time I knew that there was no point for Don was being transferred out of Iran in November.

My Dashte Behesht team which consisted of myself, Ali Akbar Kazami and Ateshe Firouz accounted for most of the major wins in the shows that season. I found myself riding two small Persian bred horses in the big events and beating my boys from the Imperial Stables on their expensive imports. I had a wonderful few months of glory. And my Dashte Behesht Team won the Aryamehr Team Event which was considered quite an upset.

An International Competition sanctioned by the FEI was planned for mid-November and knowing that I would be invited to ride, I got in touch with the Canadian Equestrian Federation to get their letter of permission to ride for my own country. James George, our Canadian Ambassador, gave me flags and emblems to sew onto my jacket and saddle pad.

Riders of international caliber from England, Ireland, France, Germany, Italy, Belgium, Switzerland and Brazil were coming to Tehran for the event.

As I expected, I received an official letter from the Federation written in Persian, inviting me to ride in this Invitational Competition. When I called Kambis to thank him and accept I told him of my plan to ride under the flag of my own country.

'Mrs. Rose, you may not do that. In our eyes you are a member of the Iranian Team and you will ride as an Iranian. That is my answer and don't you dare try to go to General Khosrodad or anyone else to try to change the decision. You are an Iranian.'

So I rode for Iran and won more prizes than any other Iranian competitor in the competition.

The night after the final day of competition there was a big party held in honor of the International visitors at La Chemine which was the most *chique* and popular night club in Tehran at that time. There was the usual sumptuous Iranian feast, along with speeches, presentations and dancing into the wee small hours.

Kambis, who made all the presentations to the foreign riders, was in fine form looking his most handsome. When he had made the last presentation I saw Pulad Mansabur go behind him and whisper in his ear; they both nodded.

'And now ladies and gentlemen, I want to make a very special tribute to someone who has been very close to me over the past few years. Someone who has perhaps done more for show jumping in Iran than any other single person. Someone who has put up with me at my worst, and that's pretty bad as most of my colleagues know. A person who has been a great diplomat for Iran though not an Iranian by citizenship, though can be as Persian as any of us. Someone I love very deeply and yet have hurt due to my foolishness during the past year. I'm sure many of you will be as sad as I am, to see Gail Rose leave Iran, as she is going, tomorrow.

'Gail, come up here so that everyone can see you.'

I did and he gave me a huge hug and a kiss on both cheeks, the Persian fashion. With tears in my eyes I heard him say more and call Don up too so that he could publically thank him for his contribution and help.

When the party was finally over the only ones left were Kambis, Avid, Don and me. We sat having a glass of champagne toasting our lasting friendship and the future for us all.

As we left La Chemine, Kambis kissed me and held me tight. 'We must stay friends forever, Gail.' he said. And we still are!

**Author being presented prize by Princess Shams
with Co. Alai and Amir Pahldad**

**Author receiving prize on Iranian horse Lady Jane, Goli Bakhtiar
on new horse looking on**

بسر میبرد.در فن سواری مهارت داشته و دارای سبک زیبائی در این ورزش است.در سال ۱۹۶۸ در بازیــهـــای المپیک مکزیکوسیتی همراه تیم ملی کانادا شرکت کرده ودر مدت اقامت خود در ایران نیز دراکثر مسابقات حضور داشته و تا کنون دو مقام اول هفت مقام دوم و پنج مقام سوم را حائز شده است.او در مسابقه جام آریامهر سال ۵٤ (دوره سرعت) عضو تیم اول اصطبل شاهنشاهی بود.

Author Picture in international program

EPILOGUE

Don was transferred out of Iran to another project so we moved to Richmond, Virginia. I bought a horse for myself to show in the jumpers and a couple of ponies for the children. It wasn't long before we bought a farm where I opened a riding school and training facility, Swift Creek School of Equitation, which became well reputed and very successful; it continues to-day still going strong under a new young owner. Don and I agreed to disagree several years after we arrived in the States. I have retired from teaching and training but keep myself involved with horses through my daughter Sulu, who with her husband Derek Reed runs a training facility and shows horses in Grand Prix events, my granddaughter who is becoming a super junior rider and my niece and her husband who train race horses.

Kambis left Iran with the Shah and his family in February 1979. He stayed with HIM until his untimely death from cancer in 1980. He continues to work for the Shabanu Fara Diba in her New York office and lives in New York City. We remain in contact and are still good friends.

Ali Reza Soudovar left Iran to live at his home in Ireland in 1976 where he supported young Irish riders. He unfortunately died of a heart attack two years later.

Fred Elghanian and his family were able to escape from Iran with the help of Kambis and myself after the revolution. He and his sons started a professional stable in Cleveland Ohio which they have run successfully importing European horses for sale in the US.

Major General Manuchehr Khosrodad, was remembered by those who knew him as a talented and effective manager, a loved and respected commander as well as a great sportsman. He had reiterated his position on the fact that the army should not be involved in politics: "We are soldiers and have nothing to do with politics. I am obedient to whoever governs the country." Never the less, the Extraordinary Tribunal found Major General Khosrodad guilty of "corruption on earth" sentenced him to death and confiscated all his belongings, "based on Islamic rules and regulations." Once the verdict was confirmed with Ayatollah Khomeini, as the "enforcer of Islamic justice" he was taken to the school rooftop, blindfolded, and executed at 11.40 the night of February 15, 1979.

General Nader Djahanbane had not been made one of the military commanders when the Shah declared martial law in 1978, due to his inexperience with internal security affairs. As a result when the Shah fled, despite the urgings from his family, his friends in the US Air Force, as well as the Shah himself, Djahanbani falsely thought that he was safe from the retaliation against the security officials who suppressed the protests, as well, he believed that the powerful air force, which Iran had, would be a testament of his loyalty to the country. However, General Shahpour Azarbarzin, who was a longtime rival of Djahanbani managed to garner the support of other generals to pledge their loyalty to Khomeini and expose that Djahanbani, (who was at that time the base commander of Doshan Tappe, The Iranian Air Force Headquarters), along with other generals, was plotting a coup d'état against him. Khomeini subsequently ordered the Revolutionary Guards to arrest Djahanbani at the air force headquarters at Doshan Tappe. He was one of the first of the Shah's generals to be arrested and was sent to a court presided by the infamous Sadegh Khalkhali. He was taken to the Qasr Prison and in the early hours of March 13, 1979 was executed. At the execution he slapped one of the guards of the revolution in the face, when he insulted him, and his last words at death were, "Long Live Iran!"

Ali Rezai continued to operate his stable of show jumpers successfully and still to-day is one of the most prominent of the horse trainers in Iran where show jumping is flourishing.

Of the djelordars, it is said that the Mullahs took over the stables at Farahabad and it was business as usual. I did get some correspondence from Ezat, Davoud Bahrami and Hosein Karimiri Majzoob when they competed at the Asian games in the early 1980s. Since then I have had no word from them. I understand having communicated with people in Iran that Show Jumping is still an important sport in Iran's society and they are well.

Author on Lady Jane

Photo by Tracy Lee

The Author, Gail Rose Thompson

Made in the USA
Columbia, SC
17 March 2019